THE REBBE

The Rebbe

The Life and Afterlife of Menachem Mendel Schneerson

SAMUEL C. HEILMAN AND MENACHEM M. FRIEDMAN

PRINCETON UNIVERSITY PRESS   *Princeton and Oxford*

Library of Congress Cataloging-in-Publication Data

Heilman, Samuel C.

The Rebbe : the life and afterlife of Menachem Mendel Schneerson /

Samuel C. Heilman and Menachem M. Friedman.

p. cm.

Includes bibliographical references and index.

ISBN 978-0-691-13888-6 (hardcover : alk. paper)

1. Schneerson, Menachem Mendel, 1902–1994. 2. Rabbis—New York (State)—
New York—Biography. 3. Hasidim—New York (State)—New York—Biography.

4. Habad. I. Friedman, Menachem. II. Title.

BM755.S288H45 2010

296.8'3322092—dc22   2009050871

British Library Cataloging-in-Publication Data is available

This book has been composed in Minion Pro

Printed on acid-free paper. ∞

press.princeton.edu

Printed in the United States of America

1 3 5 7 9 10 8 6 4 2

Dedicated to our grandchildren:

Gilboa Henry

Boaz Martin

Reut Sarah

Matan Zvi

Roʾee Yisrael

Shachar Moshe

וגר זאב עם כבש

ונמר עם גדי ירבץ

ועגל וכפיר ומריא יחדו

ונער קטן נהג בם.

And the wolf shall dwell with the lamb,

And the leopard shall lie down with the kid,

And the calf and the young lion and fatling together;

And a little child shall lead them.

—ISAIAH 11:6

We are now very near the approaching footsteps of Messiah, indeed, we are at the conclusion of this period, and our spiritual task is to complete the process of drawing down the *Shechinah* [Divine Presence]— moreover, the essence of the *Shechinah*—within specifically our lowly world.

May we be privileged to see and meet with the Rebbe [Yosef Yitzchak] here in this world, in a physical body, in this earthly domain—and he will redeem us.

—Menachem Mendel Schneerson, in *Basi L'Gani*, his inaugural talk
   as leader of ChaBaD Hasidism on the first anniversary of the
   passing of his predecessor, the Rebbe Yosef Yitzchak, 10 Shvat 5711
   (January 17, 1951)

Long Live Our Master, Our Teacher, and Our Rebbe, the King Messiah, forever and ever.

—Lubavitcher Song

CONTENTS

𝕀𝕀𝕀

LIST OF ILLUSTRATIONS

JJJ

Following page 162

xi

THE REBBES OF CHABAD

✿

Schneur Zalman of Lyady (September 4, 1745–December 27, 1812) "Alter (Old) Rebbe," founder of ChaBaD

Dovber (November 24, 1773–December 28, 1827) "Miteler (Middle) Rebbe," son of Schneur Zalman

Menachem Mendel (September 20, 1789–March 29, 1866) "Zemah Zedek," nephew and son-in-law of Dovber

Shmuel (May 11, 1834–September 26, 1882) "Maharash," seventh son of Zemah Zedek

Shalom DovBer (November 5, 1860–March 21, 1920) "RaSHaB," second son of Shmuel

Yosef Yitzchak (sometimes called Joseph Isaac) (June 21, 1880–January 28, 1950) "RaYaTZ," only son of RaSHaB

Menachem Mendel (April 18, 1902–June 12, 1994) "RaMaSh," middle son-in-law and cousin of RaYaTZ

Note: Most of the rebbes spelled their family name as "Schneersohn," however the seventh rebbe chose to spell his "Schneerson." We have followed his preference for referring to him only.

JJJJ

This is a book about Lubavitcher Hasidim and their leader, or Rebbe, Menachem Mendel Schneerson. Both the Rebbe and the Lubavitcher Hasidim became caught up in the belief that they were living in messianic times and that they could hasten the coming of the Messiah and the day of redemption through their own actions. That concern with the Messiah began with the fifth of their seven rebbes, Shalom DovBer Schneersohn (1860–1920). It was intensified in the thinking and deeds of his only son, Yosef Yitzchak (1880–1950), the sixth rebbe, who made these concerns public during the dark days of the Holocaust, and reached a climax with the seventh and most recent rebbe, Menachem Mendel Schneerson (1902–1994), son-in-law and cousin of his predecessor. This active messianism became in many ways a response to the extraordinary events of the last hundred and fifty years of Jewish history, including the ferment of European Jewish life and the erosion of the traditional world of Judaism through secularization, migration, socialist revolution, war, and Holocaust. All these, as well as the advent of Zionism and the founding of the state of Israel, along with the post-Second World War relocation of Jewry to Western democracies, convinced the seventh rebbe and the Lubavitchers that the scene was now irrevocably set for the coming of the Messiah. Under the leadership of Rabbi Menachem Mendel,[1] they saw themselves as being on a mission to transform Jewry—and indeed the world.

In time, not only would they and their rebbe be persuaded that their efforts would have a mystical effect on the world and shift the balance of reality from one in which people remained unredeemed to one in which they had prepared the world for redemption. In the course of their campaign to hasten the coming of the Messiah, they also became convinced that their rebbe was the redeemer incarnate. This book tells the story of the Rebbe, how and why his own messianic convictions ripened and expressed themselves, and what happened after he died. It is a story of the unprecedented success of a small Hasidic group that seemed on the verge of collapse in 1950 with the death of their sixth leader but replanted itself in America and gained fame and influence throughout the world in ways no one could have imagined when Menachem Mendel took over the reins of leadership in 1951. It is an account of the consequences of heightened expectations and global attention to their mission, and finally of their having to cope with the physical decline and death of their would-be redeemer and the apparent failure of his prophecies and their expectations.

This is a tale of great drama, triumph and tragedy, filled with hopes and prayers, mystery and intrigue. It is also the story of how one man and some of his followers were swept away by his beliefs and expectations and led to assume that death could be denied and history manipulated. It recounts how an ancient idea—that there is a messianic redeemer, and he will come—could be brought onto the agenda of the modern world and make headlines, of how a small and relatively obscure group of Hasidim could capture the imagination of the world and deign to transform it.

Because we believe that "what a man is may be so entangled with where he is, who he is, and what he believes that it is inseparable from them," the story necessarily also touches on some of the major historical currents that swirled around the life of this man and his movement.[2] It merges social and personal history with mysticism and religion.

The book actually began in Chicago during the early 1990s, when we were both involved with the American Academy of Arts and Sciences' Fundamentalism Project under the leadership of Martin Marty and R. Scott Appleby. During that time we were both independently researching the Lubavitcher Hasidim and their Rebbe. Our thoughts came together in *Accounting for Fundamentalisms* in 1994. Then we each independently continued to collect information about Lubavitchers and wrote papers on the subject.

In the summer of 2007, while vacationing, our wives Ellin and Tamar persuaded us to combine our efforts and at last produce our book on the subject. We had doubts that we could manage to agree sufficiently in our understanding. One of us was convinced that the Lubavitcher phenomenon needed to be understood as profoundly affected by its American context, the other was no less powerfully persuaded that it needed to be seen through the prism of Jewish and Israeli realities. Our ongoing debate on this matter is reflected in these pages. That one of us was more comfortable writing in Hebrew and the other in English also made us wonder whether we could write a manuscript that would work. But we resolved to try.

The Institute for Advanced Studies of the Hebrew University and its research group, Towards a New History of Hasidism, headed by Professor David Assaf, provided the space and intellectual environment in which we could work. Beginning in December 2007, we met daily for nine months in room 14, and then again in the summer of 2009, working and arguing—sometimes loudly. The results of these debates are to be found in the pages that follow.

We have begun the story with what everyone knows today: there are emissaries (in Hebrew, *shluchim*) who continue to engage in religious outreach activities and who consider themselves to be on a mission for the seventh Lubavitcher rebbe, Menachem Mendel Schneerson, who passed away in 1994. These emissaries today have only one another and their attachments to their Rebbe, and we describe what happens when they come together, as well as the nature of their activity. But they cannot be understood without some comprehension of the man who sent them on their mission and who even after his death continues to inspire them; his story occupies the bulk of this book. We start his story by returning to the day when Schneerson's cousin, predecessor, and father-in-law, the sixth Lubavitcher rebbe, Yosef Yitzchak Schneersohn, passed away, and detail the circumstances that led to the selection of Menachem Mendel as the next rebbe—a process filled with surprises and some tension. Our next two chapters offer an extended exploration of Menachem Mendel's life, from his birth through his coming of age and his entrance into the court of the Lubavitcher Rebbe, marriage, life in Berlin and Paris, and the outbreak of the Second World War. Chapter five details the events that snatched him from the grasp of the Nazis and their minions and brought him to the United States, exploring both the theological struggles and the personal transformations he experienced as he began his tenure as the seventh Lubavitcher rebbe. This chapter deals as well with the core themes of his leadership and the idea of emissaries. Chapter about physical dangers in their often far-flung postings, or the challenge of supporting themselves economically.

Lubavitchers are unlike other Hasidim, who remain far more anchored to the geographic and cultural boundaries of their community, fated to be born, live, and die within its "four cubits" and insulated by its customs and restrictions. While other Hasidim have tried to preserve themselves and their own version of Judaism by ghettoizing themselves, choosing Yiddish as their primary language, dressing in ways that make them seem attached to another time and place, and sheltering their young deep within their community boundaries, Lubavitchers have eschewed these limitations. Although bearded, Lubavitcher men do not wear the fur hat or *shtrayml* common among other Hasidim, preferring fedoras instead. Their married women shun the kerchief that so many of the Orthodox don to cover their hair and wear instead attractive wigs that could pass for their own hair. Thus attired—not quite looking like those around them, but also not wholly other—these couples go way beyond the boundaries of their insular communities, hoping, perhaps even expecting, to change the world.*

These emissaries feel that their power comes not from themselves alone but from the one whom they represent. Their boundless confidence has been characteristic of the movement since its early days. Consider, for example, the case of Abraham Hecht, one of the first ten students in the Lubavitcher yeshiva Tomekhei Temimim in America, who in 1939, on the eve of the Nazi conquest of much of Europe, was sent on a mission by Yosef Yitzchak Schneersohn, the sixth rebbe, to

* As for the *shtrayml*, which the Previous Rebbe still wore, see chapter two. While many married Hasidic women choose to cover their heads with kerchiefs, hats, or patently obvious wigs, the Lubavitchers were told by the Rebbe Menachem Mendel that they should in fact wear wigs: "I have given my opinion numerous times that covering [a woman's hair] with a kerchief [*tikhl*], does not in this generation, because of our many sins, work, since the woman *all the time* must stand the test of whether to cover all her hair or just a portion of it, and so on, so that she not be embarrassed by those who make fun of her (even though she sometimes only imagines them but at other times encounters them in reality). But this is not the case when she wears a wig [*sheytl*], for she cannot take off the wig [as she might feel pressured to do with a kerchief] when she's at a party and such" (Menachem Mendel Schneerson, letter of 10 Adar, 5718 [March 2, 1958], in *Igros Kodesh* [Brooklyn: Otzar Hasidim 5718 (1958)], 16:330–31, emphasis in original). We thank Maya Katz and Leizer Shemtov for help with references here.

the Lubavitcher yeshiva in Poland.[8] When the mother of one of those who joined him said she was frightened to send her son on a mission to a place where the Nazis were attacking Jews and Jewry, she was told by the Rebbe, "He has nothing to fear. He's going to go and he's going to come back and everything will be all right." That, Hecht concluded, "wiped out any doubts that we had. . . . If he said nothing to worry about, then OK."[9] The assurances of a rebbe were sufficient to allay all concerns.

In the postwar period, parents of *shluchim* were at the outset somewhat anxious about sending their children away as emissaries, especially to the open societies of the West. But the assurances of Rabbi Menachem Mendel, like those of his predecessor, proved sufficient in the end. Moreover, as the movement's missionary vocation became more pronounced toward the end of the twentieth century, young Lubavitcher couples were further encouraged to choose a joint life as emissaries by strong communal pressure no less than by the urging of their rebbe. As young Lubavitchers increasingly chose to "go on *shlichus*" and out into the world, remaining within the Lubavitcher enclave seemed increasingly like being left behind.

Lubavitcher women have not taken a back seat to men in the missionary vocation. While elsewhere in the Hasidic and traditional Jewish world women were encouraged to find a husband who ideally would be a Torah scholar studying in the yeshiva and whom they would support in that effort, contemporary Lubavitcher women are expected to go out into the world as emissaries with their husbands. In practice, much of the work falls on their shoulders, including coordinating Sabbath or holiday meals for all sorts of guests—often invited on short notice— and acting as a nurturing guide for the Jewishly uninformed. Some, such as Dina Greenberg of the ChaBaD Center in Shanghai, China, have started schools. Women in Lubavitch are not second class; they are full-fledged emissaries who have their own *kinus* and are encouraged no less than men in their mission.

One does not become a *shaliach* overnight. The training often starts in the early teens (and for children of *shluchim* it is part of their upbringing), when the would-be emissary serves as a counselor or assistant in a Lubavitcher summer camp or school in a place where ChaBaD already has an institutional presence. He or she might then graduate to the position of assistant to a *shaliach* elsewhere. Finally, after marriage, often in their early twenties, the young couple would find a posting where they were in charge. At first this might be in a territory in which they would be expected to report to a senior *shaliach*, and later they might at last find a place where they could be totally on their own.*

Typical of the *shaliach* career trajectory is the path followed by Hirschy Zarchi, a young Lubavitcher yeshiva student who had been dispatched to Boston in the 1990s to wander Harvard Square and connect with nonreligious Jewish students. He began by setting up a table and urging Jewish men to put on tefillin (phylacteries). He soon realized that he had to change tactics, as the Harvard students would not be swayed by simplistic slogans and easy rituals. So Zarchi began to engage them in deeper discussions. By 1997, after he had married Elkie, the new couple had opened a ChaBaD House at Harvard, and within six years, with the widespread support of faculty and students, they had succeeded in attaining officially recognized Jewish chaplain status on campus. Harvard's ChaBaD House defined itself as on a mission "inspired by the Lubavitcher Rebbe" and "a place where Jews of all backgrounds and degrees of observance can enjoy exploring their Jewish heritage in a warm, welcoming and non-judgmental environment." By 2003, Zarchi, a Hasid who had never gotten a college education, was marching in cap and gown at the university's graduation ceremonies. By 2008 he and his wife had added a "wisdom center" that offered everything from basic answers to questions about Jewish practice to "comprehensive, in-depth treatments of an array of subjects and issues by Chassidic scholars and professionals," as well as advice on "love, friendship, sexuality, intimacy, marriage and more."[10]

In 1999, Shalom Greenberg, Israeli-born son of and brother to Lubavitcher *shluchim*, had moved with his wife, Dina, to Shanghai, a burgeoning financial center in the new China and a magnet for Jewish entrepreneurs and business people.[11] Setting up shop in a small

---

* By the third generation of this sort of *shluchim*, the process in places almost became like a family operation, and children who could not find a posting of their own or some other mission often had to be habilitated in their parents' territory. Those who had no family connections might find entry into the mission difficult.

apartment, he began calling whatever Jews in town he could locate (there were at the time about one hundred fifty families) to invite them to a Sabbath meal, sometimes getting about twenty-five to come. By Passover eight years later they were hosting four hundred people for a seder in a new ChaBaD House in the Shang Mira Garden Villas on Hong Qiao Road. By 2008 on Sabbaths they were getting on average one hundred fifty congregants in two services and feeding hundreds. They had built a *mikveh* or ritual bath and were catering kosher food throughout China. Their school and infants' center rivaled many found in larger Jewish communities. They had expanded their operations across the Huangpu River to residential Pudong, where Shalom's brother was the *shaliach*, and they had a thriving mother-and-child center offering a variety of activities, from lunch-and-learn to a women's circle and Talmud classes.

In 2003, the newly married *shluchim* couple Asher and Henya Federman were making plans to strike out on their own. At the time Federman was teaching at a yeshiva near the Rebbe's grave in Queens and his wife was commuting to a Lubavitcher preschool program in Greenwich, Connecticut. As Asher explained, they "Googled all the remaining countries in the world without a Lubavitch presence and researched the Jewish population." Before pursuing a particular assignment they spoke to Rabbis Yehuda Krinsky, the head of Merkos L'Inyonei Chinuch, the central organization of Lubavitch, and Moshe Kotlarsky, vice-chair of the *shluchim*, and on Kotlarsky's advice they settled on the Virgin Islands, where at the Elysian Resort Beach Building they set up their outreach efforts. Here they built what they called "your soul resort in America's paradise," offering many of the same services the Greenbergs provide in Shanghai.[12]

The Zarchis, Greenbergs, Federmans, and *shluchim* like them could go to such geographically and culturally distant places and build new lives and institutions without feeling they had defiled themselves religiously, betrayed their way of life, or abandoned their own community because they were still inspired by and linked to the Rebbe, whose mission provided them with moral protection. As Shalom Lipskar, a *shaliach* in Bar Harbor, Florida, explained, "only because of a sense of self-security, pride in my Jewishness, knowing I was part of a mission, was I able to keep walking down the street without feeling totally inept and offensive."[13] By the time of Rabbi Menachem Mendel's death in 1994, there were thousands of *shluchim* scattered across the globe, in places as exotic as Katmandu, Nepal—where on Passover they organized one of the largest seders in the world for the many Jewish trekkers passing through—and as mundane as Long Island, New York, where religiously wayward Jews are aplenty. Indeed, it is increasingly difficult to find any place in the world where there are many Jews and no *shaliach*. Throughout the United States and Canada, especially on all major university campuses where Jews in any number are found—in short, wherever Jews are located—sooner or later a ChaBaD Lubavitcher emissary is at work. Indeed, at their 2009 gathering, Lubavitchers claimed that the number of *shluchim* had doubled since 1994.[14]

The collapse of the Soviet Union and its Eastern bloc satellite states in 1989 had made these formerly communist countries virgin territory for *shluchim*. The fall of communism allowed a return to the Lubavitchers' place of origin, where they had first begun their work until being forced to go underground during the early days of communism.[15] After 1989, in what many Lubavitchers saw as a sign of the coming redemption and a consequence of their rebbe's power to bring it about, they began spreading all over the former Eastern bloc in search of Jews to redeem and remake. One *shaliach*—Berel Lazar, son of *shluchim* in Italy and a former clandestine Lubavitcher activist in the Soviet Union—found his way into the good graces of then Russian president Vladimir Putin, becoming his "favorite rabbi" and eventually chief rabbi of Russia. Others were establishing themselves elsewhere throughout the old Soviet empire. In what many Lubavitchers saw as the hand of God in history, *shluchim* descended on Dnepropetrovsk (formerly Yekaterinoslav), Russia, where their revered rebbe had moved as a seven-year-old when his father, Levi Yitzchak, was appointed the Hasidic community rabbi of the city.

In Israel, where Zionism, nationalism, socialism, and secularism have competed to redefine the modern Jew, *shluchim* offer yet another model of what a Jew should be. They have entered into the competition over Jewish identity. Historically, ChaBaD had been the purveyor of a powerful anti-Zionist ideology, which (as we show) played a part in its initial relationship with the new Jewish state. But that would change. At Kfar Chabad, a village between Tel Aviv and Jerusalem founded in 1949, Lubavitchers established a stronghold and from there sent *shluchim* to establish ChaBaD schools throughout Israel.[16] They proved to be especially successful at attracting immigrant Sephardic Jews from North Africa and the Middle East, who felt left out and belittled by the Israeli establishment and were often ignored by other Jewish Orthodox groups. The Hasidim began to have increasing influence in a variety of ways. ChaBaD opened a trade school in Kfar Chabad offering instruction in mechanics and metalwork. In 1970 the village was designated an "absorption center" for Israeli immigrants, providing more opportunity for Lubavitchers to influence newcomers to Israel, and during the decade, ChaBaD *shluchim* began visiting Israeli army camps to provide support for the troops during the Jewish holidays.[17] As we show in this book, Lubavitcher involvement in Israel intensified after the 1967 war and came to influence Israeli politics and society in unforeseen ways.

It took more than messianic belief or confidence in the Rebbe to make all this possible. It required fundamental changes in the world that modern Jewry inhabited and the development of a cadre of young people powerfully committed to the ChaBaD tradition but willing to go out to transform Jews and the world. The first such change was the remarkable resurgence of religion in the modern world. Religion at the start of the twentieth century was considered an inevitable victim of modernity—"the old gods are growing old or already dead," Émile Durkheim opined, while Friedrich Nietzsche proclaimed that without doubt, "God was dead."[18] But by the end of the twentieth century, a new religious reawakening was afoot in precisely those precincts of Western civilization where modernity had been forged.[19] The second change was ChaBaD's offering young people who were Lubavitcher Hasidim a way to enter into the new world of contemporary culture—a world that most of their Hasidic counterparts tried to keep at a distance—without feeling they had to abandon all their Hasidic and Jewish attachments. Rabbi Menachem Mendel and his mission held out to ChaBaD young people the promise of, as he once put it, "a sense of respect, particularly towards those who remain steadfast in their convictions, and are not embarrassed by those who make fun of them or their worldview," but who nevertheless were ready to go out as his emissaries. [20] He assured them they could stand with their feet in both the world of their Jewish commitments and the world where those commitments were being tested all the time, where the tomorrow of change was often of greater interest than the yesterday of tradition. This mandate spoke to many of the young Hasidim, who, like all adolescents, seek, as Erik Erikson has shown us, "to experience wholeness," which they discover when they "feel a progressive continuity between that which [they have] come to be during the long years of childhood and that which [they promise] to become in the anticipated future."[21] The role of the emissary offered a way to be whole: steadfast in their Judaism but able to go anywhere in the world and define themselves anew. In the atmosphere of religious resurgence, young Lubavitcher *shluchim* and their mission have become more conceivable and acceptable, both in America and everywhere in the modern world Jews have flocked.

The third change that made all this possible stems from the multiple forces of robust economic growth, globalization, and technological advance that have led increasing numbers of prosperous Jews to travel and settle all over the world for business and pleasure. Among this group are observant Jews who need religious services wherever they find themselves, and other less observant or nonobservant Jews who Lubavitchers believe also need their religious services. Lubavitcher emissaries now in place across the globe are prepared to provide these services for Jews on the go. They do so not only for those who want these services but also for those whose desire for these services must be aroused and vitalized.

Asked whom he was there to serve more, the observant Jews who might make their way to Shanghai and needed religious services or the marginally involved, Rabbi Greenberg replied he was there clearly for the latter: "I am happy to provide a synagogue and kosher meal for religious Jews visiting Shanghai. But if I were not here, the observant Jew would still pray on his own or eat the sardines he had brought along; the Jews who are not observant, however, are praying because I and Dina are here and they are eating kosher because we supply them with it. They are the reason ChaBaD has come here, and they are the ones I have been truly sent to serve."[22]

Finally, Lubavitcher *shluchim*, especially those on university campuses or in Jewishly sparse communities, have responded effectively to the growing anxiety among many Jews in this globalized and fast-changing, seductive world that a distinctive Jewish identity might disappear as Jews assimilate into open society and the global culture. The *shluchim* have become avatars of religion and outspoken protectors of some sort of obvious Jewish identity. Their efforts have attracted economic and moral support among Jews who, while perhaps not ready themselves to be Hasidim or even fully observant Jews, are prepared to help Lubavitchers do the job. This is what makes it possible for Jewish trekkers in Katmandu, business people in Shanghai, students at Harvard, and vacationers in the Virgin Islands to come to and even help ChaBaD. These Jewish sojourners find in ChaBaD Houses around the world a ready-made and welcoming family of Lubavitchers prepared to help them with their Jewish needs and make them feel at home in an otherwise alienating and anonymous global world.

♫♫

After Rabbi Menachem Mendel Schneerson's death (his Hasidim called it the Rebbe's *histalkes,* or leave-taking) on June 12, 1994 (Gimmel [3] Tammuz 5754 in the Hebrew calendar), the mission and the *farbrengens* took on a new poignancy and meaning.* No longer was the *farbrengen* an opportunity to be in the Rebbe's physical presence, a meeting that for Lubavitchers was spiritual and religious in nature; rather, it became a time to recall and somehow reanimate that presence and revitalize the mission, if not the movement, that he helped shape during more than half a century of leadership. But there were difficulties.

The Previous Rebbe, Yosef Yitzchak Schneersohn, had asserted that the age of the Messiah was nigh and that this generation was the last in exile and would be the first of redemption, a message that his successor, Menachem Mendel, had reiterated and intensified. From his first public address as leader he had made many believe that the messianic mission was in the very process of completion. Indeed, at the end of his life, almost all his Hasidim believed Menachem Mendel was himself the Messiah. With his passing, however, much of that message and the mission

---

* Generally to avoid referring to their Rebbe's death, Hasidim simply use the phrase "Gimmel Tammuz" (the third day of the month of Tammuz, in this case the day on which Rabbi Menachem Mendel Schneerson died) as a euphemism. The use of such euphemisms for death is not unique to Lubavitchers. Traditional Judaism shies away from the word "death." Even cemeteries are commonly referred to as "houses of life" or "houses of Eternity"—*bey-shakhayim* or *beys-oylem*.

it stimulated had to be understood anew.[23] "A fulfilled prophecy makes real what one previously had to take on faith. A failed prophecy, on the other hand, demonstrates that one's faith was mistaken."[24]

But the faith of Hasidim in their rebbe can never be mistaken, for if it is, they are no longer his Hasidim. To give up faith was unacceptable to all Lubavitchers, who had built so much of their way of life and the character of their movement on their faith in the messianic message and its foremost exponent. They could not return home and give up the mission, and with it their hopes for forcing the end and bringing on the age of redemption. Continuity was a foregone conclusion. That is not to say that even believers were not plagued by doubts that surely affected their faith. The challenge was how exactly to maintain continuity. "The Moshiach is going to come," said a Lubavitcher woman, assuring a reporter—and perhaps herself as well—in the days after the Rebbe's death. "It's just not going to happen the way we thought it would."[25]

In almost all Hasidic groups, including the Lubavitchers, the death of a rebbe, like that of a king, is commonly followed by the appointment of a successor. That man might be a son, son-in-law, or in some cases an outstanding disciple.[26] There might be some tension and conflict surrounding the choice of the successor, particularly if the previous rebbe had not designated him in advance or had failed to leave a will in which he specified who would lead after his demise. Sometimes dynasties and courts might become divided, with sons or sons-in-law competing for followers, a process that in the best circumstances could lead to Hasidic diversity, a spiritual division of labor, and broader influence as rebbes established themselves in different areas of Jewish settlement, taking their names from the towns and villages where they held court (a practice especially prevalent during the period of Hasidic expansion in the nineteenth century). Such was the case with ChaBaD Hasidism in the eighteenth and nineteenth centuries. After the death of the first rebbe and founder, Schneur Zalman, his son DovBer (1773–1827), known as the Miteler (Middle) Rebbe, and Schneur Zalman's outstanding disciple, Aaron Halevi Horowitz of Starosielc, competed for the Hasidim's loyalty.[27] Even more so following the death of the third Lubavitcher rebbe, Menachem Mendel (1789–1866), better known by his nom de plume, Zemah Zedek, there were competing claims, with one son establishing a following in the town of Kapust (Kopys) and three others leading groups in Lyady and Bobriusk, all in Belarus, and one in Nezhin, Ukraine. By the time the sixth rebbe, the sole son of Rabbi Shalom DovBer, the fifth rebbe, whose dynasty had long ago taken the name of Lubavitch (after Lyubavichi, Russia, where the second rebbe, Dovber, had established the court), arrived in New York to reestablish his brand of Hasidism in America, the Lubavitcher line was largely accepted as the dominant if not the only surviving strain of the ChaBaD school of Hasidism.[28]

During this long history the Lubavitchers always found a way to continue the line through this process of succession, albeit at times with some friction. But the ascendance of the childless forty-eight-year-old Menachem Mendel Schneerson as their leader in 1951 came with the assurance that the long-awaited Messiah would arrive in time to solve any future succession questions.[29] This understanding had been implicit from the time he made his first public address as Rebbe through the time he lay comatose in a bed at Beth Israel Hospital in the weeks before his demise. But now with his *histalkes*, Lubavitcher Hasidim refused to formally make the transition to a new leader, for there was no alternative for them—after all, the Rebbe had promised his would be the first generation of the final redemption. To ensure continuity, they simply denied the finality of death and continued to see the Rabbi Menachem Mendel as their Rebbe. They could not say good-bye: "You say goodbye to your parents and create your own life. The Rebbe is our connection with God. Every day he's helping us live our lives."[30] They could no more sever their connection to him than to Almighty God. If the Rebbe had promised to lead them to the Messiah, he must still be doing so. If they could be led by Rabbi Menachem Mendel during his life in this world, they could also be led by him during his afterlife.

The idea that they could be led by a man who had died was not altogether foreign to Lubavitchers. It had a precedent. Indeed, from the beginning of his own reign, Rabbi Menachem Mendel had insisted that his predecessor and father-in-law, Rabbi Yosef Yitzhak Schneersohn, remained Rebbe—even after his earthly departure. In taking on the leadership of Lubavitch, he, Menachem Mendel, would therefore serve only as a channel, receiving and sending messages from and to the "Previous Rebbe," as Yosef Yitzchak came to be known, during Menachem

Mendel's regular visits to the latter's gravesite in Old Montefiore Cemetery in the Cambria Heights section of Queens, New York.[31] He would still refer to his predecessor as *n'si doreynu*, the leader of our generation, "who continues to serve on high and cares for his flock here" and who will lead us to receive the Messiah.[32]

This rationale for Menachem Mendel's leadership, so important at the outset and repeated endlessly by him, had gradually faded in the consciousness of many of his followers as they increasingly embraced him in the role of Rebbe. But with his death, Lubavitchers revived the idea of taking directions from a rebbe who was in an afterlife but could continue to care for and direct his flock here. As Menachem Mendel had done with *his* Rebbe, Yosef Yitzchak, so would they do with him, Menachem Mendel, with the same if not greater loyalty than they had when he was alive.

But could *they* be the channel for him? He, the holy and inspired leader, *alone* had served as the conduit for messages from his predecessor, Rabbi Yosef Yitzchak; how could a *group* become the conduit through which the Rebbe would continue to lead? And what about the coming of the Messiah? Both Rabbi Yosef Yitzchak and, even more so, his successor, Rabbi Menachem Mendel, had assured the Lubavitchers that the Messiah's arrival was imminent and the actions of the Hasidim were driven by a preparation for this day of redemption, but now both were dead and the Messiah was nowhere to be seen. How could they keep the faith? Menachem Mendel had helped restore them after Yosef Yitzchak died, but who would revive them now?

The revival process began at least partially in the cemetery. The practices associated with the commemoration of the anniversary of death began when many of the Hasidim went to the cemetery and visited the Rebbe's *tsiyen* (tomb) and brought *pidyones* (sometimes called "*pan*," an acronym for *pidyon nefesh*, "the redemption of the soul"), personal notes on which the names of the petitioners and their requests are listed. Those who give a rebbe *pidyones* are said to be bonded to him spiritually.[33]

The idea of going to the grave of a *zaddik*, or what some have called "the cult of the departed saint," has a long history in Hasidism and kabbalah.[34] This practice is driven by the belief that the *zaddik*, saint or great sage, is regarded as mediating between the divine and those among the living who had a deep connection to him, even after death.[35] This was part of a process called *yihudim* (unifications), mystical procedures by which the living continue to be attached to the soul of the departed saint. It is based on the assertion of the *Zohar*, the primary text of kabbalah, that the *zaddik* is more present "in all the worlds" after his death than during his life.[36] Indeed, the Talmud (B.T. *Hulin* 7b) in its assertion that "*gedolim tsaddikim be-mitatan yoter mi-be-hayyeyhen*" (saints are even grander in their death than in their lives) provided perhaps the ultimate basis for the notion that a rebbe could achieve more for his followers after his passing than during his lifetime.[37] Accordingly, part of the responsibility of the dead *zaddik*—and of course a rebbe *is* a *zaddik*—involves his petitioning on behalf of the living (particularly those with whom he is unified) after his passing. The *Zohar*'s categorical assertion that "without the prayer of the dead the living could not exist" serves as a basic proof text for the practice of going to the grave. It was here, according to the kabbalist Rabbi Hayyim Vital (1542–1620), that *yihudim* were best accomplished, since the lowest part of the *zaddik*'s soul, *nefesh*, was ever present, and hence the living petitioner could better gain contact with the residual presence of the departed saint at the graveyard.[38]

ChaBaD Hasidim were particularly attuned to the notion that contact with a *zaddik* could be mediated via other means. Indeed, their founder, Schneur Zalman, had told them in an epistle that became part of their most sacred text, *Tanya* (published in the eighteenth century, and whose study was meant to serve as a substitute for the close personal contact that his Hasidim expected to have with its author), that the soul of the *zaddik* infused his followers with a transcendent life force, and that even after the *zaddik*'s death, his spirit (*ruekh*) "remains truly in our midst," but only for those who are sincerely and completely bound to him.[39] For true believers, and Hasidim surely qualified, the departed *zaddik* is present even more than he was during his lifetime. That was why going to the grave was so important. And for no one was it more important than Menachem Mendel Schneerson. Now that he was no longer among the living, it was also important for his followers.[40]

While 770 had been the place to encounter Rabbi Menachem Mendel during his lifetime, "after Gimmel Tammuz," as his followers often referred to the period following his physical leave-taking, the cemetery became an intensified focus of their devotions, just as it had for him after the death of *his* predecessor.[41] Here, just east of the last house in a row of modest, single-family homes along Francis Lewis Boulevard, in a working-class and largely African American neighborhood in Queens, New York, not far from Kennedy International Airport, Lubavitchers had established a most extraordinary Jewish holy place, considered by them to be as sacred as any of the other places on earth that Jews venerate. The focus of the veneration was a small stone mausoleum (the *ohel*), open to the sky, where now the remains of the two Rebbes, Yosef Yitzchak and Menachem Mendel, lay buried side by side, surrounded by other important Lubavitchers and across a small stone path from the deceased women of Lubavitch.

To reach it, visitors pass behind the row of small cottages. Inside the house closest to the cemetery the Lubavitchers have installed a small office with several phone lines, a fax machine, and a computer equipped to receive missives and *pidyones* to the late Rebbe from petitioners all over the world—messages to be deposited on the bier. The office is manned by a gentle young Lubavitcher from England, Abba Refson, who sorts and directs the electronic supplications. It is active at all hours of day and night (the world of ChaBaD followers never sleeps).

The main cottage features a small reception room in which a video mix consisting of thousands of hours of the Rebbe's talks and public sessions, all of which have been documented, runs endlessly. Visitors can sit and watch him on reruns while they compose themselves and the written petitions they will deposit on his grave. In what was once a kitchen, people wash their hands at two sinks, in line with the tradition that all those leaving a cemetery must purify themselves, and some lave their hands in preparation for visiting the resting place of the *zaddikim*, the righteous, as the rebbes and their holy disciples are also known. The largest room inside the cottage has a library and chapel where people may pray (facing east toward the tomb and Jerusalem) and study the enormous body of literature, published talks, and letters the Rebbe produced in his lifetime and that are now part of his legacy. One Hasid among the many who visited the space on this commemorative day referred to the library as "the Rebbe in the book."

Refson often watched with bemusement as people came for the books of the Rebbe's letters and opened them at random, hoping to find on the page answers to the questions they had asked at the grave. This bibliomancy had become a common means of communicating with the Rebbe.[42] Refson was not a big believer in this, for he had seen too many people opening the book more than once, presumably when they did not find a satisfying answer the first time.[43] But among many of the visitors it remains a popular practice.

In addition to this place, the Lubavitchers have gradually purchased several other cottages nearby to accommodate overnight guests and petitioners, one in which they established a yeshiva, and a larger house on another street where they billet students who come to plumb the meaning of the Rebbe's texts. Next to this little yeshiva they have built a ritual bath for the daily immersions and for those visitors who wish to purify themselves even more before "coming into the Rebbe," as they often refer to these visits. Behind these are two Quonset huts that dwarf the houses and serve as a kind of staging area for a small opening into the cemetery and stone walkway leading to the graves. Over time the huts have been converted to spaces where pilgrims can study or pray. On the long tables in the huts and everywhere inside the house are small Lucite boxes in which stacks of blank paper and pens are available for those who want to compose *pidyones*, little notes to God and the Rebbe. In a corner there is a constantly replenished supply of cookies, tea, and coffee; the body needs a lift even where the soul is king. At the side of the hut, near the path that leads to the cemetery, are shelves stacked with spare *gartls*, the black sashes Hasidim wrap about their waists during prayer to symbolically separate the higher from the lower parts of the body and the mind from animal inclination. Underneath the *gartls* is a stack of worn slippers (and more recently Crocs) for those who wish to remove their leather shoes (a tradition when one steps on sacred ground) before entering the holy place inside the *tsiyen* (grave) or *ohel*, but do not want to step on the cold stone in their socks. Here too are some psalters whose frayed pages show the signs of the countless fingers that have traced their words in supplication.

From the hut, visitors can walk a short distance to the small section of Lubavitcher notables that surround the Rebbe's *tsiyen*. Since his death, pilgrims have been pouring in from all over the world, often on their way to or from nearby Kennedy International Airport or 770. Non-Lubavitchers, many of them Sephardic Jews of North African or

Middle Eastern origin, come seeking what they have searched for at other holy places they are accustomed to visiting: personal blessings, the redemption of their souls from evil, the intercession of the divine, cures for the ill, or endorsement of their important life choices and guidance from on high.[44] But for Lubavitchers in particular, the pilgrimage to the *tsiyen* is a way to keep close to their Rebbe. They flock there on days considered special in the ChaBaD calendar, such as Gimmel Tammuz or Yud (the Tenth of) Shvat (the day Rabbi Yosef Yitzchak died and on which a year later Rabbi Menachem Mendel ascended to his position), as well as the days preceding the *kinus shluchim*.

On the sidewalks and in the hut, everywhere around the place, there are stacks of pamphlets filled with prayers, readings, and a variety of materials meant to assist the ritual of visiting. These practices are variations on established rituals of Jewish gravesite visits, with specifically Lubavitcher customs. Arriving at the *tsiyen*, one knocks on the door, removes one's shoes, enters, and deposits one's note on the ground after tearing it above the grave, where the pile of white slips of paper is enormous. While there, one recites psalms and perhaps lights a candle, then departs. Even *Kohens*—Jews who are considered the descendants of the ancient priestly tribe and who normally cannot visit cemeteries because of death's capacity to defile their special purity—are allowed by Lubavitcher custom to visit the Rebbe's tomb, based on the principle accepted by ChaBaD that while presence near a dead body is defiling, even a *Kohen* cannot be defiled by the corpse of a *zaddik*. The Lubavitchers have found a way to make it possible under Jewish law to reach the *tsiyen* by installing red curtains on both sides of the pathway from the hut outside the cemetery to the mausoleum. The curtains ritually separate the space the pilgrims pass through from the surrounding dead bodies. The presence of these curtains seems to have a further symbolic meaning; they dramatically highlight the fact that there is only one path for faithful Jews to walk, one that leads back to the Rebbe.

For many of the faithful, the wait in the line to the tomb on Gimmel Tammuz or other holy days in the ChaBaD calendar is considered part of the experience. The waiting and all the related ritual preparations recall the mental and spiritual preparations that a true Hasid must make before approaching his Rebbe. As Rabbi Yisrael Shmotkin, a visiting *shaliach* from Milwaukee, explained, before an audience, however brief, with the Rebbe, "[you had] to get your mind and heart so that you should feel the need for the spiritual enhancement, *cheshbon ha'nefesh* [soul searching]. In fact, you never feel sufficiently prepared. The more spiritually sensitive a Hasid is, the more difficult the preparation."

Insiders understand this experience of pilgrimage not as "going to a grave" but rather as "going into the Rebbe." They go "into" him and come away charged up with "feelings" and understandings that fill their interior imagination.

"It is today exactly as it was; I go through the same preparations that I made before I would go in to see the Rebbe when he was alive," Shmotkin added, explaining his relationship to the Rebbe after the latter's death. As for the responses pilgrims such as Shmotkin expect from their deceased Rebbe, "the way you ask the Rebbe for something determines the kind of answer you get."[45] His physical absence can be "neutralized" by the attitude of the believer. He might be physically dead, but he continues to be spiritually alive in those who turn to him.[46] Over the three days of the commemoration of this anniversary of his death, Lubavitchers reported 28,000 visitors, and near 40,000 *pidyones* were faxed to the cemetery.[47]

Many of those who went to the cemetery on the anniversary of the death claimed to have received messages from the deceased Rebbe. Where once his charisma brought his disciples together, now they bonded over an intense and shared sense of bereavement and loss, as well as a commonly held commitment to continue the mission he had initiated and incarnated. In a sense, this bonding and the determination to ensure continuity have led to a kind of transformation and absorption of the Rebbe's charisma by the assembled.[48] No single one of them became the Rebbe, but in some way the collective and their assembly—their coming together—brought him to life. That was particularly evident at the *ohel*.

Many of the older Hasidim, especially those who could narrate their encounters with the now absent leader, began to exude some of his charisma during the assemblies. While the Rebbe was alive, they might have constituted a secondary elite, but in his absence they have risen to the highest tier. While gathering to commemorate their Rebbe's memory, when one of the older men begins to offer his recollections—a story, a tune, a lesson learned—younger Lubavitchers crowd around him and hang on his every word, as if straining to penetrate his memories and make them their own. They might even organize *farbrengens* around senior Hasidim whose personal histories and recollections go back to the first days of Rabbi Menachem Mendel's tenure.[49] One such episode occurred on the eve of Gimmel Tammuz, when Rabbi Berel Shemtov from Detroit, one of the oldest *shluchim* and the first to be sent out by Rabbi Menachem Mendel in America, became a magnet for a crowd of enthusiastic young Hasidim by beginning a conversation with a visitor about what it meant to relate to the Rebbe on the eve of the anniversary of his death. Shemtov's father, Bentzion, a contemporary of the Rebbe, had been a devoted Hasid of the Previous Rebbe, from even before the time he had been a rebbe, and had been a student at the Tomekhei Temimim yeshiva in Russia. His sons and grandchildren were prominent *shluchim*. The Shemtovs were as close as one could get to someone who had deep roots in the Lubavitcher saga.[50] Avremel Shemtov, Berel's brother, was now chair of Agudas Chassidei ChaBaD, the highest post in the movement in the absence of a rebbe. As Berel spoke, he suggested to his eager audience that they, the young Hasidim, were crucial to what was happening in ChaBaD. "Those who do not remember the Rebbe in life are 'bigger Hasidim' even than those who did," he remarked, "because they have to work harder to bring him back."[51]

Here was an old-timer encouraging and praising the very people in whose hands continuity rested. If they had doubts they could accomplish this in the absence of their leader, he assured them "the Rebbe gives a person the strength he needs." In fact, he argued, "a *tsaddik* lives more today than yesterday." How could that be? It was, he explained, "the Rebbe's *neshamah* [soul]" that was always the source of his ability to bestow blessings, not his physical being. And "he is a more a *neshamah* today than he was before." These were almost the same arguments that Rabbi Menachem Mendel had made after the death of his predecessor, and indeed what Rabbi Yosef Yitzchak had said about himself.[52] Now the Hasidim were making these claims. Precisely his incorporeality was what gave him a greater presence, as long as those assembled believed in his capacity to bless them.

For the Lubavitchers, then, Gimmel Tammuz had become not a day of mourning but rather a *hillula*, a day of celebration with a sense of triumph over the continuing mission and a chance for Hasidim to demonstrate to themselves and others that they could find within themselves, as a *shaliach* put it, the "collective energy that transcends and at the same time empowers the individual." Thirteen years after the Rebbe's death, tears were replaced by an excitement in the air, as if this were the eve of a festival—as in many ways it was.

If in the past the *farbrengens* provided an occasion to "reconnect with the Rebbe and interact with colleagues," in the absence of his physical presence the focus of their attention was their proximity to those who felt his absence most keenly. The *farbrengen* now would serve primarily, as one Lubavitcher put it quoting Isaiah (41:6), as a vehicle for "*ish es re'eihu ya'azoru ul'eochiv yoimar chazak*," for each and all as one to help one another and to offer strength, support and encouragement. If in the past it was the charismatic Rebbe in person who orchestrated the enthusiasms and collective effervescence of his Hasidim, now their interaction and continuing devotion to him accomplished it.

There were all sorts of signs that the group had in a sense come to embody the Rebbe. In his lifetime, beginning on 11 Nisan 5746 (April 20, 1986), his eighty-fourth birthday, Rabbi Menachem Mendel had taken up the practice of handing out crisp new dollar bills that were meant to turn every recipient into a *shaliach mitzvah*, someone who would act as his agent to give that dollar (and perhaps more) to charity and thereby fulfill the mission of doing that mitzvah. "Charity," the Rebbe had said on many occasions, "hastens and immediately causes the true and complete redemption."[53] It had become a famous practice, as for most of the rest of his life he distributed tens of thousands of dollar bills to all manner of people who came to 770 Eastern Parkway on Sundays. As the Lubavitchers gathered to mark the thirteenth anniversary of his passing at the *tsiyen*, young Lubavitcher yeshiva boys—the *temimim*, the unblemished and pure of heart, as they were called, and because they went to the yeshiva of that name— walked along the street in front of the cemetery and handed out dollar bills to all those assembled. In so doing, these youngsters, who had never seen the Rebbe in life, embodied and expressed both the future and the past. They effectively mimicked what the Rebbe had done, but with a new twist in that rather than waiting for people to line up for dollars, they went out to them.

The children, the Rebbe had often said, "were entrusted with a special mission to particularly dedicate themselves to all matters of Judaism." This included "using their own personal allowance money to give extra charity," an act that would help the Jewish people "as a whole," because the charity given by a child in particular had "special significance" in hastening the redemption. Moreover, not only should they give, they were to "inspire all their neighbors to do the same." These children were doing just that. In so doing, they were the incarnation of continuity and the vehicles for bringing the Messiah. Their dollars were the Rebbe's dollars, but now given by the group via the children to all comers. And they were doing it, as the Rebbe had told them God wanted them to, "with joy and exuberance," thus making the "world a dwelling place for God himself."[54] With obvious pride, their initiative became the talk of the day among all those who had come to the *tsiyen*.

These Hasidim also kept the Rebbe alive by continuously plumbing and internalizing the messages that were in the copious literature built up of texts their rebbes had left them. They paid particular attention to ensuring that the young studied and assimilated these words. This in fact they had done since the fifth rebbe, Rabbi Shalom DovBer, had established the Tomekhei Temimim yeshiva, at which he included as subjects of study, in addition to the traditional Jewish texts, Hasidic texts, or *khsides*, as they were often called, including the so-called *Sichos* (talks), *ma'amarim* (discourses), *Divrei Elohim Chayim* (*DACh*, in its Hebrew acronym), the Words of the Living God, as offered by their rebbe, and *Igros* (letters) of their rebbes that were taken down, studied, committed to memory, and repeated. In this way, Hasidic text, teacher, and student became one. Study of their founding rebbe's *Tanya* taught them that. The idea of accessing a rebbe by means of a text was thus a long-established principle for these Hasidim. That the Rebbe was no longer among them physically was irrelevant to this sort of encounter. Indeed, for the young ChaBaD Hasid, for whom the intellectual element was critical, the written work would be among the most direct personal encounters with the Rebbe.

ʃʃʃʃ

Through the collective energy and consciousness that such *farbrengens* stimulated, through their sharing and adopting of recollections, through their assimilation and repetition of his words, and through their emotional attachments, the Lubavitcher Hasidim thus kept their Rebbe alive. As long as the young and old remained enthusiastic, willing, and able to share in all this, they claimed they could feel the Rebbe among them as a guiding force. As Leizer Shemtov, a third-generation *shaliach*, put it, "When the Rebbe was here physically, one could feel secure by relying on the Rebbe to identify threats and opportunities and lead the response. After the *histalkes*, we no longer have that. The initial feeling is one of vulnerability and loneliness. Eventually the feeling sets in that we can do this all together nourishing ourselves from one another's strengths. That feeling strengthens at each *kinus*."[55] "Can we even fathom the collective power that we have?" asked Rabbi Ari Solish, the enthusiastic young new *shaliach* to Atlanta, addressing his fellow emissaries at the 2006 banquet.

If Gimmel Tammuz was a gathering to recall their connection to the late Rebbe, what was the *kinus shluchim*—the coming together of the emmisaries—if not a celebration of their network and their accomplishments? It is the network in which the life of Lubavitch now resides. The ability to spread the message, to engage in the mission, to learn from one's counterparts, to share experiences and wisdom, to train one another or to be apprenticed to one who is practiced in being a Hasid on the move, and even the opportunity to share memories of the past—all this is what gives life to Lubavitcher Hasidism in the absence of a living rebbe.

There is yet another way that Lubavitchers revive their missing Rebbe, and it was manifest at the 2006 *kinus*. A wall of video screens surrounded the vast hall at Pier 94 in Manhattan where the gathering was being held. The ubiquitousness of videos of the Rebbe made his voice and words very much a part of the day. On them, past and present merged seamlessly in a kind of visual metaphor of precisely what was critical for continuity. So, for example, when Rabbi Moshe Kotlarsky began the proceedings by calling on the assembled to sing a melody that Rabbi Menachem Mendel had taught them, a video of the Rebbe teaching the tune flashed on the screen. As the virtual Rebbe began to sing, the screens showed the Hasidim who were at his *farbrengen* at the time singing with him and, as the cameras at the present *kinus* panned across the hall, cross cut that image with shots of the assembled here and now also singing, thereby bringing all into the moving image. The voices of those in the past and those at the current banquet became indistinguishable. The virtual and the real, the past and the present, appeared almost interchangeable. At that moment one could be forgiven for imagining that the Rebbe was not simply an image flickering on a screen but a real person present in the room. That, of course, was the point.

"ChaBaD's attention to visibility as an essential component of its spiritual mission has proved strategic in the community's survival of a major loss," as Jeffrey Shandler has put it.[56] Countless Lubavitchers admitted they had watched the videos, which were now available online as part of a huge documentary project carried out by the Lubavitcher Jewish Educational Media under direction of a thirty-something-year old Elkanah Shmotkin. These videos enable the Lubavitchers to see the Rebbe in ways that no other Hasidim have ever been able in the past to see their previous leaders. Photographs of their rebbes had come to be important visual aids to maintaining a spiritual attachment between disciple and followers, particularly when the Rebbe was physically distant. The unprecedented number of photographs and moving images of Rabbi Menachem Mendel (which he, unlike other Hasidic rebbes, encouraged), along with the repackaging of these into the *Living Torah* series of disks on which bits of his addresses (with subtitles in English, Hebrew, Russian, French, Spanish, and Portuguese for non-Yiddish speakers), as well as a series of "special moments" and other snippets of his actions, are available by subscription or individual purchase and make the Rebbe a virtual presence everyone can have on screen on demand. Lubavitchers screen these images in some places every week at the close of the Sabbath, listening to Rabbi Menachem Mendel's remarks for that particular week. For those who were not present at the original talk, this is a chance to experience it for the first time, while for the others it is a chance to see it in a new way.

Some Lubavitchers who had experienced the original *farbrengens* in the Rebbe's presence even suggested that, while they missed his being there, watching these videos offered something more. At the original events, most of the attendees barely glimpsed the Rebbe and were often jostled by the crowd as they looked at him, or they were for some other reason unable to focus completely on what he said. Still others noted that their reverence for him had prevented them from looking directly at him. But by watching the videos they could absorb the whole experience in comfort. They could see their Rebbe's face in close view, observing in ways they never could before. Commenting on Rabbi Menachem Mendel's penetrating blue eyes, so often described by outsiders who met with him, a Hasid admitted he had never dared look directly at the Rebbe when speaking to him and only after viewing the videos discovered the "power of his gaze and the blue of his eyes." In a sense, the videos made the Rebbe closer and more present than he had been in life. Moreover, they made the encounter more intimate. In much the same way that viewers who encounter late-night television talk show hosts in real life often report they feel as if they know them intimately, because "[I have them] in my bedroom every night before I go to sleep," there is a closeness that the video image can create with the viewer that almost trumps real life.

"Through video not only can participants in the original events relive and reconnect, but for those who never met the Rebbe, it recreates the experience, touching and moving them as well," as the narrator of the trailer for the *Living Torah* series puts it. "In the words of one woman who watched a video of the Rebbe and then called her *shaliach* in excitement, 'Rabbi, I was just at my first *farbrengen*.'"[57]

Of course, for years Lubavitchers had been used to relating to the Rebbe as a video presence. Many of his talks and appearances had been beamed by satellite throughout the world via a technology he encouraged and celebrated when it was used for good. Looking at him now, it was easy to believe he was still alive and sending messages to his followers, but from "another location."

In addition, the editing of the videos, as well as the way they were organized by subject, occasion, and the like, allowed the viewers to distill the long and sometimes complicated talks with Rabbi Menachem Mendel or the hours of routine life in the court to moments and sound bites that could be translated into everything from pithy messages that anyone could understand—particularly useful in outreach work—and inspirational views that allowed one to go straight to the highlight zone.

Thus, for example, on one disk the Rebbe is seen at a *farbrengen* telling a story whose point is that an observant Jew should not be embarrassed to perform Jewish acts in front of nonpracticing Jews or even non-Jews. The story is of a successful Jewish businessman who has leased a yacht and seeks to know from the captain which direction is east, so that he can direct his daily prayers that way and toward Jerusalem. The captain, a non-Jew, the Rebbe reports, is deeply impressed by the fact that such a successful man still stops all his affairs and prays to God thrice daily. The Rebbe then observes, in a message that one can imagine many *shluchim* who were sent to impress nonobservant Jews and non-Jews alike—perhaps many of them also successful businessmen—of the importance of prayer, might want to highlight: "'In this case,' said the captain, 'I will also begin to think about God.'"

"I heard this second-hand," the Rebbe concludes, "and I don't know if the captain ended by promising that he would also pray, *but thinking about the Holy One Blessed be He is also 'prayer.'*"[58] This latter sentiment could surely be used in the Lubavitcher mission to bring the consciousness of God's presence in the Jewish world.

The videos thus could be understood "as but one means of realizing Chabad's ongoing commitment to making esoteric principles of spiritual transformation, once the provenance of a learned elite, accessible and meaningful to the entire Jewish community."[59] If once the image of the Rebbe was meant to make the viewer feel closer to the one in the picture, now that image can replace him. If at one time the living Rebbe could only be seen in one place, now the virtual Rebbe, the image, could be seen everywhere. There is something profoundly American and modern about this video packaging of the Rebbe. The Rebbe could live forever on reruns, and he could be reanimated by all who played the videos.

And beyond all this, Lubavitchers also remained tied to their leader in his afterlife by continuing to carry on the mission on which he had sent them, a mission they remained certain was still needed to guarantee a redemption for all Jews. They did that by becoming *shluchim* in ever greater numbers. That was precisely what the *kinus* and the *farbrengen* that accompanied it was meant to celebrate and reinforce.

How long, however, could the Lubavitchers remain on the mission without arriving at the moment of redemption? Could the Hasidim who expected the Rebbe to bring them to the Messiah himself be satisfied with what was becoming an endless wait? And who was this leader who had brought them to this crossroads? How had he become such a presence in his absence, in an America where Hasidism—indeed,

Jewish Orthodoxy—was expected to wither and die? Where did he come from, this man who trumpeted the Messiah and promised redemption in a world where the very idea seemed out-of-date and the Lubavitchers appeared to lead what they hoped would be legions of the skeptical and secular? To answer that question, we must first go to the day his predecessor died. There we can begin to understand how this man who stood between the old world and the new, the sacred and the secular, redemption and defilement, came to be "the Rebbe." It is to that day we now turn.

Death and Resurrection

JJJJ

Sabbath morning, January 28, 1950, Yud (the 10th) of Shvat, 5710, by the Hebrew calendar. At a time when most of his Hasidim would have been going to the synagogue to pray on this holiest day of the Jewish week, Yosef Yitzchak Schneersohn lay in his bed in his Brooklyn home at 770 Eastern Parkway. Yosef Yitzchak, the sixty-nine-year-old rebbe of the Lubavitcher community, had made 770 his home for most of the previous ten years, since his arrival in the United States.*

---

* The Rebbe had a cousin, Rabbi Moshe Schneersohn, living at 922 Eastern Parkway, an address that was very close to the residence the Lubavitchers helped purchase for the Rebbe at 770. There had been a proposal to appoint Rabbi Yosef Yitzchak as the head of the Lubavitchers in Chicago, but this never came to fruition. Had that happened, the court of Lubavitch would have found itself far from the center of the largest Jewish population in America and the locus of most of its institutions on the continent. Yosef Yitzchak had already seen the disadvantages of being remote from the center and he was not about to make the same error in America that his father had made in Europe. In fact, many years later, in 1959, Menachem Mendel Schneerson, explaining the choice of Brooklyn for the Lubavitcher court during a meeting with leaders of the Jewish campus organization Hillel, would note, "My father-in-law wanted a place where he could influence a great number of students. And this can be done more easily in Brooklyn than in Baltimore or Chicago" (see http://portraitofaleader.blogspot.com/ [accessed February 19, 2010]).

New York was also where his tutor, Rabbi Chaim Avraham DovBer Levine Ha-Cohen, known as "the Malach" (angel), had come in 1923. But he had become distant from ChaBaD and from his former student. He and his followers regarded Rabbi Yosef Yitzchak and his followers as too caught up in the contemporary movements of the day and secular knowledge. (The split may have also begun with a sense of personal slight by Rabbi Yosef Yitzchak of his former teacher.) Levine, who was dead by 1938, and his group became fierce opponents and competitors of Lubavitchers, and located in Williamsburg, Brooklyn, in the neighborhood of the fiercely insular and anti-Zionist Satmar Hasidim. That therefore would not be a place for Rabbi Yosef Yitzchak to move. See Jerome Mintz,

His oldest daughter, Chana Gourary, who lived on the third floor, had gone downstairs to the synagogue in the house's main floor at 7:45 a.m. to report that her father, who was in his second-floor bedroom, was feeling poorly. Even though it was Sabbath, when phones are not to be used, everyone understood immediately that this was a life-threatening illness, and two Hasidim who were present called the doctor.[1]

The fact that the Rebbe was dying could not be unexpected. For years he had suffered from multiple sclerosis, and at age fifty-six he had already suffered a stroke. Gradually weakened by being constantly on the run, first from the Germans in the First World War, then from the communists, and finally from the Nazis, he had two months earlier experienced what his doctors then referred to as a "mild" heart attack.[2] Moreover, he was overweight and a heavy smoker. This morning he had suffered another heart attack. Dr. Abraham (Aba) Seligson and Shalom DovBer Eichorn, the young Hasidic aide who had been on duty in the house, were summoned to his bedside and arrived in a few minutes.[3] Both concluded that the situation was now beyond help. At 8:07 a.m. the doctor pronounced the Rebbe dead.[4]

Near him at his passing were all of those who lived at 770: his wife, Nechama Dina, who had sat facing the window reciting psalms, and the Rebbe's eldest daughter, Chana Gourary, who was frantically entreating the doctor to save her father. Upon the Rebbe's death, they entered the bedroom, closed the door, and remained alone with the body for a short while. Chana's husband, Rabbi Shmaryahu Gourary, and their son, the Rebbe's only grandchild, the twenty-seven-year-old bachelor named Shalom DovBer and later referred to as "Barry," stayed in the adjoining chamber. Also in the antechamber was Chaim Lieberman, an unmarried man who since 1925 had been Rabbi Yosef Yitzchak's faithful secretary, aide, and confidante, and who now was chief librarian of ChaBaD and keeper of its keys. Lieberman lived in the house and was considered a member of the family.[5] Present as well

---

Hasidic People (Cambridge, MA: Harvard University Press, 1992), 21. See Shalom DovBer Ganzburg, *B'Kodesh P'nima* (Kfar Chabad: Yossi Ashkenazi, n.d.), 82–83.22, and Bernard Sobel, "The M'lochim: A Study of a Religious Community" (master's thesis, New School for Social Research, 1956).

was Shmuel Levitin, the Hasidic elder and very close associate who had been one of those who called the doctor.[6]

The large gothic-style mansion at 770 had been the center of Lubavitcher Hasidism since September 22, 1940, a half year after the Rebbe's arrival in New York. Downstairs was the main *Bet-midrash*, the study hall that also served as a synagogue. A few Hasidim and students from the Lubavitcher yeshiva wandered about, whispering about what they heard was happening a few floors above them. According to Jewish law and tradition, the death of a family member should affect neither the liturgy nor the sanctity of the Sabbath, a day on which most public signs and symbols of mourning are suspended. However, the normally joyous Sabbath prayers were recited with sadness, and the reading of the Torah was chanted in a melody of mourning. Those who felt closest to the Rebbe quietly ascended to his private chambers; others remained below and, following religious custom, recited psalms, to ease their leader's soul on its final journey. In spite of its being the Sabbath, a time when neither can preparation for a funeral be made nor the corpse physically attended to, news of the Rebbe's passing moved swiftly throughout this and nearby Jewish neighborhoods, and the *Bet-midrash* began to fill as the day wore on.

One of the Lubavitcher yeshiva students recorded some of the contemporaneous events in his journal:[7]

> As fast as our feet carried us, we returned to "770," climbed the stairs and began saying *Tehillim* [Psalms]. Students of the yeshivah had already filled every space. There was not a dry eye among them. Hearts beat with anguish, thoughts raced confusedly. With every second that went by the crowd swelled in number, sounds of sobbing and wailing were heard from every quarter. There was much pushing in the corridor. . . . The bedroom door was thrown open. Then we saw it with our own eyes—on the bed, under the sheet, lay our crown, our splendor. Oh, how the heart was wrung!

By nightfall and the end of the Sabbath, the streets around 770 were filled with people from outside the neighborhood wanting to find out if the rumors that had been circulating about the Rebbe's death were true.

Now that the Sabbath was over, those present at 770, especially family members, gave fuller expression to their bereavement and mourning.

Shmaryahu Gourary, the elder of the Rebbe's two sons-in-law, fainted. This man, for years his father-in-law's most prominent aide, was the nephew of a successful businessman and Lubavitcher Hasid in Rostov-on-Don who had been a close friend and supporter of the fifth rebbe, Yosef Yitzchak Schneerson's predecessor and father, Rabbi Shalom DovBer. Shmaryahu Gourary had reportedly been handpicked by Rabbi Shalom DovBer to be the husband of his oldest granddaughter, Chana. The fifth rebbe had great hopes for this marriage between Chana and Shmaryahu, a descendant of the famous MaHaRaL Rabbi Judah Loew of Prague, who had reputedly created the Golem. He did not live to see their wedding day, but they married soon after his passing. Shmaryahu Gourary had been among those few present at a reading of the fifth rebbe's will, an event of great importance, since the question of continuity and leadership was implicit in that event, and commonly those who would inherit were among those who would be present.[8] The Gourarys' son, born in 1923, the only male heir of the dynasty in the twentieth century, bore his great grandfather's name.

While Shmaryahu Gourary was swooning, his brother-in-law and Yosef Yitzchak's younger son-in-law, Menachem Mendel Schneerson, was sobbing. He and his wife, Moussia, had learned of the death from Rabbi Eichorn, who had rushed to their home a few blocks away on President Street to inform them.[9] In the diaries and recollections of those who were present during the *shiva*, the traditional seven-day mourning period, Menachem Mendel's continued weeping throughout the week and even into the year of mourning, in particular whenever the name of Rabbi Yosef Yitzchak was mentioned, stands out. The intensity of his mourning made a deep impression on the community. This man, who had seemed to be distant, who had lived far from the Rebbe and his court for years, and who even in Brooklyn had remained in a separate residence, was now evidently more openly broken up than Shmaryahu Gourary over the loss of their Rebbe. Shmaryahu Gourary had lived in the same household with the Rebbe, but judging by his frequent weeping the other son-in-law's apparent attachment to the memory of their beloved Rebbe could not be gainsaid. To whom would they now turn for guidance?

This was a huge question, for a rebbe was not simply a political or institutional leader. He was also someone who was an intermediary between his followers and the Almighty, capable of bestowing blessings as well as transmitting the will of God. Although he communicated with the Infinite, like a father, he also guided his Hasidim in the most personal decisions of their lives. Before marriage, couples came to him for a blessing. If they were anxious, they turned to him for hope. If they were sick, they asked for his prayers and advice. Only those who could bear this lonely but theologically and hefty burden and social responsibility and who could persuade others that they could, those with true charisma, qualified. That made the pool of viable candidates for the position of rebbe very small.

Rabbi Yosef Yitzchak had died intestate; he left neither a will that indicated who would receive his property, including his beloved and huge library, which contained rare books and manuscripts of the writings of previous ChaBaD rebbes as well as other rare books, nor a "moral" will that indicated who should lead the community of Hasidim after him.[10] There were unsubstantiated rumors that there had been a will (naming Barry, his beloved grandson) but that it had disappeared, perhaps eliminated intentionally. Still, people wondered why the Rebbe had left no instructions.[11]

Some supposed he had been so sure that his grandson would inherit the crown that Yosef Yitzchak concluded no will was necessary. He had once—when he had been about to be taken to prison by the Soviet authorities and worried he might never come back—famously blessed the grandson with the hope "that this child grow to be the greatest of his brothers, and stand firmly on the same basis on which his grandfather is standing," and asked that God "grant that he tread the same path that was boldly trodden by my holy forebears, for in his veins flows holy blood that is bequeathed from a father to his son, to his grandson, and to his great-grandson."[12] Since the boy had no actual brothers, the meaning clearly implied the Rebbe's hopes that his grandson would grow to take on the mantle of Lubavitcher leadership at some future time. Barry had been his assistant for years, watching the Rebbe's every move and coming whenever his grandfather rang a bell for him.[13]

Because of Yosef Yitzchak's physical infirmities during his last years, those around him were probably reluctant to tell him of the rumors circulating about Barry—that in America his grandson was choosing another path that departed from ChaBaD Lubavitch and therefore would be unacceptable as a leader to most of the community. Many understood, as Barry would later admit, that he was not interested in becoming a rebbe, an all-absorbing vocation that he learned about from his years of assisting his grandfather, a position that involved endless dealings with the personal problems and lives of the Lubavitcher Hasidim and others who approached the Rebbe for counsel. This was something that Barry, who saw other opportunities in the New World, did not want.[14] As he would tell an interviewer many years later, explaining his choice, "I decided that was not the kind of life I wanted to lead. I wanted a life more like that which was being led by Mendel Schneerson, the hard sciences life," referring to his uncle's early plans to study mathematics and engineering.[15] Of course, as we shall see, while in America Barry was thinking of studying sciences instead of being a Hasidic rebbe, his uncle, Menachem Mendel, on whom he sought to model himself, was considering abandoning that sort of life and taking on the mantle of Hasidic leadership that his nephew might have worn.

After attending Yeshiva Torah VeDaas in New York, Barry went to Brooklyn College between 1944 and 1947.[16] Ultimately he would become a management consultant, living in New Jersey.

Perhaps, as supporters of Rabbi Menachem Mendel would later speculate, Rabbi Yosef Yitzchak in his last years had decided that neither Shmaryahu Gourary nor his grandson Barry would be suitable, but because he was being cared for so closely by them, he did not want to hurt or alienate them by indicating that he had already selected his other son-in-law to lead Lubavitch in the next generation. Or perhaps Yosef Yitzchak's powerful conviction of the imminent arrival of the Messiah moved him to defer or even deny considerations of death.

This last matter was undoubtedly also among the most vexing religious concerns that Lubavitcher Hasidim had in the aftermath of Rabbi Yosef Yitzchak's passing. Their dead Rebbe had assured them until the end that the time of the Messiah was near. In the darkest days of his wanderings from the forces of the Russian Revolution and later the malevolence of the Nazis, Rabbi Yosef Yitzchak had become persuaded that the help of heaven in the form of a messianic redeemer would be forthcoming. He had told anyone among the Jews who would listen, and his Hasidim trusted in his assurance that they had the power to guarantee their redemption, for he had offered them a concrete recipe of how to accomplish this: it required arousing themselves in penitence.

"Jews," he declared upon his arrival in North America in 1940, "we must repent and save our children and ourselves from the danger. We have to observe Sabbath and the laws of *kashruth*. Men must put on tefillin and women must go to the *mikveh* [the ritual bath], children must get a religious education. Even the [so-called] religious Jews must repent, each according to his situation."[17] His motto had been "*l'altar l'tshuvah, l'altar l'geula*"—"repentance immediately, redemption immediately." Since redemption was coming straightaway, repentance was needed without delay, *if one wanted to be among the redeemed.* Indeed, for a time Hasidim were posting stickers with this slogan around the neighborhood, but it was a message whose significance at the time was not always clear to everyone.[18]

But now he was suddenly gone, and his prophecies of a religious return and redemption were unfulfilled. Indeed, if anything, American Jews seemed even less engaged with their religious traditions and observances than before, assimilating willy-nilly into the American culture of the 1950s. The Stalinist Soviet Union, his archenemy, was stronger than ever. Secular, socialist Zionism—against which he had railed—had caught the imagination of the Jewish world as thousands of Jewish refugees streamed into the new state of Israel. And there was no sign of the Messiah or redemption. "A feeling of unease," as one Hasid wrote in his journal at the time, began "gnawing at us" because "our unshakable faith that the Rebbe would lead us to meet the *Mashiach* [Messiah]" had been undermined by the reality of his death. "How could it be?"[19] These anxieties must surely have been on many Lubavitchers' minds at the afternoon funeral the next day.

The *New York Times* reported that three of the four lanes on Eastern Parkway between Kingston and Brooklyn Avenues were blocked for twenty minutes "when 3000 persons jammed the streets and sidewalks in front of 770" during the service. The original plan had been to carry the coffin on foot to the Lubavitch school on Bedford Avenue about a mile away. The body, prepared for burial by several Hasidim, who had been picked by lot, was placed in a wooden coffin constructed of planks from the Rebbe's desk. However, when the casket reached the street, "the pressure of the crowds was so great that they put it in a hearse on Brooklyn Avenue."[20]

Most of those in the crowd likely were Lubavitcher Hasidim. Few of the Torah giants or students from yeshivas affiliated with other branches of Orthodox Judaism or Hasidic courts took part in the memorial service—even though Rabbi Yosef Yitzchak had been admired within Jewry as a whole for his advocacy on behalf of persecuted Soviet Jewry.[21] Since his arrival in the United States, however, and during the last decade of his life, after he fled the Nazis in a war-ravaged Warsaw, his increasingly insistent messianism had embroiled him in controversy. His messianism carried within itself a powerful criticism of broad swaths of American Jewry, whose laxity in Jewish observance, he had argued, had defiled the world and brought about catastrophe and ruin. Only immediate repentance would ensure the Messiah's coming. In August 1941, fifteen months after his arrival as a refugee in his adopted country—a rescue brought about by Jews who were not at all Orthodox in their observance—he had argued that American Jews' "coldness and indifference . . . towards Torah and religion" were no less destructive than the fire in Europe that threatened "to annihilate more than two-thirds of the Jewish people."[22]

Many of Rabbi Yosef Yitzchak's contemporaries also understood these words to be an implicit criticism of other rabbis, religious leaders, and yeshiva heads who had clearly been *unable* to turn American Jewry toward greater religious observance. In words that stung much of the Orthodox religious rabbinate when they were published in 1941, at the time when Nazi general Erwin Rommel's tanks threatened to occupy the Holy Land, Yosef Yitzchak invited Jews to "imagine what would have happened if a few hundred rabbis . . . had appeared before the community and announced that the day of redemption is coming soon and that the tribulations of the Jewish people were simply the birth pangs of the Messiah; how powerful would have the repentance of the Jewish people been had they done so."[23] In the eyes of many Jews, he was blaming the victim.

Rabbi Yosef Yitzchak had hoped to offer a recipe for a religious revival and Jewish survival, but instead he created conditions that led to the decline of his influence in America, a decline accelerated by his physical deterioration as his life neared its end. Such statements, as well as what many of the influential considered his radical messianism, did not endear him to many of the religious leaders in America, and probably accounted for their absence at his funeral.*

Little if any mention was made of his more provocative messianic accusations at the funeral, perhaps because to do so would only remind people of the Rebbe's failures. No reference was made to his messianic beliefs in the press reports, both Jewish and general, of his death. Instead the stories recounted his preceding illness, his lifetime of travels, his successful efforts to establish yeshivas both in America and Israel, and the upcoming fundraising banquet on their behalf that was scheduled to take place within a week's time.[24] The educational institutions of the Lubavitcher community had been perhaps the Rebbe's most tangible success and legacy.

During the funeral, the family remained united in its bereavement. The women, including the Rebbe's widow, Nechama Dina (accompanied by a nurse), and the surviving daughters, Chana Gourary and Moussia (Chaya Mushka) Schneerson, followed the body in the first limousine. Behind them the late Rebbe's two sons-in-law, Shmaryahu Gourary and Menachem Mendel, Shmaryahu's son Barry, and two of the senior Hasidim, Eli Simpson and Baer Rivkin, as well as Chaim Lieberman, followed in a second. When the procession arrived at Old Montefiore Cemetery, about a half hour's drive away, the late Rebbe was interred in a back corner, where Lubavitchers had a relatively small section for their people. Following the burial, both surviving sons-in-law recited the memorial Kaddish. No tributes were offered. "Is there anyone sufficiently illustrious to eulogize him?" as one of his Hasidim asked rhetorically, avoiding explaining why none of the great rabbis of the day said a word.[25]

As the mourners left the cemetery, the question of who would take his place was undoubtedly on everyone's mind. No one had stood out at the funeral; they had been a single family in grief. By the beginning of the *shiva*, the seven-day mourning period, however, cracks in the

---

*The fact that his aggressive fundraising for his institutions was viewed as undercutting their own was probably another reason many of the ultra-Orthodox leaders, such as Rabbi Aharon Kotler, who tried to draw from the same sources, did not come to the funeral. See Joseph I. Schneersohn, *Igros Kodesh* (1982), 6:170, 173, 196–97.

family unity began to appear, and with them signs of what would become a contest over the future leadership of ChaBaD Lubavitch. With Barry, the grandson and only blood heir of Rabbi Yosef Yitzchak, no longer a realistic candidate for the leadership, the choice appeared to be between the two sons-in-law. To be sure, in the immediate aftermath both of them signed a letter telling everyone that Lubavitch would go on, and that there was a need for solidarity.[26] However, according to Barry Gourary, each of the sons-in-law "sat *shiva*" in separate rooms at 770, and consequently led independent services at which each of them recited the memorial Kaddish, a practice continued throughout the year of mourning.[27] Moreover, as was customary at such services, each of the sons-in-law would offer words of Torah (*sichos*) for those who had come to console and sit with them. That meant that during this period, each man was implicitly in competition with the other to see not only whose words could demonstrate greater insight, erudition, and acumen but also who could draw a more enthusiastic, larger, and engaged audience. In a sense, the period of mourning provided a chance for each man to reveal the extent of his Hasidic power, intellectual rigor, popularity, and charisma.

To an outsider the contest might have seemed uneven from the start, favoring Shmaryahu Gourary. As Rabbi Yosef Yitzchak's right-hand man (the one who literally sat at his right at all public events), Gourary was a familiar presence in Lubavitcher circles. The Rebbe Yosef Yitzchak had described him as a man "gifted with deep understanding" and "a man of intelligence and intellectual stature."[28] In Rostov, where the fifth rebbe had moved his court just before the First World War, he had been the one who accompanied the then new Rebbe, Yosef Yitzchak, on his periodic visits to the tomb of his father, an expression of spiritual intimacy and Hasidic significance. He had been with the Rebbe on his pilgrimage to the Holy Land and had accompanied him on his visits to physicians and spas, and even on his first trip to the United States in 1929.[29] Over the years he had been responsible for many of the administrative details of his father-in-law's leadership, served as head of the *Vaad Hapoel of Agudas Chassidei ChaBaD* (the Working Committee of the ChaBaD Hasidim), often having to enforce or deal with the mundane minutiae of what was a complex organization that in recent years had had to rebuild itself again and again. Wherever the

Rebbe Yosef Yitzchak had found himself over these years—in Russia, Latvia, Poland, and now in the United States—Shmaryahu Gourary had been there with him. As the Rebbe weakened with age and illness, Shmaryahu Gourary was often a stand-in for him on public occasions. It was Shmaryahu Gourary's review of the ten years of Lubavitch yeshivas in America, of the institutional legacy of the Rebbe, that had been prominently printed in the Yiddish paper *Der Morgen Zhornal* (*The Morning Journal*) on the day of the funeral. His son Barry was the only male blood heir of the dynasty. Surely he would be the next rebbe or interim leader.

But while Shmaryahu Gourary had been a familiar figure and perhaps in some eyes the viceroy, he had never really had an opportunity to shine on his own. Now was his chance. The question was, could a right-hand man, a man of organizational details, ascend to the throne? And if not, who would? To those on the inside, the answer was by no means obvious.

Menachem Mendel Schneerson, the younger son-in-law, although a member of the royal family through marriage and a blood descendant of the third rebbe, for whom he was named, had been largely removed from life at his father-in-law's court while he and his wife lived in Berlin for about five years and Paris for about seven, pursuing a life that was neither distinctively Hasidic nor Jewishly insular. Indeed, Menachem Mendel and his wife, who had begun the application process for French citizenship in 1937, lived in the cultural capitals of Western Europe in ways that seemed to border on the cosmopolitan and secular. Had the Second World War not occurred they might have remained in France, where, as "Mendel Schneerson," son-in-law of the Lubavitcher Rebbe, he pursued studies in engineering with the financial support of his father-in-law. Only when he and his wife arrived in New York from France on June 23, 1941, refugees from the Nazi onslaught, with any dreams they may have had to remain in Paris shattered, did Rabbi Menachem Mendel and his wife for the first time settle permanently into the Rebbe Yosef Yitzchak's Hasidic court (in contrast to the brief time before they were married, when they lived in the same apartment with the sixth Lubavitcher rebbe in Leningrad).[30] Even then, according to the Lubavitcher version of history, he at first went to work assembling electrical circuits at the Brooklyn Navy Yard, using skills he had acquired in France.[31] Unlike Shmaryahu Gourary and his family, who were part of the household at 770 (as they had been as well in Leningrad, Riga, and Warsaw when the Rebbe lived there), Mendel and his wife lived in a separate household on 1304 President Street.[32] Though she was a rebbe's daughter and wife, Moussia did not attend celebrations, *farbrengens*, or Lubavitcher women's group gatherings; indeed, throughout her life she referred to herself as "Mrs. Schneerson from President Street," almost as if to emphasize an identity that separated her from ChaBaD and the Lubavitcher court of her father.[33]

Although in the years since his arrival, Menachem Mendel had sat at his father-in-law's left side on public occasions, and there were reports—many of them emerging later, after his star had risen in the Lubavitch leadership—that he had been involved with ChaBaD and other Torah scholarship throughout his years outside the court and had carried out some "important" unheralded missions and tasks for his father-in-law during the preceding years, he remained a largely unknown figure to the rank-and-file Hasidim, especially the yeshiva boys.[34] Thus, for him, the talks during the *shiva* and into the year of mourning served as well as a kind of "coming out," an opportunity to reveal both his scholarship and any makings he might have of the charisma that a rebbe needed.

To be sure, Hasidim and others who had been exposed to him, including those few who heard him speak in Marseilles in 1941 on the eve of his immigration to America and those who gathered in Paris in 1947 at a Lubavitcher synagogue during his brief return there after the war, had been impressed both by his Jewish knowledge and his easy charm.[35] Undoubtedly, some of their reports of his capacities were known in Lubavitcher circles after his father-in-law's death. In addition, in New York he had been initiating a *farbrengen* at the end of Sabbath morning prayers once a month following the ritual announcement of the beginning of each new moon. People were eager to attend his talks, which captured the enthusiasm of the crowds.* So he was not a completely blank slate in the days after the sixth rebbe's demise.

---

* Indeed, as late as 1947, while he was in France (see below), they and he displayed an unfamiliarity with one another. See Mordecai Menasheh Laufer, *Yemi Melech* (Brooklyn: Kehot, 5751 [1991]), 2:948.

Hasidic transitions have been best handled when the community leader left clear instructions for his succession, often through the naming of a successor in a will; the model of Moses publicly naming and anointing Joshua on the eve of his passing is the paradigm here.[36] In such a case the new leader is believed to share in the personal charisma of his predecessor and grows in stature because of the charisma inherent in the office. In time, the abilities (or lack thereof) of the new incumbent lead either to the consolidation of his leadership or to the decline of the particular Hasidic sect as it loses followers. According to the rules of succession in the Hasidic world, being a son, son-in-law, or charismatic disciple might qualify one to succeed a rebbe. But in cases of competing claims and no clear chosen successor, the situation becomes complicated. In Lubavitcher succession, being a son or son-in-law of a Rebbe has been the sine qua non of leadership, but that has not always led to smooth transitions.* In such cases, after the matter of leadership is concluded (a process that might be filled with intrigue and political machinations), the victorious successor is retroactively understood or at least presented as the one who had been destined for the position all along. The conflicts over the succession are hidden, minimized, or disregarded in the revised history of the court, even though below the surface some of the tensions might still simmer, particularly among those who recall the time before the new Rebbe's ascendance. In the end, the victor is presented by the Hasidim as the most deserving leader who is truly ordained for the role. Any lingering doubts are simply banished, and even those who recall them would be expected to let them dissipate. The key was always to ensure continuity. This happened during 1950 and into 1951 in Lubavitch. And, when it was over, as the new Rebbe would later put it, "they put the key into [my] pocket."[37]

It would take some time for Rabbi Menachem Mendel to firmly establish his ascendancy and absolute authority over Shmaryahu Gourary, the right-hand man who ran so much of the organization during

---

* In ChaBaD Hasidism there were such cases that emerged after the death of the first rebbe (when matters of succession were still fluid) and the Rebbe's son Baruch competed with his father's star pupil, Aharon, for leadership. It occurred as well in the case of the third rebbe, several of whose sons established courts that ultimately withered: Yehuda Leib in Kapust (Kopys) Belarus, Chaim Schneur Zalman in Lyady, and Yosef Yitzchak in Ovruch (Ukraine).

their father-in-law's period of leadership. It would mean building on the groundswell of support among the young followers as well as gaining a new respect from many of the old time Hasidim. It would also require gaining control over the organization, which he accomplished with the help of Chaim Hodakov, whom Yosef Yitzchak had brought with him from Latvia and who would become the new Rebbe's chief secretary.

Tension rose throughout that year of mourning as the Lubavitcher Hasidim, both in America and Israel, looked for some sort of irrefutable sign of who would lead them forward. They were worried about continuity, hoping "to carry on the golden chain and to strengthen it so that it not be broken, heaven forbid."[38] The fact that Menachem Mendel was both a direct heir of the most prominent third rebbe as well as a son-in-law of the sixth was not lost on them. They sent him individual letters asking for counsel, thus indicating a readiness to be led by him.[39] They asked him outright. For example, on Purim (February) of 1950, Zalman Schachter, one of the Lubavitchers who had met him and heard him speak in Marseilles, and who was then living in New York as a student at the yeshiva, had a revealing encounter with Menachem Mendel on the way home from a visit to the late Rebbe's gravesite. In responding to Menachem Mendel's good wishes that his prayers be answered, Schachter replied, "they will if people don't get in the way. I prayed that we should have a Rebbe, that you should be that Rebbe, and that you should be blessed with children."[40] Both men wept, perhaps a sign of Menachem Mendel's agony about his childlessness and of the Hasidim's concern about continuity.[41]

This prayer for continuity was surely in the hearts of many of the Hasidim. Other branches of ChaBaD, all of which had descended from the third rebbe, had been wiped out because they did not have leaders.[42] Lubavitchers did not want this to happen to them. After composing himself, Menachem Mendel's response to Schachter and to all those who worried about continuity was a comment that deftly sidestepped the problem and that became a hallmark of his leadership. He insisted that the departed Rebbe, Yosef Yitzchak, was still leading his Hasidim: "But we *do* have a Rebbe. What difference does it make where he is, in this world or the other world?"[43]

Still, the late Yosef Yitzchak's failure to leave a will with precise instructions left everyone in a quandary. Some Hasidim went to his grave and asked for direction.[44] Others claimed to have had dreams and visions in which he informed them that his younger son-in-law would lead them.[45] Rabbi Menachem Mendel's repeated refusals and apparent reticence actually seemed to encourage his supporters, who redoubled their efforts to convince him to take up the mantle.

By the second day of the Jewish holiday of Shavuot in May 1950, the Hasidim who sought his leadership pressed him again to make a public address in which he would indicate a willingness to take over his father-in-law's role. According to one report, he refused, but added cryptically that this sort of talk need not be given specifically now; it could, he said, be offered at another time, a reply that some took as a sign that he was indeed contemplating leadership.[46]

He saw Lubavitch in a precarious position, desperately needing direction in light of the failure of Yosef Yitzchak to fulfill his promises of an end to history and beginning of redemption. He was becoming convinced that his brother-in-law could not provide an answer to the dilemma of continuity. As for himself, he saw that in 1950s postwar America, for a nearly forty-nine-year-old new immigrant there was no real career outside Lubavitch, and he was not ready to be subject to the leadership of Shmaryahu Gourary.

In Israel on 18 Elul (August 31, 1950), the birthday of the dynasty's founder, at a countrywide convention of ChaBaD Hasidim, a resolution was passed in favor of Rabbi Menachem Mendel and a telegram of *mazl-tov* was sent to him. The next day a news item in *HaModi'a*, the newspaper of the Orthodox Agudat Israel party, appeared under the headline, "The Great scholar Rabbi Menachem Schneerson was crowned as the Nesi of Lubavitch." No comment came from the candidate.

On 19 Kislev that year (November 28, 1950), the day Lubavitchers celebrate as a the New Year of Hasidism, a holiday that commemorates not only the birthday of the Maggid of Mezritsh, the most prominent disciple of the Ba'al Shem Tov, but for them most especially the anniversary of the release in 1798 from a capital sentence and imprisonment of his disciple, Rabbi Schneur Zalman of Lyady, the first of the ChaBaD leaders, the attendance at the synagogue on the lower level of 770 was greater than it had been in years. The hall was filled to overflowing. A sense of anticipation was in the air. But nothing dramatic occurred. A few weeks later, on 24 Tevet (January 2, 1951), during a community commemoration of Rabbi Schneur Zalman's passing, always a special day for Lubavitchers, once again the expectations for an announcement were raised. This time a group of Lubavitcher rabbis signed a letter called an *hiskashres*, a document asserting their spiritual bonding to Menachem Mendel, which signaled their willingness to accept his leadership. They hoped that the object of their veneration would accept the crown of leadership on the first-year anniversary, the *yarzheit*, of Yosef Yitzchak's death, two weeks hence. This petition was released to a number of Yiddish papers, which reported, precipitously, that the transition was for all intents and purposes a fait accompli. On the front pages of the January 4, 1951 (26 Tevet 5711), edition of the Yiddish papers *Der Tog* and *Der Morgen Zhornal* were headlines declaring, "Rabbi Menachem Schneerson has become the Replacement for the Lubavitcher Rebbe, of blessed memory." These announcements notwithstanding, Rabbi Menachem Mendel had not yet formally assented to his ascendance.[47]

By the first anniversary of Yosef Yitzchak's passing, a groundswell in the community in support of his ascension was well under way. Subsequent official histories of the Lubavitchers mark this day as the time when Menachem Mendel Schneerson "formally" accepted the leadership of ChaBaD Lubavitch, and it has come to be celebrated as the anniversary of that ascendance.[48] However, a closer look at the events at the time shows a more complex process. In fact, the transitional year after the sixth rebbe's death was a veritable hornet's nest of intrigue in the court of the Lubavitchers as Hasidim sought to transfer power to a new leader.

As the first *yarzheit* drew near, there was an intensification of concern among Lubavitchers regarding the future. On January 13, the Sabbath preceding the *yarzheit*, activity was particularly electric. According to Jewish mystical tradition, on the Sabbath each person gains a *neshamah yeterah*, an added soul, which couples with his normal soul and enhances the bliss of the day. After death, according to tradition, each soul must be separately recalled on its last day of earthly existence. The *yarzheit* is the day for recalling the "normal" soul, while the Sabbath preceding is the time to do so for the *neshamah yeterah*. Commonly the mourner as part of this recites the *Haftarah*, the selection from the prophets for that week. On that Sabbath, January 13, 1951, the sixth day of the Hebrew month of Shvat, as one of the Lubavitcher yeshiva students noted in his diary, Menachem Mendel Schneerson recited the *Haftarah* in the main synagogue at 770. It came from Jeremiah 46:13–28, verses that speak about exile and redemption.

"He shed copious tears on this occasion, particularly when he came to the last verse," which read, *Do not fear, O Jacob My servant, saith God, for I am with you.*[49] The idea of the presence of absence and absence of presence resonated in this phrase, and his weeping hinted at that. His tears, so often shed in the past, served to heighten the drama and emphasize the anxieties and fears they all felt about the future. Yet his capacity at last to compose himself, at least for those who watched him intently, could serve as a means of calming them too.

In 1951, Yud (the 10th) Shvat came on January 17, a Wednesday. Even though this was a far less convenient time than the Sunday on which the funeral was held the previous year, attendance was high. People would also stay for the annual Dinner Banquet of the United Lubavitcher Yeshivas, at which supporters and Lubavitchers gathered, many of whom came from out-of-town. The well-attended banquet was the following Sunday evening, 14 Shvat (January 21), at the Biltmore Hotel in Manhattan. Everyone sensed that Lubavitch was reaching an important milestone as the year of mourning drew to a close.

According to one eyewitness account, many Lubavitchers wrote *pidyones*, notes of petition for spiritual assistance, with pledges of their allegiance to Rabbi Menachem Mendel's leadership—*nesies*—and brought these to be read at the gravesite, thereby symbolically transmitting these requests to Yosef Yitzchak for his approval.* This was an

---

* *Nesi*, a term taken from the Bible, where it is used to describe the head of a tribe, is commonly translated "prince," although in Modern Hebrew it denotes "president." *Nesies* thus is best understood as leadership. The term also is related to the word for "carrying," to suggest that *nesies* means the ability to carry the burden of leadership. Lubavitchers often refer to their Rebbe as "*Nesi hador*," "leader of a generation." They play with the Hebrew letters of the word as well. Hence, *nosi* is an acronym for *nitsots shel Yaakoyv Ovinu* (the spark of our father [the patriarch] Jacob), while *Rebbe*, they say, is an acronym for *rosh bney yisroel* (the head of the children of Israel). See Laufer, *Yemei Melech*, 1138–40.

echo of a practice the sixth rebbe himself had performed repeatedly in his own lifetime, explaining, "it was clear to me that it was my prayer at the resting place of my holy forebears that had aroused God's loving kindness and compassion."[50] Afterward, several of the senior Hasidim brought them to Rabbi Menachem Mendel, much as they would in the past have brought them to Rabbi Yosef Yitzchak. At the outset, he refused to read them, as if to say that he was not the one to whom petitions were to be brought, that being something limited only to a Rebbe. In time, however, he began to open and read them and, weeping, placed them on the grave—the clear implication being that he, too, was passing on these requests to his predecessor.

Already during the high holy days of Rosh Hashanah and Yom Kippur of the year of mourning, Menachem Mendel had begun accepting *pidyones* on behalf of his father-in-law.[51] Rising to the pulpit before the afternoon prayers on Rosh Hashanah with his prayer shawl over his head, he read them there, as part of the petitions to heaven.[52] A few weeks later he was called to the Torah with the title nominally reserved for leaders, "Arise our teacher and rabbi"; he did not object. On Sundays, Tuesdays, and Thursdays, from 8 p.m. until well after midnight, he would meet with individuals, some of them Lubavitchers, but also quite of few who were not. Shmaryahu Gourary met with people at the same time, but not in the numbers who came to Menachem Mendel, which increased impressively over the year.[53] The fact that so many wanted to consult him was not lost on the Hasidim, particularly the younger ones whose loyalties were up for grabs and who clearly represented the future. People started talking about his power to affect them, about his ability to provide answers; there were even reports of how he'd helped in matters of health and welfare.

These acts alone, of course, would not be sufficient to mark his ascendance, although they were clearly freighted with meaning. More was needed. At about 9:45 in the evening on Yud Shvat, Rabbi Menachem Mendel arose to offer a Torah talk, *sicha*.[54] However, in light of the fact that he had received the *pidyones* earlier, after about an hour of this, one of the elders among the Hasidim stood up in the upstairs chambers in 770 and shouted words to the effect, "*sichos* are fine, but the congregation wishes a *ma'amar khsides*."[55] This refers to an address that is also called a *Divrei Elohim Chayim* (*DACh*, in its Hebrew acronym), the "words of a Living God," a talk filled with ChaBaD philosophy and thought that is recited in a distinctive and unmistakable singsong, punctuated by the congregation of Hasidim singing, and which in Lubavitcher practice can only be offered by a rebbe.

This occasion is described in exacting detail by Yehuda Leib Groner, a young student at the time and later one of the personal secretaries of Rabbi Menachem Mendel, who became one of his closest guardians during the final days of his life.[56] As Groner tells it, in the evening, at the *farbrengen* of the Hasidim, Rabbi Menachem Mendel received visitors from Montreal, including the distinguished Lubavitcher Rabbi Yitzchak Hendel (who years later, in 1988, would issue a ruling that Rabbi Menachem Mendel was the Messiah). They sat alone with him in his chambers for an extended period. When the party from Montreal came out of the meeting, the Hasidim waiting outside asked Hendel if they had been told anything about the question of Lubavitcher leadership. The answer was no, but then one of the Hasidim proposed that Hendel ask Rabbi Menachem Mendel to offer a *ma'amar khsides* (Hasidic talk). Rabbi Menachem Mendel, now coming into the room, overheard this and replied directly to Hendel, "Stop this nonsense."

"There wasn't a huge crowd there," as Yehuda Krinsky, then a young Hasid from Boston, would recall fifty-eight years later, "maybe around a hundred people."[57]

Rabbi Menachem Mendel began to give a talk. It seemed to be like all the other *sichos* he had been offering throughout the year. Then, as Krinsky recalled, one of the oldest of the Hasidim present, Avraham Sender Nemtzov, who was close to ninety, shouted, "'*venimtso kheyn veseykhl tov*', *der rebe zol zogn khsides*" (may we find grace and good wisdom, and would the Rebbe offer *khsides*).[58]

There was a pause, almost as if the interruption had broken Menachem Mendel's train of thought. After the few moments of silence, he began to speak again, but now he referred to the final *ma'amar* of Yosef Yitzchak and announced that he would continue on with this same subject. Switching into the special singsong associated with such addresses, Menachem Mendel at last offered the *ma'amar khsides* for which so many had been waiting and *which he had undoubtedly prepared in advance*. The drama of this vocal transition was unmistakable.

It was a bravura performance. In an exquisitely organized presentation, he demonstrated not only erudition in ChaBaD Lubavitch literature and familiarity with his predecessor's final talk, he was also able to display his understanding of the Midrash by weaving commentaries from each of the previous rebbes on its kabbalistic theme. There was a clearly implied progression. Each rebbe would in turn help draw the divine emanation of God, *Shkhine*, progressively closer to man on earth until the day of redemption.[59] Like a true rebbe, Menachem Mendel was expounding Hasidic philosophy based on the foundation of his predecessors. Then he asserted what they all needed to hear: that the prophecy of Yosef Yitzchak about the advent of the Messiah would come to pass. *The Messiah would be brought by the seventh generation in the ChaBaD dynasty, and they were that generation.*[60]

This theme would become a recurring leitmotif of the reign of Rabbi Menachem Mendel, the seventh rebbe in the ChaBaD dynasty. He explained that while Yosef Yitzchak had recognized that the period in which they lived was the dawning of the messianic age, it was left to this sacred seventh generation of ChaBaD rebbes, like the seven generations between the patriarch Abraham and Moses, who redeemed the Jews, to bring that day to full light.[61] This address, which became a key text in Lubavitcher mythology and messianic theology, would be recited each year thereafter on this date, and served as the basis of the entire Messiah campaign and the justification for all its missionizing and other activities.

But when Menachem Mendel gave this talk for the first time, all the assembled were shocked that he had at last publicly accepted the call to become Rebbe, moments after referring to such a request as "nonsense." It made it seem that he was suddenly overtaken by the spirit, and it made publicly clear that he was going to follow the sixth rebbe and become the all-important number seven. And it showed, as Faitel Levin and Allon Dahan have argued, that Menachem Mendel had absorbed and made his own the messianic idea, the essential message of Lubavitch, in ways that no one else had.[62] As time passed, Lubavitchers would come to understand how he would transform and apply this messianic idea in creative and unexpected ways. So shaken were those listening that they did not immediately stand, as would be customary when Hasidim are present at *DACh*.

If there were those who had doubts about his capacity to lead or theirs to be part of this messianic generation, he had an answer for that. "Although we have not earned it, and have not toiled for it," he said, speaking of his generation but perhaps also speaking to those who wondered how he who had for so long been far from the court and headed in another direction could have the courage (or perhaps the temerity) to take this role, "nevertheless, 'all those who are seventh are most beloved,'" and therefore "there are no inherent limitations that should cause an individual [of this seventh generation] to say that this status is beyond him or that it is accessible only to a select few."[63]

When he had finished the first section of this address, he asked the assembled to raise a cup and say *lekhayim*, to life. It is customary among Hasidim to make these toasts at a *farbrengen*, and particularly to offer this on the occasion of a *yarzheit*, for it elevates the soul of the departed to a higher kind of 'life.' As they raised their cups, Nemtzov shouted in joy, "Hasidim, repeat after me, 'we must now recite the blessing of *shehekhiyonu, vekiymonu, vehigiyonu lazman haze* [who has kept us alive, sustained us, and brought us to this moment]' that the Almighty has helped us to have a Rebbe." He then recited the entire blessing using God's name, a practice permitted only when one is engaging in a religious act. Then everyone responded aloud and with great joy, "Amen." And so did Rabbi Menachem Mendel, clearly acknowledging the significance of the blessing. Then, Nemtzov continued, "now the Rebbe will go on with his address, and we must all stand, as has always been the accepted practice when we hear such words from our Rebbes and leaders." That night, Groner concludes, the Rebbe established the foundations of his thinking and the path on which he would lead in the years ahead, telling his contemporaries that they formed the seventh generation and therefore must complete the mission of that generation—to bring the final redemption.

Yoel Kahan, an eyewitness to this scene who is a Lubavitcher elder today, reports that Menachem Mendel paused and asked the assembled to sing a tune that was a favorite of Rebbe Yosef Yitzchak. When they finished, he requested that they sing yet another tune, one with which the Rostov-based fifth rebbe had been associated. The assembled proceeded to sing songs in honor of all the other Lubavitcher rebbes, thereby connecting Menachem Mendel in a chain with all of them.

Menachem Mendel had been careful not to accept the position of seventh rebbe until he was certain there would be little or no resistance. He wanted it to build and become almost inevitable. An introvert and loner, he was perhaps not able to make the jump to Rebbe on his own. He wanted first to overcome his internal resistances, his natural shyness. He needed to feel pushed, urged forward by the expressed and almost frantic desires of the Hasidim. He wanted it to seem to himself and the world as if it had come completely from the followers rather than from somewhere inside himself too, as if he had not wanted to wrest his position from his older brother-in-law.

"In ChaBaD," declared Menachem Mendel after the singing subsided, "the rebbes have always asked their Hasidim to act on their own initiative."[64] It was a sentiment that would also become a part of the deep structure of ChaBaD in the years ahead, as *shluchim* would increasingly have to act "on their own initiative." And of course, it was a kind of license for Menachem Mendel Schneerson himself to act on his own, without the legitimacy that a will might have afforded him, and secure the leadership of Lubavitch.

As Rabbi Menachem Mendel left and returned to his quarters, the Hasidim, including many of their elders, began to dance and sing the song "For in joy we depart and in peace we return." After the singing had ended, they reviewed the content of what they had heard throughout the night, as was always the custom following a rebbe's *DACh*.[65]

But all was not settled. Four days later, at the big Lubavitcher dinner at the Biltmore, Shmaryahu Gourary held court as keynote speaker and reported on the impressive institutional success of Lubavitch. The new Rebbe, if indeed he was recognized as such, was not mentioned at the banquet, or at least in reports of it.[66] Now, if he had been "crowned" on the *yarzheit* and recognized by everyone as leader, why would this momentous development not have been a primary focus of the dinner, or mentioned in subsequent reports about it? One would suppose that on this most public occasion, the first such event following the year of mourning for Rabbi Yosef Yitzchak, the new Rebbe would be introduced, if not asked to speak to all these supporters. But this banquet was a demonstration of the empire of Shmaryahu Gourary. The absence of any mention of Menachem Mendel in reports of the dinner can be taken as evidence of Gourary's initial refusal to accept his rival as Rebbe. Indeed, throughout this first year after the old Rebbe's death, Shmaryahu Gourary and Menachem Mendel were each leading their own competing gatherings, often days apart. What happened now was simply the most dramatic example of these two parallel assemblies. Nevertheless, when the celebrations at the end of the year of mourning were over, Menachem Mendel clearly held the upper hand.

Yet even after that week, embers of resistance to his leadership lingered within the circle of Shmaryahu Gourary, though they were systematically snuffed out whenever and wherever they appeared.[67] For example, in May 1951 (Iyar, 5711), in *HaPardes*, the journal that served as the house organ of the mainstream *haredi* (ultra-Orthodox) rabbinic group of the period, an announcement appeared under the headline, "The New *ADMOR* of Lubavitch," that trumpeted the ascension of Menachem Mendel to the leadership of ChaBaD.[68] The new leader in Brooklyn was called "head of all ChaBaD-Lubavitch Hasidim in the world." While there are some errors in the description of his educational background—perhaps as a result of information given to them by Menachem Mendel's new supporters, who wanted to establish his pedigree in this most public way—the article clearly sought to associate him with much of the success that Lubavitchers had had in establishing yeshivas and strengthening Orthodoxy in America. Indeed, the article credited Lubavitcher Hasidim with launching a "spiritual revolution in America," praising the literature that the new rebbe had been responsible for promulgating in his guidance of the movement's *Merkos L'Inyonei Chinuch*, its educational publication arm. The following month, however, *HaPardes* issued a correction stressing that many of these accomplishments were actually the results of the efforts of Shmaryahu Gourary and the sixth rebbe.[69] Clearly, both sides continued efforts during this transitional period to make public demonstrations of strength.

Among the most powerful of the elements in Shmaryahu Gourary's camp were members of the immediate family of Rabbi Yosef Yitzchak, most prominently his widow, Nechama Dina. The extent of her support for her elder son-in-law became apparent in her response to a letter addressed to her by Lubavitcher supporters of Menachem Mendel in March 1951. In the letter they complained that Shmaryahu Gourary, for whom they had "the greatest respect," had "refused to agree" to relinquish control over all the "ChaBaD institutions" and assent to the complete authority of his brother-in-law, whom each day they felt "attached to more and more" and who they believed "with full faith" was Rabbi Yosef Yitzchak's chosen heir. They argued that it was necessary for her elder son-in-law to follow Lubavitcher precedent and tradition and defer to the new Rebbe, who, in the eyes of "all the Hasidim and *Temimim* [Lubavitcher yeshiva students] in all lands" as well as the lay leadership (*bale-batim*), was the new head, *nesi* (prince), and hence formal person in command of "all institutions." They expressed regret that Shmaryahu Gourary "had not [yet] agreed" and accused him of wanting "to disturb everything." They laid blame on him for walking out of the Sabbath prayers in protest rather than being present when his brother-in-law was called to the *Haftarah* reading with the title, "Our master, our teacher, our Rebbe"—a symbolic act of public defiance they found disturbing and even sacrilegious, as well as embarrassing, especially in the face of the outsiders, who often attended these services. They also expressed fear that this continuing resistance would, "Heaven forbid, cause everything to fall apart and the entire structure of Lubavitch to crumble," and avowed that this was something they "[would] not permit."[70]

Angered by this letter, Nechama Dina, who clearly favored the son-in-law who had lived in her house and had been by her husband's side in his waning years and the daughter who'd help care for her, responded in a letter of her own by calling them "*chutzpahnikes*" (arrogant). In the letter, she "refused entry into her house to those who had mocked" Gourary and claimed to consider herself the "only Lubavitcher *Rebbetzin*," or rebbe's wife.[71] Significantly, in an act of widely recognized symbolism, she refused to transfer the Rebbe's distinctive *shtrayml* to Menachem Mendel. This was the fur hat that Rabbi Yosef Yitzchak used on every Sabbath, holy day, and other festive occasions and in which he was famously photographed.* Rabbi Menachem Mendel handled this development, as he handled other challenges, with creativity. He simply removed the use of *shtraymls* from ChaBaD rabbinic practice and was forever after seen only in his trademark snap brim black fedora.

---

* The handing over of this hat is in many circles "an indication of succession." See Shaul Shimon Deutsch, *Larger than Life*, 2 vols. (New York: Chasidic Historical Productions, 1997), 1:156.

Another member of the late Rebbe's entourage, Rabbi Yosef Yitz-chak's secretary Chaim Lieberman, similarly refused to transfer his loyalty to Menachem Mendel and did not give the new Rebbe free access to the ChaBaD library, an act that over the course of years would become freighted with powerful symbolic meaning.* This became even more apparent when thirty-five years later these books, so important to ChaBaD, would become the subject of a famous trial in the New York courts that pitted Rabbi Menachem Mendel against his nephew and sister-in-law over who had ownership of the books: Agudas Chassidei ChaBaD Lubavitch, the group that represented the movement, and hence their leader, or the Schneersohn family, and hence their heirs.[72]

Barry, as the only grandchild of Rabbi Yosef Yitzchak and someone who might once have been a candidate for leadership, argued that he and his mother, as direct heirs, could claim at least a portion of the library. This claim reiterated the fact that he and his mother had always refused to accept his uncle's complete "sovereignty." Indeed, they had not even invited him to Barry's wedding.[73]

In the end, Menachem Mendel's main rival Shmaryahu Gourary himself ultimately accepted the authority of his brother-in-law (and testified on *his* behalf at the library books trial). What else could he do, where else would he go? His life was in the movement, to which he had given so much. For a long time many of the leaders of the *Vaad Hapoel of Agudas Chassidei ChaBaD*, the steering committee of the movement that Shmaryahu Gourary headed, remained loyal to him, although they ultimately dropped away. Some, like Israel Jacobson, executive director of the American branch during the period, turned on him early because they were more impressed by Menachem Mendel. Indeed, Jacobson saw Shmaryahu Gourary as one who was trying to wrest control and grab power both of the organization that he, Jacobson, had been running in America and of ChaBaD. While Jacobson

---

* That Lieberman remained the keeper of the keys to the library and the great treasures of ChaBaD is seen in a story Shalom Ganzburg relates of an instance when, after her husband's ascension to the position of Lubavitcher Rebbe, Moussia Schneerson wanted him to see the prized prayer book of the Ba'al Shem Tov, founder of Hasidism, that was held in the library. To do that, he had to get access from Lieberman. See Shalom DovBer Ganzburg, *B'Kodesh P'nima* (Kfar Chabad: Yossi Ashkenazi, n.d.), 82–83.

was willing to cede control to Menachem Mendel, he was not ready to do so to Shmaryahu Gourary.[74]

After Shmaryahu Gourary accepted Menachem Mendel's sovereignty, he never again really tried to exhibit the qualities of a rebbe, never published talks that were meant to display his erudition, scholarly acumen, or even his knowledge of Hasidic traditions; he never again tried to play the role of a holy man. Instead, the United Lubavitcher Yeshivas (ULY) remained his empire, but it was an empire that gradually shrank both financially and politically. Under the leadership of the Rebbe Menachem Mendel the *shluchim* would become the main focus of attention and activities in the ChaBaD movement, while the scholars and students of the yeshiva became secondary. For young Lubavitchers wanted more and more to go out on a mission rather than remain students or scholars within the walls of a yeshiva. In later years Shmaryahu Gourary, removed to a place on Bedford Avenue in another corner of Brooklyn, could be found smoking a cigar, opening mail, and sorting checks that came in as donations.[75] Perhaps as a reward for his loyalty, when all three of the Gourarys were dead, only Shmaryahu Gourary, who was eulogized by his brother-in-law, was buried in the small ChaBaD section of Old Montefiore Cemetery, his grave right next to the *ohel*. The others, Rabbi Yosef Yitzchak's eldest daughter and his only grandson, were denied this final resting place and consigned to lie for eternity in separate cemeteries in New Jersey. In addition, in the official published history of ChaBaD, no mention is made of Chana Gourary, her son Barry, or Chaim Lieberman.[76]

Menachem Mendel's final victory over his opponents within the movement came in the 1980s, at the end of a two-year court case in New York that concerned ownership of the ChaBaD library. The new rebbe was perhaps even more attached to the ChaBaD books and manuscripts than his predecessor, because much of his legitimacy came from his knowledge of them. The trial pitted Menachem Mendel against his nephew, Barry, and Chana, Barry's mother and eldest daughter of Yosef Yitzchak. When federal judge Charles P. Sifton handed down his verdict on January 6, 1987, favoring the Rebbe's position (a verdict upheld unanimously by the U.S. Court of Appeals for the Second Circuit on November 17 of that year), Menachem Mendel proclaimed the day a Lubavitcher holy day, calling it, the fifth of the Hebrew month

Tevet, *Didan Notzach*, an Aramaic phrase meaning "Our side won."[77] For seven days thereafter his Hasidim celebrated what they called "the triumph of light over darkness."[78]

On November 23, a number of the books that had been held in escrow until the conclusion of the legal proceedings were returned to Lubavitch, and the Rebbe directed that some of them be brought to him at his father-in-law's grave, where he was waiting for them.[79] Menachem Mendel Schneerson understood that the library was more than just a collection of books, and that the struggle over it with his nephew and sister-in-law was about his leadership. As he would tell a meeting of Hasidim at the time, "It should be understood the war [conflict] is not only over the *seforim* [books], but rather *oif dem benkel*—'over the seat'" of power.[80] Or, as Judge Charles Sifton put it in his verdict, "the collection, possession and study of a large library was part of the function of each successive Rebbe, at least from the Third Rebbe on."[81] When Menachem Mendel was affirmed as having that possession, he was finally judged to belong symbolically and legally to that succession.

In his remarks, after the initial verdict, Rabbi Menachem Mendel, speaking in the twilight of the day, began by quoting Joseph's words when he revealed himself to his brothers as recounted in that week's Torah reading, Genesis 45:8: "Now it is not you who have sent me here today, but the Lord."[82] The Rebbe often compared himself to Joseph, separated from his family for so many years only to be reunited with them as their leader, so the significance of the sentiment behind the words could not be missed by his Hasidim.

ʃʃʃ

How exactly did Rabbi Menachem Mendel win the leadership of the community from his brother-in-law, who had so many management responsibilities during much of Rabbi Yosef Yitzchak's reign and who had seemed so well poised to inherit the old Rebbe's position? To begin with, in the aftermath of Yosef Yitzchak's death, Shmaryahu Gourary's deficiencies, hidden by his shared authority when his father-in-law still lived and acted as rebbe, became more apparent when he was thrust into the limelight and compared to his impressive rival. Unlike Menachem Mendel, whose appeal emerged at this time, Gourary suddenly appeared to many people to lack personal charisma. His familiarity with the literature and philosophy of ChaBaD, as became apparent in his *sichos*, was judged unimpressive. Those who attended his talks came away with the unshakable sense that, unlike his erudite brother-in-law, he was parroting phrases from someone else's talks or books, or repeating the words of his late father-in-law. Under the intense communal scrutiny he seemed to be a man swallowed up by the minutiae and administration that had been his life, a man of rational organizational talents and a loyal assistant, certainly, but conventional, rather than stellar as a rebbe had to be. He was not one who would attract more followers to the movement or lead them toward the day of redemption, supporters of Menachem Mendel claimed, ignoring his accomplishments as celebrated at that 1951 banquet.

Moreover, they saw him as parochial in comparison with his relatively worldly brother-in-law and unable to carry on a dialogue with the cosmopolitan world. For the Lubavitcher Hasidim, it was vital that their leader be able to engage all sorts of people. They wanted to be proud of a rebbe who could speak to and impress the world beyond their own, who would be an outspoken public voice and figure, a man of initiative. One Hasid, who had been a modern Orthodox Jew and joined the Lubavitchers as a follower of Menachem Mendel early in his reign, explained his attraction: "The Rebbe had a global perspective, and that's what got me."[83] In postwar America, being worldly and cosmopolitan was valued more than it had been in the traditional Eastern European Jewish world. Undoubtedly, that ethos had seeped into the thinking of the Lubavitchers.

Menachem Mendel did not disappoint on this score. When he first became a public figure and came to the attention of America (about ten years later), he took a strong public stance on a policy matter that rankled assimilated and secular—and indeed most—American Jews. He issued a call to the federal government to provide aid to Jewish day schools and argued on behalf of prayer in the public schools, a stance that put him at odds with most American Jews who opposed both of these.[84] It would be the first of many pronouncements on the issues of the day he would make in his more than half a century of leadership, pronouncements that would increasingly be covered by the world press.

Even Shmaryahu Gourary's son and potential rival became impressed with his uncle, the man who had been to Berlin and Paris, more than with his father, who had lived his entire life at the Rebbe's side, in a Hasidic court.[85] Other Schneerson relatives who had left the world of Lubavitcher Hasidism likewise stressed the parochialism of Shmaryahu Gourary in comparison with his far worldlier brother-in-law.[86]

Related to Menachem Mendel's perceived cosmopolitanism was his "outsider" status, which paradoxically raised his standing among the Lubavitchers and enveloped him in an aura of mystery. Leadership suffers greatly from the ability to see one at close quarters, especially one whose role is administrator. But the forty-nine-year-old Menachem Mendel, whom some had seen as the outsider "student," who had never studied in a Lubavitcher yeshiva, reflected a charismatic and deep religiosity and turned out to all the Hasidim's amazement to be a scholar in ChaBaD wisdom and Jewish sources.[87] Moreover, as he spoke and thought, he seemed to observers and listeners to undergo "an internal transformation."[88]

Yet at first it was not clear to the Hasidim where he had acquired his deep knowledge. That mystification likewise charmed them. Undoubtedly, his father, Rabbi Levi Yitzhak, with whom he studied and corresponded after they separated, had managed to transmit to him a great amount of scholarship as well as kabbalistic knowledge. He had surely always studied on his own, during his years in Berlin and Paris. A look through his diary and notes reveals that he had been collecting and absorbing the myriad customs of Lubavitcher practice for years, noting all sorts of details about the previous rebbes, from how they dressed to the stories they repeated. No detail was too trifling for him.[89] And in the years since coming to New York in 1941 he had spent much time in the library at his father-in-law's court delving into the esoterica that was in it, and he had published a calendar that served as a kind of manual for ChaBaD daily practices and customs. Of course, the talks he gave once a month gave him a stage on which to shine. Yet he was not one who had simply memorized and was spitting back what he had read but rather had absorbed it so deeply that he was, as Lubavitchers said, *pnimi* (one of us, an insider who could also penetrate to the core meaning of a text). He often seemed to speak extemporaneously but with great erudition.

As Naftali Loewenthal argues in his study of the emergence of the ChaBaD school of Hasidism, a rebbe or Hasidic *zaddik* communicates and changes the people around him in at least two ways. The first is by "personal charisma," during which "contact with the man of vision transforms the ordinary individual" almost in direct proportion to how those who encounter him perceive he is undergoing an internal transformation. Second, the rebbe somehow translates "esoteric concepts into forms accessible—and meaningful—to the people," and does this with "oral teachings, or by means of texts."[90] Menachem Mendel seemed to be doing this in ways that Shmaryahu Gourary simply could not accomplish.

ʃʃʃʃ

The new Lubavitcher leader faced formidable challenges. Foremost was how to start anew while at the same time continuing the intense messianic fervor of Rabbi Yosef Yitzchak, because the Previous Rebbe, who had promised imminent messianic redemption, died without fulfilling his promise. The new Rebbe was also forced to recalibrate his community's stance toward both Zionism and America. The previous two Lubavitcher rebbes had waged an intense war against Zionism, which they had dismissed as false messianism. They opposed the idea of reestablishing a Jewish state in the Holy Land that was based on anything other than prayer and Torah study. The Zionists, for their part, wanted a society made up of "normal" people who lived and worked in a modern society. And it was succeeding; after the Holocaust, Zionism, unlike Lubavitcher messianism, had delivered on its promise to gather Jewish exiles into the first Jewish state in two thousand years. Did the undeniable success of the Zionist present not presage a future different from the one the Lubavitchers had prophesied?

America posed similar challenges for Lubavitcher ideas. At one time excoriated by the Lubavitchers and other European Orthodox Jews as a *trefene medina* (impure state), it had become a refuge that welcomed tens of thousands of Jews, including the Lubavitchers themselves. What should the new attitude to that country be? How the new Lubavitcher leader confronted these new realities seemed crucial to determining whether the movement would thrive or instead pass from the scene with the man they had buried on Yud Shvat.

Menachem Mendel's first task was to reconcile a community in mourning to the recent departure of its beloved leader. To deal with the reality of Rabbi Yosef Yitzchak's death, he declared that while it might appear that the Rebbe was dead and gone, to those who recognized a deeper level of reality (that is, those who believed in his message), it was clear that the Rebbe Yosef Yitzchak had simply moved from one realm of existence to another—one that in many ways was actually more substantive. Menachem Mendel affirmed that Rebbe Yosef Yitzchak's passing had placed him closer to God, and indeed to his followers. This message was reiterated incessantly. He would often tell his listeners that Rabbi Yosef Yitzchak was with them "in this room." And because he was still present, he was still working to assure that what he foresaw would happen; those who understood that would be his *shluchim*, or emissaries, in this world to complete his mission.

Menachem Mendel had not invented this idea of talking to a dead rebbe and claiming he was not really gone. There were many precedents to this in ChaBaD. After the death of the third rebbe, *Zemah Zedek*, his youngest son (the fourth rebbe) of the Lubavitcher dynasty, announced to his followers, "Know that father did not die, and whoever wants to make any requests [of him] can still do so. I too have done so."[91] Similarly, Yosef Yitzchak went to the grave to speak to his departed father and claimed to get replies. For these rebbes, however, such encounters with the dead were relatively infrequent. For Rabbi Menachem Mendel, it became the *basis of his legitimacy*. Perhaps it was why he would never stray further than a short car ride away from the cemetery that was Yosef Yitzchak's final resting place for the rest of his life.

In a talk to his followers in the spring of 1950, a week and a half after the death of Rabbi Yosef Yitzchak, Menachem Mendel connected his ongoing communication with his late father-in-law to the all-important question of the coming of the Messiah. The death of Yosef Yitzchak, he declared, did not have to undermine belief in the imminence of the Messiah, as many doubters in the non-Lubavitcher Orthodox establishment had been suggesting. On the contrary, now Yosef Yitzchak was in a "far better position"—closer to heaven—where he could hasten that messianic arrival. Unlike even the great Talmudic sage Rabbi Akiva, who had also sought to bring the Messiah, Rabbi Yosef Yitzchak was not doing this "for his own good" but for the sake of all of us.[92] Many other *zaddikim*, including the Ba'al Shem Tov, had promised that they would go to heaven and encounter the Messiah. They promised they would then "force" him to complete his redemptive mission. But they had all failed, giving up their struggle on behalf of those still on earth for the rewards of paradise.[93] Rabbi Yosef Yitzchak, however, would succeed where they had not. As Menachem Mendel put it, previous *zaddikim* had been weighed down by their human selfishness. But Rabbi Yosef Yitzchak was beyond this sort of selfishness. His was a totally "selfless" devotion to the Jewish people that no other *zaddik* matched.

Menachem Mendel argued further that Yosef Yitzchak, because he was no longer weighed down by mortality, could work more successfully both among his Hasidim and in heaven to lead in this world and the next, to bring on the day of redemption. He was now *yatir mibehayekhon*, "above and beyond the limitations of life," and working harder than ever.[94]

The new Rebbe repeatedly made these points in public addresses. In March 1950, he told his listeners that the "struggle to bring the Messiah" was not over, and their Rebbe in his new afterlife had thrown himself completely into it in ways that he had not done before. He would solve all the problems of the Soviet Jews, the question of the secular state of Israel, as well as the problem of the continuing presence of sinners in America. He would offer spirituality and holiness to a contemporary world that was materialistic and base. To make his case, Menachem Mendel drew on passages from Talmud, Hasidic, and kabbalistic literature. His erudition and his arguments impressed his listeners. Rabbi Yosef Yitzchak, they were told, *had* to leave the physical realm, to hurl his soul into the battle, to engage in the ultimate selflessness and self-sacrifice. Only thus would he "bring the Redeemer."

In the next month, on the last day of Passover in April 1950, he expanded on the new double life of Yosef Yitzchak. The Hebrew term for death, he explained, is *ptire*, which in its original biblical sense meant "going from one place to another, from one subject to another, from one place of work to another."[95] Thus does a *zaddik* pass from this world to the next, "from strength to strength," in a continuous ascension. This is a spiritual ascent, from lowly service on this earth toward a more divine calling. But, Menachem Mendel assured his listeners, this ascent did not mean that their rebbe had abandoned his Hasidim in his transition to the higher realms. He needed them still (as a father needs his children) and they needed him; the intimate tie remained powerful in all matters. The Rebbe would still act as their guide and master; they could still turn to him, and he would answer them "*as before*," whether in matters of the spirit or matters concerning this world. And he still needed them to act in ways that he had demanded of them so that they would remain linked to one another. The Rebbe and his Hasidim thus could remain a single intertwined entity, even after death. But since the Rebbe in heaven was now intertwined with God, this meant that all three—Hasid, Rebbe and the Almighty—were bound up together in an eternal bond.

If, Menachem Mendel continued, Lubavitchers believed that the Rebbe had not brought the Messiah and that his prophecies had proved false, it was because they had wrongly assumed he was gone forever, and thus it was *they* who had broken their tie to *him*. But since he was still present and working on his ongoing mission, no judgments could be made about the mission's outcome, nor had his Hasidim the right to give up. Menachem Mendel's words placed the responsibility of continuity squarely on the Hasidim. Those who failed to understand this and who did not continue the mission were obviously insufficiently devoted to the Rebbe. These very same arguments were invoked within the community years later, after Menachem Mendel himself had died with his own promises of redemption unfulfilled.

Repeatedly, Menachem Mendel punctuated his Passover speech with heartfelt sobs. The tears their emerging leader shed could not help but arouse natural feelings of survivor guilt in the congregation—the feeling that they had never been devoted enough to the old Rebbe. But Menachem Mendel offered his listeners a way out of these feelings. Through unstinting work, they could still help their old Rebbe make his mission a success, to bring the Redeemer and right the wrongs of history. There was no need for despair or disappointment. The battle was not over, and the late Rebbe, whose death was a tactic to ensure victory, surely would still lead his followers to the redemption and fulfill all he had promised.

In another talk the following month, Rabbi Menachem Mendel expressed the view that all the pain felt by the community over Yosef Yitzchak's death, and indeed his passing itself, was but the "birth pangs of the Messiah," which the Jewish tradition had always said were a precursor to the days of redemption.[96] Therefore their pain was not a cause for concern but rather a sign of an impending joy, just as birth pain precedes the delight of greeting the newborn. These were echoes of precisely what Rabbi Yosef Yitzchak had said nearly ten years earlier in the dark days of the Holocaust. "For those who want to open their eyes and hearts to the truth, to them we bring the joyful good news. . . . No new tribulations should . . . bring the Jews into despair! Let each Jew greet his fellow with the happy blessing: *l'altar l'geula*, [to a swift redemption]."[97]

In the immediate aftermath of Yud Shvat, the new Rebbe inspired confidence and pointed toward a future filled with promise. Their mission was still intact. The Previous Rebbe would continue to lead them. "One has to surrender oneself and become another," he asserted, adding, "I am only a stand-in."[98] In a sense, he would consider himself for the rest of his life as being on a mission for Rebbe Yosef Yitzchak, his father-in-law, even in the latter's afterlife, continuing to refer to him "in the present tense," claiming "wild men think that to die is to leave completely, this is not so."[99]

The question was how practically Lubavitchers could continue to follow the leadership of and communicate with the old rebbe. For this, Menachem Mendel would prove to be the indispensable go-between. In terms that would be echoed years later after his own passing, Menachem Mendel told the Hasidim that the connection between them and their rebbe was not a relationship between two separate individuals. Rather, as he showed from a plethora of Jewish sources, the two became a single unit. Through his emotional displays—his frequent weeping when he mentioned Rabbi Yosef Yitzchak—and his ability to interpret the message of the rebbe, Menachem Mendel demonstrated that no one more than he had become entwined with the dead rebbe.

Menachem Mendel repeatedly told the community that he continued to feel the presence of his father-in-law, and that he sensed it particularly when he visited the *tsiyen*, which he did regularly. At the old rebbe's gravesite he could not only pass on their *pidyones* and other communications to their rebbe, by reading them and depositing them on the tomb, but, more important, he could *hear* and receive replies. That capacity to serve as the channel or emissary for his father-in-law's messages would become a cornerstone of Menachem Mendel's leadership.

He continued throughout his life to travel regularly to the cemetery (and toward his final years, particularly after the death of his wife in 1988, even more frequently), his one regular journey out of Brooklyn after becoming Rebbe. Here he would commune with his predecessor. He would travel with only a small coterie of aides and remain in a small chamber adjoining the *ohel*. Indeed, it was here that he suffered his first devastating stroke in 1992.

Among his followers this practice became a key element of his authority.[100] He would often refer to "orders" he had received from Rabbi Yosef Yitzchak while he was there. Even Shmaryahu Gourary was reportedly impressed. In one account, published years after the events in question, he supposedly recounted how once he was troubled over an important decision he had to make, yet felt unable to finalize. Realizing that "my brother in law, Menachem Mendel was here, [I thought,] why not consult with him?" The latter deliberated deeply about the matter and replied that the question was so weighty that he did not deign to give counsel on his own, but as he was going that day to the *tsiyen*, "he would speak to and confer with our father-in-law, the holy Rabbi Yosef Yitzchak, may his memory preserve us, and bring an answer. And indeed, upon his return from the *tsiyen* he brought me a wondrous reply."

Demonstrating how important this capacity to communicate with Rabbi Yosef Yitzchak was as a means of accepting and legitimating Menachem Mendel's authority, Gourary added, according to the author of this account, who put the following words into his mouth: "my brother-in-law, may he be well, is not given to exaggeration. If he says he will consult with the father-in-law at the *tsiyen*, then he will surely speak to him there." Finally, as if to explain why he, once heir apparent, had deferred to Menachem Mendel, Gourary added, "I know that *I myself cannot converse with my father-in-law*. . . . If he can, then I am bound to him."[101]

What Shmaryahu Gourary was admitting here, as any Lubavitcher would understand, was that his brother-in-law's ability to converse with his father-in-law at the grave was evidence that the two Rebbes were unified, or as it might be expressed in Lurianic kabbalah, from which ChaBaD drew deeply, they were "two souls stemming from the same root," and that they therefore were unified.[102] Indeed, often if not always, when he was asked for a blessing he would reply, "I will mention it at the *tsiyen*."[103]

Other than his visits to the *tsiyen*, after assuming leadership, Menachem Mendel never again "left Lubavitch," yet he managed to spread his influence and send his emissaries far beyond its boundaries. In the end, Menachem Mendel Schneerson combined both the charisma of his office as Rebbe of ChaBaD Lubavitch and a more personal charisma, in virtue of his powerful personality and extraordinary individual magnetism.

All this was an astonishing achievement for a man born in Ukraine at the start of the twentieth century, who had to cross many geographic and cultural boundaries on a life's journey that took him back and forth from the periphery to the core of many societies, both Jewish and Hasidic as well as secular and cosmopolitan. It is to these journeys and how they brought him to his leadership of a worldwide Jewish movement with messianic overtones to which we now turn.

CHAPTER 3

Coming of Age in a Time of Transition

∭

The life story of a Hasidic rebbe is often shrouded in hagiography. To believers it cannot be that the man who stands between them and God could have had a life like any other. Even that which seems prosaic is understood as appearing so only to the uninitiated, and therefore things can never be what they seem. For believers, beneath the surface reality there is to be found a deeper truth. Only one who has the key can thus unlock the whole truth, and that key is possessed only by those who are truly Hasidim. This view seems to be defended with even more vehemence when the rebbe in question is faced with early challenges to his claims to leadership from those within the community who contest his succession. In the aftermath of such contestation, after the new rebbe's position is secure, the life before his selection and ascendance must be reframed so as to conform to Hasidic expectations of holy men. Every past act and event must be shown retrospectively to have led inexorably to his eminence and greatness, which with hindsight is revealed to have been there all along. The farther back in the rebbe's life one goes, the more difficult this becomes, and the more pressing is the need to shroud these distant events in hagiography, myth, mystery, and reconstructed memory.

Obviously, such an attitude often makes it difficult to sift through internal accounts by those who look upon the rebbe as their spiritual leader and guide, even though these are the people who are most interested in and have tried to learn as much as possible about the man, whose life and character they also consider worthy of emulation. Phrases like "little is known" or "during those years he acted anonymously" or "because of his modesty" he worked alone make their way into internal hagiographic accounts or recollections.

By contrast, the task of independent biographers is to navigate between hagiography and mystery, to analyze testimonies and documentation in order to trace the journey that took someone like Menachem Mendel Schneerson from his birthplace in the Ukrainian port city of Nikolayev on the Black Sea to Brooklyn, New York, near the Hudson River. Our goal is to follow Rabbi Schneerson's life and career from his beginnings as a child of a prominent Lubavitcher family in a sociocultural atmosphere quite different from that obtaining at the court of the Rebbe to his own long tenure as Rebbe.

𝕴𝕴𝕴

Like so much else in his story, even the date of his birth is ambiguous. While the accepted birthday, according to his own word, was Sabbath eve, April 18, 1902 (11 Nissan 5662, according to the Jewish calendar), his Soviet passport indicates an earlier date, March 2, 1895, a discrepancy having to do with the constant need of Jews born under the rule of the czars to find ways of avoiding the army draft, which many understood meant the inevitable loss of young Jewish boys to secularity and unbelief.[1] Mendel Schneerson claimed he had received a student deferment from the Russian army in 1915.[2] Perhaps when he applied for his passport in 1927 he gave the earlier date so that he could exit Russia at an "older" age, when he would no longer be as likely to be called to serve as a soldier.

His maternal great-great-grandfather, Avraham Lavut, a student of the third Lubavitcher rebbe, Menachem Mendel (known as "Zemah Zedek"), had been selected by a Hasidic entrepreneur in Nikolayev to be rabbi for the Hasidim in that city. In time, this position passed to Meyer Shlomo Yanofsky, Lavut's grandson, whose daughters, Gittel and Chana, would marry two Schneerson brothers, who also traced their roots in a direct line to the Zemah Zedek. Gittel married Shmuel, and on June 18, 1900, Chana married Levi Yitzchak (this date makes clear that the date of Mendel's birth could not be 1895, as given on his passport). The couple lived in the Yanofsky household in Nikolayev, where Levi Yitzchak studied under the sponsorship of his father-in-law. They bore three sons: the eldest, Menachem Mendel, was named after the Zemah Zedek; the second, born about a year later, DovBer (known as Bereke or Belka), was given the name of the second Lubavitcher rebbe (the so-called Miteler Rebbe); and the youngest, Yisrael Aryeh Leib (called Leibel), was born about nine years into the marriage.

In 1907, Levi Yitzchak moved with his family to 2 Mostovaya Street in Yekaterinoslav, a cosmopolitan city on the Dnieper River, where he had been offered a rabbinic position.[3] Here, on the edge of the Pale of Settlement, he would serve the city's small Hasidic community, the majority of whom were followers of ChaBaD.* Yekaterinoslav, on the southern reaches of the Russian empire in territory that had been captured during the Russo-Turkish wars, had become colonized in the last third of the eighteenth century.[4] The city attracted those Jews who wanted to share in its economic and cultural riches. Its rapidly industrializing economy and its access via the Dnieper to the shipping trade attracted a flood of newcomers by the end of the nineteenth century, including tens of thousands of Jews from villages and *shtetls* in the surrounding agricultural region. As newcomers, they obviously lacked traditional communal roots and extended family ties in the area, making them even more open to change. By 1920, the city, connected by rail link to Moscow and Petrograd (the latter also known as Leningrad and St. Petersburg) and important to the industrial might of the region, housed about 70,000 Jews, many of whom were working in commerce or the professions.[5]

Jewry had been undergoing change and ferment in Western and Central Europe in the previous generation. Secularization and political emancipation had led to the erosion of the authority and appeal of long-established traditional Judaism, its way of life, and its leaders. By the second half of the nineteenth century a similar process was overtaking Russian Jewry, but it was exacerbated by the economic, political, social, and cultural changes in the areas where they lived. Traditional religious authority and patterns of life in the Pale that had seemed immune to the changes going on in the West were now experiencing much of the same erosion and crisis. Jews were no longer forced to remain solely within

---

* The Pale was the restricted territory of approximately 386,000 square miles within the borders of czarist Russia wherein the residence of Jews was legally authorized.

the parochial and insular precincts of their religious community or to retain a strictly Jewish identity but could move into other orbits and adopt a new sort of Jewish existence—and they did.

When the Schneersons arrived in Yekaterinoslav, they joined a Jewish community beset with social change. In this new, cosmopolitan urban milieu, the appeal of traditional Jewish authority and patterns of life was rapidly eroding, especially among Jewish youth. Many who came from traditional religious homes—families that kept "Torah and mitzvahs"—changed dramatically in a short time. Instead of identifying with the traditions from which they came, they became caught up in a whole array of alternative and competing ways of seeing themselves, which they believed would offer more promise for the future. These included, on the one extreme, the secular national identity of Zionism that sought to create a new ideal type of Jew who would be a sovereign full-fledged citizen in his own country, and at the other, the embrace of a new sort of secular and socialist society in Russia that left behind all parochial and religious identities. Those adhering to either vision were no longer prepared to accept the authority of rabbis, who for generations had been leaders and guides of religious Jewry. In their place stood new, revolutionary, and typically younger guides to whom the changing Jewish society looked for leadership. Among these would be counted two of the prominent official or "crown rabbis" in Yekaterinoslav, Shmarya Levin and his successor, Emanuel Burstein, both of whom were supporters of Zionism.[6]

In the midst of this crisis of leadership, the education of the young became an issue of paramount importance and intense competition. Many came to see traditional, parochial Jewish education, with its concentration on the teaching of Torah, Talmud, and its commentaries (and for the Hasidim as well the teaching of Hasidic tracts, stories, and customs), as inadequate to prepare students for the new conditions of life. Such critics were drawn to a modern secular education that was oriented to the new economic, political, and social realities. Some traditionally religious Jews vehemently opposed the new educational trends, going so far as to forbid Russian language instruction or any practical-vocational coursework alongside classical Torah study. Other religious Jews, by contrast, recognized that without the skills and knowledge they could acquire through at the very least a secondary school level of a general secular education, they would be at a disadvantage. They, too, wanted to give their children the opportunity to succeed and survive in the modern world, and thus many among them accepted the need to broaden the education available for Jewish youth.

Even Levi Yitzchak Schneerson valued such knowledge. In a letter of recommendation written by the fifth Lubavitcher rebbe in support of his rabbinical selection in Yekaterinoslav, Levi Yitzchak was described as superior "in Torah and the fear of God," but also as someone who *"knows and understands worldly matters."** The Lubavitcher rebbe of the time understood that this last point would carry weight—this in spite of the fact that ChaBaD rebbes had generally been prominent opponents of the idea of Jews receiving a general or university education.

As a Lubavitcher Hasid and rabbi, Levi Yitzchak Schneerson was not at all averse to moving to cosmopolitan Yekaterinoslav and giving his children a sort of general education that fit within a Jewish framework. He recognized that traditional Torah learning no longer constituted all that Jews needed or wanted to know. Indeed, this "worldly knowledge" of his was part of his appeal.

By the time the Schneersons moved to their new home, Yekaterinoslav could boast of three libraries with book collections in Russian, Yiddish, and Hebrew. Residents could attend public lectures of all sorts on a variety of general topics as well as concerts of classical music and cantorial recitals, reflecting the interests of a varied and growing Jewish intelligentsia. In the large central synagogue there was a choir made up of men and women—unthinkable in traditional or Hasidic congregations—accompanied by an organ. There were Jewish hospitals, orphanages, and a Polytechnic Institute that would later develop into a university. There was the modern *Heder Metukkan* (improved school), headed by Hayyim Zuta (who would afterward become a pioneer of Hebrew education in Palestine), that stood in contrast to the

---

*He tried hard, and even went so far as to suggest that his cousin, Levi Yitzchak, try to acquire an additional ordination or at least a letter of recommendation from the non-Hasidic yeshiva head, Rabbi Haym Soloveitchik of Brisk (Brest-Litovsk) in Lithuania, indicating that the broader the education, both in Torah studies and in other matters, one had, the greater the likelihood of getting hired by the Jews of the increasingly cosmopolitan region of Russia. See letter in *Kovetz Chof Menachem-Av* (Brooklyn: Kehot, 2004), 10 (italics added), 12.

traditional *kheyder*. Unlike the latter, which featured strictly traditional Jewish learning, the *Heder Metukkan* provided instruction in subjects such as mathematics and literature and approached Jewish learning with innovations such as studying the meaning of sacred texts in Modern Hebrew rather than merely translating them into Yiddish, which had been the traditional approach. Even in the local yeshiva, pupils received training in Modern Hebrew language, grammar, and literature, reflecting a clear Zionist influence in the Jewish community. Indeed, the rabbi of the non-Hasidic traditional synagogue who founded and directed the yeshiva was himself a member of Mizrachi, the political party of religious Zionism. At the time, the so-called *kazyonny ravvin* (Hebrew: *rav mi-ta'am*), or "official rabbi," sometimes also called "Crown Rabbi," who was appointed by the community "to supervise public prayers and religious ceremonies," officiating at or registering circumcisions, marriages, and burials, was also a Zionist.[7] In fact, many of the prominent leaders of Zionism traced their roots to the city.

Although Levi Yitzchak Schneerson was not a Zionist, he and his family could not remain remote from or untouched by all these Jewish trends. His sons Mendel and Leibel—Bereke, the middle son, suffered from some form of mental retardation and was sent to an institution— were clearly affected by this extraordinarily open and vibrant Jewish environment. Their peers came from families that had already been swept up by secularization, political change, and the variety of social movements that filled the air.*

There are surprisingly few eyewitness accounts of what life was like for Mendel and Leibel in those days. Perhaps the most important and reliable one comes from Abraham and Vardina Shlonsky, whose mother and Chana Schneerson were cousins and who lived next door. Passionate Zionists who would end up living in Israel, where Abraham would go on to become a famous Hebrew poet and his sister

---

* We do not really know the attitude the Schneersons took to Berel's diminished mental status. We know that he spent most of his life in an institution. In perhaps a cryptic hint of the way Berel was viewed, we find that in April 1911, the Schneerson family gave donations in honor of their sons in the following amounts: 18 kopeks (18 is a number that is equivalent to the Hebrew word for "life") in honor of Leibel, and 27 kopeks (a life and a half) for Mendel and Berel. Who was the half? See *Ha'Ach* (a Lubavitcher monthly published in Lubavitch, Belorus), 16 Nissan 5611 (April 14, 1911), last page.

Vardina a pianist and composer, they had moved to the city around the same time. The Shlonsky and Schneerson families, although quite different in their orientations—the former intellectuals and Zionists and increasingly secular, the latter Hasidic and traditionally observant religiously—became very close. Sabbaths and holidays were often celebrated together, even though the Shlonskys were no longer strict in their attachment to the Jewish dietary laws of kashrut. The children spent much time in one another's company, moving easily between the adjacent ground-floor apartments. In spite of the fact that they came from the more religiously observant home, the Schneerson boys were comfortable with their cousins. Just as the Shlonskys enjoyed listening to the Schneerson family's Hasidic songs, so the latter enjoyed playing in their cousins' home. Dov (Beryl) Shlonsky, one of the other children, who loved to sing opera and Hasidic tunes, was particularly close to Mendel and Leibel. For a time, Abraham, who studied in the same traditional *kheyder* as the Schneerson boys and was going through a religious phase, decided he preferred eating at the Schneersons because Chana's kitchen, unlike his mother's, was strictly kosher. Vardina, his sister, recalled her older cousin Mendel, or Mekka, as she called him, as being intellectually curious, finding everything of interest—decorating his room, for example, with astronomical maps. Indeed, according to the Shlonskys' recollections, neither of the Schneerson boys lived a life insulated from the political, ideological, and social currents that swept up their Jewish neighbors in Yekaterinoslav.

At the outset, the two brothers received their primary education from a Lubavitcher Hasidic *melamed*, Zalman Wilenkin, whom their father found to instruct them in the Jewish basics and later Talmud and ChaBaD Hasidism, subjects which, as they grew older, they would study under their father's supervision. Mendel would also study later (from 1909 to 1915) in a yeshiva in Yekaterinoslav that offered courses not only in the classic Torah subjects but also in Hebrew grammar and poetry, including the work of the recognized national Zionist poet, Bialik.[8]

Despite his attachment to Lubavitcher Hasidism and his close ties to the then rebbe Shalom DovBer and his only son, Yosef Yitzchak, Levi Yitzchak Schneerson did not send his sons to the Tomekhei Temimim yeshiva in Lubavitch, as for example did the Lubavitcher parents of at least two of their schoolmates.[9] The fact that neither of the

Schneerson boys studied in the Lubavitcher yeshiva could not have been an oversight or the result of happenstance.[10] According to one internal Lubavitcher source, Levi Yitzchak did not "permit" his son Mendel to go to the yeshiva in Lubavitch.[11] On the contrary, the Schneersons obviously *wanted* their children to acquire a general education. To this end they hired Israel Eidelsohn, a confirmed socialist and Zionist, to be the boys' tutor. Eidelsohn, who would later change his name to Bar Yehuda, emigrate to Palestine in 1926, join Kibbutz Yagur, and eventually rise in the ranks of the socialist Labor *Ahdut-Ha'Avoda* party to serve a four-year term as interior minister in the new state of Israel, supported the then revolutionary idea that one could declare oneself a Jew on the basis of personal choice rather than on religious and legal criteria. (Many years later Menachem Mendel as Lubavitcher Rebbe would adamantly and publicly oppose this position.)

At the time that Eidelsohn became the Schneersons' tutor, he was already a leader of a Zionist youth organization and a student at the university in Yekaterinoslav, and worked part time in the office of the Jewish secondary school (gymnasium). He taught the boys mathematics, Russian, and other languages and mapped out a program of study for them equivalent to what they would have covered in gymnasium. Mendel was reportedly gifted both in translation and in mathematics.[12]

To be sure, the boys still devoted many hours to their Jewish studies, which made up the bulk of their day. But there can be no doubt that their close exposure to a man like Eidelsohn, who may in some way have served implicitly as a role model for them, had a profound intellectual and moral impact on them. The tradition of respecting one's teacher was deeply ingrained in the Jewish ethos that shaped the consciousness and character of homes like the Schneersons'—and that held true even if the teacher taught them matters beyond the boundaries of tradition. As the boys sought to impress their teacher in their secular studies, their horizons were opened beyond the Hasidism of their family roots. It thus came as no surprise when Leibel decided to join the Zionist youth organization that Eidelsohn headed, a development that pained his parents, who saw Zionism as a threat to Jewish tradition.[13]

Leibel and Mendel lived out their adolescence and shaped their emerging identities in turbulent times. As the Great War swept across

Europe, Yekaterinoslav was occupied by German troops. Then, as the Germans withdrew, Jews suffered attacks, against which they formed a variety of defense organizations, none of which proved particularly successful.[14] Four more occupying armies would take over the city by 1920 during the upheavals in Russia that would lead to the end of the czar's reign, a civil war, and ultimately the Bolshevik revolution. Jews went through highs and lows, believing for a time that the change would free them from the terror of pogroms and tyranny of dictatorship that had characterized life under the czar. Material conditions in the city declined, even as political activity increased, with Jews debating whether socialism and communism offered them more hope than Zionism. The repeated violence against Jews made life here difficult. In May and June 1919, for example, assaults against Jews in the city left one hundred fifty dead and about a thousand women raped.[15] By this time the city was dominated by ruin, a seemingly infinite change of authorities, and a paralysis of industry and transport; many were looking to leave. According to second-hand accounts published many years later, Mendel Schneerson claimed to have served in one of the many Jewish defense groups that protected Jews from anti-Bolshevik White Army attacks in 1919.[16] Beyond this source, we have found nothing else. We do know that he claimed in an affidavit, many years later in France, to have served in the Russian military from March to August 1915, before being released to become a student; what he did during those six months of army service remains unknown.

When at last the Bolsheviks came to power, many Jews believed that better times were coming, but they soon discovered that the Bolsheviks and their brand of communism did not offer true deliverance for many of them. In 1917 wealthy Jews in the city had their businesses confiscated, while religious repression became the norm, a severe blow to the rabbis above all others. In 1922, after the firm establishment of Soviet rule, about a thousand Jews were arrested.[17]

Despite his claim of involvement in Jewish defense groups and the Russian military, there is no evidence to suggest that young Mendel was as deeply touched and radicalized by this turmoil as his younger brother and contemporaries. While Leibel and many others were engaged in large world-building debates about the future and the politically extraordinary events of the day, in 1920, by his own account,

Mendel became an assistant, apprenticed to an engineer for the next two years.[18]

Did this young man, who would later be seen by his Hasidim as a world leader with an interest in and power to affect history and events, remove himself from history and events during perhaps what was then the most turbulent period in his life? To these questions there are no ready answers. It is clear, however, as we shall subsequently show, that Mendel drew on some of the secular ideas of this tumultuous era in his later career as Rebbe—although this would be discernible only to those who knew how to look beyond the surface of his explanations.

His interest in science, and particularly mathematics, increased during his adolescence. Being an apprentice to an engineer, however, was clearly not enough for the young man. After two years on the job and after the authority of the Soviet Union had firmly been established, Mendel began in 1923 to attend the formerly Jewish Polytechnic Institute now confiscated by the communists and made part of Yekaterinoslav University.[19] He remained there during 1924, after Lenin's death in January, and in 1925, while Stalin and Trotsky, whom his brother Leibel supported, were engaged in a power struggle for control of the nascent Soviet Union.

For Leibel, the ultimate triumph of Stalin would become life-changing, for as a Jew and a devoted Trotskyist, he would now be in danger from the victorious Stalin and his supporters. What did it mean for Mendel? We only know that he spent the year continuing as a student.

In November 1926, the year in which Stalin established himself as a virtual dictator, Mendel Schneerson left the university and the city without a degree (though he would later get a letter testifying to his having studied in Russia). The following month he departed for the newly renamed Leningrad (St. Petersburg), where for the next eleven months and with the support and encouragement of his parents he sought to advance his studies in his chosen field of mathematics and engineering as an auditor at the university.[20]

Leningrad, for many years the capital of the czars, was also the city to which Rabbi Yosef Yitzchak, the reigning Lubavitcher rebbe, had come in 1924 to reestablish his court in the wake of war, civil strife, and the communist revolution in Russia. Arrangements had been made for Mendel to live in the apartment of his cousins, the Schneersohns, on the third floor of 22 Mokhovaya Street.[21] For the first time, Mendel would live in the court of the Lubavitcher Rebbe. Here he met and actually lived in the same apartment with the Rebbe's middle daughter, Chaya Moussia, whom in time he would marry. This meant that four years would pass between this meeting and their wedding, an extraordinarily long time for an arranged marriage to be concluded. Indeed, it would be unprecedented for two people from such distinguished and related Hasidic families to carry on such a long courtship and to live in the same residence.* Long courtships are against the norm among Hasidim, nor was there any formal sort of engagement of which we can find any record.

Later Lubavitcher histories claim with hindsight that this move to Leningrad, the early connection with the court of the sixth Lubavitcher rebbe, and the marriage to Yosef Yitzchak's daughter prove beyond any doubt the strength of Menachem Mendel's Hasidic attachments.[22] Certainly, as his diaries reveal, the young Menachem Mendel used this period to familiarize himself with ChaBaD customs and usages, stories, and commentaries. It is entirely unclear, however, whether becoming his father-in-law's successor was in the young man's plans.

〽

When Yosef Yitzchak became the sixth Lubavitcher rebbe in 1920 at the age of forty, it was a difficult time for any religious leader.[23] As a result of the war and the October revolution, Russia was in a state of turmoil. So too was Lubavitcher Hasidism. It had become a court on the move—some might say on the run. Being on the move forced this Hasidic court to place far more emphasis than ever before on building and maintaining a network, with an enhanced usage of emissaries to keep their Rebbe in touch with his Hasidim. Yosef Yitzchak understood this necessity, and his successor would understand it even more so. In effect, a key element of evolving Lubavitcher Hasidic court life

---

* If we accept the official ChaBaD timeline and Lubavitcher sources' claim that in 1923 he had briefly visited Rabbi Yosef Yitzchak in Rostov and at that time the possibility of his marrying the Rebbe's daughter was explored, the interval between meeting and marriage becomes even longer.

was movement, and being a Hasid increasingly meant being on a mission from the Rebbe.

Five years before Yosef Yitzchak's ascension, in 1915, the Lubavitcher court had been forced to flee the German invasion and its longtime home in Lubavitch and moved to Rostov-on-Don, where the fifth rebbe, Rabbi Shalom DovBer, spent the remaining five years of his life. Shalom DovBer had chosen Russian-controlled Rostov in order to avoid Germany, which he saw as the ultimate enemy, both political and cultural, under whose hegemony he believed Judaism became hopelessly compromised and religiously endangered. But the diminutive Jewish backwater of Rostov with its overwhelmingly secular Jewish population could never be more than a small outpost in the Lubavitcher network of Hasidism. When Yosef Yitzchak consolidated his leadership, he understood that in order for his court to flourish in the new century and modern society, he would be better off in a city where there were many Jews whom he could attract to his court and movement. Following the revolution, Jews like others were streaming to the capital in Moscow and to the former capital of St. Petersburg, now renamed Leningrad. He chose the latter for his headquarters. And so in 1924, Yosef Yitzchak, his wife, three daughters, son-in-law Shmaryahu Gourary, personal secretary Chaim Lieberman, and the rest of his court followed them to the ancestral home of the czars.

Many if not most of the Orthodox or Hasidic rabbis who found themselves under communism decided to flee its domain wherever and whenever possible. Many went to the West; some ended up in Poland, and still others continued farther. Unlike them, however, Yosef Yitzchak stayed in Russia as a matter of principle, prohibiting his Hasidim from emigrating, particularly to the United States or Palestine, where he saw dangers to the integrity of traditional Judaism as he defined it. He maintained his contact with all followers scattered throughout Soviet-controlled territory through his emissaries, who became all the more important for him now. He sent his devoted students from the Tomekhei Temimim yeshiva, which his father had set up and which he had appointed his only son to head, throughout the main Jewish settlements in the Soviet Union. Often they came in the role of *shokhtim*, ritual slaughterers of kosher meat. As such, not only did they succeed in providing for the kosher dietary needs of Jews, they also came with a ready-made source of income: for every slaughtered animal, they were paid a fee. In time they would also set up a network of schools for the teaching of Torah and ChaBaD Hasidism.[24] This made their rebbe not only a leader but a man who controlled an important network within the new Soviet Union, a region that would in time become cut off from the world by what Winston Churchill would call an "Iron Curtain."* This made the ChaBaD leader important indeed, both as a link to the Jews caught behind that Iron Curtain and as a symbol of them.

This use of emissaries and the creation of an active network of followers and supporters answerable to the rebbe and guided by him served as a model for Menachem Mendel when he later became the Rebbe and sought a way to expand his influence beyond his local authority in the Crown Heights Lubavitcher community, through what became known as his *Uforatzto* Campaign.[25] At the time Yosef Yitzchak developed his network, however, we find no evidence that his future younger son-in-law took part in it.

Jews outside the Soviet Union saw their Soviet-bound kinsmen as victims of a tragedy, lost behind the Stalinist and hostile authority. This view of an embattled Jewish minority in communist lands served indirectly to enhance Yosef Yitzchak's stature. In the absence of almost all other Russian rabbinic leaders of importance, Jewish organizations worldwide that wanted to help and support Jewry in the USSR looked increasingly to Yosef Yitzchak and his network. He became the man to go to in order to reach that Jewry and was seen as the best hope for Jewish spiritual continuity. For Yosef Yitzchak, the growing repression of Soviet Jewry as well as his opportunity to play a role in its survival signaled the dark days of life under the communist unbelievers, but also a sign of the birth pangs of the Messiah and his chance to hasten redemption.[26] Out of the darkness, there was light—and he felt positioned to lead Jewry toward that light. He would get material help from an unlikely source.

In 1914, American Jews—the very Jews Yosef Yitzchak would later identify as sinners responsible for the travails of European Jewry—had founded the Joint Distribution Committee (JDC), originally organized

---

* While Churchill would not use the phrase until 1946 in a speech in Fulton, Missouri, the idea that those living inside the Soviet regime were being separated from the rest of the world to the West was clear early on.

to aid Palestinian Jewry in the First World War.* By the beginning of the 1920s they had begun coming to the aid of Soviet Jewry, many of whom had lost their private property, stores, and factories, and who were also counted among the famine sufferers of the time. Seeking someone inside the country who could distribute the funds they were collecting, the JDC concluded that Yosef Yitzchak would be the person for the job, for there seemed no one better positioned to reach large numbers of Jews. This control over these funds made him even more powerful, but it also made him a potential target for the communist authorities. Additionally, it raised the ire of the local Jewish establishment who resented the Lubavitcher Hasidim for gaining control over so much money and thereby over Jewish activities.

Targeting him was a task the new Russian communist secret police, the OGPU, gave to the Jews who had joined the party. To fight against religion and the structure of the traditional Jewish community, the Soviets created the *Yevsektsiya* (*Yevreyskaya sektsiya*, or Jewish section) of the Bolshevik party in the immediate aftermath of the revolution to carry out the policies of the party toward Jews and Judaism. It was led for most of its existence by Semion Dimanstein, a former student at the Lubavitch yeshiva who had received rabbinical ordination from the illustrious Hayyim Ozer Grodzinski. Dimanstein, however, had left his religious roots behind and become a Bolshevik and Yiddish newspaper editor.[27] Under Dimanstein, the Yevsektsiya's mission was to undermine and end all forms of Jewish religious behavior and organization, which it saw as an obstacle to the total assimilation of Jews into the new communist society. No Jewish activity was too minor to attract attention and be stamped out. To the Yevsektsiya, the activities of Yosef Yitzchak, which aimed at maintaining, if not heightening, Jewish religious identity and involvement, were anathema, and any successes

---

*Its founding fathers were the very successful German Jewish immigrants ambassador Henry Morgenthau and financiers Jacob Schiff and his brother-in-law, Felix Warburg, probably among the more assimilated American Jews. They sent the Russian-born agronomist Joseph Rosen to handle relief missions to the famine-starved regions, having made a deal with the Soviets to aid all Russians, but Rabbi Yosef Yitzchak was going to handle specifically Jewish needs. See Sara Kadosh, "American Jewish Joint Distribution Committee," 59–64, and Yehuda Bauer, "Joseph A. Rosen," in Berenbaum and Skolnik, *Encyclopaedia Judaica*, 2nd ed., 14:269.

he had, however limited, represented a threat.[28] This was the motive behind the Soviet OGPU's campaign against the Lubavitchers. Yosef Yitzchak was therefore denounced by the Yevsektsiya and marked by the OGPU as a "foreign agent" running a "counterrevolutionary network" that imperiled the Soviet state.

Near midnight of June 14, 1927, a detail of the OGPU, the Soviet secret police, headed by two former Lubavitchers, came to Yosef Yitzchak's home. After searching the entire premises and interrogating him and others in the apartment, including two of his daughters, they prepared to arrest the Rebbe—the only Schneersohn they wanted—to take him to "Shpalerka Prison."*

During the process, Yosef Yitzchak's middle daughter, Moussia, who had been out for the evening with Mendel, came home.[29] The fact that two were out together until the early hours of the morning is glossed over in Lubavitcher accounts of the events. Such behavior would certainly have distinguished them from a traditional Hasidic couple—let alone the daughter of a rebbe and one who "would be her husband."[30] A more traditional couple would never have gone out without a chaperon (and certainly not till such a late hour), such "dates" being rather in the style of more modern acculturated Leningrad couples. Ignoring these facts, most of the hagiographic versions of these events focus on the fact that Moussia, seeing the lights on and cars in front of the building, suspected trouble and before going inside told Mendel to wait outside on the street. In one plausible version of the story, once in the apartment, and noting the presence of the police, she signaled to Mendel (whom she had just left and therefore knew was still outside) to stay away through the pre-arranged sign of opening the window. On seeing this signal, he supposedly rushed to the apartment of the Rebbe's secretary, Lieberman (who would be arrested later as well), to alert him of the arrival of the police. Lieberman reportedly began to destroy the Rebbe's and his own private correspondence and sought to somehow protect the treasures of the Rebbe's library.[31]

---

*This is the name Lubavitchers gave it. This probably refers to Spalernaia Prison, reputedly "one of the best prisons" or "strictest" in Leningrad. See Vladlen S. Izmozik, "Voices from the Twenties: Private Correspondence Intercepted by the OGPU, *Russian Review* 55, no. 2 (April 1996): 299, 302.

Apart from Yosef Yitzchak and Lieberman, as well as Shmaryahu Gourary for a short time, none of the other family members were detained or imprisoned. Mendel remained untouched—and all the efforts in which internal sources describe his being active or wanted by the police remain undocumented. In the many letters and telegrams sent on behalf of Rabbi Yosef Yitzchak, we find none signed by him, nor is there any paper trail of his efforts. Only in Lubavitcher sources written long after the events in question do his "secret" efforts on behalf of his future father-in-law appear. Some Lubavitcher sources claim he was caught by the police while traveling between Yekaterinoslav and Leningrad but "managed to escape."[32] We have no independent evidence of this, nor do we know how it would have been effected. Why there is no detailed account of what would have been a "miraculous" event in the life of the future Rebbe, we do not know.

As the Rebbe Yosef Yitzchak was led off to jail from his home, he reportedly approached the crib of his only grandchild, Shalom DovBer Gourary, and offered the blessing we described in the previous chapter, "that this child grow to be the greatest of his brothers," and praying that God grant him a future that would allow him to follow in the footsteps of his forebears.[33] The message to those in the room was clear: if anything fatal should happen to the Rebbe during the arrest, the mantle of Lubavitcher leadership would pass to the child in time. In one version of the story, as they took Yosef Yitzchak away to prison, one of the two former Lubavitchers, perhaps with irony, offered to carry the Rebbe's bag of *talis* and tefillin (prayer articles), saying, "As my grandfather your Hasid once carried packages for your grandfather, so will I now carry them for you."[34] The Rebbe reportedly held on personally to these articles in defiance.

𝕸

Rabbi Yosef Yitzchak was imprisoned and, according to Lubavitcher versions of the events, sentenced to death. That condemnation—if in fact it occurred—was soon set aside, and the sixth rebbe was released at least in part owing to the efforts of Ekaterina Peshkov, a Red Cross activist and former wife of the famous author Maxim Gorky, as well as the heads of the Jewish JDC. Also involved were Senators Robert Wagner of New York and William Borah of Idaho, the latter a dominant member of the Senate Foreign Relations Committee who had called for American recognition of the new Soviet government and who was seen as an important friend by the USSR.[35] Borah's crucial involvement was enlisted by American Reform rabbi Stephen Wise.[36]

Following the cancellation of his sentence, Rebbe Yosef Yitzchak was "exiled" for just ten days with Shmaryahu Gourary and one of his daughters to Kostroma, a lovely and ancient city on the banks of the Volga, about 212 miles northeast of Moscow—not exactly Siberia.[37] Then, after being freed, he went to rest in the resort town of Malakhovka in the Zhitomir district of Ukraine. Afterward he returned to Leningrad, where the continuing surveillance by the secret police convinced him he had to leave, and he began negotiating his departure from the USSR with the OGPU. In the interim he paid a visit to Rostov and his father's grave, where, in a foreshadowing of what Mendel would do many years later, he claimed to receive instruction from the dead rabbi about what steps to take next.[38]

Leaving the Soviet Union was neither simple nor easy; there had to be a country and community to which he could immigrate. A range of community leaders, including Latvian senator Mordecai Dubin, member of the Orthodox Agudat Israel political party and a ChaBaD Hasid, along with German Jewish leaders such as Rabbi Meir Hildesheimer and socialist politician and legal adviser to the Soviet embassy in Berlin Oscar Cohn, as well as Reform Rabbi Leo Baeck, intervened and offered to find a place for the Rebbe in their communities.[39] In the end, on the night after the conclusion of the Sukkot holiday on October 20, 1927, Rabbi Yosef Yitzchak and his immediate family went to Riga, Latvia, where he would try to retain his connections to the Lubavitcher network in the USSR. Here he believed he could carry on activities free from the oversight and dangers of the OGPU.

Yet it was not simple for a rebbe to leave behind his Hasidim; this would have to be justified as being something truly in their service. Because a rebbe is responsible for his Hasidim, Yosef Yitzchak could not abandon them to their fate in the increasingly dangerous USSR without some explanation. Thus, in one missive after his emigration, he wrote, hinting at his concern about appearing to desert his Hasidim, "I wish to make clear to everyone that no credence must be given to the reasons advanced for my leaving the country. They are illogical in the extreme. I am *not leaving under duress*—far from it! I am doing exactly what I planned to do." A rebbe must always appear in control and never at the mercy of others. In the same letter, he concluded, "Know that I shall be with you always . . . know that what you are seeing [referring to himself] is a *neshamah* [soul], as it exists in *Gan Eden* [paradise] clothed in a body."[40] These letters were obviously intended to offer hope to Hasidim for whom connection to their Rebbe was all that stood between them and despair. In an eerie way they would foreshadow things said about Yosef Yitzchak after his death, again to keep his Hasidim from despair. With their Rebbe gone, they could not help but wonder what the future held for them.

From his safe haven in Riga he continued to send letters, remit money, and generally try to tend to the needs of his flock and work for the betterment of all Jews left under Soviet rule.[41] His mechanism for doing so was a committee known as the *Vaad L'Chizuk HaTorah V'Hadat B'Russia* (Committee for Strengthening Torah and Religion in Russia). On November 17 and 18 1927, less than a month after his arrival in Riga, he convened the first meetings of this committee, which were attended by a variety of rabbis, including Meir Hildesheimer from Germany, who had been so helpful in getting him out from under the control of the Soviets, along with Shmaryahu Gourary, his father, Mendel Gourary, and Mendel Schneerson, who had left Russia on October 25 and was now living at the Commerce Hotel in Riga.[42] Shmaryahu Gourary offered a review of the activities inside the USSR, and then Rabbi Yosef Yitzchak talked about future action, how to keep the money from the JDC flowing, and how to provide for the needs of the Jews under communism.[43] For all this, Rabbi Yosef Yitzchak would not see most of his Hasidim in the USSR again, as many of them perished either in the Stalinist terror or in the brutal murders of the Nazi firestorm. Although present at the initial meeting, Mendel is not reported to have said anything worth recording.[44]

In 1927, the year of Yosef Yitzchak's arrival, Latvia had a population of nearly 100,000 Jews who had created a diverse life, in part because the state allowed its Jewish citizens a high degree of community autonomy.[45] Not only were there the many movements that had flourished in Russia before the revolution, there were as well those that had evolved among German Jewry, including those that urged education that coupled Torah studies with secular ones. Inspired by this organizational and ideological diversity, Yosef Yitzchak adapted some Latvian Jewish institutions for his own purposes. Thus, for example, he formed Mahane Israel, a social service arm of his network modeled on similar Latvian organizations. Indeed, he would even later engage the man, Chaim Hodakov, who ran several of the latter to help do so for him.[46] All this organizational activity emphasized the Lubavitcher commitment to placing its stamp not just on its Hasidim but on Jewry in general. Of course, it also represented a broader mission for the Lubavitcher Rebbe.

Under Yosef Yitzchak's leadership, the Lubavitcher community shifted its orientation from the strictly parochial to something more expansive that reached far beyond the natural Lubavitcher constituency. That global outreach was abetted by the money and influence of the JDC. In his effort to maintain control and contact from Riga, even in the face of resistance from the Soviet authorities and the organizational difficulties of running a network in one country from another, he found himself increasingly having to deal not only with Lubavitcher emissaries but with all sorts of Jews. Yosef Yitzchak was not always successful at this and remained in many ways rooted in his own parochial vision and experience. He had been forced by circumstances to deal with the world outside his own. It would remain for his successor to find a way to embrace the idea of a universal mission and create a cadre of Lubavitcher emissaries in countries throughout the world who not only knew how to deal with all sorts of Jews but seemed to relish the idea of doing so. But all of this was yet to come. During the late 1920s, Yosef Yitzchak was still engaged in building and running his network, at a time when his eventual successor seemed to have been uninvolved in the evolving Lubavitcher mission.

⁂

What was Mendel doing during this time? We know he did not flee the Soviet Union together with Yosef Yitzchak and his family but left days later. We can trace his footsteps by reviewing his passport and travel documents.[47] Mendel Schneerson's Soviet passport, number 116277, was issued in Leningrad on October 1, 1927, the Sabbath of Repentance, which falls between the high holy days of Rosh Hashanah and

Yom Kippur. One Lubavitcher version of the events has him traveling back to Yekaterinoslav to his parents to spend the Sukkot holidays with them and leaving on a Thursday after the end of the holy days after bidding a final farewell to his father, whom he would never again see alive.[48] He then purportedly journeyed on with his mother, stopping in Kursk, where he stayed for the Sabbath. From there he went back to Leningrad and picked up his travel documents, which would give him permission to leave the Soviet Union with a legal passport that he was able to keep valid at least until 1932.[49] Departing from his mother at the Latvian border, he arrived in Riga about a week and a half after Rabbi Yosef Yitzchak. There he would reunite with the "royal family."

We know that he had clear intentions not to remain at the Rebbe's court but rather to go on to Berlin to advance his studies, because while he spent two months in Riga, he left on December 26, 1927, the last day of Hanukkah, for Germany by way of Lithuania, arriving the next day.[50] The Rebbe had preceded him, for he had spent a few days in Germany meeting with people who were anxious to help him work his network on behalf of Jews caught in the Soviet web. He wrote on November 24 to tell Mendel about this activity. Possibly he also made contacts for him in Berlin.

Why did Mendel choose Berlin, where he would study without getting any degree? Did Yosef Yitzchak, with whose daughter he had been spending more and more time, agree to his going on to Germany and university study there, in the midst of a cosmopolitan way of Jewish life against which as Rebbe he had preached vehemently time and again?[51] Yosef Yitzchak's biting opposition to the kind of instruction and the philosophy of the Berlin-based, neo-Orthodox Hildesheimer Seminary, which advocated Jewish learning alongside secular study, was well known; he cuttingly criticized it, as he put it, "with a sharp blade," and contrasted it to the "pure" (*tomim*) Lubavitcher approach.[52] We find no reliable answers for Mendel's choice of Berlin.[53] We know that from the very beginning, Yosef Yitzchak paid for his tuition costs and living expenses there.[54]

Notwithstanding the claims of Lubavitchers that he spent much time there on missions for the Rebbe, Berlin was not a place where Mendel went to act in his capacity as a Hasid.[55] Indeed, it was not a center of

Hasidic life, and few if any Lubavitchers were to be found there on any permanent basis. On the contrary, Berlin, the capital of the Weimar Republic, was a city in which Jews were able to choose among all the cultural riches of German and Western culture. Here the critical and scientific study of Judaism, *Wissenschaft das Judentums*, dominated over the traditional sort of yeshiva study. In Berlin even the Orthodox shared in an ethos that embraced general culture, as exemplified in the *Torah-im-derech-eretz* philosophy that emerged among German Jewry and that urged the study of Torah and Jewish sources alongside secular university study. As such it became a magnet for those who sought to leaven their religious attachments with the supplement of Western civilization.

The famous Hildesheimer Rabbinical Seminary, officially opened in October 1873 in Berlin, was an institution dedicated to producing religious leaders who felt equally at home in general as well as Jewish learning and in the cultures attached to each. In time it became the central institution for the training of Orthodox rabbis in Western Europe.[56] The language of instruction was German, and the school demanded of its students that they either have a certificate of graduation from a gymnasium (high school) where they pursued secular studies or demonstrate that they had the knowledge necessary to graduate from such a secular secondary school. Those seeking ordination as a rabbi were strongly encouraged to get a university degree as well, and most did so, becoming "Rabbiner-Doktor."

At the time in question, Rabbi Meir Hildesheimer, son of the founder Esriel, was head of the seminary.[57] He had worked with Yosef Yitzchak and was likely predisposed to help the Rebbe's son-in-law. The seminary, which was attracting increasing numbers of former yeshiva students from the east, would serve Mendel's needs. Neither a yeshiva student nor possessing any sort of formal diploma attesting to his secondary education, he would have difficulty gaining admission to any sort of university. A credential from the Hildesheimer Seminary was more realistic. Like many yeshiva students who wanted to attend a Berlin-based university, he needed to show he had the required academic background. Mendel began attending the seminary as an auditor—since he had no graduation diploma from a secondary school he could not enroll as a full-time student.* This made him able to solicit a letter from Rabbi Hildesheimer attesting to his study there, thereby providing the documentation that universities required for course enrollment.[58] This of course made Berlin, for someone like Mendel lacking educational credentials but seeking to further his university studies, ideal.

As his passport reveals, Mendel continued to shuttle back and forth between Berlin and Riga. He did not yet have state permission to stay in Germany for an extended period. Having entered Berlin in late December 1927, by March 8 he had returned to Riga and at last received permission from the German authorities to stay in Berlin until September 15, 1928. This would allow him to live and study in Germany. Indeed, on April 26, following the Passover holidays, which he spent in Riga at the Lubavitcher court, he left for Germany and arrived there the next day, Friday, registering for the first time as an auditor (*Gasthörer*) in courses in philosophy and mathematics at Friedrich Wilhelm University (today part of Humboldt University). He claimed on his university registration form that he was at the time a student at the Hildesheimer Seminary and provided the seminary's street address as his own, even though he was not formally enrolled there as such.[59] Mendel, who was not interested in being trained as a neo-Orthodox rabbi, never attended the seminary as an officially registered student. There is a report from one seminary student who recalled seeing him standing at the back of

---

* The Lubavitchers explain Mendel's limited studies at the university as an expression of his willingness to abide by Rabbi Yosef Yitzchak's desire that he devote "the absolute minimum of time to his secular studies" (Wolf, *Admorei ChaBaD v'Yahadut Germania*, 99). However, when given the chance later (in Paris) to become a full-time student in engineering, Mendel jumped at the opportunity (see chapter four), which makes us believe that his status as an auditor (*Gasthörer*) was a consequence of his lack of prerequisite academic credentials above all else. To be sure, in the past, these same Lubavitchers claimed that their rebbe had been a full-time student at the university and the recipient of many distinguished degrees in Berlin and later Paris (see, e.g., Laufer, *Yemei Melech*, 1:357, who claims that "it was known that the Rebbe was granted several high degrees in Berlin and later in [the Sorbonne in] Paris with several high academic degrees" or in another place that he received a degree in medicine, at Laufer, 455). However, as the evidence came out that this was not the case (see Avirama Golan, "Messiah Flesh and Blood" [interview with Menachem M. Friedman], *Haaretz*, April 21–24, 1998), this argument of hewing to his father-in-law's wishes began to be made instead.

a room and listening intently to some lectures.* And we know that he "carried on conversations" with the son of Rabbi Meir Hildesheimer as well as with Rabbi J. J. Weinberg, since he reported on these to Yosef Yitzchak.[60] A story repeated among Lubavitchers that Menachem Mendel Schneerson received rabbinic ordination (*semikhah*) while in Berlin from Rabbi J. J. Weinberg, who taught and also served for a time as a rector at the seminary, has no apparent evidentiary basis. While in his registration at the university he did identify himself once as student and later as "rabbiner" (rabbi), we find no documentation that he ever received formal ordination as a rabbi.**

Lubavitcher accounts of Mendel's days in Berlin are replete with references to his involvement in unheralded missions for the sixth rebbe. Other than a few of these which we shall describe in the next chapter, extensive activities of this sort are difficult to substantiate. There are reports of his having attended a few meetings, writing some letters on behalf of the Rebbe's court, tracking down rare manuscripts, books,

---

* One report of a sighting in class comes from Pini Dunner, who writes that his grandfather, Rabbi Yosef Tzvi Dunner, who at his death in 2007 was the final living rabbi ordained by the Hildesheimer Seminary, was asked if he recalled seeing Mendel Schneerson from his time in Berlin. He replied that "he remembered him well—he was the rather modern-dressed young man with the neatly trimmed beard who stood at the back of the shiur [class] room." Pini Dunner, "Unknown Picture of Late Lubavitcher Rebbe, circa 1930s," the Seforim blog, March 30, 2008, http://seforim.blogspot.com/2008/03/pini-dunner-unknown-picture-of-late.html (accessed March 31, 2008). But another student there at the same time, Yosef Burg, later a famous member of many Israel governments, reported (to Menachem Friedman) that he never saw him in the seminary.

** The claim is made there that he requested this ordination from Rabbi Weinberg because the "national library in Berlin" allowed entry only to those with formal documents, such as ordination from a recognized rabbi. There is no evidence of that. Indeed, as we describe below, he did use his library privileges to seek out rare books and manuscripts for Rabbi Yosef Yitzchak at the latter's request. Why Yosef Yitzchak did not ordain him is not clear. Laufer in *Yemei Melech* (1:167) claims Mendel received *semikhah* from the ChaBaD Hasid Rabbi Yosef Rosen, the so-called "Rogatchover Gaon" (1858–1936) and author of *Tzafnat Paneach* (Decipherer of Secrets), with whom he corresponded. Menachem Mendel would claim this as well in his booklet *HaYom Yom* (Brooklyn: Kehot/Otzar Hasidim, 1943, 21) on October 1924 (Tishrei 5685). To be sure, ordination, whether he had it nor not, is not the sine qua non of his becoming a rebbe, which is a position that requires nothing more than Hasidim who believe him to be one. That he was called "Rabbi" or "Grand Rabbi" even though he may not have been formally ordained, would not distinguish him from most other Hasidic rebbes. See Deutsch, *Larger than Life*, 1:83, and Wolf, *Admorei ChaBaD v'Yahadut Germania*, 103–5, 129.

and Jewish engravings in the German libraries, and on one occasion filling in for the Rebbe in Riga during the latter's absence, but not very much else.[61] Lubavitcher missions at the time were limited to seeing to the religious needs of the Hasidim who remained within the Soviet Union, and particularly to helping them to be supplied with matzah for Passover. To this end the support and assistance of rabbis and Jewish leaders in Germany, France, England, and elsewhere in Europe was needed—aid that Rabbi Yosef Yitzchak hoped would counteract the antireligious activities of his nemesis, the Yevsektsiya. But he was more inclined to dispatch his older son-in-law, Shmaryahu Gourary, on missions to build up these alliances.[62]

All the while, Mendel, engaged in his studies, continued to go back and forth to Riga, a flexibility of movement that was possible because he was only auditing courses. There are of course no grades, as auditors are not matriculated students, so absences are not registered. In July 1928 he was able to convince the Soviet authorities in Berlin to extend his passport and allow him to remain a student in Germany until October 25. At the end of the month of July, he was back in Riga, for the summer holidays—this even though Rabbi Yosef Yitzchak was now in Berlin for a few days to once again meet about matters concerning Soviet Jewry. Clearly, Mendel was not needed to help his father-in-law on this mission.[63]

And when in March 1929, Rabbi Yosef Yitzchak traveled to Berlin for medical care and to raise funds for his network and its activities, he asked Shmaryahu Gourary to remain in the city afterward and, with the help of Rabbi Hildesheimer, raise money for Passover supplies for Soviet Jewry.[64] If Mendel had been his representative in Berlin, why would he have instructed Shmaryahu Gourary—whom he described in a letter to Rabbi Hildesheimer as his *shaliach* in Berlin—to stay behind?[65] Was Mendel otherwise occupied, or did the Rebbe not believe him suited to this sort of mission? We have no reliable sources that provide an answer.

In 1929 Mendel once again spent the high holidays and the other Jewish occasions at the court of the sixth rebbe. Perhaps this is why visitors to the few Hasidic congregations in Berlin report never having seen him there at the time.[66] But what of Sabbaths and the services each day that a Jew is required to attend? There is no evidence of Mendel's presence in Berlin's synagogues during this time. We do know he was pious and perhaps as well a bit ascetic, for he would soon take up fasting as a practice while in Paris, a fact that apparently concerned both Moussia and Mendel's father.[67]

His studies notwithstanding, in the fall of 1928, Mendel Schneerson had a far more important item on his agenda than auditing university courses or serving as an occasional secretary to the sixth rebbe. In November of that year, he was to be married. The long courtship with Moussia Schneersohn was at last over. With this marriage, he would not only gain a wife but shift his status from that of a cousin of the Lubavitcher rebbe to being his son-in-law. In time, that status would prove far more important than having studied in Berlin.

CHAPTER 4

Entering the Court of Lubavitch

𝍱

The marriage of the daughter of the Lubavitcher Rebbe was far more than a personal family event. This was particularly the case for a rebbe who had increasingly been raising his profile as a world Jewish leader. When his oldest daughter, in a match made at the request of the fifth rebbe, had been married to Shmaryahu Gourary, whom his new father-in-law described as "a dear young man, learned and knowing much of Hasidism," on June 17, 1920, Yosef Yitzchak was still in mourning for his father, who had passed away on March 21.[1] His economic situation and that of his Hasidim in Rostov, like so many others after the communist revolution, was precarious, and to add to all that, the combination of famine and an outbreak of typhus served to make a large celebration of the first daughter's wedding unthinkable. That first wedding took place before his arrest by the Soviet authorities and his subsequent release, which came after world pressure. At the time, Yosef Yitzchak was still not quite comfortable with his position as a rebbe, nor was he yet a symbol of a Russian Jewry caught in the antireligious communist web or famous for running a network of emissaries behind its lines. The wedding therefore had been a relatively small affair and had gone largely unnoticed in the larger Jewish community. The bride had been twenty-one; her groom was twenty-three, a student of the yeshiva in Rostov and son of a businessman there who was a brother of a good friend of the fifth Lubavitcher rebbe. He had been called in for a blessing at the deathbed of that Rebbe. Beyond that, nothing was particularly noteworthy about this arranged marriage.

The wedding on November 27, 1928 (14 Kislev 5689), of Menachem Mendel and Chaya Moussia, however, would be quite different. Unlike her sister, whose age at marriage was in line with the common custom of Hasidic daughters, Moussia, born March 16, 1901, was at almost twenty-eight marrying at an extraordinarily late age for Hasidic brides. And she had been going out with her groom for quite a number of years, before finally deciding to wed him. Furthermore, unlike the husband of her older sister, Shmaryahu Gourary, Mendel, her new partner, was not now nor ever had been a student at the Lubavitcher yeshiva, but someone pursuing university studies, something that must have certainly troubled the Hasidim, some of whom asked why Levi Yitzchak had never sent his talented sons to the Tomekhei Temimim schools.[2] Nor was he himself a youngster. He was twenty-seven.

If in the world of Hasidim, a marriage at these ages would have been eyebrow-raising; for those who were university students or professionals, of course, this would not be a late age at all. Indeed, marriage at the age of Mendel and Moussia, while unusual among Hasidim, was a common phenomenon among young former Russians at that time.[3] Why, however, did this marriage take place at the time it did?

In all the internal Lubavitcher hagiographies, before his marriage and during what might be called a courtship, Mendel is always referred to as "the one intended to be the groom," a title that has no precedent in Jewish tradition and law. One may be what we now call a "fiancé" (in Jewish terms, *meoras*), but that is a status that has Jewish legal standing. Mendel was not that; the ceremony of formal engagement was held on the evening of November 18 (6 Kislev), nine days before the wedding.[4] The groom had come back for this on November 8 from Berlin, where only a few days earlier, on October 30, he had registered for his second term at the university. Had the engagement occurred earlier—indeed, had the wedding of this couple occurred in Leningrad, or even Rostov—then Mendel's parents, Levi Yitzchak and Chana, could have attended. But now, given that the wedding would occur outside the borders of the USSR, they could not be there. At best, they could now only send letters, like the one dated 7 Kislev 5689 (November 20, 1928), a week before the wedding, in which Levi Yitzchak urged his son to get some new clothes for himself and also purchase a gift for his future bride and "tell her, may she live long, in our name, that she should wear the gift in life and peace, joy and happiness and use it well." And when his son wrote back and asked for more details about what he should buy, the father answered, "What can we tell you from here? Whatever seems suitable to you and to Moussia, you should buy for her and give it in our name—may she wear it in health and happiness for many years together with you."[5]

Surely, Mendel would have wanted his parents, who so much wished to be with him on this day, and cared so much about him and his contentment, to be at his wedding. Mendel was, after all, the first of their sons to marry. Why then had he not wed earlier, inside Russia, when they could have come? We know that he and Moussia had spent much time together, even staying out late together on the night of Yosef Yitzchak's arrest. Mendel had stayed at the Schneersohn residence in Leningrad, and according to some ChaBaD sources he had visited even earlier, when they were in Rostov. His mother had come to Leningrad twice, first in 1924 and for a longer stay in 1926. Presumably the subject of his courtship and marriage to the daughter of the Lubavitcher Rebbe must have come up during these visits.[*] Were they not able to decide to get married while they were in Russia? Did he have to court his bride more? Did he have to persuade his future father-in-law that he was appropriate? Was the couple not certain they should marry?

We know that economic obstacles to holding the wedding earlier were unlikely to be the reason, for even in hard times in Rostov, the Schneersohns had been able to mount a wedding. Even if there were such difficulties (and a letter sent by one of Yosef Yitzchak's secretaries to the head of the American ChaBaD organization revealing financial concerns and asking for help exists), certainly if the marriage was a foregone conclusion, a formal engagement at the very least could have been held in the USSR, at which Mendel's parents could have been present.[6] Why did that not happen?

Yosef Yitzchak and his wife looked for someone who would somehow be suitable and acceptable. According to one source, Moussia had

---

[*] Interestingly, Mendel's mother Chana during her 1926 stay did *not* lodge at the home of those who would be her future in-laws but rather with the Althaus family, perhaps a further sign that the marriage was far from agreed upon at this stage. *HaRabanit*, 29.

rejected matches who she felt were too Jewishly parochial, and her father could not bend her will, any more than he could control her younger sister.[7] Eventually, each of the two daughters would marry cousins named "Mendel" (named after the same Lubavitcher Rebbe who was their forebear), both of whom were to varying degrees worldlier than the suitors their parents had once had in mind for them. Whether these men were viewed as compromises, we cannot say.** We do know that the matches took time to be completed. In the case of Moussia and Mendel Schneerson, whatever the reasons for their not wedding or formally becoming engaged in the country where they had first met and kept company with each other, by the time the couple became engaged and married, neither Mendel's parents nor his brothers were able to attend.

We know that after the arranged marriage of their oldest sister, both Moussia and her younger sister Sonia (Sheina) asserted they would not accede to such an arranged marriage.[8] They saw themselves as more independent and cosmopolitan, and would only marry men who matched these characteristics. Indeed, from an early age, Moussia's attachment to the broader culture could be seen in her embrace of the Russian language. When her father, while on a brief trip abroad, wrote a letter to his then twelve-year-old Moussia, he did so in Russian, wishing her "outstanding success in your involvement in your studies," and she would generally write to her parents in Russian rather than Yiddish.[9] Her father had also given Moussia power of attorney in 1924, empowering her to receive monies on his behalf and documents from the government or banks, a reflection of his appreciation of her worldly savvy and competence in Russian.[10]

Mendel's actions suggest he was determined to enter the court and marry Moussia, but they also suggest he was not ready to be a Hasid like all others. Leaving the USSR (for what turned out to be forever) on October 25, 1927, Mendel had followed Moussia to Riga, and he had requested permanent residence in Latvia.[11] He had spent November and

---

* The symbolism of their names was significant. Chaya Moussia (named so at the urging of her grandfather, the fifth rebbe) was the name of the Zemah Zedek's (Menachem Mendel, the third Lubavitcher rebbe, after whom her husband was named) wife. This symbolic reincarnation of this rabbinic couple was not lost on Lubavitchers, for whom names are most important.

most of December 1927 at the court of the Rebbe. He had come back from Berlin for most of March and April (Passover) to be there. From the end of July until the end of October he was there, returning to Berlin for just a few days to register at the university. He was not ready to give up his pursuit of secular education, even at this time of intensified Lubavitcher involvements. But he came back quickly from Germany for the preparations for his forthcoming engagement and wedding.

Clearly, he had been making himself a part of the court as he engaged in his courtship. His future father-in-law had already been asking him to write some letters on his behalf as early as November 1927, a year before the formal engagement and wedding, and as we said probably helped him with contacts in Berlin.[12] Whenever he could, Mendel would make notes about Lubavitcher traditions and the practices of the Rebbe, observations that would later form the basis of many of his talks and writings. All this demonstrates that Yosef Yitzchak was having some success in integrating Mendel into the court and its activities, finding some tasks for him to do—after all, he was also fully supporting him financially and had to justify this to the court. Normally, a Hasidic father-in-law would support a son-in-law in his study of Torah, as had for example been the case with Mendel's father. But here most of the money was being spent to support Mendel in Berlin and later Paris while he was primarily engaged in secular studies, activities not at all concerned with Lubavitcher affairs or Torah.

To be sure, while Mendel would during his days in Germany report on the rare Hasidic figure who came through town, once, for example, writing that he found that in the Czortków *shtibl* (small synagogue) there was barely a *minyan* (ten) when their rebbe visited, he would also write to his father-in-law about topics that had little if anything to do with Hasidism or Judaism. In these communications he would, like the first-time traveler outside of Russia, simply share his impressions of life in Berlin, describing, for example, in a letter in June of 1928 how the locals strolled the streets with a jacket on one arm and a handkerchief in the other to wipe their perspiration, "and when the sun sets, the doors all open" and families sat outside, "looking at the moon, happy with the world and in particular with themselves, their wives and children."[13]

The Rebbe Yosef Yitzchak, however, did not manage to persuade his new son-in-law to abandon completely his aspirations for secular study (which in principle he appeared to oppose) in Berlin. Perhaps this double life as both a Hasid and a student at the university was a reflection of Mendel's desires to please both Moussia and her father. Ironically, his activity as a university student, which probably impressed the worldly Moussia more than his Hasidic involvements, was what her father had merely to tolerate, while his Hasidic involvements, which never really captured her interest, was what she had to accept. Indeed, not only Mendel but also Moussia would be busy taking courses in Berlin. After they married, she would enroll in the university at the German Institute for Foreigners, as student 143 (out of two hundred), and take a course in German history.[14]

♬♬

Although Rabbi Yosef Yitzchak had been living in Riga for a little over a year, the decision was made to hold the wedding over three hundred miles away in Warsaw, Poland. Why? We know that the number of Lubavitcher Hasidim at the time in Riga was small. Moreover, Riga was a city in which religious life of the type Hasidim live was not vigorous, while Warsaw was a city in which Hasidim still dominated observant Jewry, which itself was vital and effervescent. After the collapse of religious life in the USSR, Warsaw became an even more important center of it. With Russia under the antireligious communists, Warsaw, like Poland in general, was now the preeminent location of Hasidic activity in the world. There was a Lubavitcher yeshiva here, while Riga had the Rebbe but no such yeshiva. In Warsaw, therefore, there was both a place, the yeshiva, where the wedding could be held and a location where more Hasidim could be expected to attend. Here such a wedding, which was always an event that gave a rebbe—in this case Rabbi Yosef Yitzchak—a large stage on which to present himself, would be far bigger news than in Riga.

This was important because Hasidic weddings, especially those of a child of a rebbe, were significant cultural performances, public occasions when both outsiders and insiders could discover or rediscover the essential character or spirit of whom and what they were; as such, they were opportunities to demonstrate the strength and grandeur of a Hasidic court.[15] The large wedding, in which one sees all those who have come to pay tribute to the couple and through them to the rebbe and thus to the Hasidic court and its supporters, becomes an event at which collective strength is reaffirmed and the collective consciousness and conscience are revitalized. For a group like Lubavitch, which had now been on the run as its rebbe tried to reconstitute his following and his power, a large wedding celebration could serve as a sign of its return to strength and life. Moreover, it would give the lie to any suggestions that in the face of the rebbe's "exile" from Russia, Lubavitch was now in precipitous and ineluctable decline. Of all the places possible for this wedding at this time, Warsaw, which had all the most widely read Jewish newspapers, was the only one where a celebration that would remind the world of the prestige and importance of the Lubavitcher Rebbe could conceivably be held. The Lubavitcher Rebbe was perhaps hoping that he could, with a large wedding, remind the Jewish world of his yeshiva there, which had been founded in 1921, and could use it to substitute for the Temimim educational institutions he had lost in Russia and hence establish an increasing presence in the Polish Jewish religious firmament, and become one of the stars of its Hasidism. (He of course did not know that within a little more than a decade, Warsaw and Polish Jewry would be victims of a Holocaust of enormous proportions and many of his *temimim* would be annihilated.)

Weddings are also ceremonies that symbolize continuity and point to the future. If the new bridegroom was to be a new leader, if not the future face of the court, this wedding would be the most suitable opportunity to present him to the court and the Jewish world. Furthermore, in a wedding of Hasidic "royalty," the lineage of the bride and groom is critical, for each one must be "worthy" of the other, and both families who are united in the marriage must gain social stature—or at the very least not lose it—as a result of the new union. But could this bride and groom serve as the vehicles for such a cultural celebration, and was their union going to serve these purposes?

The bride, after all, was only the middle daughter, and from all signs not one who wished to celebrate her Hasidism. In *Haynt*, one of the major Yiddish newspapers, she was described as "with an academic education."[16] She had, as we have noted, displayed an independent streak, an interest in the wider culture, in theater, Russian literature, university education, in a life as a modern European woman who yearned to move to Berlin, where she wanted to study. She had put off marriage for a long time, and one doubted that she was now, at the age of twenty-eight, going to come out as a dutiful Hasidic wife, the mate of a rebbe-in-waiting and ready to bear lots of grandchildren to the Rebbe.

The groom was also a question mark. Although descended from Lubavitch royalty and the son of a respected rabbinic leader, he was not a familiar figure in the Lubavitcher Hasidic court. Because he had never been a student at the Temimim yeshiva, they did not know either his wisdom in Jewish scholarship or his level of Hasidic engagement. There were Jewish scholars throughout the Orthodox precincts of European Jewry with important reputations who were far younger. Moreover, Mendel had not been living in Hasidic communities or pursuing Hasidic occupations (although, as noted, that was beginning to change subtly during the year before his wedding). He had moved from Yekaterinoslav to Leningrad and thence to Berlin, the capital of Reform Judaism, Jewish enlightenment, and neo-Orthodoxy, movements against which the Lubavitchers had fulminated. In pursuit of a university education, he was engaged in activity his future father-in-law had also denounced. The groom was interested in hard sciences, and he was no youngster. According to one Yiddish paper he "graduated from the university in Berlin from the faculty in philosophy,"[17] While the latter facts were completely inaccurate, it was clear that what the papers found striking was that this groom was not a standard Hasid but one who was attached to the world of higher education and refinement. Indeed, so concerned was he about his university study that while the invitations to the wedding from Riga were dated October 30, 1928, on that same day, as we have seen, Mendel Schneerson was in Berlin registering as student 187 at the university in Berlin. (To be sure, on the day of the *tena'im*, the engagement ceremony in Riga at the rebbe's court, his future bride and her mother were not present, having gone to Warsaw to shop and prepare for the wedding.)[18]

The Yiddish papers in Warsaw were struck by the anomalous character of the couple and of the celebration of their union. They noted that this affair was attended by a crowd that was quite unusual for a Hasidic wedding. The reporter for *Moment*, another of the major Yiddish dailies, wrote, "The crowd of guests is completely different from those seen at other [Hasidic] Rebbes' weddings. One sees no *shtraymls* or the black round velvet hats [typical of Hasidim]. Most are Jews clothed in

European dress and only a small number is dressed in high silk caps."[19] If Yosef Yitzchak Schneersohn wanted to impress the Hasidic world with his position as a Hasidic leader who would attract other Hasidim, this was the wrong crowd and wedding with which to do that.

He had, of course, invited other rebbes, who if they had come would have made the assembly appear far more classically Hasidic, at least as far as the Warsaw Jewish sensibility was concerned. For example, the two most prominent Hasidic leaders of Poland with the two largest courts, Abraham Mordecai Alter, the Gerer rebbe, and Yitzhak Menachem Mendel Danziger, the rebbe of Aleksander, although invited, did not attend—this even though Rabbi Yosef Yitzchak had sent two emissaries to each of them on the day of the wedding to personally invite them again.*

There were other rebbes who did attend. Indeed, on the day of the wedding Rabbi Yosef Yitzchak traveled around Warsaw and environs with his son-in-law, Shmaryahu Gourary, to "personally invite" some of them, including those of Piotrków, Nowominsk, Zlatopol, the famous Rabbi Meir Shapiro, and the rebbe of Radzin (who would be the one to read the *ketobbah* or wedding contract aloud under the canopy), bringing them along when he arrived at the wedding in the evening.[20]

Rabbi Yosef Yitzchak, the Gourarys, Sheina Schneersohn, the bride's younger sister, the groom, and a number of Hasidim had arrived early on Monday morning by train from Riga, to be met by a large delegation of Lubavitchers from Warsaw. The bride and her mother were already there. They had come two weeks earlier, on November 13, when, in line with Polish law, Mendel and Moussia had been joined in a civil ceremony.[21] While the bride and her mother remained in Warsaw for the following two weeks until the wedding to shop and make preparations, the groom returned to Riga.

At the marriage ceremony, Mendel was led to the wedding canopy by Moshe Horensztajn and his wife, Chaya Mushka, the sister of the

---

*Deutsch, *Larger than Life*, 2:226, quotes the testimony of a guest, Avraham Yosef Friedman. Perhaps the Gerer Rebbe had not come because of Rabbi Yosef Yitzchak's recent attack on the former for his support of Zionist activities in Palestine and his school, the Mesivta, which allowed its students to study secular studies for two hours a day. In general, there had been tension between the two over whose version of Hasidism was superior. See letters from Rabbi Yosef Yitzchak, "On the strength of Torah versus Agudat Yisrael," 1922, and response letter from the Gerer Rebbe, Friedman Archives.

fifth Lubavitcher rebbe and aunt of the bride's father.[22] The obvious absence of the groom's parents at the wedding (who held a parallel celebration in their community in Russia) would serve to remind everyone of the ongoing struggle and crisis of Soviet Jewry.[23]

About a week before his wedding, Mendel received a letter from his father filled with a whole series of directions for how he was to behave at his marriage. In hagiographic accounts of this letter, which has been reprinted in the collected letters of his father, much is made of how it demonstrates a closeness and affection that the father held for his son. While it does do that, a close reading of it also demonstrates a concern on the father's part for the son's proper religious behavior. It is filled with specific directions for how he should act. Among these are requests that when called to the Torah in anticipation of his wedding, he should make a special blessing for his parents; that on the day of his marriage he should immerse himself in a *mikveh* (ritual bath), a request that is explained in mystical kabbalistic terms; and that he should study only after noon and "with powerful devotion" chapter twenty-five of the *Tanya*, the primary text of ChaBaD Hasidism, and then recite the afternoon prayer along with the special confession that all grooms add on the day of their wedding "with true and powerful devotion." After explaining why this confession, normally recited on Yom Kippur (Day of Atonement), was also part of the wedding preparations, Levi Yitzchak suggested to his son that excessive weeping during these prayers and the fasting that precedes marriage "is to be praised." Then he urged him to don a silk *kapote* or *sirtuk* (the knee-length frock coat common to Hasidim), which he trusted his son had had made in line with an earlier request. He allowed that right after the ceremony, "if you wish you can wear another garment," apparently responding to an objection on his son's part to wearing such an obviously Hasidic outfit. Finally, he urged his son to "meditate with fear of God" under the wedding canopy, and after the wedding to pray wearing the special "belt" (*gartl*) that Hasidim use and forever after don an extra pair of tefillin according to the specifications of Rabbenu Tam.[24]

Are these the directions of a father to a son who knows what is expected of a Hasidic groom, who himself is preparing to lead a life of piety and devotion, who is on the verge of entering the court of a Hasidic rebbe, and who is about to dedicate himself to the rabbinate? Or are these words of guidance given by a father who is very much a rabbi and is addressing a son who he knows has embarked on a life's journey that has taken him to the heart of secular culture, the university, and the capitals of Western culture and who, the father believes, needs to be reminded of the religious nature of marriage and of the holiness of this day, a father who wants his son to remember that what matters most to him is that he abide by the religious customs of Hasidism, telling him that if he does so, as the letter concludes, "then, thou joy of my heart, if you do thus, it will be good for you all of your days." The letter closes with the plea from the father to his son that "at the earliest possible opportunity" he should dispatch a telegram to him informing him that all went well.[25]

Mendel had not wanted to wear the *sirtuk*, a garment he had eschewed, perhaps out of a desire to move about comfortably in the cosmopolitan capitals of Europe. But as we have seen, his father had written him requesting that he wear one under the bridal canopy in addition to "a new *kitel*" (the white smock Jewish grooms traditionally wear at the marriage ceremony) as well as "the *gartl* [the rope-like belt worn by Hasidim to separate the lower from the higher regions of the body during prayer] made from the garment of the Zemah Zedek" that was in his possession back in Russia.[26] While he followed his father's wishes, he was quick to remove the *kapote* after the 5 p.m. ceremony at the yeshiva on Mławska Street and before adjourning to the reception at the Weisman catering hall on Pańska Street.

In fact, while Mendel surely did all that his father asked, the appearance of the groom was especially noteworthy. In *Moment*, he was described at his wedding as "a young man of refined features, with an intelligent demeanor," while in *Haynt* he was portrayed as having a "sympathetic face and a small dark beard."[27] His attire at the wedding was explained as an odd amalgam of European dress and Hasidic finery. He wore a black snap brim fedora, a *kapote,* which was soon replaced by a brown suit, brown shoes, a white shirt with a stiff collar, tie, and fashionable white dinner gloves.[28]

According to reports of the wedding, the Rebbe Yosef Yitzchak was quite happy at the reception. In his own account of the day, Mendel would many years later report that "my father-in-law stood up from his place to give *l'chaim* [make a toast] to everyone. When I saw him doing this, I could not sit in my place while my father-in-law was going around giving out vodka. I stood up in order to go and join him, at least to hold the bottle or the cups." But the Rebbe Yosef Yitzchak would have none of that. "Immediately he turned to me and motioned that I should remain seated," a gesture he repeated when Mendel tried to ignore him and rise. When the Rebbe Yosef Yitzchak insisted the groom remain seated, the latter did so reluctantly, later reporting that he remained "*oyf shpilkes*," a Yiddish expression that denotes the nervousness of pins and needles.[29] What was he so nervous about?

To be sure, this encounter can be explained as evidence of the solicitude of a father-in-law for the new groom. But a closer look suggests an alternative explanation. As he went around from table to table, the Rebbe Yosef Yitzchak, wearing a *shtrayml*, was clearly seeking out those guests who were important to him—perhaps the distinguished among the rabbis or his supporters. To walk around with a son-in-law at his side who sported a short-looking beard, fashionable appearance, and white gloves and who carried on a distinctly un-Hasidic lifestyle would occasion at each stop a chat about the groom, his plans, and his his past—questions that Yosef Yitzchak might not have been terribly comfortable exploring at this time. Perhaps the groom was nervous as well about that.

Indeed, when at last Yosef Yitzchak arrived at the section of the hall where the *temimim*, the Lubavitcher yeshiva students, were, he asked that vodka be distributed to all of them and then turned to them and said, "The Torah remains only with those who give their life for it. Diligence in studying the depths of Torah is what causes that Torah to remain in a person's mind." And he added that they need "to suppress themselves" and all their other career aspirations in favor of such labor in the Torah.[30] Did he want to make such a toast with a son-in-law standing with him who was not one of the *temimim*, who had not spent time in a yeshiva, who was headed back to the university in Berlin, who was at that point not apparently "giving his life" and suppressing himself and all his other career aspirations to a life of Torah?

The next night, at a celebratory meal where many of the prominent rabbis of Poland were present, when he might have given his new son-in-law an opportunity to shine before this audience, Yosef Yitzchak again did not. The groom sat silently. Instead, his father-in-law gave a talk about the kabbalistic reasons for rejoicing with a bride and groom, an address that might have impressed the rabbis present with his own erudition. Then he asked for songs to be sung.

A few days after the wedding, however, Yosef Yitzchak would give a hint of what must have been on his mind, even in the midst of his joy at his daughter's wedding. On Saturday night, the day after the wedding party had returned from Warsaw, a *sheva berakhot* gathering, part of the seven days of festive meals that follow a traditional Jewish wedding, was held in Riga, a city where even the observant Jews had absorbed many of the views and institutional patterns of the neo-Orthodoxy of German Jewry. With his new son-in-law sitting near him—the same son-in-law with the trim beard who was about to return to Berlin and the university, where he and his new wife, Moussia, would take courses—Rabbi Yosef Yitzchak spoke to the assembled *Tseirey Agudas Yisroel*, the youth of the fervently Orthodox community. After two years in Riga, the Rebbe knew well the views of these young people, who had embraced higher education and secular culture as part of their worldview, who appeared in modern dress, many of them barefaced or with short beards, and who probably looked at the new son-in-law sympathetically as one who shared their values and ethos. Before this audience Yosef Yitzchak gave an impassioned sermon against the mixing of the sacred and the profane, arguing that the neo-Orthodox approach that combined religious and secular studies was only "good for those who would otherwise, Heaven forefend, be even worse," but that for those who were truly pure, the "*temimim*," this was not the way. Then he denounced those who trimmed their beards or who shaved them off altogether. All of this he said while his new university bound son-in-law with a beard that for all intents and purposes looked as if it were trimmed sat there, and his two younger daughters (one of whom was the bride), who everyone in the room likely knew shared an outlook of modernity, were in a room nearby. Did he mean that this mixing of Torah and secular learning was alright for the bride and groom because otherwise they "would be even worse"? After all, he would help support them financially when they returned to pursue this way of life in Berlin. Or was he trying to warn them against the way of life they had apparently chosen? He was of course nominally speaking to the audience, but could his message to his own children be lost on them?

Later he would report that some of those who heard his words that evening were angered by his attack but thankfully, "slowly, slowly removed the signs of their 'honor,'"—words referring perhaps to the outer trappings of cosmopolitanism—"and the hair of their beards began to grow."[31] For Lubavitchers this last image was not just a metaphor. For them the untrimmed beard had become *the* symbol of their identity as "faithful Jews," something that distinguished them from their counterparts in the non-Hasidic yeshiva world. For Rabbi Yosef Yitzchak, a long beard was a badge of honor and belonging. That his new son-in-law lacked one was no small matter (and when his youngest son-in-law, Mendel Horensztajn, known in Warsaw as a far more secularly oriented student, later would be completely barefaced, that must have surely troubled him, and it was probably the reason that that third wedding was smaller and celebrated in an out-of-the-way town.)[32]

As festive as the wedding was, it was marred by an event that made all the newspapers. Even though "ushers had been placed at the entrance . . . and only guests with official invitations were allowed to enter" the reception, during the proceedings in the courtyard of the yeshiva, the affair was mobbed by the uninvited and the curious who wanted to watch.[33] Into this crowd, pickpockets and thieves from the Jewish underworld insinuated themselves. As a result, many of the most valuable gifts that had been brought to the couple were stolen, including perhaps most prominently a rare letter from the Ba'al Shem Tov that the maternal grandfather of the bride, Avraham Schneersohn, had brought for the occasion. Purses disappeared. In addition, many of the homes of the guests—who the thieves knew would be in attendance at the wedding—were robbed. The thefts made headlines in the Yiddish press. If the Rebbe Yosef Yitzchak had wanted this wedding to serve as an opening to the Warsaw community and a means of establishing the good news of his presence among its Hasidic royalty, this scandal certainly put a damper on the effort.

⦚⦚⦚

A little more than seven weeks after the wedding and the subsequent celebrations, Mendel and Moussia Schneerson prepared to go to Berlin, arriving there on January 21, 1929.[34] Although they would subsequently claim 8 Marius Street, apartment 6, in Riga as their formal address (where they would return for the Jewish holidays and other family occasions), after January 1929 and until the end of September 1932 they spent about twice as much time in Berlin as in Riga and other places.* In a sense, they lived a kind of bifocal life: in one they were young newlyweds in Berlin, students tasting the cosmopolitan life of the German capital—a life in which they would go out together, usually on Monday nights to enjoy the city, establishing their own home together.[35] To be sure, they were living in a room in someone else's apartment, which undoubtedly gave these quarters a temporary feel (something they would not repeat when later they moved to Paris). On the other hand, they were still firmly connected to the family and court from which they came, and would return to it for holidays and family events—and on a few occasions when Yosef Yitzchak came to Berlin as part of his work they would visit with him in his more spacious accommodations.[36] Moreover, because Mendel was now largely cut off from his own family, which was trapped inside the Soviet Union, he likely transferred much of his familial attachments to his in-laws. Add to that the fact that his father-in-law was also his "rebbe," a relationship that magnified these attachments, and the likely desire that this Rebbe wanted to make certain that his children did not become swept up by the cosmopolitan and more acculturated Jewish life of Berlin, and it becomes clear that the second focus of the Schneersons was Lubavitch, memories of which Mendel would emphasize much more after he became the seventh Lubavitcher rebbe.

Yosef Yitzchak was most concerned about this Lubavitcher side of Mendel's life and continued sending letters to him (and Moussia as well), trying repeatedly to inform him about the practices and ideology of ChaBaD. His son-in-law would send back comments and questions. For example, a correspondence between the two in late 1931 and early 1932 demonstrates this double life. Mendel had sent a letter in which he asked how it was possible to call ChaBaD Hasidim the "true heirs" of the founder of Hasidism, the Ba'al Shem Tov; after all, it seemed to him, the Hasidim of Poland, Galicia, and Volhynia appeared to resemble

*The months they spent outside Germany were generally in the court at Lubavitch in Riga, as well as at their own wedding in Poland and later that of Sheina and Mendel Horensztajn.

what he knew about the founder far more in their approach and practices. Responding to this question, Yosef Yitzchak in a letter on January 3 complements his son-in-law on his involvement in "study" (presumably the study of Hasidism) and expresses the hope that he will continue to be fortified by the Almighty in his efforts. Then he explains that this "deep question" that Mendel has asked can be answered by the fact that while the Hasidim of Poland, Galicia, and Volhynia might tell stories about performing miracles, ChaBaD Hasidim "have given us an inheritance of books filled with complex, deep and intelligent elucidation of *toras hasidus*," the wisdom of Hasidism.[37] In line with these religious concerns, Yosef Yitzchak would occasionally send Mendel books of rabbinic commentary and Jewish significance.[38]

But Rabbi Yosef Yitzchak also had other less religiously or hasidically oriented errands for his second son-in-law. These had to do with the books and manuscripts that the sixth rebbe liked to collect and that throughout his life concerned him so. He wanted Mendel to help him gather facsimiles and even some original manuscripts as well as rare books while he was in Berlin. Thus, for example, late in 1932, just before the high holy days, he writes to Mendel asking him to check in the library in Berlin, consult an expert there, and catalogue the rare books and "very old manuscripts" (he even asks Mendel to enlist the assistance of his brother Leibel for this task) as well as illuminations and copper engravings of Judaica in the library.[39] His son-in-law's and Leibel's access to and familiarity with the library, as well as Mendel's permission to check out books and his linguistic abilities, which allowed him to read the catalogue materials, made it possible to enlist them both for these tasks, something simple Hasidim or yeshiva students would probably be unable to do. He could also be asked to get books that one might not expect a Hasidic rebbe to want to own, books filled with ideas radically at odds with Hasidism or traditional Judaism—books that even today are not circulated freely in the ChaBaD library. Even as the Nazis rose to power, Yosef Yitzchak was concerned with getting such manuscripts and illuminations, either in facsimile or in originals, from all over Germany.

During these years Mendel's father, Levi Yitzchak, was also concerned about his son's religious life. In 1929, for example, he sent a letter in which he reported that Moussia had complained to him that Mendel was fasting every day until the time of the afternoon prayers. "Where," Levi Yitzchak asks, did his son "acquire this practice?"[40] Entreating him to desist, he adds, "You are not a Samson in strength." Such is not "the way of Torah or of repentance," he adds, telling him that Judaism demands that he protect his health and no longer act this way. Why was Mendel fasting, what did he believe this would accomplish? We do not know for certain (though we offer a hint of an answer at the end of this chapter).

We do, however, know how his father told him to act. He should, his father explained, not only stop fasting until the afternoon, he should also eat breakfast, even before his morning prayers. "Try to preserve your health, and the more the better." In place of these ascetic habits, he suggested a Jewish study program that would be sufficient for his son's religious life, and then "you will have enough time for all your other interests." Levi Yitzchak did not deny these other interests but would continue through most of his life to send his son letters with lessons and religious advice, acting as his guide and first teacher.[41]

That Mendel managed to switch easily from one mind-set to the other, from his secular to his Hasidic interests and religious concerns, must have impressed itself on him and confirmed a belief that one could be physically and culturally distant from the court, the Rebbe, and the center of Jewish religious life yet still remain connected to it and renew those ties through study, personal behavior, letters, and periodic visits to the court. It would be a lesson he would many years later share with his *shluchim*, who would also lead a multifocused existence that would take them far from their Rebbe yet allow them to remain Hasidim, communicate with and return "home," and feel as if they had never left.

∭

Throughout their time in Germany the young Schneersons continued to be financially supported by Yosef Yitzchak (as they would for their entire academic life).[42] This support was somewhat surprising, since as we know Rabbi Yosef Yitzchak opposed university education, and according to at least one report there were vociferous arguments behind closed doors in which the Lubavitcher rebbe tried to convince the newlyweds to give up this plan.[43] These efforts were clearly unsuccessful, for the couple moved to Berlin.

Mendel continued his studies as an auditor at Friedrich Wilhelm University while Moussia registered at the Institute for Foreigners, studying German language and culture (she would later claim also to have studied mathematics), listing her address as 33 Oranienburgerstrasse with a family named Bruhn, a five-minute walk from the Hildesheimer Seminary and the Jewish Community Administration building at 31 Artilleriestrasse.[44]

Where the young Schneersons actually lived in Berlin is a bit confusing. When he first arrived, as noted in the previous chapter, Mendel gave the address of the Hildesheimer Seminary as his own. Later he registered at the university as living at 7 Hansa Ufer (at Wilensky). But in 1938 in an affidavit he would submit in France detailing his residences in Berlin he listed 40/1 Potsdamerstrasse (at Grünbaum) from 1928 to 1930, 12a Konstanzerstrasse (at Braunstein) from 1931 to 1932, and 4 Kantstrasse (at Levison) during 1933 as his sole addresses in Berlin. Why he should have done this is not clear.

If the several addresses were all true, they suggest that the Schneersons moved around like the students they were, finding housing in the apartments of Jewish families (though not necessarily Hasidic ones) who rented out rooms during the five terms the Schneersons were in Berlin. We know that while they lived in this Jewish area, they did not live among or have much if any contact with Lubavitcher Hasidim (if there were any) since years later, during the trial over the Lubavitch library, in response to the question of whether her father had met Hasidim in Berlin, Moussia testified that she did not know whether he had; she had clearly not encountered any.[45] And we know too that for holidays they commonly returned to the court of the Lubavitcher Rebbe.

What else the young couple did with their time we cannot say. But we do know that their studies were most important to them. When Rabbi Yosef Yitzchak visited Berlin in the summer of 1929 in anticipation of a planned trip to the Land of Israel, then called Palestine, and later to America, perhaps looking for a new place to establish his court, he asked Mendel, who with Moussia had met him at the train station at 7:20 in the morning and helped settle him in his room at the Central Hotel, to accompany him and Shmaryahu Gourary on the rest of his trip, hoping to enlist him in his work.[46] But his younger son-in-law refused, first because his passport did not allow him to travel to Palestine and second because he was involved in his studies.[47] Indeed, when a few weeks later Moussia considered returning to Riga for a visit, Mendel expressed his intentions of remaining in Berlin.[48]

When Rabbi Yosef Yitzchak returned in August 1929, he was convinced that Palestine was not going to work out as a place to locate a Temimim yeshiva, since Arab riots had broken out in Hebron on August 23 and 24 in which nearly seventy Jews, among whom were students of the newly established Slobodka Yeshiva in Hebron, were murdered—all this shortly after he had visited this city of the forefathers ten days earlier. Indeed, there were some suggestions that the Lubavitcher rebbe's visit to Hebron may have been a precipitating factor in the subsequent rioting there.*

Returning to Berlin, he once again turned to Mendel, who visited him on the weekend of August 25–27 in the Baden-Baden spa where Yosef Yitzchak had gone to rest after his tiring journey. After sharing with him impressions of the Palestine trip, perhaps seeking to involve him more in the affairs of the court, he once again asked Mendel to join him on the American tour.[49] Again his younger son-in-law demurred, saying he needed to prepare for exams, which presumably he hoped would allow him to gain a certificate from the university and move from the status of auditor to full-fledged student.[50] In addition, his passport also prohibited his traveling to America, and he did not seek permission.[51] In August 1930, when Rabbi Yosef Yitzchak returned from America, exhausted and in ill health, he stopped again in Berlin, after a short stay in the spa at Marienbad. By the beginning of October he had returned to Riga in anticipation of the high holy days, but Mendel did not go back with him, instead continuing the semester in school, returning only later at the end of March for the Passover

---

* There is no hard evidence that the riots were in reaction to the visit. However, the fact that Rabbi Yosef Yitzchak managed to enter holy places inside the mosque over the burial cave of the patriarchs, which at the time were off-limits for Jewish visitors, and thus jar the status quo in the place would surely have antagonized Muslim zealots in Hebron. The 1929 Arab rioters claimed that their actions were precipitated by what they saw as Jewish efforts to disturb the delicate status quo around holy places in the Holy Land. Letter to Judge Gad Frumkin, who had accompanied Rabbi Yosef Yitzchak in Palestine, in Gad Frumkin, *The Way of the Judge in Jerusalem* (Tel Aviv: Dvir, 1955), 308–11. Ehud Ein-Gal, "Ten Days before the Massacre," *Haaretz Musaf*, August 20, 2004.

holiday period.[52] If Rabbi Yosef Yitzchak had nurtured the expectation that his new son-in-law would abandon his university dreams in favor of being a full-time part of the rebbe's court and mission (as had his older son-in-law, Shmaryahu Gourary), these repeated refusals must surely have been a disappointment.[53]

For all his efforts, while he would gain a certificate of attendance, Mendel did not succeed in gaining admission as a full-fledged student in Berlin, since we find no record of his being granted a degree for his auditor status in the Friedrich Wilhelm University records. He was, however, able to use the certificate of attendance at his next academic address as part of his admission process to the engineering program there, as we shall see. While in that year he stopped being listed as a formal auditor, he did not immediately leave Berlin. Perhaps he continued to come to classes informally; perhaps he sat in the library studying on his own—he had a great capacity for doing so.

According to his own notes and other Lubavitcher sources, he spent at least some of the time doing research in Jewish scholarly sources for his father-in-law. In May, for example, in response to a request from Rabbi Hodakov (later to become his secretary), he sent a review summary of a talk his father-in-law had given while in America.[54] Yosef Yitzchak was aware of this growing knowledge and valued it. Indeed, in one reported case he asked Mendel "to add his commentary and footnotes" to a responsum of the Zemah Zedek on the prohibition of cutting or even trimming one's beard.[55] Perhaps his father-in-law hoped this work would cause young Mendel to recognize the religious importance of growing his beard longer. In pictures taken at the time, however, his beard appears trimmed.

We know from Mendel's notes, volumes of which have been published by Lubavitchers through their Kehot imprint, that he did amass a vast knowledge of ChaBaD ideas, as well as other Jewish scholarship, which would be key in his rise to prominence in the early years of his ascendance to being the Rebbe. The young man was clearly spending at least some of his time delving into the sacred literature of Judaism and, as the world of Lubavitch would later discover, was also growing particularly familiar with the customs, ideas, and literature of ChaBaD Lubavitch. For example, on October 31, 1931 (20 Cheshvan 5692), he wrote in his *Reshimos* what he had learned at the court of the Rebbe that day in Riga.[56] Yet from the actions he would take in his immediate future, it is clear he still remained primarily focused on pursuing a higher degree in mathematics and engineering. While he continued to visit the Rebbe's court in Riga on holy days, and while there acted very much as the son-in-law of a Hasidic rebbe, taking note of everything, he would always return as soon as possible to Berlin and his life there.[57]

Around this time his younger brother Leibel, who had managed to escape from Soviet Russia, where his Trotskyist sympathies had made life for him dangerous, arrived. With false papers in the name of Marc (Mordecai) Gurary, an identity he retained throughout the rest of his life, he made his way to Berlin in 1930.[58] Arriving weakened and ill, he was cared for by Mendel and Moussia, who for a brief time set up a bed for him in their rooms. By now Leibel was no longer even marginally religiously observant. As they walked around Berlin together, Mendel would wear "a beret and a well-tailored suit," while Leibel "wore a pair of slacks with his shirt out"; Mendel's "hair was short, Leibel's was long and wild."[59] By the summer semester of 1932 he too had registered as an auditor in mathematics at the university, where he listed his address as 133 Kant Strasse, not far from where his brother and sister-in-law lived. Leibel, or Marc, as he now called himself, met and fell in love with a twenty-one-year-old Jewish Polish-born nurse named Regina Milgram, who went to Palestine in 1933. She was not religious and would never be. By March 1935 he was following her and sailing aboard the ship *Palestina*, arriving in Haifa on the 27th. On his certificate of *aliya* (immigration) this no longer religious man was listed as a bachelor whose profession was "rabbi."[60] He would settle in Tel Aviv, where on August 15, 1939, he and Regina married and lived a totally secular lifestyle.[61]

His family did not accept this reality and in a letter sent by Mendel from Paris to their parents on March 7, 1939 (the last before Levi Yitzchak's arrest by the Soviets), he writes about "the black one," apparently a code name for Leibel, regarding "finding for him a *shidekh* [match] such as you wished." That, of course, would not happen for his younger brother and Regina were already an established couple. Mendel added, "I truly believe without any doubt, that you and mother, may you live long and good years deserve *nakhes* [joy] and good, beyond what you have, and even more than you wish yourselves," but it could only come "for you, for us and for the black one," he concluded, from "the Almighty." It was, Mendel added, "hard for me to write much on this subject (and these are matters you know better than I)," because he realized that the kind of joy and good they hoped for from the "black one" or the "youngest," as he was also called in letters, was not likely to come.[62]

Marc would subsequently briefly open a clothing store at 3 Nachalat Binyamin Street that quickly went out of business. Most of his time in Israel he worked at Bloomstein's bookstore on the same street, where he would engage in cynical and provocative debates with Hasidim who entered the store; he was reportedly seen on Sabbath with a cigarette in hand, a cardinal religious offense.[63] Even so, years later, when he had moved to Britain in pursuit of a degree in science, although he would enroll his daughter Dalia in Jewish primary schools (a practice not uncommon among expatriate Israelis, even the irreligious among them), he remained "removed from Judaism" and not known in the Jewish community of Liverpool, where he lived and died.[64] After his death in 1952, Regina, who had joined him in England, beginning in 1956 was listed as working part-time as a teacher of religion in a Lubavitcher school, an odd vocation for a woman not known for being religious. This position was arranged by her brother-in-law, who was now the Lubavitcher rebbe.[65] Indeed, he continued to care throughout his life for his sister-in-law and her daughter, the only grandchild of Levi Yitzchak and Chana Schneerson.

♫♫♫

By the end of 1932 it was clear to Mendel that his hopes for acquiring a degree or even academic credit in Berlin were not going to bear fruit. Even his brilliant brother Marc was not succeeding in gaining full-fledged status as a student there. During Mendel's and Mousia's periodic returns to Riga to spend the Jewish holy days, Rabbi Yosef Yitzchak undoubtedly was pointing out to them that even by their own aspirations, Berlin was not a place for them. Perhaps he hoped they would decide instead to remain with him. But that was not to be.

In the meantime, that year Rabbi Yosef Yitzchak had a new family matter to deal with, his youngest daughter, Sheina. Since 1929 she had been dating her twenty-four-year-old cousin, Menachem Mendel Horensztajn, grandson of the fourth Lubavitcher rebbe and great-grandson of the same Zemah Zedek from whom Mendel was descended. Although hailing from such distinguished Lubavitcher royalty, Horensztajn, the youngest of four surviving children, had long since stopped looking and acting like a member of a Hasidic family, as had his siblings. Coming from the resort area of Otwock, forty kilometers from Warsaw, which Hasidim liked to visit, he was clean-shaven, and in his horn-rimmed round glasses looked more like a European intellectual, which he aspired to be, than a scion of the ChaBaD dynasty. His father and mother, who had been the ones to act in loco parentis for Mendel Schneerson and had led him to the wedding canopy, were still religious, and indeed his father, Moshe, had accompanied Rabbi Yosef Yitzchak on his American trip. Nevertheless, even though there was a Temimim yeshiva in the town, the Horensztajns had sent their son Mendel to the gymnasium in Otwock, a non-Jewish school, where he had received a scholarship and graduated in 1926.[66] Accepted to Warsaw University in 1926 as a full-time student, he began in the fall to study philosophy and mathematics.

As the marriage drew ever closer, Rabbi Yosef Yitzchak tried very hard to persuade his youngest daughter's future husband to come closer to the way of life of Lubavitch Hasidism, at least to grow a beard in anticipation of their marriage in 1932, all without notable success.[67] If his second son-in-law had seemed a bit too modern to him, this new son-in-law was beyond the pale. There could be no camouflaging what he was; Warsaw Jewry knew the Horensztajn family and the fact that their offspring were moving in a secular direction, and that the new groom Mendel had studied at a general gymnasium and later Warsaw University. Indeed, perhaps for this reason the Schneersohn-Horenstzajn wedding in June 1932 was far smaller and quietly celebrated in the small town of Landvarov, outside Vilnius (then in Poland, today in Lithuania). Neither was it reported on in the press. A brief recollection is provided by Mendel Schneerson, and it subtly underscores his new brother-in-law's modernity. He describes the signing of the marriage contract, a *lekhayim* toast, and the adjourning of the relatively small wedding party to another room while the assembled waited for the arrival of Rabbi Hayyim Ozer Grodzinski, the renowned (non-Hasidic) Lithuanian sage and a head of the rabbinic council of the Orthodox Agudat Israel party. He was the most prominent guest. At the wedding, the groom, who gave his bride a gold ring, was wearing a fashionable tie (an unusual accoutrement for a Hasidic groom, as his new brother-in-law noted, which was nevertheless permitted), a gold watch, and cufflinks (the latter were to be removed under the wedding canopy). The festive wedding feast, such as it was, began quite a bit later. In a breach of custom, there were not festive meals (*sheva berakhot*) during each of the following seven days. Even on Friday night, they had to call in outsiders to complete the necessary ten to make a *minyan* for the *sheva berakhot* celebrated that once.[68]

Mendel and Moussia returned to Germany after the wedding for the month of September and then went to Riga for the high holidays. Of course, they had to get permission from the authorities for such a move. At the end of 1932, the Schneersons' Soviet passport was impounded by the Soviet consul in Riga, when the Soviets refused to extend its validity.[69] Now the Schneersons had to acquire identity cards and a *laissez-passer*, documents for those who are refugees and wish to move from country to country. On December 20, 1932, and January 3, 1933, they applied for such documents from the Latvians. Moussia got hers right away.

On January 5, 1933, they both had a *laissez-passer* from the Latvians.[70] Five days later Mendel alone returned to Berlin, in the company of Rabbi Yosef Yitzchak, staying there till the end of February.[71] But now Mendel was no longer registered even as an auditor at the university, and as of January 30 Adolf Hitler was the new German chancellor. In this atmosphere Mendel was obviously unable to make the transition to full-time study in a degree-granting program. Berlin was no longer a place for Jews like him. What then would he do?

In early March 1933, Rabbi Yosef Yitzchak made a short trip to Paris.[72] Again, he seemed to be oiling the wheels for his children. On March 13, the day after the Jewish holiday of Purim, which was spent with family in Riga, Mendel and Moussia moved to Paris. At the end of April, after the Passover holidays, the Schneersons would settle in and begin their new life in France.[73] Mendel would study engineering and she, according to one published report, architecture.[74] The Horensztajns, similarly ready to strike out on their own and separate a bit from the Hasidic orbit, were already planning to join them there.

Sheina and her sister Moussia were very close; they had been single for a long time and spent much time together, especially as their family had so often been on the move. Both must have talked about their hopes and plans for the future. Indeed, those hopes and plans coincided in the months ahead. By 1933, both couples would be living in Paris and soon would be neighbors in the same apartment building, Hotel Max, at 9 rue Boulard in the fourteenth arrondissement, a largely bohemian neighborhood. The Schneersons lived here until the end of 1938. Among their other neighbors were: Rene Bono from Italy, Te Hi Ma from China, Alexander Hozmine and Basil Djordjadzé, two painters from Russia, Ernest Faillade, a Hungarian journalist, Prival Hurad from Martinique, who listed himself in the census as a boxer, as well as a number of other students—not a particularly Jewish quarter.[75]

Hotel Max was located moments from the junction of boulevards Raspail and du Montparnasse, where at a café called Le Sélect one could find the most outrageous bohemian behavior; the Schneersons had chosen to live in what was an extremely colorful area.[76] The other nearby cafés—places like La Coupole, a favorite of Sartre and de Beauvoir, Le Dôme, and La Rotonde—were also gathering places for existentialist writers and surrealist artists. Until 1939, this neighborhood teemed with writers and artists from all over the world. Gertrude Stein and Alice B. Toklas held court at 27 rue de Fleurus, only a five-minute ride away. Philippe Halsman, the photographer, had opened a studio in Montparnasse in 1934 where people like Gide, Chagall, Malraux, Le Corbusier, and many other writers and artists came to have portraits made. Between the wars, rue Campagne-Première, two blocks from where the Schneersons lived, was the haunt of such artists as Picasso, Modigliani, Miró, and Kandinsky. Could the Schneersons and the Horensztajns have remained completely ignorant of this life around them? Did they want to be? Did they never walk the boulevards, stop in the cafés, visit the galleries, or feel the energy around them? Had this couple who stayed out late in Leningrad while they were courting and who may have attended the theater there become homebodies in interwar Paris?

We know that Moussia, like Sheina, liked to dress elegantly. In the few photographs of her that are available, she is smartly dressed, her mouth clearly sculpted with lipstick, her eyebrows plucked and made up, her hair coiffed and in some cases covered partially with a fashionable hat. Sheina and the two Mendels also appear nicely dressed, although only the future rebbe wears a trim beard and a beret at times.

Missing from their neighborhood were concentrations of Jews, and certainly Hasidim. On the other hand, the Jewish quarter, dominated by the so-called Pletzel, the square at its center, was on the other bank of the Seine and about two and a half miles away. We find little evidence that either of the Schneersons was commonly seen in this district. The famous synagogue where Russian Jews got married on the rue de Tournelles was even farther, over three miles away. Finally, a small synagogue at 10 rue Dieu, at which Rabbi Yosef Yitzchak prayed when he visited Paris and which was run by a distant cousin, Rabbi Zalman Schneersohn, was about four miles away—a very long walk for anyone who wanted to live on rue Boulard and worship on rue Dieu on the Sabbath. In fact, on the Jewish holy days and family occasions, they would, as they had while in Germany, generally return to the court of the Lubavitcher rebbe rather than remain in Paris, and once there Mendel reintegrated himself into the Hasidic, mystical atmosphere of the Rebbe Yosef Yitzchak, as we find in his diary.

The decision to go to Paris from Berlin was likely stimulated by contacts that the Schneersons had with relatives they had there and whom they'd visited over the years. Among these relatives was Edmea Schneerson, like Moussia a granddaughter of the fifth rebbe, Rabbi Shalom DovBer. Edmea would graduate with a degree from the Sorbonne, with qualification in sciences and a certificate in English.[77]

Another cousin in particular would be very important to Mendel; his name was Yitzchak Schneersohn.[78] This man had served as a Crown Rabbi in Gorodnya and later in Chernigov, both in northern Ukraine. He had also been active in Russian Jewish community affairs and education, as well as later serving as a council member and deputy mayor in Ryazan in the western region of Russia, not far from Moscow, representing the moderate liberal party. But by 1920 and the victory of the Bolsheviks, Schneersohn had moved to France and become a successful industrialist. His home became a place where Jewish leaders, many of them Zionists, mostly right-wing Revisionists, as he had become, met. By the early 1930s Schneersohn was well connected and an important contact for his cousins the Schneersons and Horensztajns. Although no longer terribly observant Jewishly, he did keep a kosher home, in large measure because his wife remained religious; the Schneersons sometimes ate there. He also ran a salon, and on Friday nights people often gathered at his home at 135 avenue Emile Zola (about two and half miles from where Mendel and Moussia lived), including some of the best-known Zionists, from Vladimir Zev Jabotinsky to Chaim Weitzmann. In a way he became his cousins' adviser; even in Russia he had been particularly concerned with getting Jews past the quota restrictions and into higher education. In the process he had made contacts with the czar and other notables, a pattern he would continue in France.[79] As his own sons, Boris, Arnold, and Michel, were students in engineering at the École Spéciale des Travaux Publics du Bâtiment et de l'Industrie (ESTP), this may have made that institution appeal to Mendel too. Moreover, there were a few Jews who taught mathematics there, and that also might have made it of interest to him.

This school, founded in 1891 and officially recognized by the state in 1921, would at last provide Mendel Schneerson with the credentials and training he would need to pursue the career he had been after since he first started studying sciences in Yekaterinoslav. This was a school, moreover, narrowly aimed at providing its students entry into the civil and engineering industries. As such, it was not so much interested in turning out intellectuals—as might a university like the Sorbonne— as much as producing employable engineers. Mendel and, later, his brother-in-law Mendel Horensztajn both secured admission there. In his application, Mendel Schneerson was able to present certificates from the Russian Academic Association and later one attesting to his studies at the university in Berlin, which undoubtedly made up for the fact that he could not show a high school (gymnasium) diploma, the minimal prerequisite for acceptance.

On April 24, 1933, thirty-one-year-old Mendel Schneerson began to attend the ESTP as an *auditeur libre*—once again an auditor—entering during the third trimester and taking secondary courses in mechanical engineering. The formal schedule for students, most of whom were in their late teens or early twenties and who came with a certificate of high school matriculation, was grueling: about forty hours a week of both theoretical and applied work. After two years of preparatory study they were examined and then either accepted for admission to the engineering school or rejected. Attendance at all classes and exercises, held in three terms from early October through the beginning of July, Mondays through Fridays. from 8:30 a.m. to about 6 p.m. and part of

Saturdays, was mandatory and scrupulously monitored. In each class there was a proctor whose task was to check not only the attendance but also that exercises and exams were completed. Tallying sixty "unexplained absences" (*absences sans excuse*) during his first term, Mendel would receive only grades in "conduct" of an average 18 out of 20. In the evaluative comments on his transcript was written that the student "did not submit any work, and did not take any examinations." The remarks concluded that "under these conditions," it was impossible for the director of the form to assess the likelihood of Mr. Schneerson's ability to fulfill his assignments.

Beginning with the next term, Mendel began an intensive course of study, including courses in French writing and translation, geometry, calculus, chemistry, and physics, as well as applied skills in electricity and design. In all he took fifteen courses and received average grades of around 14—about 70 percent—putting him in the rank of tenth and eleventh in the class out of approximately twenty-eight.[80] He particularly excelled in mathematics, not surprisingly, as he had been studying this for years, and once again his grades in conduct were excellent. But the comments on his transcript indicated that his work in design and some of the applied work required improvement (something that he accomplished in his third term, although he needed to complete assignments in the laboratory). No doubt some of his deficiencies can be explained by his continuing many absences, when laboratory work was done or exercises were due. Why these absences?

Some were certainly explained by his religious life, which demanded not only that he observe the Sabbath but also brought him back to his father-in-law's court around each of the Jewish holy days and on special ChaBaD occasions. We know, for example, that on July 30, 1933, he and Moussia went for two days to Marienbad to visit Yosef Yitzchak, who was there for the cure.[81] Sabbath was a major concern and a source of absences. From his home on rue Boulard to the school on boulevard Saint-Germain was a little over a mile and half, a distance that during the week probably took a little under ten minutes on the Metro, which he could pick up at Place Denfert-Rochereau, a block from his apartment. If he had to walk, he could probably make it in under an hour. His brother-in-law Mendel Horensztajn was following a similar career pattern, and they likely traveled together to school frequently.

We know that the schedule presented problems for Mendel. In the fall and winter terms, when daylight hours grew shorter, Friday classes, the day when many of the written exercises of the week were due, would have interfered with the onset of the Sabbath at sunset. At first he simply left early on Fridays, without explanation. On other occasions he traveled to be near his father-in-law, once again sojourning in the world of Hasidism. This double life was becoming more difficult to manage.

By the end of the of the school year in 1934, however, his absences notwithstanding, he had been granted admission to the École Supérieure de Mécanique et d'Electricité, on his way to receiving a degree. Now, on the verge of fulfilling his ambition to become an engineer, Mendel Schneerson did something curious: he failed to register for the 1934–35 academic year, although he returned and proceeded with his studies the following academic year. What did Mendel do during the academic year of 1934–35?

If we check his diary for that year (which is not really a personal chronicle but notes of his thoughts and Hasidic anecdotes and practice, punctuated here and there with entries or datelines that help us locate his whereabouts), we find some evidence of his movements. At the time of the high holy days, when children commonly visit their parents and Hasidim the rebbe, the young Schneersons (and probably the Horensztajns as well) were in Warsaw, where a month earlier (September [Elul] 1933) the sixth rebbe had moved his court from Riga.[82] Since we also find some entries marked 28 Cheshvan (November 6, 1934), referencing talks of his father-in-law, we can suppose he was noting stories he had heard on that day from him. Other isolated entries reference some days in winter when he was in Vienna, where Rabbi Yosef Yitzchak had in the past gone to the Purkesdorf Sanatorium for medical treatments, as his health had begun a precipitous decline.[83] On another occasion he noted his attendance at a circumcision, and still other visits to the sixth rebbe come at Passover, as well as on a Sabbath in May 1935 and isolated days in the summer. But the visits to the court of the sixth rebbe appear to be relatively few, throwing into question any claims made by some Lubavitchers that he was working actively as his father-in-law's assistant or emissary. Moreover, the Schneersons held on to their apartment on rue Boulard, which suggests that this still remained their home base.

Undeniably, during this period he was able to focus more on his Hasidic interests. There is some evidence (or at least ex post facto Lubavitcher claims) that he was involved with the editing of a new Lubavitcher publication called *HaTamim*; however, his name does not appear in it among the three mentioned as editors.[84] There are more entries during this year in his diary that register his Hasidic knowledge of tales and customs than in the years immediately before and after, when he was busy with his engineering studies. In the Hebrew year 5694, which coincides with the 1933–34 academic year, he made nineteen entries, while in 5695 (the 1934–35 academic terms when he was not in school) there are eighty-six. In the two following years (which are the last until 1941 [5701], the year of his arrival in New York), when he was hard at work at ESTP, there are six and four, respectively.

In retrospect, and given the ultimate direction of his life as a rebbe, the few concerns with Hasidism in 1934–35 would prove to be infinitely more important to his future than his engineering studies, though he probably did not realize it at the time. In fact, as his reenrollment into full-time studies the following year makes clear, during his "year off" he did not abandon his original plans to be an engineer. Given that fact, what is likely is that Mendel spent much of the 1934–35 academic year neither in the cafés of Montparnasse nor in Hasidic venues with his father-in-law (who continued to fully support him financially), nor even in Hasidic musings, but rather sharpening his language and mechanical design skills (in which he had received his lowest grades) in order to do well in the all-important degree-granting engineering program into which he had been admitted. He undoubtedly wanted to succeed in what he surely believed at the time would for him be the entrée into his chosen profession of engineering (what he would call his "dream" in a letter to his father, as we shall see, and something he asserted in an interview with the French when he explained that he had done "the most important part of his studies in France"). He knew well how demanding the challenge would be, given the difficulties he had in the preparatory school.[85] Indeed, in 1937 his brother-in-law Mendel Horensztajn, who had also been admitted when he had, would not manage to meet that challenge and would in the end fail the course, while Mendel Schneerson, scoring just a bit higher, would pass.

In the fall of 1935, Mendel returned to school for his first semester in the advanced degree-granting program. At first he had a hard time of it. He received a grade of about 13.5, which gave him a rank of thirty-fifth out of a class of thirty-seven. In the appended comments on his transcript was the notation, "Mr. Mendel Schneerson will have to improve in industrial design, particularly in mechanics, if he does not want to repeat the first year's courses. He will in the future not be permitted to take make-up examinations, except in extraordinary circumstances." Obviously, he had been right to take a year off to prepare, but had he studied enough? By the second term, however, he seemed to find his footing and improve dramatically, scoring almost 15 and raised his rank to twelfth out of thirty-five. Still, the comments on his transcript indicated a concern with his frequent absences and their impact on his work. According to the school's rules, after one hundred absences, one was not allowed to advance to the next year of the program.[86] By the third term, with grades slightly over 15, he was ranked tenth out of thirty-four, yet the comments focused on his need "to concentrate more on graphic statistics and applied kinetics." Nevertheless, he was accepted into the second year of the program. Clearly, Mendel Schneerson was working hard to meet the intellectual challenge of this demanding curriculum, and must have thrown himself into his studies in order to succeed. Surely, he had little time left for other pursuits— and indeed he largely neglected his diary that year. Nor did he travel often to the court of the rebbe, now in Otwock, the town outside Warsaw, where in 1935 the court of his father-in-law had relocated once again. He arrived for a brief stay on 25 Shvat (February 18, 1936) to celebrate the bar mitzvah of his nephew Shalom DovBer (Barry) Gourary.[87] The next and last time he returned was for the high holy days in September, after which he returned as soon as possible to Paris. Indeed, for Passover that year, Mendel and Mousia stayed in France.[88]

The problem of absences was troubling and hurting his progress, and he therefore tried as much as possible to avoid them; he was serious about becoming an engineer. He certainly did not want to jeopardize his status at the school; on the other hand, Sabbath was not to be denied. Once again, he began to leave without explanation (he did so thirteen times), starting on November 15, when Sabbath in Paris began at 4:53 in the afternoon. But he soon discovered this approach was not going to work. In consequence of his unexplained absence, he was suspended for two days, beginning November 18. Realizing this could wreck his career plans, he and his brother-in-law successfully petitioned the administration for permission to leave early on Fridays, explaining the reasons for their absence. Attached to his transcript was the following notation: "Messrs. Schneerson, Mendel and Horensztajn, Mendel are authorized to leave the course in applied science at 3:30 P.M. on Fridays during the winter, but they are required to submit their written exercises, which are normally turned in at the end of the class, in advance." And the note added, "They may not use this authorization to ask to do these exercises late." Mendel used this permission twenty-three times. There were another sixty-six "excused absences."

Beginning in the fall of 1936, Mendel started his final year of studies at the ESTP. Once again his grades remained largely the same: around 15, with a student ranking of twelve out of twenty-eight for the term. The following semester he again scored around 15, with a ranking of fourteenth out of twenty-nine. This time the comments were more positive; his grades were termed "very satisfactory" but they added that he must do something about his repeated absences, which were due to a *"force majeure,"* a term normally used to refer to acts of God. The comments in his last semester noted that he "had to use his semester break to complete his work in industrial accounting and commercial law." Mendel took this seriously, and the following spring he and Moussia once again did not leave Paris and return to the rebbe's court for the Passover holidays.[89] In the end, he succeeded, and on July 24, 1937, the board of examiners recommended to the minister of education that he grant Mr. Mendel Schneerson a diploma in mechanical and electrical engineering, subject to the certification of his completion of a three-month internship (*stage*) in his field. On that same day Mendel Horensztajn, who with an average of a little lower of 14 had ended up twenty-seventh out of twenty-eight, was denied qualification for a degree. While Mendel Schneerson went on to his *stage*, his brother-in-law would ultimately return to Warsaw, a decision that would have tragic consequences when he and his wife became trapped in the Nazi regime.

At last, on March 25, 1938, Mendel Schneerson, who was now thirty-six years old, received his diploma. He was finally an engineer with a degree. His pride in his new status could be seen in the fact that on the letters he sent to his parents, he marked his return address on the envelope as "Eng. M. Schneerson."[90] His internship as an engineer surely absorbed his energy, for we find that unlike in past years, when the high holy days arrived, he and Moussia did not return to the court of her father for the occasion. Indeed, that year, the Rebbe Yosef Yitzchak had to content himself with writing them a letter from Otwock with his greetings and blessings for the New Year.[91]

Writing from Paris to her in-laws in May, Moussia explained that "We want to live here as permanent residents, and we are trying with all our ability to get approval for this," for, as she concluded, "without permanence, life is very difficult."[92]

Leaving rue Boulard, they now found a place about two and half miles away in the more bourgeois 15th arrondissement on 7 Villa Robert Lindet.[93] Describing the quest for this apartment, Moussia in the letter to her in-laws wrote how hard it was to decide to rent a place because they "had no jobs and it did not appear they would get any soon," and it was therefore "unreasonable" to spend too much, but that Mendel had said "we had to decide yes or no," and therefore "finally we have rented a small apartment." She was glad they had, and reported that their "two rooms, a bath and a kitchen," on the third floor in an "elevator-building with all the services" were sunny. Her sister, Sheina, and her husband, she added, had helped in the search and found a similar place for themselves nearby, something that "for us is important."[94] They had little furniture, but they were sending for some of their linens and tablecloths which they had left at "her mother's" now that they were establishing a permanent home.

The choice of the new address was apparently not based on its closeness to the Jewish ghetto in Paris or Zalman Schneersohn's synagogue at 10 rue Dieu. Indeed, they were now even farther away than they had been while living on rue Boulard. From a distance of about three miles to the Pletzel, they were now more than eight and one-half miles away, and from having been four miles distant from rue Dieu, they were now more than five miles away.

∭

Although he had worked as an engineer during his *stage*, when he received his final certification, Mendel did not become a full-time working engineer. As he wrote his father in February 1938, a month before he received his diploma, about his search for a job, he had "many dreams regarding a position or possibly a partnership with my specialist," referring perhaps to the engineer with whom he had been interning.[95] These dreams were not fulfilled. Instead, we find that he registered in the faculty of sciences at the Sorbonne. On November 30, 1937, Mendel Schneerson signed in as registrant 2040, noting that he had practical experience in differential calculus. A year later, on November 18, he did so again. Having finally acquired a degree that could lead to the vocation he had been pursuing for so many years, he instead decided on more university study. Why?

To understand what might have motivated him, we need to consider briefly the conditions in France at the time and their possible impact on a Jewish man of Hasidic background who was still a foreign national with no passport, yet with a French degree (and who had not graduated at the top of the class but rather somewhere in its middle), who was seeking work in the relatively elite profession of engineering.

France, like much of Europe and the West, had been suffering the effects of a massive economic depression since 1933, when the Schneersons had arrived in the country. That depression would end in 1936, just a few years before the outbreak of what would become the Second World War. Beginning in 1933, Jewish refugees, many of them from Germany, had begun pouring into France. As Vicki Caron documents, "by the summer of 1933, at the height of the first refugee crisis, France had absorbed some 25,000 refugees from Germany, placing it first among the refugee-receiving countries."[96] Coupled with the economic hard times, this led to what Caron calls a series of "conservative crackdowns," the first of which came in 1934–35. At that time, "the drive to eliminate foreigners emerged as a principal strategy for dealing with the Depression."[97] Whereas on their French identity cards (which Mendel had received on March 25, 1937, and his wife had received a few weeks later in April) the Schneersons, listed their profession as students (actually only Mendel was listed as a "student in the sciences"; his wife was listed as having no profession), their nationalities were identified as "Russian refugees." Moreover, when later, in October 1937, the Schneersons petitioned the registrar of seals in the Ministry of Justice for French citizenship, they referred to themselves as "Russian refugees" who had "completely broken" with "their country of origin" and had decided to definitively fix their future in France, where they hoped to establish themselves. Their Latvian *laissez-passer* was clearly ending its term of utility. Having identity cards was no small accomplishment, as there had been a series of decrees and laws making it increasingly difficult for foreigners to obtain these, beginning in 1934. Getting work permits was no easier.[98]

By 1937, when Mendel and Moussia were trying hard to become citizens, the atmosphere in France had turned quite sour in regard to such grants. By 1938, front-page editorials in *Le Temps*, usually considered the semi-official mouthpiece of the French foreign ministry, were arguing against citizenship for "foreigners," suggesting that "the competition these foreigners pose in commercial matters and in the labor market, as well as in the domain of the liberal professions," was a source of legitimate concern among average citizens.[99] They were calling for revisions in the naturalization laws to make them more restrictive. That same year Emile Béron, a left-leaning representative in the Chambre des Députés from the Mosselle, appealed to the Ministry of the Interior to restrict future naturalization and allow it only to foreigners engaged in manual labor.[100] The entry of increasing numbers of refugees, many of them Jews, led to intensified opposition, particularly by the middle-class professional associations, to making citizenship easy. This would have made it hard for people like the Schneersons, an engineer and his wife, to find work or gain citizenship.

Recognizing this, the Schneersons subjected themselves to the extraordinarily intrusive questions at the Préfecture of Police that were part of the petition process. Mendel was deposed. Asked, for example, whether he had his own means of support, he replied that he did not but that "the family of his wife" was providing support for their studies, such that he had an income of 40,000 francs a year (a little under $2,700 at the time), out of which he paid for his rent, which he listed at 300 francs a month.[101] To be sure, he did not have to explain how a Hasidic rebbe like Yosef Yitzchak Schneerson, himself a refugee from Russia and one who claimed to oppose the very idea of university study, would be willing and able to pay these costs. Asked if he had lost all hope of returning to his native country, he answered simply "yes," even though he also reported that his parents and his thirty-five-year-old brother Berel (who he claimed was an "accountant who resided with the parents") still lived in Dnepropetrovsk. Moreover, he provided a notarized statement in which he claimed he was each month sending his parents food and clothing valued at 350 francs.[102]

Asked about his occupation and attitudes during the war years of 1914–19 and whether he had rendered any service to France, he replied that "after being called to serve under his flag," he received a release, "due to his quality as a student," in order to continue his studies, but had also served simultaneously as an aide to an engineer who was involved in war production.[103] When the interviewer asked the degree of the petitioner's assimilation to French custom and usage, he was able to conclude, as he noted, that Mendel was "well assimilated" and that he and his wife both spoke French "fluently." He noted his degree in mechanical and electrical engineering, but also the fact that Mendel maintained acquaintances not only with French nationals but also with foreigners. In the end, despite a supporting letter on behalf of the petition in early 1939, the request was denied by June 10 of that year.

The Schneersons must have guessed that their chances of remaining in France were slim, and given that their identity cards listed Mendel as a "student in the sciences" and the difficulties of refugees finding jobs in France, even with a French degree, Mendel may have decided that registering as a student in the sciences at the Sorbonne was his best move if he wanted to stay in Paris. After all, where would he go? In a letter in 1939 to his parents in which he repeated that he still harbored "dreams about a job or a partnership in his profession," he now added that "at least part of these is *only a dream*."[104] The situation for Jewish refugees in France was not improving, even for those with training like his. Yet while he had by his own statements given up hope of returning to Russia, he apparently did not now want to move to Otwock and the rebbe's court. Registering for more studies at the Sorbonne was a solution.

But did he actually study at the Sorbonne? We know he loved mathematics and that he loved to study. However, if he actually did, we find no further record of those studies; no grades, no certificates, no letters or even correspondence that would indicate that he actually attended. To be sure, the situation in Europe was swiftly deteriorating. In January 1939, Hitler threatened Jews during a speech to the Reichstag. By August 1939, the Soviets and Nazis had signed a non-aggression pact, by March Germany had invaded and taken Czechoslovakia, and in September 1939 Nazi Germany attacked Poland. In May 1940 the Nazis invaded France, and any hopes that Mendel Schneerson harbored for a career as a French engineer completely evaporated.

He would perhaps briefly entertain this engineering dream again in 1941 when he arrived in New York, but there he would discover that the prospects for practicing his profession in a country where he did not speak the language, where he had landed as a Russian refugee who was identified as a "rabbi" and was living in the newly reestablished court of a Hasidic Grand Rabbi, were unlikely. First, however, he would have to escape the murderous reach of Nazism.

Other Jewish refugees in France were also struggling with the collapse of their world. Some reacted with political activity; others turned inward and began to concern themselves with their Jewish identity and involvement.[105] Some of the former met to map strategies for resistance to fascism and anti-Semitism, while the latter tried to explore their Jewish roots and tradition. But we find no evidence that Mendel Schneerson was among either of these groups. Neither did he get involved politically, even when in May 1936 the French elected Léon Blum, their first Jewish prime minister, a man whose party instituted social reforms and who led the effort to oppose fascism, a man "whose mother was rumored to have kept a kosher home and not to have allowed anyone to work in her house on the Sabbath" and whom the editor of the Yiddish paper *Parizer Haynt* called "not simply a Jew but a real Jew, a Jew with a Jewish heart and a Jewish understanding."[106] Nor did he look to serve as a religious guide and teacher, a rabbi, for those—particularly among the immigrant and refugee population, many of whom dominated life around the Pletzel— who had made their way to Paris, at the time "the second largest Jewish community of Europe (after Warsaw)," and who on the eve of the Second World War searched "for renewed strength in Jewish tradition."[107]

Not all Jews in Paris were alike. The immigrant Jews made their Jewish life public and engaging, while the native French Jews were far more likely to put the "emphasis upon Judaism as a private affair."[108] Combing through the police archives in Paris, where those Jews who were politically active against the Nazis and who were outspoken leaders and publicly known Jews were listed by name, we find no record of either Mendel or Moussia Schneerson except on their application for citizenship. We also find no record in his own correspondence or diary notes to indicate an involvement in helping people with their theological and religious crises or renewing their attachment to Jewish tradition—something that would be so important for him when he became the seventh Lubavitcher rebbe. Instead, the Schneersons were caught up in concerns about housing, a job, naturalization, the safety of their loved ones, and the desire to find a haven from the encroaching Nazis.

𝔪

During 1937–38, we can see from his correspondence that Mendel became more active as a Lubavitcher. He spent time with his father-in-law at the sanatorium near Vienna between December 1937 and March 1938. Indeed, Yosef Yitzchak, whose health was steadily deteriorating, came straight from the sanatorium to Paris, where he stayed from March 9, 1938, until just before Passover, when he returned to the court, while Mendel and Moussia remained in Paris.[109] Mendel helped Yosef Yitzchak and also involved himself in some activities on his behalf. Checks from Lubavitcher activity in the United States, for example, were apparently being channeled via Mendel in Paris. This source of support became even more important after the collapse of Jewish activity in Germany in 1933, and Israel Jacobson, the head of the Lubavitchers in America, who would play an important role in Mendel's life in the years ahead, became even more important a contact. Thus, in November and December 1937, we find Mendel communicating with Jacobson about how to cash a check from America that was deposited into a bank that went bankrupt.[110] At the end of July 1938 and even on the eve of the high holy days in September 1938, he was sending transcriptions of his father-in-law's talks as well as commentaries on topics of Hasidism and Jewish customs while handling foreign funds. Paris, apparently, was the preferred address for these over Otwock in Poland where the court was located. At this time, Mendel helped with Yosef Yitzchak's correspondence. Hence, by staying in France as long as he could, Mendel was serving not only his own needs but also those of the Lubavitcher Rebbe and his court. As late as the end of July 1939, he was writing to Jacobson about fund transfers and asking about the "results of the convention" of the ChaBaD Hasidim that had been held earlier that summer in the United States.[111]

Clearly, as his prospects for a career as an engineer declined, Mendel's possibilities for and interest in a vocation in the court of ChaBaD grew. This, he surely recognized by the end of the 1930s, was something he could do. He had the knowledge, pedigree, and connections, and perhaps slowly he was gaining the desire to play a larger and more important role in Lubavitcher affairs. His ailing father-in-law needed more and more help. Mendel was ready to give it, although he was still far less involved in the affairs of the Rebbe than his older brother-in-law Shmaryahu Gourary.

♪♪♪

What about his family life? Levi Yitzchak, his father, continued writing to him. This correspondence reveals a closeness reflecting his dual role as both a parent and a spiritual guide. A letter on the eve of Yom Kippur in late 1938 is typical.[112] It begins with a review of the laws and practices of this holiest day of the Jewish year, complete with references to Talmud and other sacred literature, as well as the expressed hope that these lessons "will not be lost from you and your progeny forever." Then the father adds the specific blessings for both Mendel and Moussia that a father offers on this day and includes a wish to the childless couple, married now for about ten years, that "God may remember you with a son, with 'a seed both healthy and vital.'"

A child, of course, was not just of personal concern. Levi Yitzchak still had no grandchildren, no one to carry on his branch of Lubavitch. On the other side, for a daughter of the Lubavitcher Rebbe, a son would be the hope for the future of the movement. Chana and Shmaryahu Gourary already had such a son and heir. But neither Mendel and Moussia nor the Horensztajns had any children. Clearly, with Moussia thirty-seven years old, there were concerns. Perhaps that was why Mendel had begun his fasting, hoping to move heaven to "remember" him and his wife by his actions of piety.[113] Maybe his increasing attachments to the Lubavitcher Rebbe were reflections of his desire to have this closeness translate into God's blessing him with a child. For Hasidim, closeness to a rebbe is a means of effecting divine intercession on their behalf.[114] Rebbes are frequently asked for the blessings of fertility.

Mendel was becoming increasingly pious; the anxiety of their childlessness weighed heavily on the couple and their parents. On

19 Tammuz 5699 (July 6, 1939), Levi Yitzchak wrote to him about a new religious practice that he had learned his son had taken up.[115] It was a ritual that offers a sign of his increasing devoutness and an indication that some profound change was going on inside. Mendel was donning "*tefillin d'shimusha rabba.*"[116] According to standard religious practice, a Jewish adult male must strap on one pair of tefillin (phylacteries) made of leather and containing sacred scriptures on parchment inside them on all mornings except Sabbaths and holy days. Because there are some doubts as to exactly the order of placement of scriptures in these leather boxes, some Jews put on two different pairs of tefillin. An even greater level of piety extends this practice to strapping on additional types, where the order of the scripture placement includes the opinion of different rabbinic scholars, the last of these being "*tefillin d'shimusha rabba.*" Very few do this, but it is a custom that was adopted by the rebbes of Lubavitch.[117] Mendel's father had already urged him to put on two pairs; now he encouraged this practice of putting on a third, saying it would assure those who did it of "long, good and pleasant lives." To this he added that this ritual was particularly important for someone "who has no children" and that it connected to the possibility of "a woman giving birth to a son." Obviously, as his father understood, Mendel's piety was directly attached to his and probably Moussia's longing for a child.

All these concerns would be suspended when war broke out less than two months later, at the start of September 1939, and the agenda of every Jew in Europe became physical survival. That would prove to be a watershed experience for all of Jewry, and no less for the Schneersons and Lubavitch.

From Survival to *Uforatzto*

ʃʃʃ

The Nazi conquest of Europe, and in particular the Nazis' arrival in the locales where the family of Yosef Yitzchak and the court of Lubavitch had settled, threw the world in which they lived into extraordinary turmoil. Because they had found themselves in Poland as the Germans approached, the Rebbe, the Gourarys, and the Horensztajns, as well as the Hasidim who made up the court, had been put in especially perilous circumstances, worse than any they had ever experienced. Indeed, when at last, in March 1940, Rabbi Yosef Yitzchak was saved from the murderous brutality of the Nazis and brought to New York, he averred, as he was being wheeled off the ship onto American soil, "The sufferings I endured in prison in Russia do not compare to the torments of the 12 weeks I spent under *their* rule."[1]

The sixth Lubavitcher rebbe, his mother and wife, the Gourarys, and some of his entourage had been saved by the efforts of, among others, lawyers Sam Kramer and Arthur Rabinovitz (both of whose fathers were Lubavitch followers), Supreme Court Justice Louis Brandeis, and officials in the U.S. State Department, Israel Jacobson and the American members of ChaBaD, presidential adviser Benjamin Cohen, and—once again coming to his rescue)—Reform Rabbi Stephen Wise, Senators Robert A. Wagner of New York and William Borah of Idaho, along with some members of Congress, as well as Ernst Bloch, one of a group the Germans called *Mischlinge*, people of mixed Jewish-Aryan parentage. Bloch, a Nazi officer, was the son of a Jewish father.[2] Of course, a great deal of money also had to change hands for this escape to occur. Key, however, was the fact that American officials, whose help was critical, had been somehow persuaded, as Max

Rhoade, the Washington lawyer who helped organize the rescue noted, that the Lubavitcher Rebbe was "a sort of Pope" of the Jews and that his liberation from the clutches of the Nazis, along with that of his immediate family and disciples, would be an act of significant political and humanitarian value.[3] Indeed, in one communication to American officials, Rhoade actually compared him to St. Francis of Assisi.[4] As Bryan Rigg in his absorbing chronicle of the effort notes correctly, "It is likely that American officials' ignorance of the social topography of American Judaism, when combined with the political pressure exerted by well-placed politicians, may have persuaded them that the rescue of the Rebbe, described as an important spiritual leader, could yield good publicity at a minimum risk."[5]

At first Mendel and Moussia, separated from Rabbi Yosef Yitzchak and his court, were not in immediate danger. Between the initial invasion of Poland on September 1, 1939, and even after October 1, when the Nazis marched in triumph into Warsaw, Jews in France were still relatively safe. The dangers would spiral upward in May 1940 with the Nazi invasion of France. Although the young couple remained in Paris until around the time of that invasion, they realized their days there were numbered, and therefore as early as October 11, 1939, Mendel wrote to Israel Jacobson in New York (who had been in touch with lawyer Sam Kramer regarding the matter of bringing the Schneersons to America). His letter, a reply to Jacobson's request for the whereabouts and detailed birth dates of all the family, reported that he did not know the exact location of Rabbi Yosef Yitzchak and his immediate family, something that worried him. But he did add details about his and his wife's dates, indicating they too wanted to be listed among those applying for a visa for America.[6]

In the meantime, by late 1939 efforts to rescue Rabbi Yosef Yitzchak had intensified. He had fled to Warsaw from Otwock on September 5, just three days before the Nazis reached it. In Warsaw he stayed at the home of his Hasid Zalman Shmotkin until September 13, the eve of Rosh Hashanah.[7] He would move around the area throughout the month to hide but return to Shmotkin's by September 24, the day after Yom Kippur. At some subsequent point he moved to 29 Bonifraterska, the address of another supporter.[8] On the 21st, Chaim Lieberman, his secretary, had escaped to Riga to pave the way for what they hoped would be the Rebbe's return to Latvia.[9] Rabbi Shmaryahu Gourary was supposed to accompany him, but Chana, his wife, was so devoted to her parents (as was his grandson as well) that the Gourarys refused to leave Rabbi Yosef Yitzchak even for the relative safety of Latvia, which was still a neutral country and a place where many other rabbis had rushed for sanctuary.

When Rabbi Yosef Yitzchak in the late months of 1939 came to terms with the idea of leaving for America, the only refuge he considered, at the urging of his family and supporters, he tried first and foremost to include all the members of his immediate family, the Schneersons as well as the Horensztajns and Gourarys. On July 25, in a letter to Rabbi David Mayer Rabinovitz of Boston, a long-time follower of Lubavitch and leader of Tifereth Israel, a synagogue on Chambers Street in the West End (and father of the lawyer, Arthur), Rabbi Yosef Yitzchak reported that, although he had lost contact with Mendel and Moussia following the invasion of Paris, "thanks be to God" he had ten days earlier received two telegrams from them informing him they were in Vichy, the unoccupied zone in the south of France, and safe.[10] They were safe and spared the worst, that is, until March 1941 when the Vichy government set up the Commissariat Général aux Questions Juives, an organization that carried out the anti-Semitic policies of the Nazis and in some places devolved, as Donna Ryan puts it, into "a den of thieves grabbing whatever movable property remained in Jewish hands."[11] Nevertheless, as the Schneersons were not French Jews but Russian refugees, they were still in a precarious position. This was because the Vichy government "authorities were prepared to enforce the regulations to persecute 'foreign' Jews, [even though] they were often reluctant to act against French Jews."[12]

Efforts to liberate Rabbi Yosef Yitzchak and the Gourarys, as we know, proved successful. Traveling by truck and train (in first class) from Warsaw via Berlin, they spent the Friday night of December 15, 1939, at the Jewish Federation in Berlin. They probably received their necessary transit visas there. After the end of the Sabbath on the night of December 16, "they boarded another train, again in a first-class cabin, for Riga, accompanied by German escorts and delegates from the Latvian embassy."[13] The journey that in normal times would have taken more than sixteen hours was even longer, as they stopped in

Kovno, Lithuania, "where several of the Rebbe's followers met the train and danced with joy as he arrived," and then finally reached Riga on Sunday, December 17. They had been able to enter Latvia because they all held Latvian citizenship.[14] However, this was true only for the rebbe and his immediate party. His daughter Moussia and husband in France were former Russian nationals, while Sheina, her husband and his family still in Otwock were Poles.

To enter the United States, those accompanying Rabbi Yosef Yitzchak would either have to be listed as his "dependents," in order "to avoid extensive investigation into their financial resources and those of the Chabad organization and to thereby expedite the granting of visas for the entire group," or at least some of them would have to be identified as "rabbis." Under a provision of the 1924 Immigration Act, clergymen were exempt from exclusion by the quota system of the act, although many had to also prove they were employable and would therefore not become economic burdens on the state.[15] Max Rhoade accordingly needed to prove to American immigration authorities that "the Rebbe and his group were rabbis and thus 'professors' of Jewish theology who could find employment as teachers."[16] This would not be easy, particularly for Mendel Schneerson and Mendel Horensztajn, even though the Lubavitchers tried to persuade American officials that they were major religious leaders. (Indeed, to help make this case, on July 7, 1940, the American Lubavitcher organization listed Mendel Schneerson as one of the twenty members of the administration.)[17] Neither Mendel Schneerson nor Mendel Horensztajn, however, had served as rabbis in any professional capacity. Both had been engaged in engineering studies, and the former was now degreed in that field, while the latter was neither an engineer nor obviously engaged in a rabbinical life; he was barely religious.

If this approach failed, the "fact that most of the Rebbe's group were born in Russia eased Rhoade's job since that country's quota remained open."[18] Tragically, as it turned out, Mendel Horensztajn and his family as Polish citizens remained disqualified for U.S. visas, nor was anyone sufficiently convinced that young Horensztajn was a rabbi or an important religious leader who would be able to serve in that capacity in the United States.[19] Another explanation that has been offered for the Horensztajns' fate is that at the outset they still believed they might

survive the war and did not want to leave Otwock and Mendel's aged
parents, who were unable to travel. By the time they realized this was a
poor plan, however, their rescue had become impossible.[20] In the end,
the youngest Schneersohn daughter, Sheina, and her husband did not
manage to get out of Poland, and despite desperate efforts by her father and his supporters to get the couple into America, they remained
trapped in the Nazi web and perished, along with millions of Jews and
many Lubavitchers.*

At last, on March 6, 1940 (the day Finland surrendered to the Soviets and a little over two months before the Baltic states would do the
same), Rabbi Yosef Yitzchak and his wife, Nechama Dina, his mother,
Shterna Sarah, his daughter, Chana, and her husband, Shmaryahu Gourary, his grandson Barry, his secretary, Chaim Lieberman, his twenty-
three-year-old nurse, Sheina Locs, Chaim Hodakov, the educator and
pedagogue who had headed the modern Orthodox school in Riga and
had become attached to Lubavitch (even though he had spent his youth
as a Hasidic opponent), and two other Hasidim flew from Riga to Stock-
holm and traveled thence by train to Göteborg, where they boarded the
Drottningholm (the Rebbe in cabin 13) and sailed for New York, arriving
late on March 18 at Pier 97 on Manhattan's Hudson River.[21] The next
morning he disembarked, wearing his *shtrayml,* with Shmaryahu Gourary in top hat at his right, and was taken by a delegation of Lubavitchers
to the Greystone Hotel.[22] After a short stay in Manhattan, on September
12, 1940, the Rebbe moved his headquarters to Brooklyn.[23]

Now that the Rebbe was saved, attention quickly turned to rescuing
those left behind. On August 30, 1940, Shmaryahu Gourary wrote to
Henry Butler, a Washington attorney working for the Lubavitchers, and
informed him that Mendel and Moussia Schneerson had left Vichy and
were now in Nice.[24] Gourary was working hard to get his brother-in-
law and sister-in-law out of war-torn Europe, even though, as he told
his son, he knew that by doing so he was bringing his competitor closer
to the rebbe's court.[25] On September 23, the State Department reported
receiving a cable (paid for by Mendel Schneerson) from the American

---

*ChaBaD sources indicate they perished in Treblinka, but an interview with their
niece, a Holocaust survivor, suggests a different end (Friedman, July 9, 2001). According
to her, the younger and elder Horensztajns were killed in Otwock.

consul there that he was trying to arrange for their departure but that there were problems with listing Mendel as a clergyman, who would thus be exempt from quotas. He noted that Mendel was an engineer (in fact, his first request for a visa had identified him as such) and was also known as a journalist, the latter based on his writing for *HaTamim*, a Polish Lubavitcher publication in Hebrew.[26] Therefore the idea of getting him in as a rabbi would have to be dropped, and he would have to submit a request for a normal immigrant visa, which would require preparing a new affidavit. Now Rabbi Yosef Yitzchak turned to Arthur Rabinovitz to provide this. At the same time the Lubavitchers sent a certification of Mendel Schneerson's status as a rabbi to the consul in Nice, still trying to convince him that the man who had identified himself as an engineer on his visa application was truly a rabbi.

At last, despairing of success in Nice, where they believed the consul was not friendly to Jews, the Schneersons went to Marseilles, where they thought exiting would be easier.[27] In Marseilles, Mendel made contact with his cousin Zalman, who like him had abandoned Paris. He had set himself up on rue des Convalescents. There in January 1940 at Zalman's invitation on the holiday of Tu B'Shvat, Mendel, in a trim-looking beard and wearing a gray suit, tie, and fedora, gave a talk to a small group of yeshiva students. In the darkness of the war, he shared his ideas about messianic redemption to the young refugees who were there *farbrengen* over soup and couscous. At least some of those who heard him at the time did not know who he was, even after his talk in Yiddish. Nevertheless, as those terrible days closed in on him, he was thinking, as were so many who looked into the dark abyss of what in time would be called "the Holocaust," about the hope of ultimate redemption, and he was beginning to talk very much like a disciple of his father-in-law.[28]

On January 18, 1941, Rabinovitz asked Eliot Coulter, a State Department official, to transfer the Schneersons' visa to Marseilles. He also telephoned and wrote to Breckinridge Long, the State Department official in charge of matters concerning European refugees and an extreme nativist with a particular suspicion of Eastern Europeans, and asked for visas for the Schneersons and Horensztajns as well as thirty-four more people, including twenty-eight Temimim students then caught in Yokohama and six who were in Poland.[29]

On February 7, 1941, Long wrote to the visa department the following: "Mr. Arthur Rabinovitz advises me that Rabbi Mendel Schneerson's visa application was transferred from Nice district to Marseilles district, and he is now refused non quota visa by Marseilles. We authorized issue of visa. Consul at Marseilles suggests immigrant visa. I see no reason why he should not be granted immigrant visa even though we authorized non-quota."[30] This meant that Mendel Schneerson, while referred to as a "rabbi" in Long's message, had still not convinced the immigration authorities that he *was* a rabbi. (Perhaps he had been unable to produce a satisfactory document of ordination or any convincing record of his having served as a rabbi.) Nevertheless, it seemed from Long's reasoning that Mendel and his wife would be allowed to enter the United States as normal immigrants—a prize that few other Jews in Europe could get at this time, and certainly very few with Breckenridge Long's endorsement. At last, the Schneersons received immigrant visas 2635 and 2636, issued in Marseilles on April 17, 1941. They were very lucky to do so. "Because Marseille was virtually the only legal location for emigration, applications swamped the U.S. consulate there," and many applicants often waited for hours, only to be disappointed at the end of the day.[31]

Leaving in June, they, like most of those fortunate enough to get passage out, probably "traveled by train through Spain to Portugal, where they could arrange passage across the Atlantic from neutral Lisbon."[32] Departing from Lisbon on June 12, they arrived eleven days later on the morning of June 23, 1941, when the *Serpa-Pinto* docked in New York. Mendel (who the immigration official noted "wore a beard," noteworthy to Americans at the time) and Moussia stepped onto the streets of Manhattan, met by Israel Jacobson, Shmuel Levitin, Eliahu Simpson, and Shlomo Aaron Kazarnovsky—Lubavitchers all—and were taken directly to Crown Heights, Brooklyn, where Rabbi Yosef Yitzchak had now located himself and his court; only three days later did Mendel meet with his father-in-law.[33] His and Moussia's lives would never be the same again.

∭

What Mendel Schneerson did next is not altogether clear. Although he had a degree in engineering, he had no real professional experience.

He spoke little or no English. Moreover, his beard—too short for Rabbi Yosef Yitzchak's preference but too long for the Americans, as we see in the notation by the immigration official—set him apart from most other Americans at the time. To them he was probably little more than a Russian or French refugee and a Hasid—whatever that was, as in 1940s America, and even New York, the sight of Hasidim was not yet common—but definitely *not* the American image of an engineer. While some reports have him working for a subcontractor to the U.S. Navy at the New York Navy Yard in Brooklyn, his position there, if indeed he held one, was certainly not one of major responsibility. The U.S. Navy was hardly about to give important war work to a foreign national, a non-English-speaking refugee who formerly held a Soviet passport or an immigrant whose record as an engineer was limited to a short period of *stage* or internship and whose grades put him in the middle of the class in a French technical college that probably no one had heard of in America. According to one account, he was given some computations to do, a task that would square with his mathematical abilities and would not require English language skills. In all events, such work would surely not be the fulfillment of his long quest to be a professional engineer. If anything, it would force him to rethink his life.

As he reflected on his situation, he could not help but realize that his plans to settle in Paris, become a French citizen, and live as a Jew of Hasidic background pursuing a career in engineering were now a shambles. Moussia, too, who would forever look back on her years in Paris as among her happiest and freest, as she often told friends, realized those days were over.[*]

Leaving aside these vocational questions, which were personal but relatively minor in light of the events of the last few years, the experience of the Holocaust and his flight from Europe (as well as his childlessness) must have been monumental in his life. The Horensztajns, to whom he and Moussia had been so close in Paris, were dead. His brother Berel,

---

[*] Moussia Schneerson would make a two more trips abroad, once to Paris, Zurich, and possibly England (where she visited her widowed sister-in-law, Leibel's wife, and niece) in 1953 and several years later to Switzerland in 1958. But by then she had realized that the Europe of her past was a changed place and she was no longer free to live a life there as she had once done. For one thing, she was now in these places without her husband. See *HaRabanit*, 49, 79, and Ganzburg, *B'Kodesh P'nima*, 79 n. 111, 91–93.

who had remained behind in Ukraine, had been murdered by the Nazis in Dnepropetrovsk. This was their standard approach with all those they considered mentally or physically "defective." His brother Leibel as the no longer religious Marc Gurary was living with Regina in Palestine, where he had arrived, escaping from the Nazis. His mother was still caught behind the Iron Curtain; his father had been arrested and sent to Kazakhstan by the Soviets in 1939. His long correspondence with his father now stopped, as had the packages of clothes and funds of around 350 francs he used to send.[34] In prison for ten months, Levi Yitzchak was released to spend his remaining years in internal exile in Kazakhstan, where his wife Chana joined him. By 1944 the father whom Mendel had seen for the last time more than seventeen years earlier would also be dead, probably from cancer, and buried in Almaty.* Mendel's whole world had collapsed. Now he was a childless refugee in America nearly forty years old with little or no English facility, with no job prospects in what had been his chosen field.

Most of European Jewry had been crushed and burned. The Jews in the Soviet Union were trapped and seemed lost, while those in Palestine were locked in a battle for survival, and he was safe in New York. Surely this evoked in him deep religious questions and perplexity, perhaps even disorientation. Did he now feel guilt or have second thoughts that when others had been working against the Nazis and the Soviets and on behalf of the Jews, he was nowhere to be seen or heard? Did it concern him that he was not in the battle for Jerusalem or in Israel with his brother? Did he wonder why his fellow student and cousin Mendel Horensztajn and his wife Sheina were dead, while he and Moussia were safe in America? He and Moussia were now in a place they never expected to be. He must have been deeply disconcerted by all these developments. What was the meaning of his survival?

---

*While the initial arrest and exile in 1939 of Levi Yitzchak Schneersohn by the Soviets was looked upon as a total misfortune when it occurred, ironically, this arrest, which sent him to Kazakhstan, to which his wife followed him, ended up saving them from the Nazis. Their son Berel, who remained behind, was killed by the Nazis, while Chana Schneersohn survived the war precisely because she had been in the East with her husband. See Shmuel Marcus and Avraham D. Vaisfiche, *Rebbetzin Chana Schneersohn* (Brooklyn: Merkos L'Inyuinei Chinuch, 2001), and http://www.chabad.org/library/article_cdo/aid/133640/jewish/Rebbetzin-Chana-Schneerson.htm (accessed April 9, 2008).

The theological difficulties this raised for him must have been disquieting as they were for many survivors, especially those who were religious believers and even more those who had taken Rabbi Yosef Yitzchak's messianic message seriously. Like so many of his contemporaries, he could not deny the tragic condition of the Jewish people, the horror of the Holocaust and what it meant about God's relationship to the Jews and the promises of redemption that his Rebbe, Yosef Yitzchak, had made so vigorously in the preceding years. Some of these concerns, doubts, and even frustrations are hinted at in a letter the forty-six year-old Mendel Schneerson wrote on April 22, 1948, as the battle over Jerusalem raged and once again he saw Jews taking heavy casualties while fighting for their survival and for the state they would hopefully declare less than three weeks later.

"*Gevalt* [for heaven's sake]," Mendel wrote, "the Messiah told the Ba'al Shem Tov that he would come with him when he spreads the wellsprings to the outside. And this task was given to us, to lead—and what are we doing about it? We are suffering in exile even though the Rebbe *shlita* [may he live for many good years, amen] in his *maymer* promised that the redemption would come quickly in our days."[35]

These are not the words and sentiments of a man planning a career in France, living on the Left Bank and looking forward to being an engineer. This "*Gevalt*" is a cry from the heart of a man whose life has been turned upside down and around, a man convinced that God is acting in history in unprecedented ways. They are the words of a man who must be feeling desperate in his anxiety, loneliness, confusion, and survivor guilt, whose prospects are unclear, looking for a way out, an answer from God. The messianic message of Rabbi Yosef Yitzchak, which seemed to have been denied by the facts, actually fit Mendel's own situation: it solved the dilemma of what the future would hold for a barren couple. It promised redemption to all of the Jewish people. If the Messiah was coming, there was no need for children and heirs or even for a career; the end of history was upon us; Jews just had to work harder to hasten that day. He would often say that he believed "that nothing happens by accident."[36] That the Messiah had not come *yet*—as Yosef Yitzchak had predicted—required an explanation of how his arrival must somehow still be imminent. That explanation would turn out to be essential to Mendel's thinking and theology for the rest of his life. It would be the answer to the conundrum of his survival and the unexpected turn in the circumstances of his life.

♫

After receiving his U.S. citizenship on November 14, 1946 (the only nationality he had and would hold the rest of his life after losing his Russian passport in 1932), Mendel had a freedom of movement he had not had in years. He used it in the early spring of 1947 to return to Paris (his only trip away from America after his arrival in 1941). Flying from New York, he arrived there the third week in March, just before the Passover holiday.[37] His widowed mother had managed to escape the Soviet Union and by way of Poland and Germany to arrive in Paris, staying with her cousin Rabbi Zalman Schneersohn in his 10 rue Dieu home. Reuniting with her after a twenty-year break, Mendel would bring her back with him to New York. According to at least one report, there were a handful of Lubavitchers in Paris at the time, and on Sabbaths they would gather for prayer at rue Dieu.[38] Particularly sensitive to the fact that "he could not perform the commandment of honoring his parents for a long period," he wept when he met his mother and compared himself to the biblical Joseph, who left as a young man and who had likewise been separated from his parents while he became a great leader in Egypt, and according to rabbinic commentary had felt guilty for his long separation.[39] But of course, Mendel was not yet quite the viceroy that Joseph had been, although perhaps in 1947 he was beginning to see himself as such. Two Lubavitchers, Bentzion Shemtov and Yaakov Lipskar, were there to assist him and called on him regularly, seeing him as an important prince of a court that had miraculously survived the Holocaust.

On his visit to Paris this time he stayed in the second arrondissement at the Hotel Edward VII, about two and a half miles away from where his mother stayed in the tenth arrondissement.[40] According to Mordecai Laufer, the Lubavitcher biographer of the Rebbe, Mendel largely kept himself closeted in his hotel "and did not come in much contact" with the Lubavitchers in the city.[41] Maybe so, but perhaps he actually took the time to reacquaint himself with the Paris he had fled in the midst of war and consider whether he could again resume the life he had left there. If he did so, the answer was obviously negative. The world had been unalterably changed by the war. Moreover, he was now in Paris fully in his Lubavitcher incarnation, receiving letters from his father-in-law and working on his behalf, particularly in the matter of refugees who were getting out of the Soviet Union.[42] He surely understood that for all his hopes to be a Parisian and an engineer, it was Lubavitch that had saved him and welcomed him with open arms, and was now giving him more and more to do. Even in Paris in 1947, where he celebrated the Passover seder and later the night of study on the festival of Shavuot, activities on behalf of the court took most of his time.[43]

To his widowed mother, who had lost one son to the Nazis and another to socialism and secularity, Mendel, her first-born, was the only one who seemed able and willing to take up the heritage of his father and his Hasidic ancestors, and of this she was obviously proud. That too must surely have played a role in his thinking. Indeed, on June 8, two days before his departure, a "*tzetkha le'shalom* [bon voyage] event" in his honor was held at 10 rue Dieu, to which invitations were sent out by the Lubavitchers.[44] After a formal talk and reception at which he was able to act as a stand-in for his father-in-law in ways that perhaps he never had before, he stayed until around ten, long after those who were not Lubavitchers had left. Now he managed to ignite the enthusiasm of those who remained, demonstrating an ability to remember people's names and using the occasion to offer little sayings that connected those names with the unique characteristics of each person, an exercise that totally charmed those in the room. It was a virtuoso performance, and he knew it.[45] By the time Mendel boarded the *Mauritania* with his mother, he must surely have realized his future and destiny were in and only in the Lubavitcher movement. As he would tell an interviewer later, "We need engineers and chemists, but engineering and chemistry are not the most important things."[46] Arriving in New York after a six-day crossing from Cherbourg, France, on June 16, 1947, he was ready to be a full time Lubavitcher, and perhaps also its leader.

He had found a new home just a couple of blocks away from what would become the world headquarters of ChaBaD Lubavitch. This was now his neighborhood, and would become his world. In 1944, unable to attend his father's funeral, Mendel recited Kaddish for a year, and it was among Lubavitchers that he did so morning and evening and found consolation, an experience that could not help but arouse in him more feelings of closeness to these people from whom he had been distant for so much of the time he was in Germany and France. In his first years in a new country, no one else looked on him with the same favor. Indeed, on the register of its officers submitted on November 14, 1940, to the State Department by Agudas Hasidei Chabad, he was listed as third in the hierarchy, superseded only by the Rebbe Yosef Yitzchak (president), Shmaryahu Gourary (first vice-regent), and Chaim Zalman Kramer (second vice-regent).[47] On June 6, 1941, just days before his arrival in New York, he was already listed not simply as a journalist for *HaTamim* but as its editor.[48] A man in his forties, married with no children, forced to start life again in a new country, whose prospects in all other spheres were limited; he must surely have begun to understand that in the world of Lubavitch, he could find a position of honor and usefulness. In 1943 he published under the Lubavitcher imprint, *Ha'yom Yom*, a booklet with a Hasidic saying for each day of the year.[49] A letter in 1948 shows a man thinking and writing in Hasidic terms, a man who had for almost seven years been ensconced in the court of Lubavitch, living with Hasidim more than he had done in years. He was now totally in a Lubavitcher environment and trying to find his bearings and redirect his life. Although on 14 Kislev 5714 (November 21, 1953), the twenty-fifth anniversary of his wedding, he would as their new Rebbe, and perhaps still trying to establish his credentials as their leader, tell his Hasidim that that day a quarter of a century earlier, "bound me to you and you to me," it was really these years between 1940 and his 1947 stay in Paris when he probably truly felt first new stirrings of those bonds.[50]

His father-in-law also had to get his bearings, to deal with many of the same questions, with the fact that he had left so many of his followers behind twice, first in the hands of the Soviets and then in those of the Nazis. He had to explain the presence of all this evil and his inability to crush it. By now he had to recognize as well that what Lubavitcher ideology had called the "false Messiah" of Zionism was increasingly becoming the true hope of more and more Jews, a hope that would be realized with the establishment of a Jewish state of Israel in 1948, and his own version of the messianic age seemed to be out of sight and perhaps even a matter of doubts.

Although ill and exhausted after what would become his final flight from peril and effort to reestablish his court once again, this time in

Brooklyn, Yosef Yitzchak understood that he must offer some answers to the religious and existential questions that the events through which Jewry was living had raised. His answer to all of this, as we have suggested earlier, was that these agonies were the birth pangs of the Messiah, the suffering that precedes redemption. All that was happening aimed to encourage Jews to repent, an act that by itself could hasten the day of redemption. His son-in-law Mendel seemed increasingly to share these convictions.

The idea that the Jewish people were entering the messianic period was one that Rabbi Yosef Yitzchak had inherited from his father. Shalom DovBer Schneersohn had been overwhelmed by the rapid decline of traditional observant Jewish life at the turn of the nineteenth century.[51] The secularization and political and social emancipation, the assimilation of European Jewry, and the increasing interest among many in a secular Jewish Zionism were for him unthinkable. How could Jews abandon the genuine faith of their fathers? This, the fifth Lubavitcher rebbe argued, could only be a sign that the Messiah was preparing to come. Messianism was for him a way out of the dilemma of his inability to prevent this erosion of the traditional Jewish life in which he believed. The Messiah's arrival would restore the control and dominance of traditional Judaism over Jews and the world. Of course, Rabbi Shalom DovBer did not live to see this happen

For his son, the belief that the Messiah was near remained a cornerstone of his theology and understanding of the reality that he encountered in his lifetime. This meant that the Bolshevik revolution, which had forced him into "exile" from Russia and trapped his many Hasidim and other Jews in its godless regime, was a sign of the pangs that preceded the birth of the Messiah. The rise of the Nazis and the outbreak of the Second World War and its murderous impact on Jewry—and on his own family and followers—could for him only underscore his conviction that such suffering and pain had to accord with a divine plan.

As early as 19 Kislev 5699 (December 12, 1938), the so-called New Year of Hasidism and one of the most celebrated days in the ChaBaD calendar, Rabbi Yosef Yitzchak asserted to his followers, "We need to talk about the Messiah."[52] Again in war-torn Warsaw, under the rain of German bombs and bullets, he reiterated this belief when he published pamphlets asserting that as worrisome as the war was, it *had* to be seen as evidence of the imminent arrival of the Messiah. Jews were not at all powerless, as they believed. Hitler would be defeated only by Jewish acts of repentance, and they had the power to repent. These ideas were swiftly promulgated, and the news moved around the world, including the Jewish settlement in Palestine.[53]

Shalom DovBer and Yosef Yitzchak were not talking of the Messiah in a vacuum. As Rodric Braithwaite and others remind us, at this same time, in the supposedly "godless" Soviet Union, "religious commitment increased: more than half the peasants took the risk of identifying themselves as believers in the 1937 census." Among them, as early as the late 1920s, "tales of the forthcoming Apocalypse began to spread," and the conviction was that the "reign of the Antichrist was at hand, so the rumours said, and it would be followed by Armageddon and the Last Judgment."[54] In this atmosphere of apocalypticism, whether they were aware of what the Orthodox Christian peasants believed or not, the Lubavitcher rebbes were expressing almost the same beliefs.

After Yosef Yitzchak's escape from Europe, these messianic ideas resurfaced in America, but as we have seen, they were harder than ever to defend. How could he explain his arrival here? He had claimed the Messiah was coming while he was in Poland, in the thick of the war. He had claimed Hitler would be defeated by repentance. But now he had run away to safety and well-being, even as he told his followers to remain in place in Europe and the Soviet Union. How could that be?

To answer the doubts that his situation must certainly have provoked in his mind, if not in the minds of those who listened and looked to him for guidance, he had to somehow insert America into his theodicy. In Rabbi Yosef Yitzchak's thinking, as the body of Jewry was being burned in Europe, in the new world the Jewish soul was being destroyed by the fire of American Jewish heresy.[55] But if that was nullified by repentance, spurred on by the arrival of the Lubavitcher rebbe, then America would ineluctably lead to the final redemption.[56]

Four weeks after his arrival in New York, on the eve of Passover, he dispatched a letter "to the Jewish people of America and Canada" with what would be his solution. It was filled with imagery of the Jewish people being "like a ship sailing on stormy seas" (perhaps recalling his own recent ocean crossing) in which "every Jew, not only the Jews of Europe, are in danger of drowning."[57] Only if North American

Jewry observed Sabbath and the Jewish dietary laws of *kashres*, the men donned tefillin, the women used the *mikveh* (ritual bath), and the children received a religious education would the plague be ended and the redemption come.[58] That was what he saw as his mission, and to accomplish it, the Almighty had plucked him from the fires of the Nazi regime and brought him to America.

On October 20, 1940, seven months after he walked onto Pier 97, he founded *Mahane Israel*, an organization that would further his messianic mission. This organization "thought of itself as a religious safety zone protected from the *Hurban* [destruction], a Biblical 'Goshen' ('Only in the land of Goshen, where the children of Israel were, was there no hail,' *Exodus* 9:26). It believed it could end the *Hurban* through religious activity and bring about the redemption (*Geula*)."[59] At the same time, Rabbi Yosef Yitzchak and the Lubavitchers believed that God had sent the Jews into exile in the "Diaspora to hurt and to become martyrs."[60] In fact, "the degradation of exile was intended by God to create a receptivity" to redemption.[61] Hence, behind the suffering, the "plagues of Nazism, like those before, were ultimately traceable to a divine plan and were intended to bring the people back to God."[62] Lubavitchers read and assimilated these ideas, particularly in *Hakriya v'Hakedusha*, the publication begun in 1941, to promote these messianic ideas.

Destruction and redemption were dialectically connected; "life followed death."[63] Indeed, he believed that only a profound fear of total Jewish collective death—precisely what the Nazis and their allies were providing—could precipitate a collective atonement and return to religion, the necessary prerequisite to messianic redemption. God had arranged history to lead to this moment so that Jews would be forced to turn away from sin.

American Jews were crucial to this turning. They were "*Galut be'tokh Galut*," the lowest level of exile, nearly completely assimilated and secularized, barely observant at all.[64] As Lubavitchers noted, "seventy-five percent . . . are Reformers, or free-thinking working class Jews, [or] ignorant and heretical business types, [or] American-born youths who were committed body and soul to baseball and movie heroes but were totally ignorant about our father Abraham. Twenty-five percent do not want to hear about *Teshuva* [repentance] because it meant they would have to start praying again."[65] In a proclamation on June 24, 1941, Rabbi

Yosef Yitzchak "condemned those who ignored his call for *Teshuvah*. He referred them to Aaron's sons Nadav and Abbihu, who brought an alien fire to the Temple altar (*Leviticus* 10:1), profaning the sacred fire, and were burned alive for doing so. American Jews compromised messianic belief by failing in *Teshuvah*, and they would fall victim to divinely ordered suffering in the form of Amalek's (the paradigmatic enemy of Israel) anti-Semitism."[66] Again and again he repeated versions of these themes, on the one hand telling American Jews and those who led them that if they mended their ways, they would open the door to the Messiah, but on the other hand if they failed to do so, then all "non-pious Jews would be killed," on "a day of fire [*a brenenden tog*]."[67] What was happening in Europe would happen in America too.[68]

These ideas did not endear Rabbi Yosef Yitzchak to American Jewry or its leadership. The man the Jews of America, many of them "non-pious," had worked so hard to free was now rewarding them with the news that they would burn if they did not repent, and that they were responsible for ending the suffering in the world. This was not a message designed to make friends and influence people in America—or anywhere, for that matter. It raised more questions than it answered. Why was suffering a prerequisite for redemption? Why had so many religious Jews who held on to tradition, including many of his own Hasidim, been burned in the Nazi crematoria? Why had the "sinful" Jews in America survived? If exile was a punishment by God, how could mankind be allowed to hasten its end? What about those who did repent? Why had some of them also been victimized? He promised hurt and martyrdom in the diaspora, though he himself had avoided it; why?

When Menachem Mendel Schneerson later took up his own "Moshiach" (Messiah) campaign, he would reframe the messages of his predecessors so that these questions became moot. He made clear that redemption did not require any further death and suffering as a prerequisite, no more birth pangs or martyrdom. His was not a messianism of pain and catastrophe. His was a messianism of promise. He stressed the ability of the converted sinner to change the cosmic balance and bring the redemption, a Messiah whose footsteps (*ikveso dimeshikho*) could now be seen.[69] As for answering the questions raised by the Holocaust, his response "took the position that the Holocaust could not be comprehended during the present," and that "comprehension had to await redemption."[70] Just as the Holocaust could not be grasped, so its counterforce, redemption, could not be understood completely in advance.[71]

For Rabbi Menachem Mendel, the evidence of the imminence of the Messiah, an idea he adopted from his two predecessors, was not the torment that preceded his arrival but rather the Jewish revival that was breaking out all over, a revival he and his emissaries would be part of if not lead. It also solved the problem of his childlessness, which had tormented him for the past several years, as it did for his followers, who surely wondered why their Rebbe had no heir. The messianic future would be miraculous. All nonpious Jews would *not* burn in his vision of the future; they would instead be made pious, and the Lubavitcher *shluchim*, who would be his children and whom he would send out throughout the world, would see to that.

These ideas would be expressed after he became Rebbe, a role for which he had to reinvent himself. He would do it by stressing his knowledge of Lubavitcher sources and by using mystification to enhance his charisma and the charisma of his office—audiences with him began at 10 p.m. and ran into the wee hours of the morning, so that people who came to see him had to walk through abandoned streets when the rest of the world was asleep and specially prepare themselves and remain awake for the encounter.[72] Of course, he would also use all the tools that were part of a rebbe's kit: the taking of *pidyones*, the recitation of Torah and DACh (often late into the night), the giving of blessings, and the like. He would with one hand distance himself and with the other draw people near.

America, where so many immigrants had reinvented themselves, was the perfect place to do this, and the 1950s and early 1960s were the perfect time to start such a process. These were years when America was "starting over" too, an America filled with promise.[73] Throughout Western culture, the twentieth century, after its false starts of two world wars, economic depression, and culture shock, after periods of mass migration and mass murder, was beginning again. In these new beginnings people wanted to forget the turbulent past, to come home, bring their lives to some kind of normalcy, get an education and a job, build families (leading in America to the now famous postwar baby boom), and give their children all the opportunities they themselves never had.

In this atmosphere of increasing economic prosperity and the rise of the welfare state, which gave people a sense of security, the five-day workweek, which gave people family time and a day to devote to worship and allowed even the Sabbath observer to be part of America, the despair of so much of the preceding decades was replaced by feelings of optimism and renewal.[74] This new beginning and its affinity for personal reinvention would be crucial for this new Rebbe, his followers, and the people he and his emissaries would serve and try to reshape.

In America, like other immigrants before and since, Menachem Mendel Schneerson started his life anew. For those who came during or after the Holocaust, moreover, this need to reinvent themselves was also connected with the realization that those they had left behind were not simply elsewhere, they had been murdered. Hence, for many of these survivors reinvention was coupled with a desire to somehow honor those dead, to counterbalance the troubling feelings of survival and loneliness with a new life that would fulfill some of the elements of those whose lives had been cut off. For Orthodox Jews, this sometimes resulted in a conviction to create a new kind of religious life that would end not in Holocaust but rather in some sort of redemption. This too must have played a part in his life, especially because the idea of redemption was so deeply a part of Lubavitcher theology.

Synthesizing all these feelings, he would become *a renewed almost reborn person in America*; he would no longer be Mendel Schneerson, would-be French engineer and student. As we have seen, by 1951 he would be reinvented and remade. No longer the shy introvert, he became the self-confident extrovert and leader, emerging as Grand Rabbi Menachem Mendel Schneerson, *shlita* [may he live for many good years, amen], the seventh Lubavitcher rebbe.[75] He would be the channel of the late Rabbi Yosef Yitzchak, now called "the Previous Rebbe," with whom he would hold frequent "conversations" at the *tsiyen*.[76] He would take the language and the mechanisms of ChaBaD Lubavitch, the traditions and the beliefs, and reengineer them, redefining what they could do and what it meant to be a Lubavitcher Hasid.

He understood that this would not be easy for older Hasidim. As he would write in 1962, "it is difficult for a person in the prime of his life, or in more advanced age, to radically change his whole outlook and reexamine the whole approach in which one has been trained and

148

steeped, in the light of contemporary conditions in the United States."[77] He knew how difficult it was because he had had to do so himself. But the young Hasidim, who would be shaped by America and modernity, would be his foot soldiers and his best and most enthusiastic emissaries.

Menachem Mendel understood that he would have to go slowly at first, framing his ideas in the terminology of continuity, even though his goal would be radically new, even revolutionary. This couching of the new in ChaBaD traditions, explanations, and practices would be the theme of his leadership. From being a somewhat mediocre mechanical and electrical engineer he would become an outstanding social and spiritual engineer who would offer his recipe for the redemption of all the Jewish people. To a significant number of his Hasidim, he would by the end appear to be the Messiah himself.

We have already described briefly the way Menachem Mendel Schneerson outflanked and superseded his rival, Rabbi Shmaryahu Gourary, for the crown, but that victory was not instantaneous or complete for quite a while. Establishing his bona fides took longer, and it required finding just the right combination of continuity and innovation. His first Hasidic talk, *Basi L'Gani*, did just that. As we have already seen, it took the title and themes of the previous rebbe's final address and plugged into them new ideas and meaning.[78] Throughout the years Menachem Mendel spent much of his time interpreting his predecessor's final talk, showing how he had penetrated it, explaining, as we have noted earlier, that there had been seven generations of sin: Adam's, Cain's, Enosh's, the generation of the flood, the one of the tower of Babel, the people of Sodom, and finally the Egyptians living at the time of Abraham. Each of these had led to the gradual departure of the *Shkhine*, the Divine Presence, from the world of human beings to the Seventh Heaven. Each of these generations of sin, Rabbi Yosef Yitzchak had argued, would be reversed by the actions of seven generations of righteous fathers and sons—Abraham, Isaac, Jacob, Levi, Kehath, Amram, and Moses—who would, in a series of steps, gradually return that Divine Presence to dwell in this world. They could do so because there was an inherent longing of God to return and reveal himself in the mundane world, as the founder of the ChaBaD dynasty, Schneur Zalman of Lyady, had explained, "to create a dwelling place [for Himself] among those in the lower realm [*Dirah b'tachtonim*]."[79] That included especially bringing God to the part of the world from which he had been completely missing until now, the Western Hemisphere, what ChaBaD called "*Chatzi Kadur Tachton*"—the other side of the globe, "the [spiritually] lowest hemisphere," the "exile of America."[80] Indeed "there is a kabbalistic belief that before the coming of the Messiah, the Torah of Hasidism," which ChaBaD saw itself as spreading, "would be revealed in the [spiritually] 'lower half of the world.'"[81]

In a sense, this view of Schneur Zalman was not particularly messianic, for it emphasized that God sought to be perpetually present among those on earth rather than a being who would arrive only in the aftermath of an extraordinary one-time historical appearance of the Messiah.[82] It required mankind to prepare the conditions for God's dwelling among them. That was the task that the Lubavitchers had taken on for themselves. *This* was "spreading the wellsprings," the necessary preliminary work, which according to the Ba'al Shem Tov was what would lead to a spiritual ascent and bring the Messiah.[83]

But, Rabbi Yosef Yitzchak had argued, mankind's continual sinning made that seem impossible. Indeed, could God have been more distant from humanity than he was for so much of the first half of the twentieth century and most recently in the Holocaust? And could God be missing anywhere more than in the world that remained after it, a world that had, as Rabbi Yosef Yitzchak argued, been all sin? That was why repentance, here in this place that was spiritually the lowest point on earth, *khutse she'eyn khutse mimenu* (the extreme outside), was so essential to bringing him back.[84] When God was allowed to return to dwell among his people, then redemption would be at hand.

That work of spreading the wellsprings Rabbi Menachem Mendel said had to be done by another seven righteous Jewish leaders, for God cherishes sevens, as the Midrash put it.[85] Those seven were none other than the leaders of the ChaBaD Lubavitch dynasty, and the last of them would, like Moses and his generation, bring the Divine Presence with the Messiah back to earth.

As he explained, "the seventh's primary quality lies in his being seventh. In other words, he is cherished not on account of his choice, desire, or spiritual service but because he is seventh—and this is something that he is born into."[86] He and his generation who had the destiny and responsibility to complete the mission of their antecedents and at last bring God back to the people were "capable of doing the divine service and fulfilling the mission of the first," a mission that would draw back down the spirit of God "into this lowly world."[87] They did this not because they were especially suited to the task but because they were ineluctably destined to do it by virtue of being the generation of the Messiah's arrival and the one living in the spiritual abyss, America (*takhtn she'eyn takhtn mimenu*).

The message was unmistakable for those who saw Menachem Mendel as that seventh rebbe. It was not his previous service or his desire to be the leader that enfranchised him; it was simply his destiny, as it was as well the destiny of those in this generation.[88] Applying this Midrashic idea to himself, as if he were Moses, and his generation was the key element of this talk, he told Lubavitchers that they were now on a mission to rebuild themselves and the world. He provided them with direction and their raison d'être.

This seventh generation would accomplish all this by getting the rest of their generation to mend its ways, and then they, the Lubavitchers, would lead all Jews to the true Promised Land of the messianic age, supplanting the false messiahs of materialism, communism, and Zionism. Whether they wanted to or not, he and this generation could not flee from their religious responsibility, even if they were reluctant to take it on. As one of his followers put it, "his Mission Statement was clear: To bring Moshiach."[89]

These were not completely new messages. Each element could be traced to a talk or idea of his predecessors, all of which he knew as well as or better than he knew the formulas of mechanical engineering design. But what Menachem Mendel did with these ideas was to apply them to the historical situation and social context in which he found himself. He would engineer a revolution with the language and ideas contained in Jewish kabbalistic tradition and ChaBaD Hasidism. He would do it with the help of the young but couch it in terms that would enable even the most conservative of elders to accept it.

One cannot understand this message without reflecting on the fact that the man who offered it had seen his whole life changed by the circumstances of history over which he had no control. For years he had fled the public stage of life, active engagement in his Hasidic heritage, and life in the Lubavitcher court while seeking a secular education, a degree in engineering, and a cosmopolitan existence in Paris. He had escaped from pogroms, communists, many of the missions of his father-in-law, and now the Nazis. Yet as he considered his life at this point, did he not conclude that he could no longer flee his destiny? He could not help but realize that in the end, he was here in "Lubavitch," and all his other plans would have to be set aside, not because he wanted to give them up (whenever he found a visitor able and willing to talk about technology or engineering or mathematics and science, he still hungered for conversation about it) and not because he felt particularly suited to be the Rebbe (though he would soon get over that doubt) but because he believed that God had steered him to this new life.*

At first only Lubavitchers who had been tuned to the Previous Rebbe's messianic ideas and who were struggling with how to continue in a new place and in the face of the Previous Rebbe's death could accept this message. Indeed, when some of the other Orthodox Jewish leaders read or heard these words, their response was less than enthusiastic. One rabbinic head at the Torah VeDaas Yeshiva, one of the premier non-Hasidic Orthodox institutions in New York (where Barry Gourary, Yosef Yitzchak's only grandchild, had been a pupil) was reported to have said (in Yiddish) of the man who offered this message, "he is either a prophet or a pretender; and I do not think he's a prophet."[90] Clearly, the new Rebbe's ideas would have to be fine-tuned, and ways would have to be discovered to spread them to the rest of the Jews and the outside world. That would take time, an organized campaign, and a leader who had learned how to speak to the modern world. The early nineteen fifties were, however, not yet that time. But this decade of re-invention was an ideal time to start.

Events would occur that would make this message find a more receptive audience in the world beyond Lubavitch. Life in America, Western Europe, and even Israel began an extended period of economic growth,

---

* When, for example, in the early 1960s he met with a couple before their impending marriage and learned the groom was working for IBM, he spent almost the entire visit, which he extended, asking for the young man's opinion about the merits of FORTRAN and other computer languages, even as the line outside his office grew longer and his assistants tried to urge him to conclude. Matthew Schein, in discussion with Samuel C. Heilman, March 28, 2008. Matthew Schein was the young man who had this conversation.

social change, and cultural ferment, as well as structural change, driven especially by rapid, almost unbelievable, technological development.* This gave people a chance to assimilate into the surrounding environment and Western culture as perhaps never before in Jewish history.

Opportunities abounded, and many took them. No segment did so more than the young, whose numbers boomed after the war. Whether in America, Europe, or Israel, they became part of the new society and culture, feeling an almost native attachment to it. But because of the economic boom times in all these places, they could also luxuriate in their youth, extending that period of adolescence (often by attending university) that allowed for the postponement of responsibility and commitment, extending the stage of life that psychoanalyst Erik Erikson called the "moratorium."[91] These adolescents would be the target of the new Rebbe and his emissaries, for they had not yet taken irrevocable life paths and still contemplated the "great questions," which after all was what the issue of redemption was; they might therefore be open to changing their ways.

But the matters of redemption and repentance were matters of profound religious meaning. In 1950s America, from which the Rebbe's call would go out, religion was rather bland and shallow. Even though (or perhaps because) the immediate past had seen terrible tragedy and suffered extreme dislocation, many at this time were willing to forget it and the theological questions it raised, turning instead to a kind of nondescript homogenized civil religion that asked little of God other than that he allow people to live their lives in peace and comfort.[92] In 1954 the words "under God" were added to the Pledge of Allegiance to describe the American nation, and in 1956 "in God we trust" was adopted as the official national motto.[93] But the God in question was rather featureless and undemanding. That suited people of the time; they wanted a moratorium on worry and a nice quiet God in heaven. For Orthodox Jews—and Hasidim were part of that group—whose God was far more demanding and distinctive, this was a time to remain quiet, keeping their distinctiveness camouflaged.

---

* The Jews behind the Iron Curtain were isolated and would not become a part of this story until the last quarter of the century.

This was not easy. After the Holocaust, this more religiously committed and observance-focused Judaism had first to come to terms with the human and institutional reality of its extraordinary losses. Many if not most Orthodox Jews were survivors or immediate relatives of survivors.[94] While they built Jewish day schools, yeshivas, synagogues, Hasidic courts, indeed whole communities, they largely remained invisible during the immediate postwar years. Most put an emphasis on making it in America, on surviving by being integrated or at least adapted to its culture. Many sought to share in the American dream, become professionals, move to the suburbs, and send their children to universities. Others, the *haredi* sector, argued that such efforts at integration were dangerous and would lead to assimilation and decline. They condemned the so called modern acculturative Orthodox as indistinguishable from the rest of American Jewry, which they saw as losing its Jewish identity and on the road to disappearing into the fabric of America. While the Modern Orthodox claimed one could remain loyal to Jewish observance and be part of America, the *haredi* Jews (at the time a small minority) said one had to choose one way or the other. These Jews argued for a more contra-acculturationist orthodoxy that took pride in standing out and apart from American culture and Western norms and values.[95] Lubavitchers were in many ways connected to the latter group, like all the other Hasidim who made their new lives in the new world. And as their leader, Menachem Mendel Schneerson at first embraced the idea of standing out and apart from contemporary assimilationist tendencies—as we saw in his call to fund Jewish education and endorse prayer in public schools.

But, unlike the other Hasidim, Lubavitchers would in time also embrace many of the open and the integrationist elements of adaptive Modern Orthodoxy, as they sought language with which to connect with all kinds of assimilated Jews. In doing so, however, they would act as agents provocateurs, people who *seemed* open to modernity and America but only in order to change it, to come down to the level of the lost soul in order to retrieve and redeem it by getting it to repent and return.

♫♫

This was the past and the future into which Menachem Mendel Schneerson inserted himself when he announced a new campaign at a *farbrengen* on 12 Tammuz 5718 (June 30, 1958), the *holiday of redemption* that Lubavitchers celebrate because this was the day Rabbi Yosef Yitzchak had been freed from prison in Russia, enabling him to once again spread the word of ChaBaD. The seventh rebbe now felt secure enough in his position as leader of Lubavitch to break out on his own dramatically; and this he did when he proclaimed a new policy: the years of *Uforatzto*.[96] He began with a commentary based on verse 10 in Numbers 23, from the reading of the Torah for the forthcoming Sabbath: "Who hath counted the dust of Jacob?", a question that refers, according to the traditional exegesis, to the young of the house of Jacob, the children who are compared to the dust of the earth.[97] This led to a discussion of how important it was to focus attention on the youth, on the future of Jewry. They, he explained, were the source of his concern, and they were the object of his campaign. He went on to cite Genesis 28:14, the verse in which the Almighty, who identifies himself as having communicated with Abraham and Isaac, promises their son Jacob, in the famous dream that Jacob has as he is about to leave the Promised Land for what would be the first "Jewish exile," that "your offspring shall be like the dust of the earth and you [i.e., they] shall burst forth [*uforatzto*] to the west, east, north, and to the south." That is to say, Jews would go to the four corners of the earth, and the Lubavitchers would follow them there in order to retrieve them for Judaism and thereby prepare for the impending redemption whose coming, they would explain, was in their hands.

The Rebbe would often refer to this narrative, for he saw in it a message that was relevant to his plan to promote the idea of his young Hasidic followers' leaving their parents' homes and the Lubavitch community to bring the message of Judaism (or ChaBaD's understanding of it) to the world. Thus, he would often repeat a version of the following commentary to his Hasidim: "'And Jacob departed from Beersheba. . . .' The way we think about this in the Torah of Hasidism: Jacob leaves his life in Beersheba, in the Holy Land and goes to a foreign place, but notably *there* in exile in particular does he set up a *bayis neemen*, a faithful Jewish house, with twelve godly tribes [children] and . . . when he goes home with them, he goes with a complete family who are the 'children of Israel.'"[98] The message was transparent: leaving for exile (and for any Hasid, parting from the rebbe is like exile) could bring them to the very place where they could succeed in building up a *bayis neemen*. At the end of days, they would lead the godly tribes they had generated back home to true Judaism, following in the footsteps of the Messiah.

"And," the Rebbe would add, telling them about Jacob, "it was particularly after 'he departed from Beersheba' that he received the blessing of '*uforatzto . . . ,*' noting that boundless blessings would come from this act and because of it 'all the families of the earth shall bless themselves by you and by your offspring.'"[99]

His Hasidim should not doubt they were going far away from home (and not necessarily just in geographic but also in spiritual terms); this was a true exile. He added another more mystical gloss on the concept of the dust of the earth, explaining that when your offspring descend to the level of the dust—when all trample upon them, when they have fallen as low as they can go (*takhtn she'eyn takhtn mimenu*)—there, most especially, the King Messiah will burst forth.[100] This was the world of the second half of the twentieth century. The fact that the Hebrew word *foratsto*, when translated by the mystical process of Gematria in which letters are converted into corresponding numbers, equaled 770, the address on Eastern Parkway from which his call came forth, he added, was a sign of the connection of this Lubavitcher mission with the biblical prophecy.*

He had been thinking about this idea already in 1950, when on December 12, in a letter, he had written that one had to burst forth and "conquer the outside," for failure to do so was what was "holding up the redemption."[101] Now, however, he was the Rebbe and could put this idea into practice; he could make things happen. He could send out *shluchim*.

On what would have been the seventy-eighth birthday of his predecessor, the twelfth of the Hebrew month of Tammuz 5718 (June 30, 1958), about seven years after he took on the mantle of leadership, Menachem Mendel, now firmly established as the Lubavitcher rebbe,

---

* The number and building 770 had taken on a kind of quasi-sacred character, referred to by many followers as "*Bais Rabbeinu Sheb'bavel*," "our rabbi's house in Babylon" (i.e., the Diaspora), because their leader had rarely left its vicinity and it thus shared in his charisma, becoming an easily recognized symbol or iconic representation of his reign.

pressed his policy of *Uforatzto*, "you shall break out." He explained his idea at a *farbrengen* by noting that "in the old days there was a person in every town who would light the street lamps with a flame he carried at the end of a long pole. On the street corners, the lamps waited to be lit. Sometimes, however, the lamps were not as easily accessible. . . . [T]here were lamps in forsaken places. Someone had to light even those lamps so that they would fulfill their purpose and light up the paths of others. Today too, someone must be willing to forgo his or her conveniences and reach out to light even those forsaken lamps. . . ." [102] The objective was to have the *shluchim* transcend and break "all barriers and boundaries" in order to light "even those forsaken lamps" that other Hasidim ignored, and thus spread the word of Judaism and Hasidism, which from his point of view were identical.[103] This was a plan for Lubavitchers to reach out to the Jewishly illiterate, the nearly assimilated, the young, college students, as well as those with barely concealed feelings of religious guilt, those who had second thoughts about the value of secularity and Western society, and light them all with the enthusiasms of Lubavitcher Hasidism. And the people who would do this were the young *temimim* who had not yet set their future, who were in their own period of moratorium.

In a sense, this idea had theological, mystical, and philosophical antecedents in the Rebbe's first address, *Basi L'Gani*. There he had talked about the *Dirah b'tachtonim*, the desire, almost a craving, that the Almighty had to descend to dwell among those furthest from him. This was a transformation of what this idea of *Dirah b'tachtonim* had meant in earlier ChaBaD thinking. There it had been understood as the desire of God to have man surmount his physicality, animal nature, and material being and thus make space for the Divine Presence to enter into him, into this lower form of existence, and hence raise it to a higher level of existence. But the new Lubavitcher rebbe had turned that idea around. It was God who wanted to descend to man's level, to transform that mundane reality into his dwelling place.[104] He did not want to be out there somewhere beyond the mundane world; He wanted to be back here, everywhere, in the mundane world, in even those places where no one imagined He might go. Were the *shluchim* who would go out to meet the Jews who were at their lowest level of Jewish consciousness and involvement and make their homes there where other

Hasidim might never go not emulating this very process? To be sure, they would have to work hard and long to raise those among whom they found themselves, to get them to observe sufficient mitzvahs so as to make it possible for God to dwell among them and hence bring the redemption by purifying and refining the mundane.

But the Lubavitcher rebbe was not completely insulated from the world outside or affected only by Hasidic and mystical ideas. In March 1961, he, like so many other Americans, had heard and was impressed by the new and young president John F. Kennedy's call for a cadre of volunteers to fan out across the globe and join a "Peace Corps."[105] Kennedy had forewarned this "pool of trained men and women," who were "committed to the concept which motivates the Peace Corps," that

> Life in the Peace Corps will not be easy. There will be no salary and allowances will be at a level sufficient only to maintain health and meet basic needs. Men and women will be expected to work and live alongside the nationals of the country in which they are stationed—doing the same work, eating the same food, talking the same language. But if the life will not be easy, it will be rich and satisfying.

The next day, the holiday of Purim in the Jewish calendar, the Rebbe, echoing these sentiments, referred again to his *uforatzto* campaign in a talk to Lubavitchers. "Don't convince yourselves," he told them, "that you can live off the fat of the land and reside in these few blocks . . . [where you have] fresh milk every day and you can shower twice a day and there is no shortage of kosher milk and kosher bread and you can serve God and remain here. Listen! There is a 'desolate land' which is thus far undeveloped spiritually. There are Jews there who don't even know that they lack anything. You had the unearned privilege to be brought up with Torah and Mitzvahs." Then he urged them to go forth from their land of material and spiritual plenty, and stay in those desolate places "for a day, a week, a month, a year, ten years. You won't have nice clothes and a comfortable home? The Jews in the place to which you are going also manage without them. Why should you be better?" And then, in words that would become a credo for Lubavitcher *shluchim*, he concluded, "If you have not used your treasures for this, it must bother you. And if you are not pained, then you are lacking in your love of God, His Torah and Mitzvahs. . . . The love of a Jew applies to a Jew across the world whom you have never seen."[106] The *shluchim* would, in short, be a kind of Jewish peace corps, sent out by the Rebbe.

Later, he would tell his young emissaries that as they prepared to depart for their many destinations: "Before you leave you should sing '*Uforatzto*' with enthusiasm."[107] They had turned the verse into a song that they repeated again and again, like an anthem. The need to sing it with enthusiasm was important and understood by those in his community who at the outset might have been reluctant and even anxious at the thought of young Hasidim going away from the Rebbe's court and community and off to live in places where Jewish life was weak or nonexistent and where few if any observant Jews were to be found. Yet they were to be enthusiastic, for, as they were being told through the story and example of Jacob, in spite of their exile, they would be blessed where they went (and those who sent them would be blessed as well) with Jewish children, who would come home safe and sound. As a reward for their efforts, boundless blessings would come, and "all the families of the earth shall bless themselves by you and by your offspring."

As they went on the mission, moreover, he told them they should keep in mind that wherever they were they would "be living examples of how it is possible" to be observant Jews and Lubavitcher Hasidim, people who study Torah and Hasidism and who bring these to action, observing God's commandments with devotion.[108] He argued that "our Hasidim can be sent into any environment, no matter how strange or hostile, and they maintain themselves within it."[109] This was a radically new view—that observant Jews could be surrounded by unbelievers and the unobservant but would change the environment rather than assimilating into it. He believed this possible based on his own experience of being distant from the heart of Jewish life and yet remaining tied to his Hasidic roots. And he was convinced it was possible because there was a new cultural atmosphere in the modern world that was willing to accept Orthodox Jews in its midst.

In advocating this approach, the Rebbe was distinguishing himself powerfully from most other Hasidim in Brooklyn, and perhaps none more than the Satmars, who were now in nearby Williamsburg. They, under the leadership of their rebbe, Yoel Teitelbaum, argued that

America was impure and destructive of Jewish traditions and religion. and that to protect and preserve their faith and way of life they needed to keep America at a distance, to fight against its values and seductions by convincing their followers that what they had was better, but also by making sure they understood the dangers of the outside world. They created an enclave culture in which it would be difficult for their young to navigate the outside world, keeping them talking in Yiddish and limiting their knowledge of and contact with those radically different from them.

But with his *uforatzto* message, Menachem Mendel Schneerson was taking an opposite approach. He shared the belief that the outside culture was corrosive and seductive. But he was not content to keep it at bay (though they tried to do that in their local Crown Heights neighborhood, where all the outsiders, most of whom were of Caribbean origin, had little if any direct contact with Lubavitchers). He wanted to engage it and change it, driven by the messianic conviction that he and his emissaries could do so. The mandate for that descent to the world outside their Jewish one was explained in a parable he liked to repeat: it was the story of a king who sent his son far away "in order that he should have more delight when the son returned," but who then discovered that the son did not return and instead forgot his royal origins. "The king sent a message to him—but he refused to come back. Then a wise minister discovered the secret of how to make the prince return." That minister therefore "changed his garments and his language, to be like the son. He came close to him, on his level, and brought him back to his father."[110] That was to be the approach of the *shluchim*.

The idea of looking far afield for followers of course did not originate with Menachem Mendel Schneerson and his *uforatzto* message, but the situation in which he found himself surely helped encourage it. As the Lubavitcher leader looked around and saw all the Hasidic courts reestablishing themselves everywhere in Brooklyn, he realized at a certain point that there was no reason to compete for followers in his borough where there were already so many Hasidic groups trying to attract the Orthodox when one could compete for all the Jews in the world. It was an idea that his followers understood, and perhaps no one more so than Chaim Hodakov, the Riga administrator who had by now became his Hasid and one of his closest confidants. Whenever

Hodakov was asked how many Lubavitchers there were in the world, he would reply with a smile, "How many Jews are there in the world?"[111] For Hodakov and his Rebbe, all the Jews in the world, whatever their background and knowledge and wherever they were, would be targets for their message of redemption.

At first this message of redemption was only for his Hasidim. But within a relatively short time, as the emissaries went out and began to establish a presence in places where no one else had, this message would strike a chord among Jews of all sorts who were beginning to be anxious about the Jewish future, about their children, who they thought were being eaten up by the counterculture, among those who were having second thoughts about the secular world and its promise and who perhaps felt guilty that they had left behind the traditions of their parents or grandparents and those of the many who had died in the Holocaust. And all this happened on the eve of what would become a time of a religious reawakening in America, a time when the young would seek to find meaning in their lives and ultimate purpose.

ﬗ

The sending of emissaries as we have noted, had a long history in ChaBaD, beginning in earnest with the fifth rebbe and used extensively by the sixth, particularly in Russia but also in the United States. They had taken the Temimim yeshiva students and sent them as emissaries to other Hasidic communities and other parts of the traditional world to spread the word of ChaBaD. Indeed, Rabbi Yosef Yitzchak had even sent his two sons-in-law from New York to France in 1947 as emissaries to his Hasidim, many of them Soviet refugees, to show them he had not forgotten or abandoned them.

The new rebbe understood, as had his two predecessors, the potential inherent in a young religious avant-garde that had been educated, prepared, and organized from an early age in a total institution like a yeshiva. But unlike those earlier rebbes, the seventh rebbe would send his young Hasidim (and their wives) as emissaries to the four corners of the globe to retrieve the assimilated and the young who had *never* learned what it meant to be a Jew. *His* emissaries would go not just to the converted or the already traditionally religious. Nor would they act simply "as interpreters and popularizers of the obscure discourse of the *Rebbe,*" as had emissaries of earlier Lubavitcher leaders.[112] His *shluchim* would be sent to those who were nearly lost in the depths of the spiritual dust, communicating teachings of inspiration and Judaism and thereby try to kindle the light of their Judaism and thus bring them back to observance, so that the Messiah could at last come. They would do it by being model Hasidim whose enthusiasm was instructive and infectious. That was what it meant for this Rebbe to spread the wellsprings.

He would push his *shluchim* with the enthusiasm of a convert, driven perhaps by the overflow of energy that a man who has changed the course of his life after going through crisis feels. And they would respond with the corresponding energy that they felt, as part of a movement that had discovered a new meaning for its existence and a new life after what had seemed to be a collective crisis. Chased from their historic origins in the Old World, they were now breaking old boundaries with a renewed sense of mission in this new one. It would take some doing to get all the Lubavitchers to make their Rebbe's fire for this campaign their own and become the new kind of *shluchim* the Rebbe was shaping, who would be willing to leave the core community near the Rebbe in Brooklyn and their parents and settle in places where they would be all on their own.[113] But when in time they caught the enthusiasm of the project, they would see to it that the rest of Jewry, and indeed the world, became aware of it.

1

A group photo of about three thousand *shluchim* in front of 770 Eastern Parkway, the headquarters of the ChaBaD Lubavitchers, on the occasion of the 2008 *kinus*. © TheRebbe.org/Chabad.org.

2

Mendel Schneerson in his university student days. © TheRebbe.org/Chabad.org.

3
Mendel Schneerson on holiday, circa 1933. Courtesy of Library of Agudas Chassidei Chabad/ TheRebbe.org.

4
DovBer (Barry) Gourary on his bar mitzvah, February 18, 1936. On the bar mitzvah boy's right is his grandfather, Rabbi Yosef Yitzchak Schneersohn, the sixth Lubavitcher rebbe, on whose right sits Barry's father, Rabbi Shmaryahu Gourary. © The Rebbe.org/Chabad.org.

5
Chaya Moussia Schneerson
on her wedding day,
November 1928.
© TheRebbe.org/Chabad.org.

6
Mendel Schneerson
in the week following
his wedding.
© TheRebbe.org/
Chabad.org.

7

Mendel Horensztajn, husband of Sheina
Schneersohn, youngest daughter of Rabbi
Yosef Yitzchak, and brother-in-law of
Mendel Schneerson.

8

Arrival of Rabbi Yosef Yitzchak, the sixth
Lubavitcher rebbe, for his first visit to
New York in 1929, flanked on his right by
Shmaryahu Gourary, his eldest son-in-law,
and on his left by Berel Chaskind, the future
father-in-law of Barry Gourary.
© TheRebbe.org/Chabad.org.

9
Nechama Dina Schneersohn,
the wife of Rabbi Yosef Yitzchak
and mother of Moussia
Schneerson. Authors' collection.

10
Rabbi Yosef Yitzchak, the sixth Lubavitcher rebbe, after settling
in New York, flanked on his right by his elder son-in-law Shmaryahu
Gourary and on his left by his younger son-in-law Mendel Schneerson.
From the Pini Dunner Image Collection.

11
Moussia Schneerson, U.S.
naturalization photograph.

12
Shmaryahu Gourary. © TheRebbe.org/Chabad.org.

13
The house at 1304 President Street, home of the seventh
Lubavitcher rebbe and rebbetzin. Authors' collection.

14
Envelope from
"Eng[ineer]
M. Schneerson,"
from Paris.
© TheRebbe.org/
Chabad.org.

15
The new seventh Lubavitcher rebbe, Rabbi Menachem
Mendel Schneerson. © TheRebbe.org/Chabad.org.

16
Rabbi Menachem Mendel carrying a bag filled with *pidyones* on his way to the *ohel* and the grave of his predecessor. © TheRebbe.org/ Chabad.org.

17
Barry Gourary with his Mother, Chana Gourary, eldest daughter of the sixth Lubavitcher rebbe. Authors' collection.

18

Entrance to Lubavitcher yeshiva on Eastern Parkway, festooned with yellow Messiah flags and a large poster, 2009.

19

Bus shelter sign, Crown Heights, during the week of the *kinus shluchim,* 2007. Authors' collection.

20

Lubavitchers writing notes or *pidyones* to be placed on the *tsiyen* of the Rebbe
at Old Montefiore Cemetery in Queens, New York, 2007. Authors' collection.

Standing in line to enter the *ohel*, Gimmel Tammuz 2007. Authors' collection.

22

Inside the *ohel* at the *tsiyen*, the gravestones of the sixth and seventh Lubavitcher rebbes, covered in *pidyones*, 2009. Authors' collection.

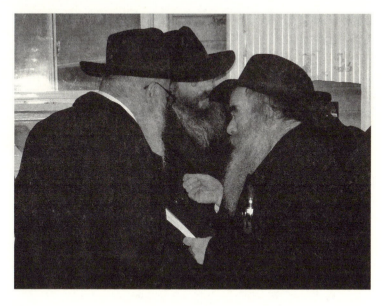

23

Avremel Shemtov on right, speaking with other Lubavitchers at the chapel near the *ohel*, 2007. Authors' collection.

24

Kingston Avenue, Crown Heights, 2009. Note the sign welcoming the Messiah.

25

Inside 770 Eastern Parkway, Chanukah, 2008. The words
over the menorah are "Long Live our Master, our Teacher,
and Our Rabbi, the King Messiah, forever and ever."
Authors' collection.

פ"נ

הבחור התמים יר"א
מגזע אראלים ותרשישים
המהרש"ל, החכם צבי,
והצדיקים הק' מזלאטשוב, ליזענסק, ראפשיץ,
צאנז, שר שלום מבעלז, פרימישלאן נבג"מ

זכה לקירוב נפלא ואבהי
מכ"ק אדמו"ר רוח אפינו משיח ה' שליט"א
ונתחנך על ברכיו
זלה"בהל"ח
מהרבנית הצדקנית
מרת חי' מושקא ז"ל ע"ה
שקד באהלה של תורה
ועסק במסירות ובזריזות בהמבצעים

הקדוש אהרן יוסף הי"ד
בנו בכורו של
יבדל לחיים טובים ארוכים
הרה"ת משב"ק
ר' חנניה, סיני דוד שליט"א

הלברשטם

נהרג על קידוש השם בדמי ימיו
בן ט"ז שנה
כ"ג אדר
ה' אלפים תבוא שעת נקמת דמי ליצירה
ת' נ' צ' ב' ה'

26

The gravestone of Ari Halberstam, a young boy killed by an Islamist in New York. The inscription describes him as one who "merited wondrous and fatherly intimacy from the holy and honorable, our master, our teacher and our rabbi, the breath of our lives, the Messiah of God, may he live many long years, amen." Authors' collection.

27

The place of the missing cornerstone at the synagogue adjoining 770 Eastern Parkway. The cornerstone was removed by those who objected to the words "of blessed memory" that had followed the name of Rabbi Menachem Mendel. Inset: the missing cornerstone, with "of blessed memory" scratched out. Authors' collection.

CHAPTER 6

On a Mission from the Rebbe in Life

〰〰

At first, Menachem Mendel Schneerson appeared to the general public mostly as a dynamic but largely parochial leader. When news of his activities occasionally reached the general press (commonly buried in the local New York section) and hence the population at large, it mainly focused on celebrations of the Lubavitcher festivals—the commemoration of a former rebbe's release from imprisonment or the celebration of a *yarzheit*.[1] In America in the 1950s, the activities of Hasidim and their leaders were not of concern to very many people outside the boundaries of Jewish Orthodoxy. Here, as indeed in the new state of Israel, the assumption was that these sorts of Jews were relics of the past, destined to fade away with time.

By 1962, however, he had begun to make a name for himself in the larger Jewish community in America, when his written call for additional aid for parochial schools from the government was printed and reprinted in Jewish publications, as was as well his public objection to the newly instituted U.S. Supreme Court ban on school prayer.[2] Taking a very public position so at odds with the one most American Jews embraced made him stand out, not only in America but also from the rank and file of Jewry; that *was* news.

As he established his leadership over Lubavitch and set the direction it would take, Menachem Mendel Schneerson, who knew well the history of his movement, understood that the world he inhabited was altogether different from the one in which his immediate predecessors had lived and led their Hasidim. Theirs was a world in which Jews were chased and persecuted, in which the move out of the orbit of Hasidism and tradition seemed to be absolute for those who chose it. Theirs was a world filled with adversaries, conflict, and despair—to which the coming of the Messiah was a solution.

In contrast to the past, the world into which the seventh rebbe and his generation were taking Lubavitch was one in which society was extraordinarily open to the Jews, where secular society did not see itself as ineluctably antagonistic to religion, and where persecution was limited to those caught behind the Iron Curtain (and even that would end in time). In America and the West, the risks were not that Jews would be chased to their death or that they would despair, but rather that they would be embraced and loved to death, that they would be so accepted and happy that they would assimilate and become indistinguishable from the cultures in which they found themselves. This was a world in which being Jewish might become so vague and amorphous as to lose all distinctiveness. Even in the Soviet Union, where Jews might not be happy, there would also be significant assimilation.

The new Rebbe saw all this and was at first flummoxed by it. In 1964 he wrote that "the house of Israel is on fire (May God have mercy), and the young generation, as things now stand, is largely trapped. You are surely not unaware of the 'dry' statistics of intermarriage and assimilation in this country [the United States] and the subject is similar in other countries."[3]

Yet as disconcerting as this reality might be at first glance, Menachem Mendel understood that it was possible for a Jew to move into the outside world, to leave behind tribal Jewish ties, to aspire to a career and a life far from the precincts of Jewish tradition and practice, to become an acculturated cosmopolitan citizen of the world—and yet be retrieved and redeemed. He knew, moreover, that some Jews were able to stand with a foot in both the precincts of religious observance and the general culture, as they had done in the Hildesheimer Seminary in Berlin and as many were doing in the growing number of Modern Orthodox day schools of America, some in his own Crown Heights, Brooklyn, neighborhood.* He believed that this journey away

---

*The Crown Heights yeshiva had a coed student body and offered secular studies along with Jewish ones. Even the Crown Heights Mesivta, although only a boys' school, offered secular studies in the afternoon. The state of New York required secular studies and that students pass state Regents exams, so all schools had some sort of secular studies.

from parochial Jewish identity, belonging, and practice was not irreversible or permanent. One could be made to abandon those aspirations, to counter-acculturate and turn back to the most parochial of Jewish identities, to escape the seductions of contemporary culture and embrace the tradition and old practices even more powerfully. He knew that being and looking traditional in America—even looking like a Hasid—could be acceptable, even laudable. He understood that a Jew could now choose to be publicly religious even in a so-called secular environment.[4] He knew all this because he had experienced it himself.

Yet while he had come back on his own (and not from such a great cultural distance as those he would try to retrieve), forced by destiny and history, as well as by mystical forces that he was still figuring out and that placed on his shoulders the mantle of leadership and showed him the way, he believed that now he had to burst the boundaries of the past, to the four corners of the world, to the farthest margins of Jewish life to bring back others. No one was beyond the pale or out of reach.

The tool for this outreach would be, as we already know, his emissaries, young Lubavitcher men *and* women (going as couples), who were his strongest backers. These young people who learned to share his messianic beliefs, whom he could shape and make living instruments of his vision, would become an enthusiastic cadre of followers. He urged them to reach into themselves and be publicly and proudly Jewish in places where others were not, and to teach others to share his beliefs and carry out the practices he was convinced were vital. They would do this even among and ultimately with those Jews who were completely ignorant of what it meant to be Jewish. By their example and enthusiasm, they would light fires of redemption and offer religious and cultural counter-seductions that would bring back all the prodigal children. They could change and "purify" the world and the mundane and prepare the way for the Messiah as no one had done before

Unlike the fifth and sixth rebbes, who had remained within the cocoon of Lubavitch even when they were on the run, this Rebbe had been on the periphery. While both Rabbi Shalom DovBer and his son, Rabbi Yosef Yitzchak, remained far more distant from those who inhabited the world beyond their own and could only imagine it through the prism of their sheltered experience, this new Rebbe had firsthand knowledge. Because of their far more sheltered and insular situation, the previous two rebbes "could not see the future" as it was, only as they wanted it to be.[5] Menachem Mendel, however, could see the future because he had been living in it. He had been in Montparnasse and he had been in Berlin, where the prodigal sons and daughters were living. And he knew how to recognize them still, even in post–Second World War America, Europe, and Israel.

Someone who has forever lived entirely within a single closed system or culture is generally unlikely to be the instrument of change. Rather, his thinking is likely to remain loyal to what is the accepted wisdom and way of acting. One who comes from the outside, on the other hand, will often radically alter the conventional.[6] Menachem Mendel Schneerson was neither the former nor the latter. He was instead someone who was a bit of both. Accordingly, he would become an innovator, but one who always used the language and instruments of what appeared to be traditional ChaBaD Lubavitcher thinking and practice. So while he used emissaries as had his predecessors, he sent them on a new kind of mission and to places Hasidim had never gone. While he accepted the Lubavitcher idea of messianism and redemption as coming from the lower realms (*tachtonim*), he refashioned it so that it would be presented in a thoroughly contemporary mode.

Like everyone at the time, the new Rebbe watched young people in the United States get involved and excited by the presidential campaign for John F. Kennedy (both he and his wife were reading the daily papers) and as we have said saw them fired up by his exciting new idea of a peace corps that would send out devoted volunteers throughout the world to work "in areas like education, youth outreach and community development"; later he saw them become engaged by the civil rights struggle and campaigns for racial equality and witnessed their peace campaigns against the Vietnam War.[7] Could his *shluchim* not draw on the same youthful enthusiasms and work in parallel fashion, but for a far more "important" cause? Witnessing the young people of this generation bursting the bonds of the conventional past in order to shape history and society, persuading their peers to join them, he realized that his young Lubavitcher *shluchim* could do no less in a *campaign* on which their new leader would send them.

The first of these would be a "mitzvah campaign." Mitzvahs, acts of Jewish observance, rather than votes, were what he sought to inspire and accumulate. Rabbi Menachem Mendel followed the founder of the ChaBaD dynasty, Schneur Zalman, in sharing the rather radical view among Hasidim that the deed itself is what counts, not the motivation.[8] He shared the belief as well, as had the Miteler Rebbe, Dovber, in "the messianic power" of mitzvahs, which he held were a kind of "practical action" that enabled communication with God and whose accumulated performance resulted in a mystical connection with the infinite that went "beyond meaning."[9] Convinced of these acts' capacity to change, purify, repair, and "conquer" the world, the seventh rebbe added to this doctrine the argument that these "physical, mundane actions directed towards G-d [sic] represent the acme of religious endeavor."[10] Moreover, he argued that, in contradistinction to the Hasidic doctrines that asserted that spiritual ascent was best achieved by "turning one's back upon the world [and] negating the material dimensions of existence," for the ordinary person, mitzvahs—material, physical acts—had the capacity to "bring man to the greatest spiritual heights, beyond the reach of what are generally considered more spiritual forms of worship."[11] He would therefore try to get the Jews of his day to enhance their spiritual lives by observing and carrying out such physical and practical Jewish acts. And he could articulate this all in the terminology of America and of his times (to keep it simple): Hence a mitzvah campaign.

The idea of sending young Lubavitchers away from the protected cultural preserve of the ChaBaD enclave on a "universal mission," but at a grassroots level, as we have previously noted, was not immediately embraced by their parents.[12] They worried that their children would be lost to them, subject to acculturation in the places of their posting, becoming victims of religious erosion or even worn down by the seemingly impossible task of turning contemporary Jewry back to Jewish observance.

Besides encouraging and nurturing emissaries, the Rebbe and his associates could also "punish" those who showed their lack of faith and declined the role after being selected. Thus, for example, when early in the campaign the parents of a young man, asking about how long and where he would be sent, implored the Rebbe "not to send their son on a mission," they were given to understand that no one would be "compelled" to go but that this sort of reluctance was "a breach of discipline" by someone who was considered one his troops.[13]

"I thought he was *my* soldier," the Rebbe wrote to the parents, "and that I could assign him. . . . However it emerges that before he makes a decision, he must listen to his mother and his family. Obviously, this is not the behavior of a soldier—to inquire about conditions and time periods and then to ask his family's opinions of the matter."[14]

The Previous Rebbe, Yosef Yitzchak, had also been "devoted to the general cause of strengthening Judaism" and had sent out emissaries to many who "had become completely estranged from Judaism."[15] Not only had he reached into the Soviet Union but also back into Europe after 1945 and to Morocco.[16] And he had even sent out two emissaries, Shlomo Carlebach and Zalman Schachter (who would become famous after they left Lubavitch), to "the universities."[17] The two men had come for *farbrengen* on the Lubavitcher celebration of 19 Kislev. Carlebach and Schachter were standing outside the Rebbe's office that day in December 1949, a few days before Hanukkah, singing some tunes. The Rebbe Yosef Yitzchak was quite ill by this time and so remained closeted in his office for much of the time, where only a few Hasidim at a time would be allowed in to be with him.

As Schachter tells it: "They didn't allow everyone to come into the *farbrengen* because the Rebbe was frail. We would stand outside the door and sing *niggunim* [melodies], and sometimes the Rebbe's secretary would come and would open the door and call certain people to come in."

Berel Chaskind, acting at the request of the Rebbe, called Shlomo and Zalman in.[18]

We approached the Rebbe's table and the Rebbe gave a big *lekhayim* [toast to life], and he said, it would be "*Keday ir zolt onheybn forn tsu colleges.*" [It would be worthwhile for you to start visiting the colleges.] He suggested we start with Brandeis, and offered us a little bottle of schnapps that was sitting on his table to take along with us. That was it.

But, he hadn't told us what to do. So, we decided to start on Hanukkah and make a tour of the Boston colleges (because I lived in Massachusetts), starting with Brandeis, and going on to Boston University, and the others.

I had collected from the *shul* [in Fall River, where Schachter was serving as a pulpit rabbi] 13 pairs of *tefillin* that people had dropped off because no one was using them. I rehabilitated them. I had some translations I'd made of the Rebbe's teachings. I had one of the first tape recorders. They were big reel to reel. . . . I recorded several hours of Hasidic music.

It was the middle of the week, Hanukkah. It was snowing when we arrived, and we had to *shlep* the accordion, tape reorder, *tefillin*, and boxes of papers all the way up the slippery steps going up to "the castle," a cafe at Brandeis where a dance was in progress. The lights were out. A guy with spotlights was hitting couples in the dark and a jukebox was playing. The two of us come in, the spotlight hits us. Pretty soon we put the lights on in the corner. The dance stopped. I set up the tape recorder to play Hasidic music, Shlomo starts to tell stories on one side, and I'm assisting, bringing people to Shlomo. First, they listened to the music, and then they started to ask questions.

That first night at Brandeis, the new Jewish-sponsored university that at the time was barely a year old, was a big success; the students stayed with them until the early hours of the morning. Zalman made a deal: anyone who learned to put on the tefillin and take them off three times would get to keep one. "We gave out 13 pair, all we had."

𝆑𝆑𝆑

Clearly America, and especially its young people, were ready for this sort of Jewish outreach. But it would fall to the seventh rebbe who with energy unmatched by those who came before him to seize upon the opportunities that emissaries like Carlebach and Schachter saw. He was the leader who would enlist "an army" of his followers, a new type of *shluchim* who would find a postwar population and atmosphere that would in time make outreach the best-known activity of his reign.

Beginning in the late 1960s, particularly after the Six-Days War in 1967, and gaining traction in the next decade, this campaign sought to insert traditional Jewish religious behavior and more specifically concrete mitzvahs into the public square and onto the Jewish agenda. The importance of transforming the individual was at the core of every campaign. Rather than overwhelming the target population with the full range and complexity of Jewish practice and tradition, the initial goal appeared first simply to raise Jewish awareness that observances could have spiritual and cosmic importance. Thus, instead of reminding Jews of the need to observe 613 mitzvahs along with their myriad details that, according to Jewish tradition, were mandatory, the Rebbe chose to focus on ten concrete acts, a kind of echo of the Ten Commandments of which everyone had heard. By doing these acts, the people would begin the process of allowing God to be revealed in the reality of the physical world and in their lives.[19]

It would also, as we discuss in greater detail later, serve as an alternative to what seemed to be happening in Israel, where military victories by the Israel Defense Forces who had regained the Temple Mount in Jerusalem and all of the biblical territories appeared to have taken the initiative in Jewish messianic dreams. They, the armies of the secular Zionist state, seemed again to be bringing the messianic age and now the return to Jerusalem. The Rebbe needed to reclaim the advantage. To prove his point, he initiated his massive outreach effort to persuade believers and unbelievers that Lubavitchers, and not the Zionist state of Israel, would lead to the end of history. He aimed to do that everywhere—even in Israel.

Ten mitzvahs was easy, doable, and a simple number to remember. But his ten were not the famous ones. His included lighting Sabbath candles by all females over the age of three, getting males over the age of thirteen (bar mitzvah) to don tefillin, getting mezuzahs on every doorway in a Jewish home, some daily study of Torah (which would include ChaBaD Hasidic texts), giving charity, owning holy Jewish books (including those by ChaBaD authors), observing Jewish dietary laws (*kashres*), loving one's fellow as oneself, getting a Jewish education, and observing the ritual laws of "family purity," meaning exerting control over sexual relations among the married, including getting women to use the *mikveh* or ritual bath.[20] These mitzvahs had to be made palatable, and some of them fared better than others in the public square. Several became signature practices of Lubavitch.

We have already suggested that a conviction of the imminence of the messianic redemption, the atmosphere of youthful activism, evidence of other campaigns, a sense of urgency about Jewish youth who were on the verge of assimilation, with growing intermarriage rates and widespread Jewish illiteracy, played key roles in the campaign's timing. In an age when most of the "People of the Book" could no longer read that book or any of the commentaries on it in their original Hebrew or even cared to do so, the Lubavitcher Rebbe decided a clear ten-step program for Jewish revival would work. What began as the *Uforatzto* initiative easily morphed into the mitzvah campaign. It would bridge the period of rebellion, when the conservative stability of the immediate postwar years had given way to a growing counterculture that challenged many of the assumptions of the previous decades, and last into the next period of religious revival and returning conservatism.

At the outset, this campaign and the precursor outreach efforts sought to counteract the new antinomianism that reigned supreme in the era of sex, drugs, and rock-and-roll when young people regarded the establishment as the enemy. Religion was part of that establishment, and most of the young wanted no part of it. Lubavitchers, who with their beards and black hats did not look or seem to be part of the establishment, tried to coax them back. They would go to those places where they believed the challenge was greatest: the college campuses.

Consider the following example. At Brandeis University in the mid-1960s, the school sponsored by Jews and with a large number of them in the student body, a campus known at the time for its radicalism, where among others the future counterculture hero Abbie Hoffman and students who shared his willingness to challenge conventions were undergraduates, several Lubavitchers came for the weekend, guests of the Hillel campus group.[21] The main Lubavitcher speaker, reputed to be an intellectual and one who valued higher education (unlike so many other Hasidim, whose conservatism, cultural insularity, and anti-college stands were by now well known), was willing to come to this hot bed of the counterculture to speak at a Friday night forum and again at Saturday morning lunch about general matters of religious openness and the importance of allowing all ideas, including Jewish ones, a voice in the university. The turnout was good if not great, because at this time in the mid sixties a Hasid taking such an unusual stand at Brandeis was a curiosity that went against type.

By Saturday afternoon, as twilight and the conclusion of the Sabbath neared, his message, however, would change. Gathering in the lobby of the anthropology building, where primitive masks and totems were on permanent display, students and Lubavitchers sat around several long tables that had been set up for the mystical closing meal of the Sabbath. As the evening gave way to night and he was joined by dozens of other Lubavitchers in the Boston area who, with the end of Sabbath and its restrictions on travel, had driven in to the campus for the occasion and joined the crowd, there was a lot of singing of Hasidic melodies and at last a big circle during which the remaining students and the Hasidim all danced rather incongruously around the pagan masks and totems, singing praises to God and repeating over and over the melody of *uforatzto* that the Lubavitchers taught them.

Most of the Brandeis students had by the close of the Sabbath left for the Saturday night activities that were so much a part of campus life. The Lubavitchers surrounded the few remaining students whose interest had been sufficiently piqued to stay. Now they lowered the lights and recited the *havdalah*, the separation ceremony over a candle and wine by which they formally ended the Sabbath and segued into the numinous *melave-malke* gathering with which Sabbath was ushered out and the week inaugurated. In their remarks, the Lubavitchers, now outnumbering the students, had changed their tune; speaker after speaker urged those who had stayed to give up the heresies they were certain they had been learning in college and come "home" to our Judaism and hasten the day of redemption. Even though he had been a university student himself in his earlier life, now Menachem Mendel Schneerson had "decided that America's college campuses would have a detrimental effect" on Jewish life.[22]

Such visits, just beginning in those years, would become more frequent and would be repeated with greater subtlety on many campuses and later wherever students and young people congregated. Students, separated from their parents, homes, and communities of origin, living on campus in a liminal period of becoming, were a perfect target audience for initiating change, and Lubavitchers understood that. The *shluchim* would try to convince them to change, to become like them; but until the change came, they would accept them as they were. Ultimately these emissaries of the Rebbe would become a permanent presence on or near the campuses, building over 250 ChaBaD Houses into which they invited students and others, hoping to provide them an alternative Jewish home where the Lubavitcher couple would be like parents or older siblings and with their children would represent a kind of model Jewish family with which visitors could share a warm environment, Sabbath meals, ideas, and a Jewish life, without a commitment in advance to total Jewish observance. They would also often offer a *lekhayim*, sanctification of life carried out over drinks, where the alcohol flowed freely. Young college students could thus mix the excesses of liquor (always a campus pleasure) with the excuses of religion in an atmosphere of camaraderie and friendship that the *shaliach* and the others in the ChaBaD House provided. This was often an irresitble draw for those searching for a haven from the insecurities of adolescence and the loneliness they might have felt on campus.

The goal, as the Rebbe would put it on Hanukkah in 1986, was that every ChaBaD House would be a Jewish home and every Jewish home "a place worthy to be a Chabad House."[23] Judaism and ChaBaD constituted a single indivisible whole. That meant that in his mind, his brand of Hasidism was not a variant of Judaism; it aspired to be the very essence of Judaism. This approach was by no means limited to America.

In Western Europe, although the tensions of the cold war would rise and ebb, the Common Market, established in 1956, had led to a society that in many ways emulated the American model of coexistence among individual states, allowing for prosperity and peace. Quite surprisingly, Western Europe achieved "political and social stability by the mid-twentieth century after two great, destructive wars and the intervening upheaval."[24] Nevertheless, or perhaps because of this stability, student uprisings and culture in the late 1960s in France, Italy, and Germany were not altogether unlike those in the United States. The year 1968, when those whom François Truffaut at the time characterized as the daughters "and sons of the bourgeoisie" rebelled and protested against everything, was a wild year on both sides of the Atlantic.[25] There developed in the European Union a population that would be no less receptive to the Lubavitchers' campaigns than those in America. In these countries, peace, increasing prosperity, and security permitted people of all ages to think about matters other than their fears and allowed their children to extend their youth, just as their counterparts in America were doing. Lubavitchers would approach them in the same way they had their American peers. In Europe, Jewish assimilation was no less the case than in America. Hence the Lubavitcher Mitzvah Campaign could and would be launched as an international effort. Moreover, since the young of these societies were on the move, the Lubavitchers would follow after them—even reaching the extreme of the extreme, whether in Katmandu, Nepal, or in outposts in the Far East as well as in South America, Australia, Alaska, or other places where young Jewish trekkers, particularly Israeli youth who in their post-army-service adventure trips around the globe, would travel. These young adventurers would often turn up at ChaBaD looking to rendezvous with friends and peers, often at Passover time, and be treated to a seder (none larger than in Katmandu). Far from home, Lubavitchers would be welcoming, offer a no-strings-attached chance to observe Judaism ChaBaD-style—an offer many found easy to accept.

But not only adventurers and students found their ways to ChaBaD. By the last twenty years of the century, when a backlash against the excesses of the counterculture took hold, and as the rebels of the sixties aged, finally moved into their adulthood and careers, and began their own families, many from the liberal era of the counterculture found refuge in religion. At the same time, fundamentalist variants of religion resurfaced. Led by new Christian fundamentalists, this resurgent religion often spoke to the needs of those who had been disappointed by the unfulfilled promise or emotional letdown of the radical counterculture. Often those who had in their youth been radicals against religion began to take it up in their middle-years. At the other extreme, so-called "New Age" religion and spirituality, an open exploration of faith and belief, also captured the imagination of many, allowing people to either explore religious roots they thought had long been torn out or establish new connections to ancient or novel religious practices. From studying kabbalah to using crystals or practicing feng shui, these New Agers turned religion into a kind of therapy. What both extremes shared was a willingness to be public and assertive about their religion and to take their places in the public square. This fit perfectly with what the Rebbe had urged his *shluchim* to encourage, and it would create a place where Lubavitch could increasingly insert itself and its public form of Jewish practice and identity.

♫♫♫

In the late seventies and early eighties, as the counterculture receded, the Mitzvah Campaign did not. The Rebbe and his emissaries created a mitzvah tank corps to further his campaign. The tanks (really caravans and mobile homes emblazoned with a variety of Lubavitcher logos and slogans), which the Rebbe believed would be more successful than the Israeli army tanks in their wars in bringing about the messianic age, traveled everywhere. Menachem Mendel Schneerson wanted an alternative army to the Zionist one, one that did not move by fire-power but was driven by spiritual power, one that he commanded and which brought not destruction before victory but mitzvahs before redemption.

On Hanukkah of 1980, the Rebbe commissioned a local artist, Michoel Schwartz (with whom he had worked in 1944 on a logo for the Merkos L'Inyunei Chinuch publishing house), to create an insignia for the newly formed "*Tzivos Hashem*" (Army of God). This boys' organization was to march against assimilation under military banners and symbols that, as art historian Maya Katz notes, created "a coat of arms reminiscent of the national emblem in Israel." The Rebbe insisted the emblem "should be inked solid blue and red, and the symbols of the sun and the moon should be removed because of their association with idolatry in the Talmud."[26] This army would be an instrument of God, working to get people to observe mitzvahs, and unlike the Israeli one, would bring true Jewish final victory.

Over the years the religious Zionist and Lubavitcher version of what was messianic and what was not would blur. For the former, a return of Jewish sovereignty to the Biblical homeland and Jewish settlement there were the signs of the approach of the Messiah , while for ChaBaD the return of Jews to mitzvah observance would be the key signal. Of course, to the Rebbe the victories in Israel and the settlements were proof his activities were working. For him it was critical to persuade his followers and the world that *his* troops and *his* ideas were the crucial elements in the triumph of the Jews over their adversaries, and that they alone were bringing the Messiah.

℈℈℈

The Rebbe's placement of his *shluchim* all over the world also coincided with a change in the condition of Orthodoxy. This Jewry that in the immediate aftermath of the Holocaust had been quiet and insular had gradually become more and more engaged with the modern world. Orthodox Jews—especially those who called themselves "modern"— had reconstituted themselves and felt triumphalist about their capacity to do anything they wanted in the modern world. They traveled everywhere, and ChaBaD was often there to meet them and share their sense of being able to do more than simply survive modernity. Lubavitchers provided these Orthodox Jews with places and a support system for the effort to be Jewishly observant everywhere. They helped travelers and those who found themselves far from home to get kosher food and find Jewish services everywhere in the world (some wags even joked that there would be a ChaBaD *shaliach* on the moon, if Jews started to travel there). This, of course, tied this peripatetic Jewry increasingly to Lubavitchers and made them view the *shluchim* positively, in the process raising their Rebbe in their estimation.[27]

During each subsequent decade, Lubavitchers, under the direction of their Rebbe, would continually adapt to the changes that went on in society, and sometimes they even seemed to anticipate them. The matter of women in Judaism was one of these.* As the Rebbe explained often, the Israelites had been redeemed from Egypt, the Talmud (B.T.

---

* Indeed, in 1953 the new Rebbe had already organized a Lubavitch women's organization. In a marked departure from an entrenched tendency to limit high-level Torah education to men and boys, he addressed his teachings equally to both genders, maintaining that women share the obligation to study and master the esoterica of Torah and Hasidism. When he would later send a young married couple out to the front lines of his war on assimilation, he expected the wife to wage the battle alongside the husband, reaching out to fellow Jews and reintroducing them to their heritage. See http://www.chabad.org/therebbe/timeline_cdo/aid/62170/jewish/1953-Chassidic-Feminism.htm (accessed April 6, 2008). Ada Rapoport-Albert demonstrates that concern for the education of women dates from the 1930s and Rabbi Yosef Yitzchak. See her article, "The Emergence of a Female Constituency in Twentieth Century Habad Hasidism," in *Studies in the History and Culture of East European Jewry Dedicated to Immanuel Etkes*, ed. David Assaf, Ada Rapoport-Albert, Israel Bartal, and Shmuel Feiner (Jerusalem: Shazar Institute, 2009). See also B. J. Morris, *Lubavitcher Women in America* (Albany: SUNY Press, 1988). In 1952 (Menachem Mendel Schneerson, *Hisvadus 5712* vol. 1, p. 307), he reiterated publicly the ruling of Rabbi Schneur Zalman (*Shulkhan Arukh HaRav, Orakh Khayim*, §271: 2) that in certain situations women

Sotah 11a) asserted, because of righteous women who lived in that generation; so too women would be essential to the redemption to come.[28] Among the emissaries, the women would in many ways be even more the instruments of change than their husbands, as they shaped the character of life inside the ChaBaD Houses and pre-schools, which they often directed. Indeed, Menachem Mendel had understood—perhaps because his wife, Moussia, had been such an independent woman and so assertive in her youth—that women could and would be important to the Lubavitcher message and mission. Already in 1947 while in Paris he had tried to see to it that the education Lubavitcher girls received was organized and developed.[29] Indeed, during the reign of Rabbi Yosef Yitzchak, education for women was considered important.[30]

The matter of women and their role in Judaism continued to be of great concern to Menachem Mendel. In the United States the new feminist movement began as an outgrowth of the civil rights struggle. Perhaps the publication of Betty Friedan's *The Feminine Mystique* in 1963 and the presidential executive order in 1967 that prohibited federal agencies to discriminate on the basis of gender might be pointed to as key markers of its start.[31] By the start of the next decade, with the emergence of *Ms.* magazine in 1971 and the effort to pass an equal rights amendment in 1972, the idea of women's rights and prerogatives was firmly part of the consciousness of America. Jewish women, who were among the leaders of the movement, soon applied the principles of feminism to Judaism. As part of that, they sought a greater role in public Jewish life, in the synagogue, and in Torah study. In 1972, twenty-six-year-old Sally Preisand was ordained the first female rabbi by the Reform movement. Soon other movements would follow.

Orthodox Jewry seemed to be far more reluctant to embrace feminism, not knowing exactly how to do so. Yet the fact was that in some ways, females had already been more empowered in Orthodoxy of the twentieth century than they had in all the preceding years. In America, Jewish day schools were following the lead of institutions like the Maimonides School in Boston (founded by Rabbi Joseph B. Soloveitchik and his wife Tanya) or the Flatbush Yeshiva and Ramaz

---

could recite *Kiddush* (the sanctification over wine) on behalf of men. See also Eldad Weil, "Tekhilata shel Tekufat Nashim," *Akdamot* 22 (Nissan 2009): 61–85.

School in New York that taught girls the same Torah studies it taught the boys. In ChaBaD, through the Beth Rivkah and Beth Chana schools, girls had been receiving a Torah education, albeit not identical to the boys', since at least the time Menachem Mendel came to the United States.[32]

As Orthodox women became better educated Jews and in the cultural atmosphere of American feminism, they unsurprisingly began to seek a greater role in public Jewish life. While not as radical as the expectations and desires of women from more progressive movements, the Orthodox nevertheless began to demand more than their mothers and grandmothers. The Rebbe understood this desire and tried to demonstrate his willingness to respond to these wishes, at times even before they were articulated. In 1974, as part of his campaign of outreach, he urged even unmarried girls to take up the observance of lighting Sabbath candles, although in typical fashion for him claiming it was really not a radical innovation but only the spreading of a custom that was already extant in some communities.[33] And of course, women served as emissaries in his outreach program—so much so that the Rebbe made it a practice to address them separately—and ultimately the women would have their own *kinus shluchos* gatherings to discuss strategy and the like.[34] While for the most part, he pressed women to stress their role in the family, in line with what most Orthodox rabbis were saying in response to the emerging feminist revolution, there is reason to believe he would have gone even farther in allowing women a great degree of involvement in Jewish religious observance had he not discovered a fundamentalist-like backlash within the Hasidic and Orthodox world he inhabited. This belief comes from an episode that occurred in 1972.

In that year, Shlomo Riskin, a young Yeshiva University–ordained rabbi, who had taken a pulpit at New York's Lincoln Square Synagogue, a new Manhattan congregation that he was trying to shift into the Orthodox orbit, came to him with a dilemma. Regularly consulting with Rabbis Soloveitchik, Schneerson, and the rabbinic head of Agudath Israel of America, Moshe Feinstein, Riskin had made progress in getting the increasingly popular congregation to move toward greater Jewish commitment and traditional Jewish practices. Among those in his synagogue were some women who had been involved in intensive and "serious Torah study."[35] In 1972 many of these women came to Riskin on the eve of the holiday of Simhat Torah and asked for his permission for them, like the men, to hold and dance with the Torah scroll in observance of the day. After much soul-searching about allowing this unprecedented and obviously feminist request, he agreed, permitting them to hold a separate set of dances behind closed doors. After the holiday, he went to the Lubavitcher Rebbe and later Rabbi Soloveitchik for retroactive approval. The latter replied that "from a halachic [Judeo-legal] standpoint this was perfectly alright," and to confirm his approval of the synagogue subsequently came and lectured there.[36] The Rebbe also met with Riskin privately; he had often opened his door to him and had followed the developments in the synagogue closely, for its outreach efforts were important to him and his mission. After nearly an hour's conversation he was persuaded by Riskin that while his position in the congregation allowed him in the future to prohibit such dancing, were he to do so, he might "lose that large group of women that might thereby be offended and consequently move to the Conservative 'temple'" and out of the Orthodox orbit.* Considering this, the Rebbe emphatically replied in Yiddish with his permission, adding, to Riskin's surprise, "Not only may you do this, but you *must* do it." The Rebbe clearly understood the need to reach out to these women and to provide them with what they needed and wanted in the cultural atmosphere of the day. Indeed, six years later, he joined in celebrating at his congregation in Crown Heights the writing of a Torah scroll, in which each of the 304,805 letters in the work would have as a sponsor a girl or woman who was attending or had attended one of the Lubavitcher-run Beth Rivkah schools around the world.[37]

When subsequently a rabbi of another Orthodox synagogue about a mile away from Lincoln Square publicly objected to the women's dancing, labeling Riskin's congregation "not Orthodox," and others in a backlash against what was seen by the most traditional and retrograde elements of Orthodoxy as a surrender to feminist demands also

* In the July 16, 2008, interview by Heilman, Riskin denied using the word "temple" but confirmed he did express the belief that he would lose some women to the Conservative movement, and that threat was the "hook" that helped persuade the Rebbe to support his initiative.

began to jump on this condemnatory bandwagon, the Rebbe appeared to reframe his verbal advice. He sent a letter (published much later) in which he found reason to suggest that perhaps he had been too hasty in his blessing of the practice, for it was not a good situation to change "current established custom," as today's Jews "have no power or authority to direct innovations."* This, of course, was the classic Orthodox position when objecting to all liberal religious movements.

Yet a close look at the letter also left room for others to draw alternative conclusions. In it the Rebbe hinted that only if the women experienced "a *great* sadness" over their exclusion from the synagogue activity was there precedent for granting their desire. That judgment was a sociological and psychological rather than a religious one, and Riskin understood it as such.[38]

Indeed, his reported comment to Riskin at the time of their conversation that "the matter of women is one of the greatest challenges that confront us in this time" was not contradicted by the Rebbe's actions. Whenever he could, Menachem Mendel would try to find a way to include them in his mission and activities, as well as to provide a place for them to study Jewish sources and become more engaged by their Judaism.[39]

The replacement of the melting pot ideal by that of multiculturalism, a reflection of the rise of the unmeltable ethnics in the West, gave Lubavitchers and the Rebbe an additional opportunity to assert their presence in the public domains. They could claim to belong to the fabric of American life no less than any other group that stood apart from white Anglo-Saxon Protestant culture. This became even more the case in the 1980s and 1990s, as cultural and religious differences in society were increasingly acceptable, even if they were often only symbolic in character.[40] This too worked for Lubavitchers, who would revel in public symbolic acts of religious engagement and involvement.

---

* The rabbi of the other synagogue, the Young Israel of the West Side, was reportedly urged on by several of his congregants, who objected not only on religious grounds but on institutional ones as well. As the Lincoln Square synagogue became more popular, the Young Israel lost members. The fact that women were being offered more at Riskin's synagogue would undoubtedly lead to more young couples and women choosing to be members there and not at Young Israel. Indeed, that is precisely what happened. Letter in *Kfar Chabad* 1111.

Nothing perhaps more brilliantly articulated this effort than the practice of lighting Hanukkah menorahs in public squares and places as a symbolic act of Jewish identification. Beginning in 1974 as a practice that Philadelphia (and D.C.) *shaliach* Avremel Shemtov had initiated at the foot of the Liberty Bell (and later in 1979 in front of the White House), Lubavitchers were able to play with the symbols of American liberty and the Jewish desire for religious expression and continuity.[41] The idea of the public lighting that Shemtov fashioned , as he put it, "out of a reality that the Rebbe created," a situation in which the idea of reaching the masses was encouraged via some visible Jewish symbolic act, caught on and in 1975, *shluchim* in San Francisco lit a 22 foot lamp in Union Square.[42] In 1979, Shemtov was lighting a menorah with President Jimmy Carter. In 2000, at the lighting in front of the White House, Deputy Treasury Secretary Stuart Eizenstat referred to the menorah "as a symbol of the pluralism and religious liberty that are such a precious part of our American heritage."[*]

The particular figure of the Lubavitcher menorah would also play a part in the Rebbe's campaigns. Designed by London artist Hirsch Pekkar according to principles laid out by the Rebbe, the menorah with its now recognizable Y shape made its debut on Hanukkah in 1982.[43] It was modeled on what Menachem Mendel believed, basing himself on the twelfth-century scholar Maimonides' minority view, was the true shape of the original candelabrum in the Holy Temple in Jerusalem.[44] It also presented a visual and symbolic alternative to the menorah that had become the most visible and recognized symbol of the state of Israel, which had become a Zionist symbol, as well as the infamous image on the Arch of Titus, where the Romans who have destroyed and pillaged the Holy Temple and exiled the Jews are depicted carrying a semicircular menorah into Rome. The Rebbe wanted the Lubavitcher menorah to stand in distinction to these, as he wanted his vision of what redemption would mean to stand in contrast. It would be defined

---

*U.S. Treasury, Office of Public Affairs, press release, December 21, 2000. Ironically, pluralism was something that Lubavitchers embraced in America but contested in every way in Israel. When Shemtov lit the menorah in the presence of President Jimmy Carter during the Iran hostage crisis, the latter saw the act as a way of "removing the darkness" of those times (Avremel Shemtov, personal communication to Samuel C. Heilman, August 13, 2008.

neither by the Zionist state nor by a symbol of exile and of Jewish degradation.[46] It would compete with them and become perhaps more recognizable. Ultimately, the Rebbe's menorah would become the closest thing to a public brand for Lubavitch.[46]

Lubavitchers had taken the Hanukkah menorah that in its historical source was meant to emphasize Jewish survival and deny acculturation and pluralism to take advantage of it—after all, the Maccabees, whom Hanukkah celebrated, opposed the pluralism of Hellenism. Now the ritual had become a symbol of Jewish identity in a contemporary multicultural American society.

Certainly, Lubavitchers wanted this also to serve as a way of showing that being Jewish in public, even or especially at Christmastime, was acceptable, even if one wore a beard and was a Hasid. This gave them confidence to do the same elsewhere in the world. Indeed, the lightings were not limited to the United States, where by the end of the century they would be held in forty-five states and Puerto Rico.[47] Lightings of the menorah occurred everywhere, from Red Square, where a film of the Rebbe's lighting in Brooklyn was shown, to Bangkok, where a menorah would be placed atop an elephant.[48] To be sure, not everyone accepted the insertion of this symbol into the mainstream of society, and the lighting in public places would face many legal challenges over the years.[49] But these were overcome one by one.

To the Rebbe, the Hanukkah menorah was in many ways like the mezuzah, both being placed by the doorway, the former on the left and the latter on the right. In a sense, both served proudly to let the world know that Jews lived where these were found. But more than that, the mezuzah was highly symbolic, for, as the Rebbe explained, it represented all the mitzvahs.[50] Lubavitchers took to affixing large and very visible mezuzahs on doorposts, and made it a practice to check their contents, to make certain the handwritten scrolls inside were complete and perfect, and if not seeing to it they were replaced. This action, they assured Jews, would protect those who lived in homes on which the mezuzahs hung. *Shluchim* would travel to the most distant places just to get a Jew to put up a mezuzah on the door of his or her home.

The mezuzah and the menorah highlighted the importance of symbols in the Lubavitcher program of outreach. Of course, the latter had not been one of the ten mitzvahs the Rebbe had chosen for his campaign, even though in a way it eclipsed many if not all of the ten. To understand how and why it did, we need to consider the reasons for some of the other mitzvahs that were chosen for the campaign and how they were part of the rise of symbolic ethnicity and religion that emerged in the last quarter of the twentieth century.[51]

Lighting Sabbath candles was a way to remind people that it was Sabbath, and when the Rebbe stressed that even young girls should do this, he understood that by getting the children to lead them, he might bring about a change in the Jewish family so that it would perhaps choose to observe the Sabbath that followed that lighting. Moreover, candle lighting was something everyone had to do at the precise onset of the Sabbath. ChaBaD took to posting that time everywhere they could, for years putting it on the front page of the *New York Times* on Fridays. The idea was that if every Jewish home kindled the lights at the same time in each location, as the sun set on Friday, there would perhaps be a spiritual solidarity of each with all and the Sabbath, a way of moving of heaven and earth in a mystical way that would not only kindle the lights but also the Jewish souls of those who were doing so. Jewish engagement and solidarity would, the Rebbe imagined, become inevitable. Giving charity, another key part of the mitzvah campaign, would likewise bind Jews to one another.

♒

When Lubavitchers began to implement the Rebbe's mitzvah campaign, the idea was to encourage these practices among the general public, including those who were far from observance or Jewish consciousness. In fact, Menachem Mendel had been urging the performance of some of these acts for a while in his advice and counsel to supporters. As early as in a letter he wrote on 25 Iyyar 5711 (May 31, 1951) to a correspondent who wanted his blessings for his family, he responded that after taking the request to the grave of his father-in-law, he now advised the petitioner to "make sure that all the mezuzahs in his house were kosher, that before Friday night candle-lighting he give charity, that your sons should put on tefillin daily," and this would help him.[52]

Menachem Mendel had been thinking about the matter of tefillin for a long time. In June 1944, when he was not yet Rebbe, he had written a letter in his role as head of *Mahane Israel*. In it he refers to the donning of tefillin as an act that daily binds hand, heart, and head together—a kind of combination of action, feeling, and intention that was precisely what a Jew needed to recall each day.[53] And we have already seen how important they were for his personal piety.

When he decided to spread his advice in the form of a campaign outward, he simply took practices and advice he had made in private and now began to offer them to outsiders. But to get the latter to embrace this advice would require marketing the likes of which Hasidim had never engaged in before.

The campaign for tefillin, which the Rebbe first ordered shortly before the Six-Day War in June 1967, vividly captures this effort. Young Lubavitcher men would set up a table on which they had laid out tefillin. It was taking the program the Zalman Schachter and Shlomo Carlebach had conceived impromptu in 1949 at Brandeis University and institutionalizing it so that it could be taken out on the road and in public everywhere. Lubavitchers set up tables with tefillin on the street or, later, in a mall, airport, or next to a mitzvah tank, and they would stop male passers-by and ask, "Excuse me, are you Jewish?" That question alone was jarring when the campaign began, for Jews were still living in a time when standing out as Jews in America and Europe seemed if not dangerous, as it had been during the Holocaust, then at least uncomfortable. If the person responded that he was a Jew, the Lubavitchers would ask him to put on the tefillin with them, an act that would publicize their Jewishness in an almost exhibitionist way.[54]

By May 1968, the tefillin campaign had been immortalized as the Lubavitcher counter-response to the counterculture. The *New York Times* headlined the story, "Hasidic Jews Confront Hippies to Press a Joyous Mysticism."[55] It described a "tefillin-mobile" and published a large picture of the scene in Greenwich Village's Washington Square Park under the banner, "Do a Mitzvah: Put on a Pair of Tefillin." As a hippie shouted "let's drop out," the Lubavitcher was quoted as saying, "let them drop into the Old World." The campaign was well under way.

From a social point of view, one may define the wearer of tefillin as a total "other," someone entirely apart from the non-Jewish world. For the non-Jew, tefillin are on the contrary completely "Jewish." Lubavitchers understood this well. When a passer-by in the modern city identified himself as a Jew to the young ChaBaD Hasidim, they immediately took him aside, thereby isolated him from the non-Jewish surroundings. At first no apparent change seemed to take place; he still resembled all the other passers-by. However, once they placed tefillin on his arm and his now covered head, he was transformed from a "non-Jewish" Jew to a committed one whose Jewish identity had an unambiguous public manifestation. This was the starting point: to transform the uncommitted Jew into a person identified as a Jew to himself and to others. This objective was achieved when the subject agreed even temporarily to "abandon" his non-Jewish identity and to put on tefillin in public. Once he acted out his Jewish identity so blatantly, there was a chance, however slight, that he might continue to do so by attending meetings and ultimately "repenting" and "enlisting" in ChaBaD. This, of course, was just what the Rebbe wanted. He would often repeat his belief that "a person should not be ashamed to live his day-to-day life as a Jew."[56]

There was also another "internal" explanation connected with ChaBaD's mystical-kabbalistic conceptions. Its Jewry-wide mission of "dispersing the wellsprings" sought to purify the Jewish soul, the source of holiness, of the dross of the non-Jewish environment. The Jew who lit Sabbath candles, put a mezuzah on his doorpost, or put on tefillin had crossed from one domain to the other, from the profane to the sacred, the non-Jewish to the Jewish. That was the mission of the *shluchim* who engaged in the kabbalistic tasks of "arousing the sparks of holiness dispersed in the valley of impurity" as a condition for the coming of the Messiah and complete redemption.[57] Getting Jews to perform these mitzvahs was a first step in cleansing the Jew of his non-Jewishness, releasing the spark of holiness from the captivity of impurity.

The Lubavitcher rebbe was focused not just on America and Western Europe (and later the Soviet Union and what it would become). Israel, the place where so many Jews had put their hope for the future, the product of what his forebears had seen as heretical Zionism, was perhaps an even more important target into which his emissaries would go to reengineer Jews and Judaism. In Israel, where Lubavitchers would in time become a major force, reinvention was the name of the game. For the first half of the century, the struggle was to create a new settlement and new sort of Jew in the ancient homeland after an absence of more than two millennia. War, Arab riots, and the difficulties of immigration, coupled with economic hard times, made the years until 1948 enormously difficult. The victory over their enemies at the armistice in 1949 made Israelis who had declared their independent state in 1948 realize they could defend themselves against all odds. Now they had to create a new society that was overwhelmed with immigrants, including Holocaust survivors, refugees from Middle Eastern Muslim states who had fled or been expelled from their communities, and those who felt drawn by the Zionist dream and a chance to build the new Jewish state. This massive "ingathering of the exiles" required the new country to create a welfare state that would secure its citizens and offer them an opportunity "to build and be built up by" (*livnot u'lehibanot*) a new society and culture. They created myriad institutions and provided an economic and social environment in which people could create a new life and identity for themselves. In a country that by 1967 had a little more than 2.7 million citizens, there were seven universities, suggesting that this society could provide its young people with opportunities not only to study but also to extend their period of moratorium no less than their peers in Europe and America did. The fact that most of the youth also preceded their studies with several years of mandatory army service further expanded this period.

In the spring of 1967, the Jewish state suddenly found itself facing the greatest threat to its existence since its founding nineteen years earlier. After the Egyptians had got the United Nations to remove its forces from Sharm el Sheikh on the Red Sea and on May 22 closed the Straits of Tiran, threatening Israel with a naval blockade, they and other Arab armies began to mass their forces in preparation for an attack. The Israelis, who looked to their allies, found themselves suddenly alone. De Gaulle and the French offered no encouragement or help; Johnson and the Americans, although expressing the belief that the blockade was illegal, found it impossible to organize an international flotilla to test it, and consequently advised the Israelis against any military action, with the clear implication that if they did so, they were on their own.[58] For many Jews, this apparent abandonment of the Jewish state by the world reverberated with the anxieties they had felt during the Holocaust, and indeed many of them the world over feared a repetition of that catastrophe. When some of the Orthodox Jews in Israel who harbored theological doubts about the Zionist enterprise had begun fleeing to the airport to escape in anticipation of the war, this only intensified the feelings of fear that many felt. At this time, at a parade in Crown Heights on the occasion of the Jewish celebration of the holiday Lag B'Omer (May 28), the Lubavitcher Rebbe spoke out, both in public and on the following Sabbath in a talk to his Hasidim, urging confidence and encouragement that the Jews and the Holy Land would not be harmed and therefore they should not abandon it and rush to the airport; it was a message to many of the *haredi* Jews in particular.[59] The instrument of defense that he advocated was the tefillin.

In his words, "Jews in the Land of Israel should remain there in confidence, for God had promised that [Leviticus 26:6] 'I shall bring peace to the land.'" That peace required as a precondition that Jews accept the Almighty as their God and then, if they did so, "He would lead his people forth with his full, open and holy hand ... soon in the true and full redemption by means of the Messiah."[60] But did this inspire confidence? Actually, since most Israelis were not religious believers at that time, might such a message not add to their anxieties rather than allay them, or was it aimed to get them to repent at this critical time?

A few days later, on the Sabbath, he offered a recipe for everyone who was worried about the future. Now he argued that "in the current situation, we must pay great care to see to it that every Jew will put on tefillin, for this is a mitzvah that has great power to bring the Jews out from their difficulties in peace." Then he quoted the Talmud (B.T. *Menachot* 44a) that all who don tefillin are guaranteed long life and (B.T. *Brachot* 6a) the Talmudic interpretation of the verse (*Deut.* 28:10) that "all nations will fear you" as a reference to the tefillin that are placed on the head. He concluded that the sight of every Jew wearing tefillin would throw the fear of heaven into all those who see him. "Every Jew who would don tefillin on behalf of those who are in the army [presumably a reference to Israeli soldiers] would thereby help them so that they would live long and the fear of them would fall upon all those who surrounded them."[61]

When after six days the unanticipated military triumph of the Israelis led not only to survival but also to their regaining the ancient Temple Mount in Jerusalem and the biblical lands of what would be called Judea and Samaria, the Rebbe could claim the victory as his, arguing that it was the sight of soldiers donning tefillin that had miraculously frightened the enemy. Now Israel, once the product of Zionist accomplishments, could be reclaimed by ChaBaD, and its rebirth after 1967, stronger and bigger than ever, could be portrayed as the result of the Rebbe's campaign and the Lubavitcher plan for redemption.

Israel had been the subject of Lubavitcher settlement already in 1949 when Rabbi Yosef Yitzchak, with the help of, among others, Zalman Shazar, gained a foothold at Kfar Chabad, an agricultural settlement on the road between Tel Aviv and Jerusalem. Its founders were Russian Lubavitcher refugees with no other place to go and whom the sixth rebbe had wanted to keep together. The village, established with the organization of a few *shluchim*, would in time grow to about five thousand inhabitants. Shazar, born Schneur Zalman Rubashov in Belarus to a Lubavitcher family (and named for the first rebbe), had after immigrating to Palestine taken his initials and made them into a new last name; he would become an important figure in Israeli government, finally serving as president between 1963 and 1973. While his help to the sixth rebbe was limited, his assistance to Menachem Mendel would be far more important. The seventh rebbe wanted more than a small village for his followers. In 1967, after the end of the war, Menachem Mendel had far greater objectives in mind. He did not want simply to inspire and guide the people of Kfar Chabad alone (where a duplicate of his 770 headquarters would be built brick by brick); he wanted to direct the entire state of Israel, whose destiny, politics, and religious culture he would seek to control in his campaign for redemption. In place of the Israeli army he would send his *shluchim* to do the work.

As Israel played an increasingly larger role in Jewish consciousness, especially after the "miraculous" victories in the Six-Days War of 1967 and later the remarkable turnaround in the October 1973 Yom Kippur War by the Israeli army, ChaBaD was confronted with a dilemma. How could it celebrate the miraculous victories of Zionist nationalism and the Israeli army—in the classic Lubavitcher ideology, false Messiahs—without strengthening these very same false Messiahs? Israelis, particularly the Orthodox among them, and other religious Jews were increasingly arguing that the establishment of the state of Israel was the "first flowering of redemption," and now, with the retaking of the ancient biblical heartland, they were certain that what had been given to them came with the help of God acting through the Israeli army and state. Many were sure this was the true sign of the of Messiah's impending arrival. Suddenly, it seemed the false Messiah of Zionism was going to steal the faith of the Jews that Lubavitchers had been working so hard to arouse.

Responding to the 1967 war, the Rebbe urged his emissaries to "speak about returning to tradition and they will listen. Ask them to don tefillin and they will roll up their sleeves."[62] He argued that it was not simply a military victory that had regained Jerusalem and the biblical homeland. Rather, the fact that some soldiers had donned tefillin was what made the Arabs flee. He wanted the Six-Days War to be a Lubavitcher Jewish victory, a miracle based on his mitzvahs.[63]

It was possible to make such claims as Israel became increasingly intertwined with America. Just as the American government and American Jews sought to play a larger role in Israel, so in parallel the Lubavitcher Rebbe from his "world headquarters" in Brooklyn sought to do the same. But his control had as its purpose not simply this-worldly realpolitik; it rather sought to hasten redemption. Of course, there were religious Zionists who would try to do the same, arguing that only settlements could do that. But the Lubavitcher Rebbe, who supported increased settlement in the biblical areas, argued that these settlements were not the *cause* of what seemed an irresistible march toward the coming of the Messiah. They were instead the *evidence* that the Lubavitcher campaigns, which were the "true" engine of change, were succeeding.

In the coming decades he would continue to intensify his work in Israel. Not only did he send *shluchim*, he also tried to create ties to Israeli generals and politicians. These men began to make pilgrimages to 770 and the Rebbe. In time, Yitzchak Rabin, Menachem Begin, Ariel Sharon, Benjamin Netanyahu, and President Zalman Shazar made the trip, as did a host of army officers and other Israeli officials.

In 1972 Menachem Mendel sent two hundred of his own Lubavitcher "soldiers" to the fronts along the Egyptian border and to the Syrian one in the Golan Heights to get the Israeli soldiers to put on tefillin, arguing, as his emissary from Crown Heights, Hershel Hecht (who brought along a reporter from the *New York Times*), put it, "tefillin gives strength to soldiers and provides them with spiritual protection."[64]

Perhaps one of the most striking encounters occurred in 1973, during the last days of the Yom Kippur War. The day was Simhat Torah, the last of the holidays of the season and what would be five days before the end of the war. The Rebbe was speaking, as usual in Yiddish, about the war and the question of Israel's place among the nations of the world, but his comments were filled with allusions that were recondite and particularly puzzling to the Israeli diplomats and representatives who had come for the occasion. They were not used to such discourses that mixed Hasidism, biblical glosses, and rabbinic references. Following his remarks and just before the traditional dancing of the day, the Rebbe called over the Israelis and asked why their troops had not taken Damascus. He then offered answers to his own questions, most of them based on mystical and kabbalistic texts, which, he asserted, favored such a move. He then directed one of the Israel representatives, Aryeh Morgenstern, to contact Moshe Dayan, the defense minister of the sovereign state of Israel, and share this counsel with him. Amazingly, Morgenstern did contact Zevulun Hammer (a member of the Knesset foreign affairs committee), with whom he worked, and asked him to pass on the message to Dayan. Clearly, the Rebbe saw himself as taking a commanding position in current events. Moshe Dayan and the Israeli government, however, were not persuaded.[65]

In 1974, again seeking to usurp the charisma of the Israeli army, the mitzvah campaigns were carried to the public by mitzvah tanks.* In the aftermath of all the Middle East wars, it would not be the Israeli army and its tanks that brought the Messiah; it would be the soldiers and tanks of Lubavitch, the Rebbe's army.[66]

Over time the Rebbe would, as his mitzvah campaign gave way to the Messiah campaign, see himself as controlling events not only in Israel but also in many other places in the world. In that campaign, Israel and his relationship to it would occupy a central position.

---

* Actually, before these caravans were called tanks, they were used and identified with another task and name. On November 23, 1963, the *New York Times* on p. 24 reported a "Mobile Library being used by Hasidic Jewish Group," calling it a "Jewish Bookmobile" in which there would be a "mobile library, bookshop, and reading room with bookstacks" that would visit a variety of the Jewish communities and serve also "as an information center and synagogue," and that it was under the sponsorship of the educational arm, the Merkos L'Inyonei Chinuch, which had been the Rebbe's first responsibility when he arrived in Brooklyn. See http://www.chabad.org/therebbe/timeline_cdo/aid/62178/jewish/1974-Mitzvah-Tanks.htm (accessed April 9, 2008).

♒

A turning point in this campaign was the decision to go to the Jewishly unschooled. A large part of the "spreading the wellsprings" had always been teaching all Jews the lessons of Torah and ChaBaD Hasidism. To accomplish this, the Rebbe had to explain to his emissaries that one *could and should* now teach these lessons not only to those who had been schooled in its esoterica and who were insiders but to everyone.[67] In time, he would reiterate and repeat often that this meant "spreading it in the widest way, to the furthest extreme, with neither attenuation nor limitations, for if there were any such attenuation or limitation (however small) that would not be true 'spreading.'"[68]

In a sense, this opening of access to the masses of what was once teaching limited to elites was not unique to Lubavitch. While the world of Jewish learning and observance was always a meritocracy—whoever had the intelligence and capability to study Torah and observe religious precepts could do so, whether they were children of the poor and uneducated or members of the elite—that meritocracy had been decimated by the countless Jews who had abandoned traditional religious life and observance in the late nineteenth and early twentieth centuries, and was finally devastated in a particularly large way by the Holocaust, in which so many Orthodox scholars and yeshiva students had been annihilated.

After the Holocaust, a generation or more of Torah scholars and even of learned laymen who would have come of age in the previous generation were missing (either because they had been killed or because they had lost interest in Torah). If Jewish study was to continue, a new cadre of learned and practicing Jewry had to be rebuilt. Orthodox Jews and Hasidim in particular had shrunk dramatically in numbers, because those who remained in Europe had been easiest to single out by the Nazis, having followed their religious leaders' advice not to assimilate or leave Europe for America or the Land of Israel, where if they had arrived early enough they might have survived in far greater numbers. In the Holocaust, these traditional Jews sustained proportionately greater casualties than the rest of European Jewry. In the aftermath of the war and its tragic consequences for that traditional world in particular, the Orthodox survivors, particularly but not only the *haredi* ones, realized they could no longer remain so selective and exclusivist about who could study Torah and its myriad holy texts. Accordingly, they were ready to offer the most intensive Jewish education to anyone, whether they were suited to it or not. In yeshivas and, later, Jewish day schools, Talmud and myriad other sacred texts were part of a curriculum in every school. Some day schools, as we have seen, building on and enhancing what had begun in the prewar period, offered study to girls as well as boys.[69] After all, in the new world and its welfare state, every child, boy and girl alike, was required to get an education. The Jews could not do otherwise, even in their private schools.

In synagogues the situation was even more open. In the past, among Orthodox lay people who in their adult lives studied Torah in the synagogue as an extension of their religious life, such study had been hierarchically organized. Making up the top tier were those in the *chevra shas*, the group assembled around the study of Talmud and its associated commentaries and glosses; this was only for those with the requisite skills. Below them were those who gathered to review only the narrative portions of the Talmud; they were the *chevra Eyn Yaakov*. So it went on down to the lowest rung, the *chevra tehillim*, those who gathered simply to recite the Psalms, not necessarily understanding their full meaning or studying their poetry. But after the Second World War, there was a whole generation of Jews even among the Orthodox who during the years when they might have been acquiring Torah learning skills instead had been trying simply to stay alive. As refugees they were now living with an American Jewry, many of whom had not yet acquired great capabilities in Jewish learning. Moreover, in America, the idea of hierarchies was undermined by a kind of democratizing ethic. All this led to opening Torah learning, from the Talmudic to the simplest level, to *any and all* who wanted to study. If the material was opaque, translations and English versions of texts and commentary were provided, and nearly every synagogue and primary school allowed everyone access to these once recondite volumes.* In time, even women, who were always excluded from Torah study by traditional

---

* The rise of Mesorah publications and the Art Scroll series of translations, among others, in the late twentieth century reflected and reaffirmed this trend. These books were written for people who could not gain access to the recondite Hebrew or Aramaic (and even Yiddish) texts but wanted to study them in English.

Jewry, would gain access to even the most esoteric texts, even within Orthodox circles. A market grew for these books; especially as those who read them became increasingly middle class and had the money to purchase them.

This was largely because such study had by the twentieth century come to be seen as a vehicle for enhancing Jewish commitment and attachment. Studying Jewish books was a way to link oneself with generations of the past, venerated texts, and what seemed a living experience of being Jewish.[70] In the effort to restore the ties to the ancient sacred texts and to allow people to act in a distinctly Jewish way in the post-Holocaust world, Torah study of all sorts was democratized. No text, however esoteric—from Talmud to Kabbalah—was now closed to anyone who wanted to study it, regardless of his or her abilities and background.

Rabbi Menachem Mendel, living in this reality, planned to do the same with ChaBaD Hasidic teachings, a practice made possible by Lubavitchers through a massive program of publication of all their basic texts, as well as the writings of their rebbes (and even descriptions and summaries of their gatherings). Even before he became Rebbe, he had been appointed to lead the publishing effort. As we have already noted, he paid attention to logos and decided what books to print, giving special care to presentation and showing a "preference for modern typeface and design."[71] He saw to it that the basic text of ChaBaD, *Tanya*, was published everywhere in the world, with editions that were produced in some of the most exotic locations. In time, as the Lubavitchers point out, "Kehot Publication Society and Merkos Publications, the publishing divisions of the Lubavitch movement brought Torah education to nearly every Jewish community in the world." By the end of the century, ChaBaD would be all over the Internet, posting writings and videos for the entire world to see. Almost everything was being translated into all sorts of foreign languages. The whole idea was to symbolically demonstrate that everyone and everywhere in the world had access to these teachings. In this way they were spreading the wellsprings abroad.

One could reveal all the esoterica because in these days preceding the imminent arrival of the Messiah, in order to hasten that day, one "spent the treasury." This was a time when one no longer acted as in the past, parceling out knowledge only to the privileged few. Now the information served as a form of connecting with people. More than that, it was a vehicle for protecting Jews from the onslaughts and seductions of contemporary profane culture and society. As he put it in a letter in 1962, "particularly in our generation, when we can see the Messiah's footsteps [*ikveso dimeshikho*], the role of the yeshiva is not simply to be a place for learning Torah, but rather—and this is most important—a place for education about the foundations of the Torah and Mitzvah, an education of the true internal meanings [*pnimi*] that will [lead people] not to fear all those currents in the world and stand up to all trials."[72] Education was now more than learning; it was spiritual fortification and protection. The Rebbe pressed it forward as essential.

⁂

And what of the Rebbe personally? While his emissaries were out preparing the world for the Messiah, the man, Menachem Mendel Schneerson, who was at the apex of this worldwide mission was all alone. By 1964 his widowed mother, whom he used to visit every day, had died. Now he was largely devoid of close family. His father was dead. His brother Berel, as well as Mendel and Sheina Horensztajn, had been murdered by the Nazis. His only surviving brother, Leibel, with whom he had once been so close, had died suddenly at age forty-three in Liverpool, England, in 1952. His relations with the Gourary family had soured when they were taken out of a leadership position and their son and heir was removed from being close to the *nesies*. When he could, the Rebbe wrote to and helped relatives, even those who did not share his worldview or life, as he did with his brother's widow and daughter, whose welfare concerned him and to whom he sent presents. But they lived "far" from him in every sense of the word. Never having attended a Temimim yeshiva, he knew no Hasidim with whom he had grown up as friends or fellow students and who might now be intimates. When he had entered the court, he had been part of its "royalty," and even then he had absented himself to Berlin and Paris, where once again he had lived distant from Lubavitchers. Now, as Rebbe, he was surrounded only by subordinates, assistants, and Hasidim—but they could not be his "friends," precisely because they were his *Hasidim*. However close they felt to him, as one Hasid explained, "he's not my friend; he's my Rebbe."[73]

Moreover, the Rebbe was increasingly sending some of the best of his Hasidim away as *shluchim*. His wife, Moussia ("Mrs. Schneerson from President Street"), did not take an active part in his Hasidic activities and barely functioned in any formal way in the court. (She was a very "private person," as the Hasidim often explained). No longer able to live the private life she had had with her husband in Berlin and also with the Horensztajns in Paris, she experienced much solitude, reading the newspapers, watching television, going about New York on her own, or visiting with a small circle of friends who spoke Russian and discussed literature.[74] Russian, of course, was the language she spoke to her husband frequently and to her sisters.[75] She would drive herself to a variety of places, and often went to the library and out shopping, or occasionally to the ballet.[76] She sometimes reached out to children (she reportedly "adopted as her special children" the offspring of her Hasidic assistant, "Chesed" Halberstam) and remained particularly close to another assistant, Shalom Ganzburg, who lived and ate with the couple in their private quarters and was treated like a family member.[77] Indeed, perhaps answering the unspoken question as to why she did not have children of her own, she would reportedly comment in Yiddish, "*Ale khsidim zaynen dem Rebns kinder*"—"all Hasidim are the Rebbe's children."[78] But the pattern of her life was not the pattern of her husband's.[79] Spending endless hours in his role as rebbe, he would be with her only a few hours of the day or in the very early mornings and occasionally in an afternoon for companionship—indeed, by Lubavitcher tradition, she was not expected even to eat at the same table (although they did not hold fast to that rule).[80] As she had once said of her father that "he belonged to his Hasidim," so she could say the same now about the man she married.[81] The Rebbe had no children with whom he could share his innermost feelings and affection or who could talk to him intimately, which must have saddened him mightily (whenever he was seen around children his face would light up).[82] Nor did he have children who could have given him the lessons in humility every parent normally receives from offspring, who do not see their parents as the giants they sometimes imagine themselves to be.

Indeed, the only person Menachem Mendel could really talk to and with whom he could expansively share his inner thoughts and feelings was a *dead man*, his father-in-law, whose grave in Queens, New York, he visited religiously and regularly, a place where he spent increasing hours alone. But the responses he got from this dead man were all inside his own head and heart.

Given this sort of personal isolation and solitude in the midst of the excitement of a campaign and a growing coterie of people who nearly worshiped him and revered his every act, statement, or thought, what must have happened to his sense of proportion? To whom could he turn for counsel and advice? He claimed he was getting it from his late father-in-law, but what could be the nature of such communications? Could they have connected him to reality, or would they instead have reinforced his sense of being all alone in the world? Was he, moreover, becoming a person with so much power and influence that he was now too heavily anchored in his own vantage point and unable to see beyond it? With no one around him who dared or could contradict his view of the world or reality, was he getting lost in a culture of messianic delusion?[83]

CHAPTER 7

From Resurrection to Death

WE WANT MOSHIACH NOW

〽

As the Rebbe's campaign succeeded far beyond anything his father-in-law ever managed, his reputation throughout the world grew. Every success his *shluchim* registered was a reminder of him and his message as well as a measure of his own success. This ability to bring Lubavitch, its message, and its various campaigns to the world stage not only gave him confidence, it convinced him that the currents of history were leading toward the fulfillment of the promise that the Messiah would come in his generation. Increasingly, he was so caught up by this idea that his wife on more than one occasion said of him, "He thinks everybody cares about the Moshiach as much as him," but of course that was not the case.[1] Yet he and his emissaries would try to make it so.

〽

For a long time Rabbi Menachem Mendel believed that the secular Zionist state of Israel was a huge obstacle and challenge to this program of redemption. Even though Lubavitchers benefited from the state—it had given them Kfar Chabad and autonomous schools within the state-funded public religious educational system, while *shluchim* were beginning to spread their wellsprings everywhere—Menachem Mendel began his reign with the traditional ultra-Orthodox (*haredi*) negative attitude toward the Jewish state, seeing it as the heretical challenge to Jewish tradition and God's plan. Like those Jews, he took what he could to sustain Lubavitcher needs, but wherever possible he undermined the Zionist enterprise because, he argued, Judaism's greatest danger lay in Israel, where Zionists "have invented substitutions and replacements" for religion that they falsely claimed freed the spirit and the soul but that in reality only fostered a base desire to be no different from the Gentiles. The situation in Israel, the new Rebbe argued at the time, was even more dangerous for Judaism than was the Soviet Union.[2] This was because the state of Israel was an entity that had inserted the "feeling of exile" into the land of redemption.[3] Unlike the religious Zionists, he refused to see it as in any way *askhalte digeule*, the beginning of the redemptive messianic age.[4]

In 1958, on the tenth anniversary of Israeli independence and seven years into his tenure as Rebbe, Menachem Mendel made this explicit: "We must not see in the establishment of the state [of Israel] the beginning of redemption, for the Messiah has not yet come." Addressing Israelis directly, he asserted that their country had become "a place where there is the desecration of the Sabbath in public," and then he hurled the following accusation: "When in 5708 [1948] you changed the name 'the Land of Israel' to 'the State of Israel,' you stole from the People of Israel the name that was written in the Torah; you established the secular state in opposition to the Holy Land of Israel. In 5708, a sin was committed against the People of Israel . . . and brought exile to Tel Aviv and Jerusalem. Yet it was called freedom and 'independence.' In place of acting according to the statutes of the Torah . . . you sought to be like all the other nations." He concluded, "Zion and Jerusalem are not ours. This is not the Zion for which we yearned." Indeed, he would never refer to the *state* of Israel.*

---

* *Diglenu*, Iyyar 5718 (May 1958), 2. The name *Medinat Yisrael*, "State of Israel," coined by Aharon Reuveni, a writer and the younger brother of Israel's second president, Yitzhak Ben-Zvi, was based on less ideological grounds. As Reuveni explained his reasoning in the magazine *Moznayim* on December 5, 1947, "It cannot be called 'Land of Israel' because it will not occupy the whole land, or most of it, or even half of it—and even if it were to occupy half the land. . . . [T]he fact of the matter is that even after we have a state in part of the land, we will not cease calling the other parts of the land, and the entire land, by the name of the Land of Israel. And thus we will cause a confusion of terms. Everyone who says, 'Land of Israel'—will be compelled to offer an interpretation of what he is referring to: the state or the [entire] land?" Reprinted in *Haaretz*, May 7, 2008, B6. In his comments, Menachem Mendel ignored all this; it did not fit his ideological argument that "state" as a secular entity had no religious meaning.

Perhaps no episode exemplifies this belligerent attitude toward Zionism more than his unheralded role in what came to be known as "the Yosele Schumacher affair."[5] In 1960, the secular parents of six-year-old Schumacher, immigrants to Israel from the Soviet Union, had asked the mother's parents, Breslov Hasidim, to take care of their young son for a while. But when they came to retrieve the child from the grandparents, the latter refused to give the boy up, hoping to prevent the Schumachers from raising him as a secular Jew. The child was subsequently smuggled out of the country by various elements of the ultra-Orthodox anti-Zionist community and finally locked away in Brooklyn with a Hasidic family and not allowed to leave. A tempest raged in Israel over the case. The boy's grandfather was put in jail for his role in the affair. Some of those who hid him were also arrested. Gradually other links in the chain of people tied to the case were uncovered by the Mossad, the Israeli spy service. In Israel, the case caused "tensions between secular and religious Israelis to reach an all-time high. Secular Jews were known to scream '*Efo Yosele*? (Where is Yosele?)' in the streets of Jerusalem," for they saw this as an example of how the ultra-Orthodox were trying to fight against the freedom of the secular state and of Israelis to choose how to raise their children.[6]

In fact, the prime mover in all this was not the elderly grandfather but his son, Shalom, the boy's uncle, a Lubavitcher Hasid in constant but secret and indirect contact with his Rebbe, Menachem Mendel.[7] It was the latter's desire to see this child, and any others he could, "redeemed" from the secular state in any way possible, even through unlawful means that undercut the state authority. Some believe that the Rebbe was convinced that had the child not been abducted, his parents would return with him to the godless Soviet Union, a state and prospect that to Lubavitchers was anathema. Shalom was ultimately caught and arrested in London and spent a year in a British prison, after which he was transferred back to his home in Israel, where he spent another fifteen months under arrest.

He would have remained in prison longer had not the new president, Zalman Shazar, elected in 1963, offered him amnesty immediately upon taking office. This act, from a sympathizer who had earlier helped the Lubavitchers get approval from the state authorities for Kfar

Chabad, was a sign of Rabbi Menachem Mendel's growing ability to influence both the politics and the cultural and religious life of Israel.[8]

The Rebbe's relationship with President Shazar (as with the state of Israel) was a complex one of competing authorities. During the summer of 1966 Shazar was visiting New York and wanted to meet with the Rebbe. By the rules of protocol, as Israeli head of state (*nesi*), Shazar could expect that the Lubavitcher leader would come to him in his presidential suite in a Manhattan hotel. But the Rebbe refused, explaining that he had received a message from the late Rabbi Yosef Yitzchak during his most recent visit to the *tsiyen* in which his predecessor had "informed him" that "we do not leave Lubavitch." Having received this injunction from beyond the grave, the Rebbe (the Lubavitcher *nesi*) in effect treated the president of Israel like nothing other than a Hasidic follower and summoned him to Lubavitch headquarters in Crown Heights. What the one *nesi* demanded, the other had no choice but to do. The Israeli president complied. Six years later American-based Lubavitchers suggested, only half in jest, that "President Shazar comes to see President Nixon so that he will have an excuse to visit the Lubavitcher."[9]

Such power was all the more remarkable in light of Menachem Mendel's steadfast refusal throughout his life to visit the Holy Land. "Everyone," he explained, "needs to find himself in a place where he can be most useful. Here in the United States," he explained, "one finds the key to global influence; here is the steering wheel of the world. Here there are historic changes that can affect the destiny of nations, among them Israel. Here we find possibilities of influencing matters for the benefit of Israel, and from here we can influence as well the situation of religion in the Land of Israel," and therefore here he and Rabbi Yosef Yitzchak would remain.[10] America, he reasoned, was a global power, and so from here, he and his *shluchim* could be no less powerful globally and steer events throughout the world.

Of course, had the Rebbe gone to Israel, he might have been expected to go to visit the president of the state or the other powers that be. And as the one who would be a symbol of the redemption, he could only come at the last step, with the coming of the Messiah. So he remained in "Lubavitch."

ʃʃʃʃ

This sense that Lubavitchers and their Rebbe from their home base in America were somehow responsible for all Jews everywhere in the world was a key message that received ever-stronger emphasis throughout his reign: after all, the redemption of which he spoke was not a local concern but rather of universal consequence. By the end of the 1950s it was already clear that, as one non-Orthodox supporter put it, "nobody is more concerned with the fate of the Jews—every Jew— than the Rebbe."[11] They were, as a spokesman would in time explain, "very much involved in matters of the world and knowledgeable about all aspects of it."[12]

All the world's Jews were their constituency, and that was behind the mitzvah campaign. As his emissaries spread across the globe, wherever even a few Jews could be found, his mission was inevitably seen to be more and more international. Even the building at 770 would be not simply their place in New York but their "world headquarters," the spiritual capital of the Jewish people, that is, the center of Jewish life in the Diaspora until the Messiah's arrival. It was the place to which the Messiah would come first and from which he would lead the return of the Jews from exile to the Holy Land. This was a radically new idea in Jewish theology: a Messiah coming by way of America.

ʃʃʃʃ

The Holy Land obsessed him all the more after the dramatic events of 1967, which moved the Rebbe deeply. Menachem Mendel was certainly not alone in seeing the events surrounding the Six-Days War through a religious prism. A war that had begun as a battle for existence ended as one defined in religious terms, and afterward even the secular Jews and Gentiles were inclined to speak of it in the language of faith, as a 'miracle' or a sign of the end of days.

Yet unlike those who in the aftermath of the war saw God's will working through the actions of the Israel Defense Forces, and the religious Zionist followers of the Rabbis Kook, who now read into the I.D.F. victories messianic meaning, the Lubavitcher Rebbe perceived the real significance in what had happened as emerging in the days *before* the outbreak of the war, when the world appeared once again to abandon the Jews. For him the fact that the Jewish people had been left alone, deserted by everyone, including the world powers, and faced another possible Holocaust by the Arab armies massing for war was of great consequence. In his view, this abandonment was the sign that God alone had helped the Jews in the Land of Israel emerge victorious, just as he had at the Exodus from Egypt in biblical times. This for him was the true meaning of the Six-Days War.[13]

The abandonment by the world was part of what the prophet had understood as the prelude to greatness; he had seen it following their exodus when he looked upon their encampment and before bestowing his blessing on them had pronounced, "Lo, the people shall dwell alone" (Numbers 23:9). Menachem Mendel often made reference to this verse and the aloneness of the Jewish people, for example quoting it in a letter of 26 Tishrei 5723 (October 24, 1962). He used it to highlight Jewish uniqueness in the world, its blessedness, and the ubiquity of anti-Jewish hatred, facts that he saw as ineluctably connected.

That anti-Jewish loathing could be effectively countered and turned into blessednesss only if Jews attached themselves to the "everlasting Torah," spread its message, and strengthened their Jewish observance— this "alone will protect us."[14] Therefore, the power that protected the Jewish people in the Land of Israel was not its military. Their survival was instead the result of their acting Jewish rather than like Gentiles. They won the war because they had donned tefillin (with the help of the Rebbe's *shluchim*), recited prayers, and performed mitzvahs. The war and the subsequent victory were an opportunity to demonstrate, as the prophet Zechariah (4:6) put it, that "Neither by might, nor by power, but by my spirit, saith the Lord of hosts" would redemption come.*
The Rebbe perceived the footsteps of the Messiah in the combination

---

* This belief was not limited to the Lubavitcher rebbe and his followers. Christian preacher John Hagee, founder and senior pastor of the Cornerstone Church in San Antonio, Texas, a nondenominational, evangelical church with more than 19,000 active members, argued in a sermon that "this is God's plan, because he wants the Jewish people in Israel and around the world to know that *He*, the God of Abraham, Isaac and Jacob, saved them, not America." The sermon was rebroadcast on the "Fresh Air" program, National Public Radio, on May 16, 2008. See also http://www.jhm.org/ME2/Sites/dirmod.asp?sid =&type=gen&mod=Core+Pages&gid=27AAA6C53C0949FC85078AEDE43C4AA0&Site ID=8112722C039B4E508F0AB8552B898895 (accessed May 28, 2008).

of the abandonment before the war and what he saw as the God-given Lubavitcher-led victory of the nation of Israel.

If Menachem Mendel had harbored any doubts about his understanding of the unfolding of events and his power to direct them, the developments in Israel after 1967 helped wipe them away and increased his confidence in his and his late father-in-law's role in ushering in the age of redemption. This led him, as we shall see, to make ever more grandiose and extravagant claims. History no longer was a mystery but became instead the revelation of a plan for salvation that Lubavitcher rebbes—presumably the primary prophetic leaders of the Jews—had been pushing. And if the end was near, then, just as Menachem Mendel had promised in his *Basi L'Gani* talk at his crowning, this generation and its leader would be the ones to bring the Messiah. Here was grandiosity combined with ideology.

Israel, whose borders after the war had grown to biblical proportions and in whose domain the holy Old City of Jerusalem and the Temple Mount now were to be found, was no longer an obstacle to his messianic message. Instead, it would increasingly become its proving ground. The fact that at the time this campaign in Israel took off the president of Israel, Zalman Shazar, was publicly identified as a follower of the Rebbe, even if this fact was not altogether accurate, enhanced the general impression there that Menachem Mendel was able to influence Israel in significant ways.[15] As we have seen, by 1973 he was even summoning Israeli diplomats and sending messages about military and political actions in the midst of the war, for he viewed the 1973 Yom Kippur War as a warning from God that if Jews did not do more to hasten the Messiah, he would take the land he had given them back and stave off redemption. More than ever, the Rebbe was convinced that he had the capacity to engineer events to prevent such a catastrophe, which was why he had the confidence to urge Jews not to abandon the Land of Israel in the dark and anxious days on the eve of the 1967 war.

Notwithstanding the increasing importance of Israel, in the mind of the Lubavitcher Rebbe, action remained indispensable. For him, Lubavitcher activities had unquestionably accelerated religious repentance and return, and that consequently altered the direction of Jewish life in Israel (and the world). And because he believed increasing numbers of repenting Jews would hasten the day of redemption, the efforts of his Hasidim would have to be intensified—and they were. After 1967, *shluchim* and their outreach became ubiquitous, while the Rebbe's messages and instructions—and, over time, his image on posters and billboards in America and Israel—were too. In typical fashion, one in particular declared, "The Rebbe has promised—the Rebbe will deliver." The ultimate promise, of course, was the fulfillment of a plan for redemption, in which the Messiah would lead all Jews into the Promised Land. And who would that be? As he would repeat always, it would be none other than "his honor, my teacher, my father-in-law," the man to whom he was inextricably linked and whom he could channel, "will lead us to the complete and *true* redemption."[16]

The world aided and abetted what many saw as this grand delusion by increasingly hailing the Lubavitchers and their Rebbe. At the twentieth anniversary of his ascension, Menachem Mendel was being acclaimed in America as a leader of Orthodox Judaism, if not quite all Jewry.[17] Indeed, he was being consulted not just by his Hasidim but by some of the most forward-looking modern Orthodox rabbis.[18] The number of his followers was being touted in the press as in the hundreds of thousands—even if no one could really prove these numbers, which were difficult if not impossible to confirm demographically.*

The Rebbe's increased frequency of contact with politicians— American, Israeli, and those from elsewhere—further added to his growing stature as a world religious leader. Often with the help of his *shluchim*, like Avremel Shemtov and others whose worldliness and political savvy was growing, his influence among government officials increased. Described by a prominent national columnist as "a charismatic religious leader," the Rebbe was portrayed as a magnet "for all sorts of people, including politicians and business leaders," and his headquarters in Brooklyn as a destination for "pilgrimage."[19]

This was undoubtedly affected by the fact that Jewish voters and political activists were becoming ever more important in the American political arena. In order to signal to Jewish voters that they cared about

---

* 770 could, after all, hold at most 2,500 people, and the white non-Hispanics listed by the U.S. Census in the Crown Heights neighborhood barely reached 7,000, even during the 1990s. Nevertheless, press reports frequently would wrongly insist that Lubavitchers were the largest group of Hasidim in the world. What they should have said was the Lubavitchers were the Hasidim spread across the widest territories in the world.

them, politicians often chose to meet and be photographed with iconic Jewish figures. No one fit the bill better than a Hasidic rabbi; Menachem Mendel, with his intelligence, charisma, and long beard (which he had unfolded and let grow bushier since his days in Berlin and Paris), as well as his increasingly global view and seemingly benign message of a coming redemption, was ideal for these photo opportunities.

The parade of politicians from America joined those from Israel and in time from other countries and made their way to 770, which became a mandatory stop for many a prominent leader who wanted to speak for or to the Jews. Nearly every statewide elected official (and those who wanted to be one) from New York came to be seen with the Rebbe, as did all the mayors and would-be mayors of New York City, as well as ambassadors and even some foreign ministers. All important Israeli politicians headed for Crown Heights and the Rebbe. They thought a picture and meeting with the Lubavitcher Rebbe would help them with their constituencies, and it probably did. Of course, the truth was that the advantages went both directions, for his stature grew with every VIP who made the pilgrimage to see him.[20]

Even those put off in principle by religious orthodoxies and fundamentalist-type movements could find nothing objectionable about the Rebbe's 1972 call, on the occasion of his seventieth birthday, for "devotion to the cause of spreading kindness and goodness," seeing it as part of his role in "awakening in everyone the potential that he has," as he explained to a *New York Times* reporter.[21] This sounded almost like New Age spirituality.

Moreover, the fact that the Rebbe was in New York City, the media capital of the most important country in the world in that domain, increased his visibility and the perception of his importance. When in earlier years he had gone to the court of his father-in-law in Riga for the high holy days, it was only of significance to Lubavitchers. Now, however, when his Hasidim came to him for the same occasion, it was news for the world. His *farbrengens* at the time of the high holy days with his *shluchim* were making headlines in the *New York Times*, which more and more reported on who he was, who visited him, and what he was doing the world over.[22]

Even more than the personal and political power this gave to the Rebbe, however, was his sense that his rising international prominence and admiration was another sign of the coming messianic age. All the attention fulfilled the words in the Jewish prayer that speaks of what will happen at the end of days and is part of the high holy day liturgy, and since the thirteenth century has been recited as the closing prayer in every Jewish service: "that all the inhabitants of the world will realize and know" of God Almighty's power. If the powerful from among the Gentiles were coming to him, who was the harbinger of that Almighty, that too was for him and his followers a sign of the changing nature of the world and of history. He was, some of his supporters would claim, responsible for the economic boom times, which in America coincided with his reign.[23]

The Rebbe and his *shluchim* were not satisfied to affect life in the spiritual wasteland of America and the secular Zionist Israel only; the Soviet Union, where they began, would have to fall into line as well. Like his predecessor Yosef Yitzchak before him, Menachem Mendel would seek to maintain a clandestine network of emissaries inside the communist empire. He would, near the end of the Soviet regime's rule and the opening of the era of *glasnost*, send them in "the guise of tourists and business travelers."[24] Like Yosef Yitzchak, he sent in supplies of matzah for Passover, prayer books, and tefillin. The number of people who cared about these things was rising because the Jewish consciousness of many Soviet Jews had been raised by the events of the 1967 war (what the Rebbe thought was *his* war) in Israel.[25]

For Lubavitchers, the slow but steady return of the Jews from the Soviet Union to Judaism, the emergence of the refusenik community—Jews who demanded to leave the Soviet Union and sacrificed job, reputation, and position just to be Jewish in Israel even though they were refused an exit visa—was one more sign of the coming redemption.

"We felt," said one of these Jews, "that this was a miracle of the same grandeur as was the Six-Day War."[26] That many of these Jews were supported and sustained by Lubavitchers, including some of the most prominent among them, was for the Rebbe another sign of his role in the shifting of the world.[27] The Lubavitchers saw their Rebbe's intervention in the communist world as responsible for the slow but steady crumbling of the Soviet empire. As Herman (Yirmayahu) Branover, a a professor of metallurgy and among the most prominent Soviet Jews who became disciples of the Rebbe, described it, "When the Rebbe summoned me in April 1985 and told me I should call whomever I can reach by phone in Moscow and Leningrad and tell them that before too long the Soviet Union will collapse . . . I was flabbergasted. At the time the Soviet Union seemed invincible. Yet the Rebbe unraveled the precise details of the unbelievable changes that were to take place in Russia."[28] What the Rebbe actually did say at the time is unclear, but the perception among Lubavitchers was that he was able to see the events in advance—even more clearly than the Soviet leaders themselves. In time, after the fall of the USSR, he would transmit his message to Russia, at one point on a huge screen in Red Square. Where once Stalin and all his successors had reviewed parades, now Lubavitchers gathered to light a giant Hanukkah menorah, while the former Red Army Band played the Lubavitcher song, "God Is One and His Name Is One."[29] Was this not the victory of the Messiah over the dark forces of the evil empire, believers asked?

⁂

And what of the Rebbe personally; what was happening to him during this time? While all this world activity by his *shluchim* at his instigation was increasing, he was aging. The fact that he had no successor was something not talked about openly by his followers, but it was surely a matter of concern. Outsiders who took a growing interest in this ever more public man and his Hasidim, however, were not as discreet. Thus, for example, on the occasion of the Rebbe's seventieth birthday, a *New York Times* reporter who had managed to secure a private audience just before dawn raised the issue of the Rebbe's childlessness by asking, "Who is to be the eighth Lubavitcher rabbi?" The Rebbe replied, "The Messiah will come and he will take all these troubles and doubts," and then added with a smile, "He could come while I am here. Why postpone his coming?" This would be the answer all the Hasidim gave whenever the question of continuity came up. With this, their anxieties about the future were to be put aside. Then they would echo the comments with which the Rebbe on that occasion concluded his answer: "My intention is to live many years more, and the Messiah can come tomorrow or the day after tomorrow."[30]

To hasten the arrival of that event, he moved to open seventy-one new ChaBaD Houses, places where Jews would be brought into the orbit of Lubavitcher activities and influence, in the course of the coming seventy-first year of his life.[31] To eliminate any insecurities his *shluchim* might have about their ability to succeed in this, he took repeatedly to quoting the prophet Malachi (3:10), saying, "test me now in this." His use of this expression of Malachi's, whose name means "My (God's) Messenger" and whom some call the last of the ancient biblical prophets, subtly identified the Rebbe as the one who would continue in that prophetic line. Indeed, as the years passed, many of his Hasidim began to refer to him as "the prophet of the generation." He in turn would respond that his predecessor, "my teacher, my father-in-law," whose place he held and with whom he was identified, was the true prophet.[32]

It seemed as if nothing that happened of significance to Jews was beyond his reach or concern. Thus, for example, in August 1976 he combined ChaBaD celebrations of the fiftieth anniversary of the freeing of Rabbi Yosef Yitzchak from Soviet imprisonment and the freeing of the Alter Rebbe (Schneur Zalman, founder of the dynasty) from his second imprisonment by the czar (which had actually taken place on October 7, 1800) with the success of the daring raid a month earlier that freed Israeli hostages from their imprisonment in Entebbe, Uganda.[33] It was as if all these "miracles" were God's victories that Lubavitchers had instigated.

But even as his empire grew and his influence spread, there was no denying that the Rebbe was no longer a young man. In 1977, a dramatic reminder of his mortality would shake them all. It was the night of Shemini Atzeret (October 3, a holiday of joy on which Lubavitchers, like other Hasidim, make seven circular dances [*hakofes*]). The evening had been filled with extraordinary messianic enthusiasms. According to Lubavitcher sources, at the start of the third *hakofe*, the Rebbe turned to his loyal longtime aide and Hasid Yoel Kahan, the very same man who was there at his ascension to the throne and who now was his *khoyzer*, the one who could and would repeat from memory all his talks, and asked him to lead the circle. The assembled began to chant an unusually explicit chorus: "Soldiers of our master, our teacher and our rabbi, soldiers of our righteous Messiah who will lead us with his tanks to our land with the campaigns and the ammunition in our possession."* As

---

* *Beit Chayenu*, no. 3 (102) vol. 4, 1 Cheshvan 5738 (October 13, 1977), JNUL PA11337, 8. The tanks were the Mitzvah tanks, and the Hebrew word for ammunition, *neshek*, was

they sang, the Rebbe clapped his hands, "and looking in all directions hinted that they all should clap and dance too."[34]

By the start of the next circle, the atmosphere in the synagogue at 770 was still animated with messianic fervor. Again the dancing was intense. Suddenly the Rebbe suffered discomfort in his chest. He tried to ignore it at first; as his wife once said, "He has no fear of pains," that is, he believed he could ignore his mortality.[35] His unwillingness to see a doctor was well known, and in the past his wife would have to use subterfuge to get him to see one. So when she felt ill and he would press her to call a physician, she would agree only on condition that the doctor examined him as well.[36]

As the Hasidim danced the set of dances, the afflicted Rebbe took his traditional position leading the procession. From the diary of one of his secretaries, we pick up the description.[37] "In the middle of the fourth Hakofo the Rebbe didn't feel well and became very pale. . . . [He] asked me to bring his chair closer and sat down caressing his heart. I immediately asked that the doctors who were there to come over but the Rebbe did not let them check him." Perhaps he did not want to show human weakness in front of his congregation. "Meanwhile they brought the Rebbe water but he didn't want to drink it saying that he had not yet made Kiddush [the holiday benediction over wine]. . . .

"The doctor asked the Rebbe if he feels pain around his heart and the Rebbe answered, yes, . . . [adding] 'I am not going to the hospital.'"[38] Hospitals were places where one becomes passive, loses control, and is defined as sick; none of these roles or identities suited the leader of messianic redemption.

The pain, however, persisted, and he sat down. He remained in place for the rest of the service, but much of the room was emptied so that he could get some air. At the end of the dances he went up to his office, and "his face turned yellow."[39] The Rebbetzin, who had by now arrived from President Street, was told by the doctor that it was a heart attack. Asked if her husband should be sedated and taken to the hospital when he fell asleep, she replied, "in all my life, I never saw my husband not in total control, and if he says he wants to stay here, I can't overrule that."[40]

---

also used by Lubavitchers as an acronym for the Rebbe's campaign to get girls and women to light *neros shel shabbos kodesh* (candles of the holy Sabbath).

He was taken neither to the hospital nor to his home on President Street. Instead, he remained in his stronghold, the Lubavitcher headquarters at 770, where a mini-hospital was constructed.* From there he sent a message: "Tell them that I will not budge from 770 and if something has to happen let it happen in 770." His refusal to leave was symbolic of his unwillingness to relinquish power, and to his followers a sign that he was still in charge. For the next five weeks he remained at 770 while doctors treated him. Although he did not appear in public, he continued to deliver talks and discourses from his study via intercom, to underscore his undiminished strength.[41]

Nevertheless, after his massive heart attack, both he and his followers could not ignore the possibility of his mortality. Were they once again going to find themselves in the situation they faced on 10 Shvat 1950, a rebbe with a promise of redemption lying dying and no Messiah in sight? While Menachem Mendel had saved them once from the apparent failure of prophecy, resurrecting their Rebbe, renewing their mission, becoming their savior, and promising them that they would yet witness the fulfillment of Rabbi Yosef Yitzchak's promises, could he do it again? What if he died?

When he emerged after five weeks of self-imposed medical isolation, many thought he was a changed man. To chase away all doubts, he needed to explain to himself the meaning of the heart attack. For him, it was more a metaphysical than a physical event, fraught with spiritual and messianic meaning. He understood it as a warning that he and his Hasidim had not been doing enough, and so he redoubled his efforts and work, encouraging his followers to do more as well. The *farbrengens* that before the attack he had carried on only once a month (and on Lubavitcher festivals and Jewish holidays), he now carried out weekly.[42] They were broadcast over radio, along with an English translation of his remarks and a color commentary of the proceedings by Rabbi Jacob (Yankel) Hecht.[43] Increasingly, the Rebbe used the technology of mass media to press his message

---

* According to Yehuda Krinsky in the same interview, all the local doctors demanded he be hospitalized and would not take responsibility for his treatment if he refused. When at last they contacted Dr. Ira Weiss in Chicago, whom they knew via one of the emissaries and who agreed to treat him at 770, explaining that stressing him by demanding he go to the hospital against his wishes could actually exacerbate his condition, they flew Weiss in to be his physician.

and mission. Unlike other Hasidic rebbes, who shied away from such media, Menachem Mendel embraced them as a vehicle for doing what he viewed as his holy mission.[44] Beginning in the early 1980s, he began to have his talks beamed by satellite to cable stations in Israel, England, and throughout America.[45] His face became a recognized and familiar image, no less so than the televangelists who had perfected such cable broadcasting around the same time. Testing himself, his stamina, and the engagement of his "troops," he remained "extraordinarily active," working "day and night."[46] Nevertheless, perhaps in an acknowledgement of his physical condition, from then on he and Moussia would spend Sabbaths and holy days in the library building that was connected to 770 rather than walking back and forth to President Street.[47]

♪♪♪

As he and his followers saw it, his increased activity made a difference. In May 1977, in an election of historic proportions, Menachem Begin and his opposition nationalist Likud party were swept into power in Israel. The victory of this more traditionally religious man (some Orthodox Jews half-joked at the time that Begin was the first 'Jewish' prime minster of Israel) over the secular socialist Labor party was perceived as a sign of the imminence of messianic times. Less than a month after becoming prime minister on June 20, Begin traveled to the United States to meet with President Jimmy Carter. During that visit, the new prime minister (described simply as "a public figure" in a picture in a Lubavitcher biography) made the pilgrimage to 770 and the Rebbe.[48] The latter used the opportunity to urge Begin not to bend under the growing American and world pressure to withdraw from the land taken in 1967. Steadfastness in maintaining hold of all land associated with the ancient biblical territory of Israel, he told him, would be rewarded.[49] Begin, the Israeli nationalist, of course shared that point of view, and said so.

In November 1977, when Egyptian president Anwar el Sadat made his unprecedented visit to Jerusalem in what would become the first step toward a peace treaty with Egypt, the Rebbe in a special radio broadcast made clear his view that his earlier counsel of steadfastness had borne fruit. Sadat, he noted, acted on his own in coming to Jerusalem to visit the new right-wing Israeli leader. Begin had publicly made no prior concessions, yet his enemy had nonetheless come to sue for

211

peace. Although the Rebbe made this claim, in truth the Israeli foreign minister had made a prior secret trip to Morocco, where he promised in advance that Israel was ready to withdraw from Sinai. The fact that Sadat appeared to act independently of his Russian and Arab allies in his going to Jerusalem to visit the new Israeli premier was also seen by Lubavitchers as a sign of the Rebbe's insight in his counsel.

The Rebbe now asserted that one could "settle all the territories in Judea and Samaria along the eastern border of the Land of Israel, swiftly and in one day," as long as "institutions of Torah" were established that would purify the region and make possible the lasting peace that would come with the final redemption. As for Sadat's desire for the return of the Sinai, the Rebbe readily gave his blessing to Israeli leaders to broker a deal, as he considered it devoid of religious and redemptive meaning. The question of what to do with it, he said, was up to military "experts"—some of whom, of course, he had been consulting with when they came to 770. For him, as he would later explain to visiting retired Israeli general Shlomo Gazit, the messianic era demanded a kind of trinity: *shleymes hatoyre, shleymes ho'om,* and *shleymes ho'orets.* That meant that Jews—true Jews, over whose Jewishness there was no question, and who observed the Torah and mitzvahs—should be sovereign over the entire Land of Israel.[50]

In 1981, on the thirtieth anniversary of his selection as Rebbe, he promoted the initiative of a new children's organization: *Tzivos Hashem,* Army of God (organized in September of the previous year), which was announced in a broadside headlined "All those who are seventh are most beloved."[51] This Seventh Generation's army's mission was to fight a battle even more important than the one for land that the Israelis had fought. This army would make possible the coming of the Messiah. As the Rebbe explained, the enemy with which it contended was the evil inclination, which had to be fought with Torah and mitzvahs, and the children, he asserted, "who are free from all other concerns and can devote themselves completely to the supreme and fundamental battle," would lead the way, as, according to the Midrash, they had done when Moses led the Israelites out of Egypt.* Now, as another Moses figure

---

* For the Midrash, see *Yalkut Shimoni,* 164, 245. Only one who had not raised children could assert that the young "are free from all other concerns." Of course, if the children

took them to the Promised Land, the children would shout, "We don't want to wait anymore; we want Moshiach [Messiah] now."[52] By 1988, the Rebbe would stand under a banner proclaiming this very message for the entire world to see.[53]

Throughout the 1970s and 1980s the Rebbe's *shluchim*, learning on the job, became ever more adept at making their marks locally and as such served to magnify his position. No one was more successful in this regard than Avremel Shemtov, the emissary in Philadelphia, who later expanded his territory to include the District of Columbia. Not only had he sparked the Hanukkah menorah lightings, but in 1977, with the help of the Philadelphia Friends of Lubavitch, he managed to enlist the aid of Polish-American industrialist Edward Piszek in trying to retrieve from Communist-controlled Poland Lubavitcher books and manuscripts left behind by Yosef Yitzchak during his escape in 1940. Six crates of material were returned to ChaBaD in 1977.[54]

By 1982, Shemtov was running what the papers called a "well-oiled [political] machine" in Washington that got Congress to declare April 4, Menachem Mendel Schneerson's eightieth birthday, a National Day of Reflection.[55] Shemtov had approached willing lawmakers who had well-organized Lubavitcher communities in their districts, including then House Speaker Thomas P. O'Neill Jr. (whose chief legislative aide was the modern Orthodox yarmulke-wearing Ari Weiss). At the same time, he spread the word to sixty Lubavitcher centers in thirty states, and instantly Lubavitchers and their supporters were calling their senators and congressional representatives. Barely a week into the lobbying effort, Rabbi Shemtov had close to two hundred congressional co-sponsors on board, and the congressional declaration was assured. This too was seen by Lubavitchers in a messianic context.

In 1984 the Rebbe stepped up efforts not only to return more Jewish people to the performance of mitzvahs but also to focus the rest of

---

were enthusiastic, the future of the group was assured. See Samuel Heilman, *Defenders of the Faith: Inside Ultra-Orthodox Jewry* (Berkeley and Los Angeles: University of California Press, 1999), for a discussion of the role of children in the ultra-Orthodox community. As for their armaments, an example could be found in their use of the so-called four species they sought to get Jews to hold on the Sukkot holidays: the citron was the "bullet," the palm branch was the "rifle," the myrtle a "knife," and so on. Menachem Mendel Schneerson, *Hisvadus*, pt. 1, 5744, 268–69.

the world on the need to observe the Seven Noahide Commandments, those directives demanded of Noah and his offspring for eternity.[56] If the Gentiles acted in accord with these demands, that too would prepare the way for the Messiah. This kind of concern about non-Jews and their moral and religious behavior was practically unprecedented in the modern Hasidic world.

♫

The Messiah, as the Rebbe described him (following the assertions of the medieval codifier Moses Maimonides, whose tract on the subject he often cited and the regular study of which he instituted in 1984), would be "a real human being" and not "something abstract," a great leader and scholar who studied and observed Torah and mitzvahs but would not immediately be recognized by the world at large.[57] He would at the outset guide the Jewish people "in ways of kindness and peace" but in the end would "not operate according to the principles of democracy" but rather force them to comply with God's laws, while he would fight the Lord's battles.[58] Looking around for such a man, many of his followers were convinced that their Rebbe had to be that Messiah. He too had not at first been recognized by the world at large but had turned out to be a scholar and great leader; he had at the outset of his reign launched his kindness campaign. For the more conservative of them, it was sufficient to say, as his secretary since 1957 Yehuda Krinsky did, "If I were asked in this generation who was the most suitable [candidate for Messiah], beyond any question in my mind, it would be the Rebbe."[59]

In making this case, they would argue that his scholarship, as much in science and general knowledge as in Hasidism and Torah, and his ability to speak so many languages were extraordinary. His access to world leaders and the press, as well as his growing fame, were no less so. That was why Lubavitchers for a long time sought to exaggerate his accomplishments even outside the Jewish realm; what once might have been seen as a liability was now presented as an asset. The greater his accomplishments in the outside world, the greater was the importance of his abandoning them in favor of his mission. Finally, his piety and his ability to foretell if not control the events of history, as well as his capacity to fight the "battles of God" and thus to prepare the people for redemption, were for his supporters proof of his grand status.

At first they received little open encouragement from the object of their veneration for this conclusion and therefore deduced that for the present, "the Rebbe has not agreed to reveal himself." His Hasidim would have to request and plead continually until such time as he would explicitly agree. This was the same pattern that occurred in 1950, when they were pressing him to become Rebbe. Then too he had seemed to shy away from accepting, but in the end had been 'persuaded.' Now again, he seemed to shy away from accepting. Indeed, on one occasion, perhaps as early as 1970 or even earlier, one Hasid had been heard to cry out in Yiddish at a *farbrengen*, "Lubavitcher Rebbe! Jews have suffered after such a difficult and bitter war [i.e., the Holocaust]—it is time that you reveal yourself." Menachem Mendel responded at the time, "Do not talk like that for you will force me to leave the room."[60] Yet this belief, which at first the Rebbe did not want to discuss in the open, would grow among his followers with each passing year.

ﬓ

Each Hebrew New Year now became filled with growing anticipation. The Rebbe and his Hasidim would look at the Hebrew letters coinciding with the numbers of the year and seek to find in them a mystical acronym that hinted at redemption. Thus, for example, in 5743 (1983) they saw the phrase, "May this year be the one of the Messiah revealing himself." Even the White House seemed to be involved when that same year President Ronald Reagan honored the Rebbe on his eighty-first birthday with a kosher-catered party at the White House. The Rebbe was not expected to come to the Oval Office, as other such honorees commonly did—"We do not leave Lubavitch." The president of the United States, however, was satisfied to allow the "president" of ChaBaD to remain at 770 and linked by satellite to the proceedings, where all the hoi polloi gathered around Mr. Reagan, who read the Scroll of Honor for the Rebbe, while an image of Menachem Mendel was projected on a screen.[61]

When he accepted these honors from President Reagan via satellite, he assured his followers, "Our Messiah is coming soon."[62] Then he pointedly added the word *mamesh*, which means "in fact."[63] His Hasidim interpreted this last word as an acronym for Menachem Mendel Schneerson and as a hint that *he* would reveal himself soon. The Rebbe knew this was their interpretation, and afterward he used the phrase often, once adding that he meant *mamesh*, "with all its interpretations."[64]

By the mid-1980s this belief in his messianic character began reaching the public beyond the Lubavitcher community and became part of the reporting about the Rebbe. This was a leap; declaring it in the public square constituted a crucial change. At first the news came via indirect means in a popular book about the community. Written by the *New Yorker*'s staff reporter Lis Harris, it described how Hasidim, whom she called "Messianic advance men," believed the Rebbe to be "a potential Messiah." In a long review of the book in 1985, the *New York Times* put the question out in its first most public form: "Is it possible that the Lubavitchers feel they do not need to worry about a successor because the Rebbe himself will be the Savior?"[65] Soon, the assertion would be everywhere, promoted in public by the Lubavitchers themselves.

Yet once again, in the midst of all this growing messianic activity and anticipation came a reminder of his limitations and of a lingering challenge to his leadership. It began quietly in the winter of 1985 as his nephew and the only male heir of the Previous Rebbe, Barry Gourary, and his mother made claims on precious books in the Lubavitcher library. The library, containing many manuscripts that were part of ChaBaD and Hasidic history and thousands of books, had been collected over the years by previous rebbes. As we have seen, it was especially important to Rabbi Yosef Yitzchak, and the subject of correspondence and concern throughout his life. Much of it had been confiscated in 1924 by the Soviets (and as late as 2009, 12,000 books were still being held in the Moscow State Library).[66] Although Rabbi Yosef Yitzchak had tried to repurchase it, he was unable to meet the financial terms of the communists and instead in 1925 purchased the personal library of Shmuel Weiner, the former head of the Asiatic Museum in Leningrad, whose contents he added to the manuscripts and letters he had managed to hold on to despite the Soviet confiscation.[67] To get this library and the documents in it out of Nazi Europe via an American diplomatic pouch, he had been forced to declare that it was not his but rather the property of the American ChaBaD organization.

"I have no apartment," he had written in November 1939, "and I find myself living with friends with my entire family in one room; consequently, I have no space for the books which Agudas [Chasidei]

ChaBaD loaned me for study. I would be pleased if Agudas ChaBaD were to take these books back." His lawyers and ChaBaD officials in America used this letter to persuade the U.S. State Department that the library was thus American property and therefore removable by the diplomatic pouch from where it was in Poland. This ploy succeeded at least in part; some ninety boxes of books arrived in the United States in 1941.[68] Moreover, as a judge would later rule, the letter and subsequent actions had the legal effect of transferring ownership of the books and manuscripts to the American ChaBaD organization.

Nevertheless, the family of Rabbi Yosef Yitzchak, like him, had always considered the library to be their personal patrimony. Indeed, Chaim Lieberman, to whom the original letter was addressed and who served as guardian of the library, generally saw to it that the pages of items in it were stamped "from the personal library of the Lubavitcher Rebbe." Against this background, Barry's claim and actions unfolded.

On his way to and from his parents', Chana and Shmaryahu Gourary, apartment on the third floor of 770, Barry gradually removed about five hundred books, some from the family quarters, and began to sell a number of them, reportedly as many as one hundred.[69] Arguing that the books, many of which he had personally helped carry on the family's flight from the Nazis, belonged to the *personal* library of his grandfather, he claimed them as part of his and his mother's legacy as his direct heirs.[70] Along with his Aunt Moussia, he therefore asserted a shared ownership of them. Barry and his mother were challenged by the Hasidim and their leader the Rebbe, who claimed the library belonged not to the Schneersohn family personally but to Lubavitch, and as such its Rebbe had absolute control over all that was in it. The Gourarys had as their main witness Chaim Lieberman, Rabbi Yosef Yitzchak's faithful secretary, who now was seen by Lubavitchers as an adversary.

All those involved understood that this was not a dispute about books alone. It was about the future and the leadership of ChaBaD, and in the end it was also a feud between two sisters—Chana, eighty-six at the time, and the Rebbe's wife, Moussia, eighty-four—and their families. Even though Barry, then a sixty-three-year-old management consultant from Montclair, New Jersey, was clearly not going to be the next Lubavitcher Rebbe, the growing messianism of the movement surely played a role in this episode. Barry was quoted as saying that Lubavitchers "had acquired many characteristics of a cult."[71] The claim on the books was thus a way to show its leader was not only not Messiah; he could not even control the library. It was also, in a way, evidence that the both Barry and his mother never fully accepted the leadership of Menachem Mendel, even if Shmaryahu did. To believers, the case was seen as an attack by retrograde forces of darkness that would restrain the day of redemption.

At several *farbrengens*, the Rebbe spoke emotionally about his father-in-law's books. On one occasion he called them "bombs" that would explode unless they were returned to 770 Eastern Parkway, and on another he referred to them as "sparks of holiness" that had become parts of his predecessor.[72] Barry charged that after one of his uncle's talks in July, "an inflamed follower of the Rebbe broke into his parents' home and beat his mother, fracturing her hand, nose and palate."[73] The Rebbe did not respond, nor did he visit his badly wounded sister-in-law.

Ironically, the main arena in which the Lubavitchers sought to do battle with the forces arrayed against them was the federal courtroom of Judge Charles P. Sifton. Suddenly the great rabbi was simply a litigant in a nasty family squabble over books estimated to be worth approximately $100 million. The fact that these litigants were using the secular courts rather than their own was not lost on people who were used to thinking about their Rebbe in purely religious and spiritual terms. In the proceedings, Moussia, the "very private" Rebbetzin, was forced to testify and answer questions about her personal life and her and her husband's personal history. It was surely unthinkable to Lubavitchers that the same thing would happen if the grand rabbi himself were to be put on the stand and cross-examined.

But before that could happen, the Rebbe emerged victorious.[74] Judge Sifton was persuaded that the library belonged to the Hasidic court, and in January, 1987 declared that "while each of the rebbes appears to have treated the library as personal property . . . , there can also be no question that the library came to be conceived as one to be used for the benefit of the religious community of Chasidim by the leader of the community, the Rebbe."[75] For the Lubavitchers, this court victory too was a sign that their Rebbe had the Messiah on his side—and that his leadership toward the redemption could not be thwarted.

A year before Judge Sifton's decision, the Rebbe proved that at the age of eighty-six he was still an innovator. In 1986 he initiated a practice that enhanced his fame further and brought thousands to his Hasidic court. One morning during that year, as his Hasidim were finishing their morning prayers, word spread through the congregation that "the Rebbe is giving out dollars for tzedakah [charity] at the door of his study!"[76] Within moments, a line of hundreds had formed. One by one they filed past the Rebbe, and each received a brief blessing and a dollar to be given to charity. Thus began a practice repeated weekly on Sunday evenings, during which Menachem Mendel would stand for hours—testing himself physically and spiritually—while handing out dollars and speaking to thousands. It was a brilliant idea. In place of his private meetings with Hasidim and other visitors, which took a great deal of time, he could now see many more people and would have to spend only a few moments with each. He would give them a dollar to give to charity, furthering his mitzvah campaign and in effect turning everyone who came to him into his emissary in the act of giving charity. He would also not have to shake hands with the many, for they would be given the bills instead.* He would be a tower of strength, leaning on his podium, taking bills handed to him by Leibel (Yehuda) Groner, and offering them to petitioners, who stood for hours in the long line for just moments with him. As they waited, their sense of his importance and majesty grew. The fact that the high and the mighty also stood in line only heightened the importance of the encounter once it happened. Whom else would people wait so long to stand before for just moments?

𝕀𝕀

By the 1980s, the Rebbe and Lubavitch were becoming familiar to much of the world. Their menorah became a familiar brand, as did the image of 770, which Hasidim and supporters had replicated in places as far afield as Israel, Australia, and Brazil. Above all else, the Rebbe's visage had become so familiar that no name needed to be appended

---

*It was also possible to hand them to women, whose hands, in a sign of religious modesty, the Rebbe would not touch.

to it. Even the sculptor, Jacques Lipchitz, buried in Jerusalem by Lubavitchers, dedicated his last sculpture, "Rebbe and his Hasidim," to the Lubavitcher.[77] His repeated exposure in photographs and news stories, helped by posters on which he appeared, made his image iconic. "People are fascinated by the Rebbe's face," said his secretary Krinsky to a reporter. Moreover, the fact that his image was everywhere also played into the notion that he was the Redeemer, for Lubavitchers had no doubt that, as the Jewish pundit Leon Wieseltier once put it, "When the Messiah comes, he will be on CNN all day long."[78]

When a famous poster on which Rabbi Schneerson was visible atop the words "King Messiah" emerged in the 1990s, most who saw it understood the reference. Soon his visage appeared in the center of a banner that read in Hebrew, "Welcome King Messiah." A shop called the Moshiach Store opened on the main commercial avenue in the Crown Heights neighborhood. The Rebbe was now fully engaged by the messianic campaign, committed in private, among his Hasidim, and in public, to the world. He sensed he was approaching the climactic moment. After all, he was not a young man any longer, and he had promised that his generation would be the one to greet the Messiah.

This growing insistence on the imminence of the Messiah was also a denial of death. Ernest Becker has argued that to deny death is at its root "to deny one's lack of control over events" and to reject any feelings of powerlessness and impotence in the face of reality.[79] The suppression of awareness of impending death, Becker explains, plays a crucial role in keeping us functioning. The messianic campaign accomplished this both for the Rebbe and for his Hasidim. It was no less a way of escaping the unspoken feelings of vulnerability and mortality that were surely present in a movement whose leader had no obvious heirs and was approaching ninety. The Moshiach campaign sustained the belief that they were all part of something invulnerable and eternal.[80]

This assumption must surely have been shaken on February 10, 1988, the day the Rebbe's wife of nearly sixty years, Chaya Moussia, or "the Rebbetzin," as they called her, died. She had of course been the key to his entering the court and becoming Rebbe. Had he not married her, he would have been just another relative of the rebbes, but not its central figure. Without the connection to Rabbi Yosef Yitzchak she brought him, would he have been the subject of successful efforts to get him out of Nazi-controlled France?

Perhaps, but throughout their years together he had outflanked her in his importance for ChaBaD, while she receded into privacy. As the years passed, the Rebbe spent more and more time at 770 and with his Hasidim and mission; she recognized, as she said in her deposition at the trial over the library, that like her father before him, her husband now "belonged to the Hasidim."[81] She was a reminder of his previous life and his youth. But she was not, it seems, prepared to be the wife of the Messiah. If Menachem Mendel was Messiah, what would her status be? Was the Messiah supposed to have a wife? Could the Messiah's wife have remained the private Mrs. Schneerson from President Street? Now, however, she was dead, and those questions no longer needed answers. On the other hand, if the Messiah was going to come in this generation, and if the Rebbe was himself that Messiah, would he have allowed the Rebbetzin to die?

Many Hasidim looked for signs in her death and how it happened that would suggest that this was not a random event but something foreseen and part of the grand plan, and which their Rebbe and his Rebbetzin understood.[82] She had begun feeling ill two days earlier. On Tuesday evening Dr. Robert Feldman, who had an office at 1401 President Street, was summoned. His initial diagnosis was a bleeding ulcer, and he suggested hospitalization. Like her husband, Moussia refused to go. Other physicians were called, and the following evening they gathered for a consultation with the Rebbe at his President Street residence; all agreed on the need for hospitalization. After the meeting, at which she was not present, she was informed of the decision not by her husband but by Schneuer Zalman Gourary, one of his assistants, whose area of specialty was dealing with physicians. He told her that the Rebbe himself had sent him and agreed with the decision. Moussia asked that the Rebbe enter her room and tell her himself before she was taken to the hospital, and he did so for a few minutes. In the meantime, Shlomo Zalman sent his daughter Esther on ahead to the hospital to prepare the way for the Rebbetzin's imminent arrival.[83] Then, according to one account, the Rebbe walked his wife downstairs to the waiting car in which Yehuda Krinsky would drive her, accompanied by her doctor and two Hasidim, Shalom DovBer Ganzburg and the aforementioned Shlomo Zalman Gourary, to Cornell Medical Center in Manhattan. In another account, Menachem Mendel took her as far as the veranda at the front door and watched her departure from there.[84] As the car drove off to the hospital, the Rebbe went back into the house, turning to go over the written text of a recent talk that was to be published.

In line with his request, Ganzburg had been keeping the Rebbe updated on her condition with calls every fifteen minutes.[85] There was no doubt the situation was grave. At the hospital, while undergoing an admission interview and examination, Moussia abruptly grew pale and suddenly expired. The Rebbe was apparently on the line as her situation deteriorated, but he did not budge to rush to the hospital, even when Ganzburg, who did not want to be the one to report her death, stopped calling. Instead the women of the burial society were sent for, and Leibel Groner was asked to go to tell their master what had happened. But when he and another Hasid approached the house, they found Ganzburg waiting outside. He told them the Rebbe had prohibited anyone from entering the house, so they remained frozen outside.

They were the Hasidim who were among the closest to the Schneersons, who saw them in their most personal and intimate moments, yet they hesitated to tell the Rebbe this news. Why? Because they were not his close friends or family; they were his Hasidim and as such understood themselves as on another level than his, and therefore unable to reach across the divide at such a particularly personal and human moment. So there he remained, the man who was to lead the generation to redemption, all alone in the world inside his house, bereft of the last person for whom he was not just a Rebbe.

Finally, Dr. Feldman called him from his car and delivered the news. Reportedly, his reaction was to say, "We have to tell the children, the *shluchim*."[86] It was as if to say, "I am *not* alone in the world nor childless; my *shluchim* are my family."

When the body arrived at 1304 President Street, it was brought into the kitchen to be prepared for burial. Menachem Mendel sent in a ring that Moussia had received from her late sister Sheina (whose name was later appended on the tombstone), as well as a small white handkerchief in which was another object, and asked that they be placed in the coffin.* Later he would see to it that his niece, Dalia, selected some of Moussia's dresses for herself.[87]

♒

The news of the Rebbetzin's death left the community of Lubavitchers, and especially the *temimim*, "in a state of shock."[88] Commonly, the death of an eighty-six-year-old woman might be considered sad but not altogether surprising or tragic. But when the wife of a man who promises that the redemption is upon us, and whom many consider able to steer the destiny of the world, dies—reminding all of his followers of the fact that these people are mortal, and that not even the revered rebbe could prevent her passing—that surely constitutes a shock to their beliefs and worldview.

The yeshiva boys were gathering outside and in groups of ten entered through the back door to recite the Psalms. That this inner sanctum, the Rebbe's home, a place that for other rebbes was commonly open to their Hasidim but in this case was off limits when the Rebbetzin was alive, part of the *mysterium tremendum*, was suddenly breachable after her death also added to the feelings of the extraordinary.**

At the graveyard, the Rebbe watched the burial; later, as he recited Kaddish, he was held on to by his cardiologist, Ira Weiss, again reminding onlookers of his mortality. He stopped for a moment and wept. When the burial was over, he stepped across the path and entered the *ohel*, the resting place of his father-in-law, and remained alone there a few moments. His weeping could be heard from outside. For those who watched, this would no doubt be a reminder that even the great and important of Lubavitch had all ended their days here. And the question that hung in the air but could not ever be asked was whether this man, whom they revered and followed, would avoid the fate of all the others. Would the Messiah arrive in time? In any event, the question of what role the wife of the Rebbe would play in all that messianic

---

* In general, Jewish law frowns upon any inclusion of such objects in the shrouds, for the custom is that all people, rich and poor alike, the mighty and the powerless, are to go to the grave in equal fashion. Apparently, an exception was made here.

** Indeed, to this day, the house on 1304 President Street remains a kind of sacred space, untouched since the Rebbe left it and closed to everyone except a select few.

activity was now no longer on the agenda. Fate had removed her from the picture.

As if to demonstrate, however, that he and his Hasidim would not be stopped by her death, on the first Sabbath after the funeral, at the singing of "Soldiers of our Master," a Lubavitcher anthem, Menachem Mendel encouraged them repeatedly with his hand in the way that he often did to sing louder and with more enthusiasm—as if their voices could rouse the Messiah. Their Rebbe was pushing himself and his Hasidim out of their mourning in order to work harder to continue his mission. To be sure, he would spend much of the year of mourning closeted in his President Street home, only going on Sabbaths to 770. The Hasidim respected his privacy. But in the end, he would emerge even more dedicated to hastening the redemption.

Now that he was all alone, he had the plants his wife had cared for sold and the locks on his house changed.[89] With his last connection to his previous life buried, Menachem Mendel belonged completely to his messianic campaign. There was nothing any longer to bring him back to President Street, no one with whom he could recall the days before all this. Over time, he moved entirely to 770, where he would live until his own death.

He concentrated even more on the world stage, and looked at political events through the prism of his messianism. "Messianism," as Anson Rabinbach has suggested, "demands a complete repudiation of the world as it is, placing its hope in a future whose realization can only be brought about by the destruction of the old order."[90] For Menachem Mendel, the old order was one in which secularity and other ideologies governed Jewish life. This had to be ended. It also required making certain that the people who were called Jews were truly Jewish, according to the strict demands of Jewish Torah law. The controversial question of who and what was a Jew, which had obsessed him since 1983, now moved to the top of his agenda. Accordingly, in 1988, shortly after his wife's burial, he opened a confrontation with the Israeli government and with world Jewry over the question of who was truly a Jew.

In the always simmering cauldron of Israeli coalition politics, in late 1988 the matter of who is a Jew came to a boil. The presence of large numbers of recent Russian immigrants, many of them the product of mixed marriages, made the religious parties, foremost among them the ultra-Orthodox Agudat Israel, call for a new government that would finally establish the legal definition of who is a Jew, enshrining forever the hold of Orthodox rabbinical courts on this question. The Rebbe chose this moment to make his move, pushing for this change in the law.

Aiming to unite the entire Jewish people, he in fact created conditions that exacerbated splits among them. Many secular and liberal groups took issue with his proposed changes. Even among the Orthodox he created discord. The centrist Rabbinical Council of America urged the removal of the divisive issue from the political agenda.[91] His support for Agudat Israel, whose campaign literature became adorned with his photograph, caused a split in *its* ranks and led to the formation of a new ultra-Orthodox group, Degel HaTorah, that opposed this confrontation. These opponents were headed by Rabbi Menachem Elazer Schach, head of the Ponevezh Yeshiva and also the Council of Torah Sages of Agudat Israel, who in his antagonism followed the lead of the late Aharon Kotler of Lakewood and the yeshiva heads who for generations had opposed the Lubavitcher messianic fever. They had been roiled by Rabbi Yosef Yitzchak's messianism and even more so by his successor's. They recalled the traumas of past false Messiahs, especially the Sabbateans, and wanted no part of such a movement.[92] But the Rebbe pressed on, because he believed he was acting in accordance with God's will and therefore could not compromise. The redemption was at stake, and the question of "who is a Jew" was central to his messianic plan.

To get his way, he was willing to lock horns with all sorts of people, some of whom argued that by allowing only the Orthodox courts to determine who is a Jew, many of them would be defined out of the Jewish people. Ironically, many of those who opposed this move, particularly in America, were the same Jews to whom Lubavitcher *shluchim* had been reaching out and trying to bring closer to Torah and whose support they needed for their many activities. Now, suddenly a confrontation was set up with them. Many were hurt and angry, arguing that the Rebbe did not consider them Jews anymore.

Jewish Federation leaders, most of whom were neither Orthodox nor in favor of continuing the divisive debate, met in New Orleans that year. In a dramatic moment, one of them stood up in the New Orleans Convention Center and lambasted the efforts of the Rebbe and others to give the power of defining a Jew to Israeli rabbinical courts: "I came out of Auschwitz, a place where they decided 'who is a Jew,'" he said as the convention center fell silent. "I didn't think I was going to live to see the day when it was decided in Israel."[93]

Many appealed to the Rebbe to compromise, but he remained steadfast. He pushed his supporters in Israel to go to the polls in the 1988 election, offering them his blessing if they voted according to his directives. But the new unity government under Prime Minster Yitzhak Shamir did not make the change that would resolve the issue to his satisfaction. And yet his spokesman Yehuda Krinsky declared a victory of sorts when he claimed that "the message has gotten out." Those converted by non-Orthodox rabbis, he said, "are going back to them and saying, 'You have deceived us. You told us we were Jewish when we were not Jewish.'" These people," he continued, "are seeking Orthodox conversions 'by the thousands'"[94] This was wishful thinking. No such outpouring of Orthodox conversion took place. This particular battle was lost.

𝕴

In late July 1990 the Rebbe, breaking with his normal practice of forty years of visits, uncharacteristically went to the gravesite of Rabbi Yosef Yitzchak on the first day (*rosh hodesh*) of the Jewish month of Av, remaining secluded there for several hours.[95] Since each movement of their Rebbe is of cosmic importance for Hasidim, this unprecedented behavior of going on *rosh hodesh* caused a stir. He already had been acting unusually when two months earlier, on May 26, he had announced that the following Hebrew year would have special significance. Such announcements commonly came on the eve of the Jewish New Year, in late September. But apparently he had been troubled by an unfulfilled prophecy he had offered the previous year when he characterized 5750, whose Hebrew name he said was an acronym for "this will be a year of miracles." So he therefore announced early that 5751 would be, according to *its* acronym, "the year I shall *show* you miracles." If the miracles in the first of the two years remained hidden, those in the second would be revealed and apparent to all.

On the Sabbath following his visit to the cemetery, he quoted and commented on Deuteronomy 11:22–23: *For if ye shall diligently keep all these commandments which I command you, to do them, to love the*

Lord your God, to walk in all his ways, and to cleave unto him; then will the Lord drive out all these nations from before you, and ye shall possess greater nations and mightier than yourselves. As the first Gulf War loomed, he spoke again on the second night of Sukkot (October 5, 1990), quoting an ancient passage from the *Yalkut Shimoni*, a fourteenth-century anthology of Midrashic literature: "In the year that [Judaism's] King Messiah will be revealed, nations will challenge one another. The King of Paras will challenge the King of Aram ... and the entire world will panic and will be stricken with consternation.... Israel will also panic and will be confounded." The Rebbe went on to explain that the King of Paras referred to the present-day Iraq and the King of Aram to the world's superpowers (for Aram is related to the word "ram," which means "uplifted"). This ominous situation, he assured all, actually heralded the ultimate good of the coming of the Messiah and the final redemption.

This talk was taken by his listeners to be part of a prophetic message that, in retrospect, they would see as evidence not only of his prophetic but also his cosmic power. He was trying to read the events of history through his understanding of what he viewed as the inerrant text of the Holy Scriptures.

When Iraq's army acting under Saddam Hussein's orders attacked Kuwait eleven days later precipitating the American-led invasion and the first Gulf War, the Hasidim saw these events as connected to their Rebbe's words, for to them he had long since proven his ability to predict, affect, and fathom world events.

Like many Jews, the Lubavitchers were especially concerned about the war's effect on Israel, which the Iraqis threatened should the Americans attack them. The Americans had warned Israel not to counterattack lest the military coalition it had assembled fall apart. Now the Rebbe's words about Israel being "confounded" began to make sense to his followers. When Israel, frozen militarily by the Americans, was attacked in its population centers by thirty-nine scud strikes from Iraq but "miraculously" no one was killed, the Rebbe (or at least his Hasidim) could claim he had prophesied this result.

Indeed, so confident had Israeli Lubavitchers been in the powers of their rebbe that when on the eve of the war he had assured them that nothing would harm them, they had not even bothered to get gas masks, even as all other citizens were taking those the government was distributing throughout the country.⁹⁶ When the war was over, the world would see their confidence was not misplaced.

Throughout the war, the Rebbe had gone to the *tsiyen* to visit the tomb of his late father-in-law. Often he had stayed there deep into the night rather than returning to Crown Heights before sundown for the evening prayers. And when he was late, the Hasidim would wait for his return and put off the prayers until he came, sometimes reciting the afternoon *minkhe* at nine at night, a normally unimaginable deviation. But the Rebbe "was above time," as some Hasidim put it, and these were extraordinary days.⁹⁷

By the holiday of Purim (February, 1991), which celebrated the fall of the evil enemy Haman (whom many traditional Jews who read the Scroll of Esther saw as the prototype for Saddam) and the reversal of his genocidal plans for the Jewish people in times of old, the Gulf War was over, the "King of Paras" was beaten, and the Rebbe could claim perhaps his greatest victory. The "miracle" of this Purim, he declared, was even greater than the one on which the holiday was based, for in ancient Shushan the hand of God had only been only clear to the Jews,whereas this time the miracle was far more public, revealed to all the nations of the world, as hinted in the acronym of the year.⁹⁸

The message was unmistakable: when the Israeli army fought battles, there were casualties, but when the Rebbe "fought" as he had now, no Jews died. As if to acknowledge this power, the secular prime minister of Israel at the time, Yitzhak Shamir, donned a yarmulke and gathered with Lubavitchers and danced in their celebrations. The picture of the prime minister surrounded by Hasidim was plastered on the cover of a *Kfar Chabad* special issue.⁹⁹

♫

Here then was the Rebbe at the peak of his powers. The war meant to usher in the messianic age had been fought and won. This time the Messiah would come without holocaust, torment, or pain. No doubt this victory, for which he and his followers took credit, increased his hubris. "Hubris," as Ernest Becker has reminded us, "means forgetting where the real source of power lies and imagining that it is in one-self."¹⁰⁰ It tends to grow particularly in one who lives in an isolated human consciousness, a condition that seems to define the situation in which the aging leader, bereft of wife, family, and intimate friends, whose followers saw him as a messiah, increasingly found himself. To the believers these were not delusions of grandeur; they were evidence of grandeur.

Already from the beginning of the new Jewish year, the Hasidim, as one put it, sensed that "this year would be different, that something was happening, something was in the air."[101] On Simhat Torah of 1990, during the dancing and merriment, one of the Hasidim began singing a popular Israeli children's tune known as "Barba-abba," but in place of the original words sang "the Rebbe, *shlita* [may he live for many good years, amen], there's no one like you in the world." The ditty ended with the words, "the one who will bring the Redeemer, the Rebbe, Chief of Staff of the world." At first, when the young Hasid began to sing alone, there was silence in the hall. Once before a Hasid had sung something that made reference to the Rebbe in this way, and he had been quieted by the leader, as if he were acting in excess. But this time the Rebbe turned around toward him and waved his hands as if to urge him on. In moments, the whole crowd took up the song. This was the year that all would at last see miracles.

In the month between Purim and Passover, the expectations reached manic proportions. Every Sabbath was filled with talk about the impeding arrival of the Redeemer. On the Rebbe's birthday, a few days before Passover 1991, the anticipation was hard to contain.[102] Many Hasidim were certain that by Passover, they would all be in the Holy Land with the Messiah. Passover, the festival that recounts the miraculous exodus from Egypt, when Moses began the transformation of the Israelites from slaves in exile to a nation redeemed and on the way to entering the Promised Land, the holiday, also called "the Season of Redemption," was now imminent. Some young Hasidim wondered how they would be transported: would they go on planes, or would they be carried aloft by the clouds? The sense of joy that had permeated Purim seemed to grow beyond all bounds.

In his first talk as Rebbe, Menachem Mendel had hinted that the leader of his generation paralleled Moses. The redemption from Egypt was the archetype of the ultimate messianic redemption. As tradition had it, and as Lubavitchers were fond of recalling, "In the month of

Nisan [when Passover occurs] they *were* redeemed and in Nisan they *will* be redeemed."[103] Surely this year at last, as the Rebbe had promised, the final redemption was coming.

With the approach of Passover 5751 (1991), the sense of anticipation was electric throughout the precincts of Lubavitch. As Stark and Fink have observed, "the higher a group's level of tension, the *higher* its *average* level of member *commitment*."[104] In that sense, the general level of commitment at Lubavitch had undoubtedly reached an unprecedented peak.

But Passover came and went, and the Messiah was nowhere to be found. Why did the "Moses of our day" not reveal himself, the Hasidim wondered? They wanted "Moshiach now." So did their Rebbe. Where was the sign he expected?

Five days after the end of holiday, on a Thursday, 27 Nisan (April 11, 1991), the Rebbe went in bewilderment for a "conversation" with his father-in-law at the *tsiyen*. He stayed there for a very long time. We do not know what he said or what he heard. When he came out, the world was unchanged: the earth was as it was, the sun still shone and the stars were visible at night, it was a day like any other. The utter sameness was crushing for one who expected the Messiah.

Surely, this was a time for soul-searching. Menachem Mendel Schneerson had been touched by history and the great events of the twentieth century. No one would be surprised if he was wondering about where his life had taken him. Long ago in Russia, he had watched people around him infected by Zionism, nationalism, socialism, communism, and the currents of migration, but only the last of these had caught him. His marriage and the hopes of having children were now history. The Holocaust had broken the trajectory of his dreams of becoming an engineer and living in Paris, and had forced him to America. There must have been a purpose to all this. He had found that purpose in his mission as a Rebbe and in his conviction that he was charged with bringing the Messiah. He had breathed new life into a Hasidic movement that most observers thought had been crippled if not undone by the blows of Zionism, communism, Nazism, and Americanism. He was viewed as a charismatic leader, an oracle, *if not the Redeemer himself*. But he needed a sign that the redemption was here, and he looked for it from his dead father-in-law—but no sign was forthcoming.[105] His frustration and his sadness overwhelmed him.

He rushed back to 770 and unexpectedly called his Hasidim together for an urgent talk. After the evening prayers that night, he suddenly tried to turn his large pulpit around so that it faced the congregation. Commonly in advance of a talk, a table was set up and a microphone put in place. But no one expected this tonight. In moments, a few Hasidim had shifted the lectern and set up loudspeakers. The Rebbe began to address his flock: "How can it be that until this moment, we have not been able to bring about the coming of the Messiah?" With no alternative answer, he put the blame on his Hasidim, concluding that if those who truly wanted Moshiach to come would sincerely "plead and cry," the Redeemer would have come. They had to really mean it. Here was an echo of the sentiment he had expressed nearly a half-century earlier when he had accepted their call to be their leader: "In ChaBaD the Rebbes have always asked their Hasidim to act on their own initiative."[106]

"How can it be," he continued in desperation and perplexity "that you have not yet succeeded in this time of grace to actualize the coming of the righteous Messiah?"[107] At last, sounding like Moses coming down from Sinai, he cried out, perhaps out of a sense of frustration and maybe even failure: "What else can I do so that the Children of Israel will cry out and *demand* the Messiah come, after all else that was done until now has not helped since we are obviously still in exile, and even more so in an internal exile from truly serving God?"[108] Then he added, sounding almost like Abraham pleading before the destruction of Sodom and Gomorrah, "may it be God's will that at least there be found ten Jews who will persist in demanding of the Holy One" to bring the Messiah immediately, and concluded, "I have to hand over the task to you: Do all you can to bring the righteous Moshiach, *mamesh*."[109]

Abraham, whom the Rebbe had invoked in his first *Basi L'Gani* talk forty years earlier, had been one who, he had told them then, "made others proclaim" the name of God, and thus spread Judaism.[110] He too had for all these years been doing the same. Now, in a desperate tone he was again telling them it was up to them to proclaim their desire for the Messiah *now*, and to get others to do so too.

This desperate cry from the heart soon echoed throughout the neighborhood. It was recorded and its substance was spread beginning the next morning throughout the Lubavitcher world by way of posters, cassettes, faxes, and word of mouth. On the following Saturday night, the final drama unfolded. As the Hasidim gathered at 770 for a *farbrengen* to hear more about what was next in the Messiah campaign, one of the Hasidim called out, "As we know that the Rebbe, may he live long and good years, is the *zaddik* [righteous man] of the generation and our rabbis of blessed memory have told us that that when a *zaddik* decrees, the Holy One Blessed Be He must fulfill—then why does the Rebbe not simply decree that the Redemption come?" This was, after all, what Menachem Mendel had told them that his predecessor was doing in heaven, and he was now the living channel for that Rebbe. A dead silence fell in the hall, as all the Hasidim waited for their leader's response.

He looked at them sharply. "As for bringing the redemption," he exclaimed, visibly rising to the occasion, "*I know* myself well what to do, and I am doing all that is in my hands to do." Then with a powerful rejoinder he concluded, "And in any event, rather than using this opportunity to find new tasks for me, it would be better that each of you decides what is upon *you* to do."[111]

At the end, the Hasidim understood that it was now completely up to them to force the Messiah to reveal himself. A couple of days later a delegation of Lubavitcher rabbis from Israel came to get orders that the Americans already had. They began to spread the news and work with an unprecedented frenzy.

On Sabbath, April 20, 1991, David Nachshon from upper Nazareth took out a bottle of liquor he had prepared the day before and, standing before the Rebbe, announced that with this drink they all would toast the Rebbe our righteous Messiah who would redeem them on the next Sabbath at the rebuilt Holy Temple in Jerusalem, and then he cried out, "Long Live our Master, Teacher and Rabbi, King Messiah, forever and forever," and everyone joined in while the Rebbe waved his hands in time to the singing.

The next day, some Hasidim led by Nachshon, reflecting this passion, came with a manifesto that they wanted all Lubavitchers to sign. It would call on the Rebbe to declare himself Messiah. Only one Hasid held out: Yoel Kahan, by now one of the key old timer Hasidim. He thought the Rebbe did not want such petitions. If Kahan, who had been with the Rebbe so long and who was responsible for repeating his every talk, would not sign, the letter could not be considered legitimate. As the Hasidim prepared to present their petition to the Rebbe in the dollar line that night, Kahan at last was persuaded that his Rebbe would not reject such letters and signed.[112] It all seemed an echo of the actions leading up to his accepting the crown of Lubavitcher leadership forty years earlier. Later the women of ChaBaD would submit their own letter. But these petitions did not lead to the wanted declaration.

Lubavitchers and their supporters began placing ads, costing hundreds of thousands of dollars in newspapers, like the full page announcement from the "Friends of Chabad-Lubavitch" on June 19, 1991 appearing in the *New York Times* declaiming, "The Time for Your Redemption Has Arrived," and urging readers to "appreciate a miracle when it happens before us," and waiting "actively" for the Messiah by means of Torah study, charity and increased Jewish observance.[113] They began telling reporters "the redemption is near."[114] They put up billboards heralding the Messiah's arrival.[115] On August 17th, early in the month of Elul and on the eve of the High Holy Days, Menachem Mendel once again proclaimed "everything necessary for the redemption has been completed," and that "all should stand ready." He explained "the uniqueness of the time in which we are living" was such that "as a preparatory step" for Messiah's coming, prophecy had returned. The rebbes who were "spreading the wellsprings" of Hasidism, he asserted, were the individuals through whom prophecy had returned. Of course, that meant he was the prophet of this generation, the one in which the spreading of wellsprings outward had "been completed, reaching a level that can be comprehended by a person who is extremely remote and having been extended to all corners of the earth." That had been the task the *shluchim* had taken upon themselves under his direction. He asserted that the Previous Rebbe was a prophet and that he, the seventh rebbe, was the prophet who testified to this effect. Then he concluded, "this concept has to be publicized to everyone in this generation. It must be made known that we have merited that G-d [sic] has chosen and appointed a person who of himself is far greater than the people of his generation, to serve as a judge, adviser, and prophet to the generation."[116]

On the final day of 1991, as they commemorated the anniversary of their founder's passing, another letter signed by some of the most respected Lubavitcher rabbis and *shluchim* appeared to accept his status and promised their allegiance "as one" to accept the sovereignty of the King Messiah should he reveal himself.[117] They urged others to sign on. They took on the task of "crowning" the Messiah themselves.

On Sabbath, June 22, the Rebbe offered yet another talk on messianism and concluded, speaking like Moses and sounding like a prophet, "'Those who lie dead in the dust will wake up and shout for joy' [*Isaiah* 26:19], and the Master of Redemption among them and at their head, together with all the Children of Israel—healthy souls in healthy bodies—'We shall go with our young and our old; with our sons and our daughters [*Exodus* 10:9],' flying with 'the clouds of heaven [*Daniel* 7:13]' to the Holy Land, to Jerusalem, the Holy City, to the Holy Mountain, and to the Third Holy Temple, the place, O Lord, which Thou has made for Thine dwelling [*Exodus* 15:17].'"[118] Hearing these words, his listeners, especially the enthusiastic youngsters among them, could hardly restrain their expectations.

Yet no matter how hard they called for "Moshiach now" and how many songs they sang, how many petitions, ads, billboards, or stories about the Messiah they got into the media, the Redeemer remained elusive. As explanations for his tarrying, they looked for additional signs of events that had to precede his arrival.

The final collapse in 1991 of the Soviet Union, the empire that had been so evil and sought to destroy Lubavitchers and their work since its rise to power, was certainly one of those signs. ChaBaD was swift to take advantage of its disintegration, opening its institutions everywhere and even, as we noted earlier, getting so far as establishing its *shaliach* Berel Lazar as chief rabbi of Moscow and perhaps the most powerful rabbinic leader in Russia. Some surely saw in this the hand of their Rebbe. But missing still was the revelation of the Messiah himself. As 5751 gave way to 5752, a new acronym and message had to be found in the letters of the year to explain this. The Lubavitchers declared 5752 the "year of blessings in everything."

This would be the year, the Rebbe promised, that "the world would become united under the flag of the Messiah," and all would be repaired.[119] His Hasidim prepared just such a flag on which a black crown on a yellow background hovered over the Hebrew word *Moshiach*. Later that year, when the Russian Supreme Court ruled in favor of the Lubavitchers and ordered the release of 12,000 volumes they claimed were stolen from them and placed in the Lenin Library, one of the *shluchim*, Boruch Shlomo Cunin, asserted that getting these books "that were the spiritual tools of the Rebbe" represented "the last of the evil being boiled out of the system, a kind of spiritual cleansing," before the final redemption.[120]

The Rebbe had often told his followers, "There can be no King without a nation that will crown him."[121] His "nation," the Hasidim, therefore now crowned him in what would become a series of such events. On Saturday night, January 4, 1992, a panel of Lubavitcher rabbis at 770 thrashed out the matter of the Messiah's arrival and concluded with cries of "Long Live the King Messiah." They beamed their meeting by satellite around the world. Others issued a legal verdict that the Lubavitcher Rebbe was the Messiah.[122] Still, nothing happened.

At the end of the month, when the United States and the Soviet Union signed a bilateral nuclear disarmament treaty, the Rebbe declared this the fulfillment of the "blessings in everything" and of Isaiah's (2:4) prophecy: "they shall beat their swords into plowshares, and their spears into pruning hooks: nation shall not lift up sword against nation, neither shall they learn war any more." But the messianic interpretation of these events, while persuasive to believers, also frustrated them, for once again it did not lead to the expected revelation.

Following a talk filled with new hints of his being the Messiah on February 1, the Hasidim concluded the only solution to their frustrations was to say that they knew who the Messiah was but they had not been able to get him to acknowledge the fact openly.[123] By now, even more Hasidim were calling for their leader to admit he was the one, and even the most restrained Lubavitchers began to aver to outsiders, as one did around Passover in 1992, that while they would "not officially" state that the Messiah was their Rebbe "or that it is he who will soon become the Messiah," they believed it "inconceivable that the Messiah could turn out to be someone else or that [Rabbi] Schneerson could die before the beginning of the Messianic era."[124] In private, they were far more certain.

Yarmulkes emblazoned with the declaration of the Rebbe as Messiah on them were donned by many Hasidim and supporters. References to

Menachem Mendel were now made by quite a few with the title, "His honor, the holy Master, Teacher, and Rabbi, the King Messiah, may he live many good years, amen." Petitions by the hundreds to God to send the Messiah speedily and in our days were signed and sent to him, urging his revelation.

To most of the other rabbis in the world, including other Hasidim and Orthodox clergy, the messianic campaign was excessive and overdone. In that same February 1992, the dean of the yeshiva world and the Rebbe's contemporary, Menachem Elazar Schach, declared to his followers what many others thought privately: that Lubavitchers who proclaimed "behold we have a Messiah" were promoting a "false messiah."[125] One source even quoted him branding the Rebbe "a heretic."[126] Lubavitchers ignored his criticism.

As Rabbi Menachem Mendel approached his ninetieth birthday, which in the Hebrew calendar would fall on April 14, 1992, just a few days before Passover, he remained a remarkable leader. He had come a long way since his days in Russia, Germany, and France. Yet he was more solitary and alone than ever, atop a pyramid of Hasidim, floating beyond their reach. He seemed indefatigable, with unknown reserves of energy, of which Lubavitchers made much. He continued to stand each Sunday evening at the head of the dollar line until late in the night, proving himself to be up to all challenges. He spent enormous amounts of time speaking and editing his writing, and more and more hours sitting at the *tsiyen* under the open sky communing with his predecessor. He met with the high and mighty, planned campaigns, and oversaw what could only be called an empire that stretched over the entire globe. No other contemporary Hasidic leader, most of whom were at best parochial heads of groups that might have greater numbers of followers but narrower visions, could compare. His Hasidim marveled at his accomplishments even as they remained increasingly anxious about the end toward which he had been driving them.

On March 15, 1992, the Rebbe was featured on the cover of the *New York Times* Sunday Magazine under a headline calling him "The Oracle of Crown Heights." For the Hasidim, the fact that he was becoming so celebrated in the press as a seer was yet another sign that he was the Messiah, for they believed that upon his arrival, the Messiah would grab headlines, and his face would be everywhere.

As his birthday neared, he was spending more time at the graveyard. Those around him reported that he seemed depressed and lonely.[127] On March 2 he left for the cemetery, as always eating nothing beforehand but drinking a glass of tea before his departure.[128] At around 3 p.m. he went as was his custom alone into the small chamber in the stone enclosure. No one wanted to disturb him during these hours, for they believed that he was engaged in a dialogue with Heaven, via Rabbi Yosef Yitzchak, "his prophet," and who he was certain was struggling with God to bring the Messiah.[129] Like Moses on the mountain, Rabbi Menachem Mendel had to remain unaccompanied during this encounter with his now in-corporeal predecessor. As the hours wore on, his faithful aide Yehuda Krinsky waited outside.* Commonly, the Rebbe would come out in time to make the return trip to Brooklyn and arrive for the afternoon *minkhe* prayers that had to be recited before sunset, which was around 5:35 p.m. that day. But the Rebbe remained inside past that time. Had he become entranced? Had he ascended to heaven with his father-in-law to argue with God? Was this at long last the end of days, the day the Messiah would emerge? Finally, at 5:40, unable to hold back, Krinsky knocked on the door. When no answer was forthcoming, he opened it.[130]

The Rebbe had collapsed. The Oracle of Brooklyn, whose followers thought he was Messiah, was immobile and silent. He had suffered a stroke, and the damage was substantial. Those who saw him then did not yet realize it, but he would never again make another speech. There was no way to know how long he had been stricken, for he had been all alone inside the *ohel* for over two and a half hours. Had the time for prayers not come, he might have remained in there even longer. Had he not been who he was, he would perhaps have been discovered sooner and treated more quickly—something that was essential in limiting the damage of a stroke. But tragically and ironically, because of who he was, he lost that time.

Krinsky called *Hatzoloh* of Brooklyn, the Orthodox paramedic ser-vice. It was now rush hour, and without the miracles of a Messiah, that

---

* According to Yehuda Krinsky (interview by Samuel C. Heilman, May 10, 2009), he accompanied the Rebbe into the *ohel* but because all that we have learned about the "meetings" at the grave and the intimate and private nature of them, we find it difficult to square this testimony, fifteen years after the event, with other sources.

would surely slow things down. According to Krinsky, the ambulance suffered a dead battery and another had to be summoned. The Rebbe's doctors, who also had been contacted, decided he needed to be hospitalized. But the Hasidim, recalling his reaction to his heart attack, knew that their Rebbe did not like to go to hospitals. While they waited for the ambulance to navigate through the narrow pathways of the cemetery and precious minutes passed, they debated the matter. A stricken Messiah does not go to a hospital, there to follow the orders of physicians and nurses, stripped of his clothes and his dignity. In the end he was taken to his "palace" at 770.[131]

By the time the ambulance reached Eastern Parkway, word had begun to spread about what had happened. As the day gave way to night, the feelings of hope among the Hasidim gave way to dark foreboding and fear.[132] From this moment on, the leader of Lubavitch became a captive of his Hasidim and his movement. Immobile and mute, he would be secured by his closest aides, doctors, and therapists. The sad charade that he was still leading them would be kept up, as reports were circulated about his remarkable strength and powers of healing.

The "realists" were praying. About 4,000 people recited the entire cycle of 150 Psalms together at 770 while a smaller band of yeshiva students continued the effort throughout the day and night in a twenty-four-hour marathon of prayer in hopes that God would grant their rebbe a full recovery and allow him to fulfill the prophecies he had adopted from his predecessor.[133] In Israel, where two weeks earlier the cornerstone was laid for an exact duplicate of 770 to be built in preparation for the Rebbe's arrival with or as the Messiah, and barely weeks after Lubavitchers "trumpeted the Messiah's imminent arrival on a hundred billboards and thousands of posters and bumper stickers bearing the image of a rising sun and the legend, "Prepare for the Coming of the Messiah," prayers were now being recited for him at the Western Wall.[134]

The man who was now silenced and paralyzed seemed to be the incarnation of a failed prophecy, his situation a demonstration that their faith in his promises was mistaken.[135] As Rodney Stark and others have shown, "other things being equal, failed prophecies are harmful for religious movements. Although prophesies may arouse a great deal of excitement and attract new followers beforehand, the subsequent disappointment usually more than offsets these benefits."[136] The Lubavitchers were faced with a situation that was fraught with difficulty. Because of this, it was critical for them, and particularly for the *shluchim*, who were on a quest to increase followers, to deny their disappointment and rev up their enthusiasms. They had to diminish the cognitive dissonance between the all-too-apparent weakness and limitations of their speechless and crippled rebbe and his promises to the world that he and his generation were controlling history and would lead humanity to the ultimate redemption.[137] All that disconfirmed the promise had to be deflected.

More than forty years earlier Menachem Mendel had taken on his mission from Yosef Yitzchak, resurrecting the hope and sense of purpose of ChaBaD after the latter had been stricken with immobility and silence in his last days. But now that the same had happened to him, who would or could accomplish such revivification? There was no replacement for the seventh rebbe; the Messiah was supposed to have come and taken leadership by now. But there was no one present who could follow Menachem Mendel. As broken as he was, he would have to remain their Rebbe.

As the Hasidim sorted through the new reality, three types of reactions would emerge: adaptation, reaffirmation, and reappraisal.[138] The first tried to maintain that one could adjust to the situation and maintain continuity "by appealing to a number of post-hoc rationalizations."[139] Reaffirmation, in contrast, involved the insistence that the new developments did not contradict prophesies but actually were built into them and that the Messiah was still imminent. Reappraisal, which would come later, aimed to come to terms with what had happened by looking for a new way to go on.

While the much-diminished Rebbe languished at 770, the adapters among his Hasidim still celebrated his birthday with grand affairs in Washington, Jerusalem, and throughout the globe.[140] In New York, the Lubavitchers marked the day with a convoy of ninety mitzvah tanks fanning out in the metropolitan area.[141] Efforts were made to minimize in public the effects of the stroke, for how could the man who was the Redeemer be so cruelly stricken? Expressing this approach, Krinsky announced that the Rebbe's prognosis was "excellent," adding, with a touch of forced humor, that he was, however, "not keen on this enforced hiatus." As for his inability to speak, that was not a cause for worry. "The Bible tells us that even Moses had a speech problem," as one follower put it.[142]

As adaptations became more difficult when the broken condition of their leader became clearer, new explanations needed to be articulated; hence the efforts at reaffirmations. True believers (and at the start, most Lubavitchers were among them) looked to what they "knew" about the coming of the Messiah for some guidance. They insisted the blow to his health, whose severity became impossible to camouflage, was part of the suffering the Messiah would have to endure before his arrival, as prophesied in *Isaiah* (53:4–5), where the wounded Redeemer is esteemed though stricken, smitten by God and afflicted. Some "referred to the writings of Maimonides to argue that the Rebbe himself had chosen to become ill and had taken on the suffering of the Jewish people."[143] This conviction was not unprecedented in the reactions of believers to the suffering of their messianic leader.[144]

Instead of giving up their campaign, calls for the afflicted rabbi to reveal himself grew to a fevered pitch. "In some seventy cities from Canada to Israel, rabbinical judges (all of them Lubavitchers) issued a joint declaration calling on all Jews to recognize Schneerson as 'the Rabbi of all Israel' and to beseech God "that this generation should merit that he be revealed as the Moshiach." Others again decreed that he really was Messiah and would live forever.[145]

To support these reaffirmations of imminent messianism, the Midrash, the great treasury of legends and folklore that was used to supplement Jewish knowledge, became an important resource. It told of the struggles the Messiah would have to undergo in the end of days and how his "tongue would cleave to his mouth." Was this not what now had happened? The Rebbe Messiah's illness was, as his predecessor's death had been explained to them forty years earlier, really part of a life-and-death struggle with Heaven to force the redemption. Their leader was not fighting for himself and his own health, but for the Jewish people. At the end, surely there would be a happy recovery and a day of true redemption. The agonies the Rebbe was suffering were simply a trial to see if those who believed in him were sincere in their faith in his message. Did the sufferings of the Israelites not intensify just before they were freed from their bondage?[146]

In another act of reaffirmation, some Lubavitcher Hasidim also argued that while the days before the stroke were a time in which the Messiah was about to reveal himself, the days after were a time of occlusion. "The Rebbe is now in a state of concealment. The Jews could not see Moses on Mount Sinai and thought he was dead," as one Hasid explained, warning what the consequences of lack of faith were in the days of Moses. "They built the golden calf and had a vision of him lying dead on a bier, whereas he was in fact alive and in a state of concealment." Their Moses, Menachem Mendel, was doing the same. He had been on the edge of revealing himself and now had retreated behind his illness because "the spiritual energy required to bring Moshiach is very great and his body is depleted of energy."[147] This period, some suggested, would last three months or so until the Rebbe's birthday, at which time all would be set right. Indeed, there was a whole series of calculations that sought to find in the calendar explanations for events and signs of the future.[148]

Other explanations were also sought as the Hasidim became manic about their study of even the most obscure sources and commentaries on the Messiah, hoping to find answers that would help them square the reality with their beliefs and allow them to reaffirm the harmony between them. Sometimes this required them to tamper with reality, suggesting the Rebbe was not crippled and mute but still sending messages out to them and the world. After all, he was not hospitalized, so that must mean he was not so incapacitated.[149] When all other reasoning failed, there were those who simply claimed that because their Rebbe was "beyond the boundaries of nature," they could expect healing that was likewise beyond those boundaries.[150]

But the stroke had done massive harm, and while some believers were persuaded by these efforts to reframe the illness in terms that did not contradict the messianic hopes, others were finding it increasingly hard to adapt. Both those who chose adaptation and those who sought reaffirmation could not make the transition to the rehabilitation that their leader needed, the first because they wanted to make it seem that little had changed, the second because they expected miracles.

In fact, the Rebbe required physical, occupational, and speech therapy. Post-stroke rehabilitation demands compelling the often reluctant and depressed patient to work very hard and cooperate in his recovery.

Stroke victims are not always easy to handle, nor do they necessarily embrace rehabilitation with gusto, especially at age ninety or when they expect history to end momentarily. How could a Rebbe—or a Messiah—be forced by his Hasidim to do what he did not want to do?

In the absence of family who would make decisions about the treatment of the Rebbe, and in light of the fact that he had never created a council that would run things with absolute and clear lines of authority in the event of his incapacitation, his secretaries, primarily Yehuda Krinsky and Leibel Groner, but also Binyamin Klein and Shalom Mendel Simpson, took over. But they often quarreled over what was best. Without an active Rebbe in control, they fought about who would make decisions. By 1993, as the Rebbe's condition deteriorated, the intrigues and rivalries at the court that swirled around him seemed to know no bounds, and a deluge of machinations flowed over Lubavitch. Phones were tapped, conspiracies suspected. Doctors of all sorts were being brought in by different groups of Hasidim who believed they knew the right doctor who could be of help.[151] Chaos reigned; there was no overall organization to these efforts, and it was not clear whether the doctors or the Hasidim—and if so which—were in charge. The frustrations and confusion often spilled into the street. There were no ultimate authorities.

In the meantime, the Rebbe, once thought to be the Redeemer of the Jewish people, lay helpless in his bed at 770 in a room filled with hospital equipment and tended to by a twenty-four-hour-a-day rotation of Hasidim. Unable to speak, nourished via a feeding tube, and lacking almost any kind of intellectual stimulation or very much in the way of rehabilitation, he was a prisoner of his body and of his situation. The screams that were occasionally heard from behind closed doors, which no one managed to be able to properly interpret, were sometimes audible on the street and only intensified the sense of chaos. These screams, it would turn out, were not the birth pangs of the Messiah but rather the death rattle of a dream of redemption and the sundowning of its prophet.

〰️

When the Rebbe returned for the first time to the congregation, on Rosh Hashanah, he was no longer a leader; he could only watch in silence. It was left to his handlers to inform the world what he was feeling and thinking.[152] They would become the channel through which the Rebbe would 'speak' and show the way. But only the truest of believers could trust that the directives that emerged were genuinely his will.

The days, weeks, and months became filled with a seemingly endless series of pseudo-events that promised further revelations, coronations of the Messiah, and reinterpretations of reality.[153] In all these, expectations rose and enthusiasm was overflowing, crowds were assembled and the press summoned. But absolutely nothing really happened. By January 1993, some Hasidim were promising there would be a true and miraculous coronation of the Rebbe as Messiah.[154] The special Torah scroll that had been readied for the occasion was placed in the ark. Overflowing crowds were gathered at 770—Hasidim had taken to wearing "Moshiach beepers" that were to signal them when the Messiah was to appear so they could get to the synagogue for the blessed event.[155] The most ardent of the followers—often those who had invested the most emotionally in the prophecy, who had internalized the charge their Rebbe had given them to really want the Messiah to come—were getting ready for the "dead to rise from their graves" and for the journey to the Holy Land and the rebuilding of the Holy Temple in Jerusalem. Some women had taken to carrying tambourines, a reminder of Moses's sister Miriam's striking of such an instrument when the sea split and the Israelites were miraculously freed by God from their exile in Egypt.[156]

A satellite feed was prepared. The Rebbe, brought out to sit among his aides on a small balcony built to look out over the synagogue, stared blankly as the Hasidim pushed to see him and repeated for more than eight minutes, "Long Live Our Master, Teacher, and Rabbi, the King Messiah forever and ever."[157] Some interpreted his imperceptible movements as signs that he approved, while others saw nothing but a broken victim of false prophecy and misplaced hopes.

Those who celebrated the occasion were organized by a new group of Lubavitchers calling themselves "the International Committee to Bring the Moshiach," headed by Shmuel Butman, who was able to get the press to buy into his extravagant media event. Others, including Yehuda Krinsky, who had learned to adapt to their disappointments, called this assembly of coronation "dishonest, dangerous, confusing, sacrilegious," and "a horrible exploitation" of the situation in which they all found themselves.[158]

Rabbi Menachem Mendel's trusted and longest-serving aide, Chaim Hodakov, had died at ninety-one on April 23, 1993 (some Hasidim claimed he had done so to go to the Heavenly Court to argue on behalf of his rebbe and ask for his healing and the fulfillment of his mission).[159] The Rebbe was now the last survivor of his generation. But now his life was the subject of frustration and broken promises mixed with hopes and prayers.

Adaptation and reaffirmation competed with one another. Representatives of each reaction jockeyed to determine the nature of Lubavitch—and the Rebbe seemed buffeted between the two, a king who had become a pawn.[160] On the day of the coronation, Krinsky's adaptive reaction was that the gathering was simply "a day that the Rebbe wanted to be with his people."[161] Nothing had really changed. For Butman and the messianists he represented, the coronation was a reaffirmation of the Rebbe's campaign for Moshiach, an event bringing the end of days another step closer. Yet regardless of these debates, nature took its own course.

♒

On March 8, 1994, the Rebbe was hospitalized with seizures he had been suffering from for two days.* His person was now completely under the control of others. Two days later he suffered another massive stroke and was transferred to intensive care at Beth Israel Hospital in Manhattan. The Hasidim "converted the medical center's meditation room as well as the hospital cafeteria into a makeshift yeshiva, yet another outpost for a group that survived world wars by uprooting itself and going into exile."[162]

A third stroke followed on the sixteenth His condition was described as critical by hospital spokespeople, and Krinsky issued a written bulletin that indicated "deterioration."[163] A vigil formed outside,

---

* His taboo on hospitals had already been broken when he was brought in for gallbladder surgery in 1992 and again in early 1994 when he underwent cataract surgery. David Gonzalez, "Lubavitcher Grand Rabbi Hospitalized After Seizures," *New York Times*, March 9, 1994.

where crowds in the streets gathered to pray and wait. At 770, petitions to God were desperately composed and signed, demanding that the Almighty allow the comatose rabbi to rise and reveal himself. Again the Hasidim sent out a caravan of mitzvah tanks and tried to get Jews to put on tefillin; the Rebbe had always seen these as a source of blessing for him. The *shluchim* were now piloting the campaign on their own initiative.

"It takes a lot of courage to participate in this today," said Rabbi Avremel Shemtov, the Rebbe's emissary in Washington and now one of the senior voices of the movement and today chair of Agudas Chassidei Chabad. "The mood is not there, but it is done because we know this is what the Rebbe wants."[164] The *shluchim* knew, and *they* were running the show.

Then, at last, it was over: Sunday morning, 1:50 a.m., June 12, 1994, Gimmel Tammuz, 5754. Within hours he would be buried, no member of his family present to mourn him or attend his funeral; the Hasidim, following a decree of their rabbinic court, instead tore their clothes in the traditional sign of mourning that surviving family members are required to display.[165] Few of the rabbinic royals from other Hasidic groups or from the yeshiva world were there. Just as they had turned away from Yosef Yitzchak and failed to attend his funeral, now they remained notably absent at the burial of his successor. They had never liked his messianic campaign and the clear implication that he was the one who outshone them all or that he alone knew what Jews had to do to hasten the Messiah. None had accepted the claim that he was the Messiah incarnate. Politicians, who knew no such distinctions and who had long ago been persuaded of the Lubavitchers' importance, were sprinkled throughout the crowd.

When the Rebbe's body finally was brought out of the door, borne in a casket made from planks of his study table, it passed through a sea of his Hasidim. A gasp followed by a scream went out from the crowd that washed across Eastern Parkway. In short order the coffin was whisked into the hearse, and after a brief cortege as it parted the multitude and left Brooklyn, it was put into the ground so quickly that most of the thousands who had followed the hearse to Old Montefiore Cemetery where he now lay in the *tsiyen* next to his predecessor had not been able to witness the internment. Perhaps the Hasidim did not want to see what would remind them that their Rebbe had after all been flesh and blood, and that he was truly dead.(Indeed, there would be some who would deny he was really deceased.) Or perhaps there were fears that the messianists would not allow the burial to take place, and would demand more time for him to rise. But moments after the body was placed into the ground, the fresh grave, which thousands now lined up to visit, was covered with earth and handwritten notes, requests for blessing to and for the Rebbe.

Some still could not assimilate the reality. "We heard his heart had stopped beating, but nobody was really alarmed," said Devorah Cadaner, a Lubavitcher true believer, to a reporter, "We just figured he'd pull through."[166] Quite a number "expressed the idea that he would be resurrected," finding Jewish sources for their belief, which struck many as dangerously close to the approach that had been identified for generations with Christianity.[167]

Others expressed opinions that echoed with the arguments that the Rebbe himself had made when his predecessor had died. "I don't believe the Rebbe has forsaken us yet," said Zalmen Marozov, who came with his family from Montreal. "Once he is out of the body, it is the soul and you have no more limitations. Hopefully he can accomplish everything he wanted to now."[168] "The Rebbe has great power now," a teenage Lubavitcher said, adding, "His spiritual presence is even greater now in all the world."[169]

Still others stressed that their faith was not undermined. "The fact that the Rebbe obviously passed away and is not in a position to be the Redeemer has nothing to do with the concept of the Redeemer himself," explained Sholom Weinberg at the cemetery. "At any second the world could turn good and the Messiah could come," the Hasid said, accounting for his continued optimism.[170] The world now had to do more to merit that arrival.[171]

Articulating the attitude of reappraisal, Manis Friedman, a *shaliach* from Minnesota, argued, "Without the Rebbe there to provide that spark, we have to be self-propelled. We are going to develop a little more imagination and initiative."[172] This meant they would now be trying to imagine and intuit what their missing Rebbe would want. *They would be the messengers carrying the message that was now becoming more and more their own. Following their Rebbe's example, they* would begin to channel him as he had his Rebbe. As they saw it, the Rebbe might have been taken from this world, but he had not abandoned his people, nor would they abandon him. As he had been on a mission for *his* Rebbe in the latter's afterlife, they would do so for their Rebbe until the arrival (or perhaps the "return") of the Redeemer.

CHAPTER 8

On a Mission from the Rebbe in His Afterlife

𝄢

In the immediate days and months following the Rebbe's passing on Gimmel Tammuz, as had happened after the stroke, his Hasidim continued to be divided mostly into those who tried to adapt to the new conditions and those who with perhaps a forced enthusiasm sought to reaffirm his mission and prophecies. In general, the latter came to be known as the "*meshikhistn*" (messianists), hard-core believers in the messianic message and that their Rebbe remained the Messiah despite his physical demise, while the former were inaccurately termed the "non-*meshikhistn*." We say "inaccurately" because they still accepted the prime directive of their rebbe's mission, which defined their activities as driven by a desire to and a conviction that they could hasten the coming of the Messiah and the day of redemption. They continued to believe what he had promised them: that this day was coming in the foreseeable future, and he would lead them. But while the *meshikhistn* continued to press this messianic idea in public and insisted nothing had changed, the others preferred to downplay the subject of messianism in public and focus instead on maintaining the vigor of the mission while adapting to the new realities. They did not insist on stressing the supernatural element of their beliefs or that nothing fundamental had changed since Gimmel Tammuz, as did the *meshikhistn*. The non-*meshikhistn* did not continue to argue openly that the Rebbe was the Messiah and would reemerge to claim his throne, leading the world to the Promised Land and redemption. They believed that "while the scenario is possible, it should *not be a public position*."[1] We shall call this "restrained messianism."

Yet the simple adaptation of restrained messianism grew increasingly difficult in the immediate years of the Rebbe's afterlife, because of the energy and attention that the *meshikhistn* generated with on ongoing series of events and a very public campaign to convince themselves and others that the Rebbe was still with them and controlling reality. Moreover, *meshikhist* enthusiasm, driven in part by the need to reaffirm a belief that seemed so obviously belied by reality, energized Lubavitchers with an effervescence that filled the Lubavitcher synagogue in Crown Heights. In many ways, this is precisely what Leon Festinger, Henry Riecken, and Stanley Schachter had argued in their famous study of what happens when prophecy fails.[2] In a book by that name they had explained that in the face of disconfirming evidence but a continuing desire to maintain faith in a prophecy that seems to have failed, believers may often intensify their belief and try to convince even more others of its truth, in hopes thereby to persuade themselves and banish doubt.

Both groups claimed they were carrying out their Rebbe's wishes and that they were certain what he wanted of them now. In a sense, both borrowed from Menachem Mendel's own responses after the death of *his* Rebbe, Yosef Yitzchak, claiming that the Rebbe did not die but was simply struggling to bring the Messiah more than ever with new tools and under new circumstances—and that he could and did send them messages and answers as he had when he was physically present among them.[3] The absence of his presence had somehow to be overcome.[4]

However, while the *meshikhistn* resisted any form of revision of the Rebbe's message and its final interpretations, seeking to maintain the high sense of anticipation of his final years; their opponents moved gradually toward a routinization of the charisma and a reappraisal and systemization of the mission, which took on a life of its own. In time these differences would grow and lead to something like a schism within Lubavitch. It would take some time to ripen, but when it did, it was unmistakable.

Perhaps the most visible and in many ways most symbolic expression of these divisions was a dispute over control of the headquarters building at 770 Eastern Parkway. Other than the Rebbe's image, the building had become perhaps the most concrete representation of his continued presence in Brooklyn. That structure, owned by Agudas Chassidei ChaBaD, now headed by Avremel Shemtov, since its purchase in 1940, and the adjoining buildings at 784–788 that had become part of the 770 complex in 1942 were now being shared by both groups. The *meshikhistn*, who quietly incorporated themselves as the "Congregation" in 1996, gradually gained effective control over the main Lubavitcher synagogue and study hall at the 784–788 address. That control was challenged in a legal case that began a few years later and was heard in New York's Supreme Court.[5] That the lawsuit, officially pitting Merkos L'Inyonei Chinuch (chaired by Yehuda Krinsky) and Agudas Chassidei ChaBaD versus Mendel Sharf et al. or the Congregation, was not simply about the building was made manifest by the lead *gabe* (Congregation official), Zalman Lipskier, who in an affidavit stated that "the real issue in dispute involves conflicting views on how our faith views the passing of the Grand Rebbe Schneerson and whether or not at this time he may be referred to publicly as the Messiah."[6]

The case began over the subject of a cornerstone on the building that was placed following Gimmel Tammuz. In the words of the court documents, "the true extent of the schism was realized when a plaque previously installed at 784–788 shortly after the Grand Rebbe's death which contained the 'of blessed memory' phrase [following his name] was defaced to the point that the controversial phrase was obliterated. To messianists, who insist that the Grand Rebbe never really died or would soon be revealed as the Messiah, the 'of blessed memory' reference and its implication that the Grand Rebbe is deceased is tantamount to blasphemy."[7] The *meshikhistn* therefore defaced the cornerstone, ultimately trying to remove it altogether. Those who opposed them took them to court, hoping thereby to eliminate the *meshikhist* influence over the synagogue. But they did not go to a rabbinic court. Lacking the ultimate authority of their Rebbe to determine who was truly following his wishes, they sought the authority of the Supreme Court of the State of New York to decide on the matter.

At first the *meshikhistn* ignored this move. Because they constituted the vocal majority among the daily attendees, they had effective control over the synagogue and had independently removed the offensive plaque. They resisted any change in their beliefs that the Rebbe was the Messiah and would soon return. Typical of this resistance were the comments of one *meshikhist*, Yitzhak Fuchs, who, like many of the other worshippers filling the main synagogue, wears a small yellow lapel pin with a crown and the word "Messiah" in Hebrew, and when asked about the Rebbe insists that he had only disappeared "but he's not dead."[8]

In December 2006 the *meshikhistn were* threatened with contempt for failing to appear in court.[9] In March 2006, Judge Ira Harkavy ruled that Agudas Chassidei ChaBaD held title to the property and could put up any plaque it chose on the building, and that the Congregation could not prevent it from doing so or damage or install its own plaque. To ensure this decision was enforced, the judge granted a permanent injunction against the Congregation, dealing a blow to the *meshikhistn*. On December 27, 2007, the same judge ruled on whether the Congregation could be ejected from the building. He found "that Agudas and Merkos are to be awarded judgment granting them each immediate possession of the synagogue space."[10]

In April 2008, the dispute returned to the Supreme Court, this time because Krinsky and Merkos were apparently trying to install a "security upgrade" to the synagogue premises, presumably in order to lock out the *meshikhistn*.[11] With no living Rebbe to settle the dispute, different groups of Hasidim continued to battle one another, each claiming to represent the true will of their leader and gain control of the building that represented his last worldly abode. But, as we shall see later in this chapter, the ongoing dispute over the building was not the only consequence of the absence of an ultimate authority.

◊◊◊

Despite the ongoing differences between *meshikhistn* and those who do not share their point of view, neither group has as of this writing utterly broken the ties to the other. Local communities and even families may be divided in their understanding of what it means to continue to be a follower of the Rebbe. Nevertheless, the common devotion to him and his mission, a reluctance to create an emotional breach within families, as well as the absence of another single individual universally accepted as their rebbe, has allowed all of these people to continue to identify as members of ChaBaD Lubavitch. Whether this common identification will be enough to avoid the emergence of completely different streams of ChaBaD—as was the case in the past history of this Hasidic group—each with their own leadership, customs, and beliefs, remains to be seen.

Each group has its synagogue bulletins and newsletters, the *meshikhistn* with their *Sichas HaGeula* (Talk of the Redemption) and the others with *Sichas HaShavua* (Talk of the Week).[12] Each group celebrates Gimmel Tammuz differently. *Meshikhistn* tend to see this as a day that should reaffirm the messianic status of the Rebbe, while the others see it as a day to celebrate their continuing attachment to his mission and principles. Until now, they have held their gatherings in different locations: the *meshikhistn* using the synagogue at 770 and the others using a variety of larger venues. Yet despite these differences and others, the instances of bitter outbreaks of conflict have for now been relatively limited. A group as small in numbers as full-fledged Lubavitchers cannot afford a full-blown schism. Moreover, all Lubavitchers continue to want to bring on the day of redemption.

As we suggested in the opening pages of this book, this belief carries with it a denial of death, a repudiation of reality, abetted by the powerful belief in messianism. At the heart of the Lubavitcher effort to "bring on the end" is a relatively simple recipe for action, at least as promoted widely in the media. According to their Rebbe's cosmic calculation, as we noted earlier, the birth pangs of messianic redemption are over, ended by the Holocaust. The Moshiach campaign essentially revealed the ultimate purpose of the mitzvah campaign. In ads and distributed leaflets, Lubavitchers provided a checklist of activities to which Jews should commit themselves. These ads began before the Rebbe's death, but they have continued afterward as well. They suggest that all it takes to tip the scales from exile to redemption is for all Jews to study traditional Jewish sources on what is meant by the messianic age, "broadening and deepening one's study of other areas of the Torah" (that is say, to explore its kabbalistic esoteric meaning, which ChaBaD thinking had opened to all Jews) and, of course, "undertaking the practical observance of mitzvahs," as well as "increasing one's daily contribution to charitable causes." Those written commitments are then to be sent to headquarters at 770 along with the signers' names in Hebrew and English, mother's name, address, and a request for more information about the Messiah and redemption.* There were even toll-free phone numbers that Jewish people could call for immediate commitments; operators were standing by.

These promotions of the messianic age had become intensified during the final years of the Rebbe's life, in proportion to the conviction among Lubavitchers that their generation was living in "an era of miracles." The miracles they had witnessed included, in the words of the ads, "the unforeseen collapse of the iron curtain and its satellite regimes [and] the epoch-making ingathering of hundreds of thousands of suppressed and stricken exiles, converging on the Holy Land from undreamed-of directions." The celebration of the latter as a sign of the coming of the true Messiah of course ran in the face of what we have seen were years of Lubavitcher assertions that the Zionist state was anything but a sign of genuine redemption. But after 1967 that opposition had become muted, once the Rebbe and his Hasidim came to believe that what happened in the Holy Land was the product of Lubavitcher activities.

In the last years of the Rebbe's life, believers could still point as well to the swift victory over the tyrant in Iraq ("Babylonia," as they sometimes termed it) in the first Gulf War, and in particular the fact that no Jews were hit by the missiles that he and his armies had launched against Israel. These miracles, the Lubavitchers argued, still had to be complemented by actions on the part of Jewry that would push the age toward the tipping point and hence move the world from the era of miracles to the one of final redemption. That last push was what the *shluchim* were still hard at work trying to bring about.

History, however, continued to unfold, and time took its toll on both groups. More than fifteen years after their last Rebbe's death, while the *shluchim* were, in spite of everything, continuing his mission, "going from one place of work to another," the era of miracles was no longer quite as lustrous or obvious, and the operators were no longer standing

---

* A typical ad appeared in the *New York Times* on June 18, 1993, and included on the checklist "studying the Torah regularly, giving my children a Jewish education, purchasing new Torah books, learning more about Moshiach, lighting candles on the eve of every Shabbat and holiday (girls over 3), doing more to honor my parents, putting on tefillin every weekday, putting up kosher mezuzahs on all my doorposts, observing the laws of Jewish family life, doing more to treat my neighbors kindly, doing more to live in accordance with the Code of Jewish law." There was also a write-in item labeled "other."

by.[13] The flow of immigrants to the Holy Land had slowed to a trickle; the second war in the Gulf has been far from a swift victory, missiles rained down on the Holy Land from Lebanon during a conflict in which many Jews were killed on the home front while the Israeli defending forces seemed helpless and even the Palestinians were dispatching rockets that landed daily without surcease. The King of Paras was more powerful than ever, and the new Hamans (Ahmadinejad and Khamenei of Iran) with their nuclear ambitions threatened the Jewish people and their state more than ever. Swords had *not* been beaten into plowshares. Peace and the Day of Redemption seemed further than ever.

Perhaps most strikingly, the high hopes they had for their Rebbe's role in leading the redemption had been severely tested by his death. The expectation of his immediate resurrection that so many had held had begun to dissipate except among the hard core *meshikhistn*. Some Lubavitchers saw this turnaround as the result of backsliding caused by unbelievers and Israeli leaders who had betrayed the message of the Rebbe.[14]

Jewish history is littered with messianic disappointments. Once again, the powerful conviction that any minute the Redeemer would appear had given way to more waiting and disappointment. These in turn had morphed among many *shluchim* into the assumption that the work was difficult indeed but had to go on for the foreseeable future, even if the end was not imminent. Now the attitude was, as one emissary explained, quoting the Talmud (*Avot* 2:16): "It is not incumbent upon you to finish the task, but neither are you free to absolve yourself from it."

Nor was the work getting any easier: "You have to ignite the *neshome* [soul]," a *shaliach* said in January 2008, explaining why he was willing to live so far from home still trying to save Jews whose intermarriage rate was skyrocketing. He admitted that the work was often "like lighting a match under water."[15] Said another about his Far East posting, "if I [were] an ex-pat or diplomat, I would leave ASAP," but as he was rather an emissary of his rebbe, he could not and would never leave.[16]

With their Rebbe gone and no one but themselves to channel him, *shluchim* revivified themselves not only by coming together but also by reinvoking a basic principle of Jewish law, one that became the official theme of their annual gathering in 2006: *shlucho shel adam kamoso* (B.T. Kiddushin 41b), meaning a person's *shaliach* is like himself and the *shaliach*'s actions and accomplishments are attributed to the one who empowered him to act in his stead.[17] It was a principle enunciated by the Rebbe to promise his emissaries that they would not fail in their mission because they carried his power with them. It was repeated frequently in many of the missives and publications that Lubavitchers sent out to their supporters, youth, and *shluchim*, the answer to how and why they must keep going on, even so many years after the Rebbe's *histalkes* and failure to reappear except on video reruns.[18] According to it, messengers were required to continue their mission until its completion in full measure according to the expectations of the one who dispatched them. Or as Ari Solish, the *shaliach* from Atlanta, put it, "this is our power; this is our calling."[19] That meant that, until the arrival of the Messiah, no matter when that day came, they had to continue doing what it was the Rebbe had sent them to do; even in his afterlife, he had a right to expect them to carry out his will, and their accomplishments continued to be attributed to him. As Rabbi Moshe Kotlarsky put it in his introductory remarks to the *shluchim* at their annual gathering, "a *shaliach* reflects his Rebbe."

As time went on, some even argued that this had all along been Menachem Mendel's plan, to disperse them everywhere he could not be in order to maintain his mission and give life to his ideas, and hence to serve as the local rabbinic guides and leaders. They did not need another rebbe; together each was a piece of the whole, as we have seen. Just as he had been on a mission for his Rebbe Rabbi Yosef Yitzchak even in the latter's afterlife, so now they continued his mission in his afterlife. They would represent him and in his name continue that same mission—*kamoso*, as if they were him. As long as they kept on, he was not dead. Or as another Hasid put it, talking about the Rebbe: "If I am connected to him, he is connected to me."

Such thinking undoubtedly mitigated the anxieties of continuity that his Hasidim had always felt when they reflected on the fact that their Rebbe, Menachem Mendel, had no children or no clear heirs, when they wondered about the future. But now that they had learned how to relate to a missing, even dead, Rebbe, they could lessen the disquiet they felt, but who knows for how long?

A debate emerged among the Lubavitchers whether they should begin calling themselves "*shluchim* of the Rebbe" rather than "ChaBaD *shluchim.*" Those who advocated the first argued that, after Gimmel Tammuz, the former was appropriate, for it stressed they were still carrying out their leader's will.[20] This argument in a sense represented the *meshikhist* point of view that sought to reaffirm the Rebbe's primary role in their mission, while those who favored the latter title emphasized the corporate identity.

There was a kind of internal contradiction in this role of *shaliach.* On the one hand, emissaries had to be themselves, drawing on inner strengths and personal talents to carry out the mission. That often meant taking personal initiatives, finding creative new solutions for unexpected eventualities. It meant working with and looking benevolently upon Jews whose level of observance and commitment to Judaism was weak or nonexistent, "even though," as Rabbi Menachem Mendel had put it in his very first talk as Rebbe, "the person to whom he was benevolent was not in the category of his 'equal in Torah and mitzvos' and did not compare to him at all."[21]

On the other hand, true *shluchim* were simply messengers; people who turned themselves into an instrument fashioned to carry out the will of the one dispatching them. They needed to limit themselves by remaining absolutely faithful to the mission on which they had been sent. Only in that sense could one say, "The *shaliach* receives the great and compelling strengths of the Rebbe."[22] As Yosef Chaim Kantor expressed it before nearly three thousand of his fellow emissaries in 2006, "The key to our tomorrow is our constant striving to be true *shluchim* of our dear Rebbe."[23] If the messenger deviated even slightly from the aims of the one who sent him, "he ceased being a *shaliach.*"[24] The tension between these two elements would sometimes lead to conflict and confusion that was not always easily resolved in the absence of the dispatcher and his absolute authority.

Whatever the differences among them, however, all Lubavitchers did *not* retreat to localistic concerns or revert to the insularity that is characteristic of other Hasidic groups. Yet since the end was no longer apparently around the corner, there could be a more organized, routinized, methodical preparation for it and an expansion of the territory to be covered. If anything, after Gimmel Tammuz they enhanced the system of emissaries, in which they had invested a great deal institutionally, socially, culturally, financially, and religiously. It became more like a well-oiled corporation that was organized by territories, with a strictly controlled hierarchical structure within regions and a definite career path for becoming a *shaliach*.[25]

By the late twentieth century the role of *shaliach* had become a kind of expected and habitualized career path for many Lubavitchers. Committed to the mission, as their Rebbe had charged them, they continued to go "after every single Jew," wherever he or she might be. If they gave up, what would become of them and their raison d'être? They would therefore continue lighting matches under water, trying to find even the solitary Jews on the margins of the community, endeavoring to fill the world with more mitzvahs than transgressions. When that was done they hoped the Messiah would reveal himself and begin the redemption.[26] If the essential sense of urgency that had been there during the Rebbe's lifetime, particularly in his closing years, had in his afterlife become routinized, that did not alter the fact that almost everybody who was anybody expected to go on some sort of *shlichus*.

In a sense, it was a brilliant plan. Why revert to competing for followers in Brooklyn, where there are already so many Hasidic groups trying to attract the Orthodox, when they could continue to compete for all the Jews in the world? With a cadre of people who had a sense of mission, a message they believed they could translate to the level of all Jews, and an ability to raise enormous funds from all these Jews and others, they were sure they could succeed where other Jewish movements had failed.

To accomplish this, of course, they had to identify and isolate their target audience; that was why Lubavitchers, like their Rebbe, remained always scrupulous about making sure that the standards of who was called a Jew remained rigorously Orthodox, even after their Rebbe was gone from this earth. When they stopped someone and asked if he or she were Jewish, they wanted to be able to take yes for an answer. They could not work with "half-Jews" or "Jews by choice." Even Gentiles, for whom the Noahide laws could be invoked, were an easier population than the children of mixed marriages. The Rebbe had been passionate about the definition of who was a Jew, whether that required involving himself in Israeli politics or even in the matter of people coming out of the Soviet Union.[27]

𝄢

By the twenty-first century, *shlichus* was a professional career track for successful Lubavitcher Hasidim, be they young men or women. Every official *shaliach* had to get the approval of "Merkos," but the control was not as absolute as in the past. About three thousand *shluchim* were at work. Men still had to dress in the uniform and grow the beard. Women still dressed modestly and looked to marry and raise many children. But all that no longer was sufficient. The Lubavitcher women for their part tended to look for a husband who understood what being an emissary meant and who could succeed at it. No longer were they only interested in finding a husband who was a scholar or one who knew all the wisdom of ChaBaD, as perhaps they once had. This made the young Lubavitcher couple significantly different from any other young Hasidic couple, or for that matter any other young Orthodox couple. By now a generation who, as Yehuda Krinsky explained, "never saw the Rebbe, never heard the Rebbe—maybe even their parents were not Lubavitchers" would feel driven to do this kind of work because they sensed it was "very fulfilling" and "a great way to live."[28]

The head *shluchim* in a region became like CEOs of corporations and others in the territory became like sales managers, while the local *shaliach* ran the storefront in the ChaBaD House. Their goal of bringing the Messiah, while in the deep structure of what they did, was often hard to perceive in the rush of activities and responsibilities, which included raising funds, running schools, recruiting volunteers, doing social work and counseling, working on the college campus, lighting Hanukkah menorahs, and getting involved in politics and public relations. Indeed, only by restraining the radical messianic message could the *shluchim* be successful in connecting to all sorts of Jews and others and not be rejected as some sort of a bizarre messianic sect.

Education, of course, remained a key concern. Although accurate numbers are hard to establish beyond all doubt, Lubavitchers claimed that as of 2007, they had served more than 71,000 students, who were enrolled in about 630 ChaBaD-Lubavitch schools throughout the world, and that did not include institutions not affiliated with the movement in which some teachers or principals were Lubavitcher *shluchim*. They declared there were 40,000 in after-school programs, and many in pre-schools.[29] However, educational researchers report that at least as of the 2003–4 school year, there were 8,609 students enrolled in ChaBaD day schools between the fourth and twelfth grades in the United States.[30]

Increasingly, the *shluchim* tried to standardize much of what went on around the world at the ChaBaD Houses and in the learning there. One such effort, the Rohr Jewish Learning Institute, part of the Merkos L'Inyonei Chinuch, sought "to inspire Jewish learning worldwide and to transform Jewish life and the greater community through Torah study . . . to create a global network of informed students connected by bonds of shared Jewish experience" to provide a series of courses that would be coordinated in more than three hundred locations in the world, so that one could travel throughout the ChaBaD network of emissaries or houses and continue the same course of study no matter where one found oneself in that network.[31] With endorsements from such non-Lubavitchers as Alan Dershowitz and Natan Scharansky, as well as a variety of academics, CEOs, and Israeli officials, the appeal was no longer that of a parochial or openly messianic cult. Clearly, ChaBaD outreach was shaping itself to those it wanted to reach. Individual *shluchim* today might, for example, offer five-minute Torah talks via cell phone to busy executives and professionals, or run to provide religious instruction in boardrooms—all the while acting in ways appropriate to their circumstances and targeted to their audience.

In the process of outreach, then, the influence is not altogether one-sided. Missionaries are "talkers (preachers) and people who bring about change (converters)."[32] But successful missionaries also "acquire a vast and detailed knowledge" about the community they seek to convert, for they aim to approach the others "from below" and "from within."[33] For Lubavitchers, this has meant they must not just learn about the people they wish to convert but also learn to speak to them in their language, even to be able to look at the world through their eyes. That often requires them to move very far from their own values and understandings of the world—even to suspend them in some way. To some *shluchim* this means being forced to accept at least provisionally the lowest level of Jewish engagement in the people they seek to change. This tolerance of what in their own communities and lives they would find absolutely unacceptable is necessary, given the nature of the Jews they are seeking to retrieve from below and from within.

On the other hand, although the *shluchim* spend much if not most of their time trying to missionize among and convert Jews who are very far from religious observance, and they hold on to (albeit frequently in a restrained manner) their radical messianic ideas, they themselves remain scrupulously attached to an Orthodox—even ultra-Orthodox— way of life, regardless of where they find themselves and how tolerant of others they seem to be. In all their outreach, Lubavitchers and the Rebbe never deviated from a commitment to being part of Orthodox Judaism, even as they hold what some have considers scandalous and unorthodox messianic ideas.

Indeed, this personal commitment to Orthodox practice often forces *shluchim* to send their young children away from home and place them in Lubavitcher centers where they can provide them with a ChaBaD education and insulate them during the key years of their socialization from the risks of outreach. (Of course, the children know well what is going on at home, and see it when they come for visits.) Without their powerful efforts to remain personally Orthodox down to the smallest detail, including maintaining their obvious Hasidic appearance and commitments, they run the risk of acculturation and becoming more like the people they serve. In short, Lubavitchers, even those who hold the most radical messianic beliefs, continue to see themselves as legitimately within the domains of Orthodox Jewry, because they do not deviate in their religious practices and observances of mitzvahs.[34]

No doubt, for *shluchim* their greatest successes have come in their ability to draw some of their "converts" completely into the Lubavitcher orbit. These are mostly young Jews, still in the age of identity development, often unmarried, who are persuaded to change the course of their lives and become Lubavitcher Hasidim, often relocating into ChaBaD enclaves. Yet looking at their numbers (since those who call themselves Lubavitcher Hasidim have not grown as much as much as some of the other Hasidic groups), one would have to conclude that such "converts" are not necessarily the people who make up the bulk of those they serve.[35]

But beyond this relatively small number of total converts, the *shluchim* also serve the needs of Orthodox Jews on the move. With the emergence of a middle-class Modern Orthodoxy, which travels throughout globe for business and pleasure, there has arisen a need for providing these people with basic religious services in far-flung places—requirements like kosher food and synagogues (especially on Sabbaths and holy days). ChaBaD *shluchim* find themselves ideally situated to provide for these Jews. Naturally, therefore, when calls have come for these same Orthodox Jews to repudiate ChaBaD because of its radical messianism, especially the belief in a dead Messiah who would be resurrected, they have largely ignored such calls. To repudiate ChaBaD who is so welcoming and helpful to them throughout the world would be to bite the hand that feeds them. Besides, no one else is there to provide for the Orthodox Jewish world traveler and his needs, sometimes even at risk to their lives, as was the case of Rabbi Gavriel and Rivka Holtzberg, the *shluchim* murdered in November 2008 in the terrorist attack on the ChaBaD House in Mumbai, India.

In addition, the children of the modern Orthodox and other traditionally oriented Jews who attend university are often served by ChaBaD Houses and *shluchim*, who the parents see as protectors of their children's religion and necessary barriers to the temptations and seductions of the permissive environment on campus—even if ChaBaD's version of Judaism does not parallel their own. The presence of these Hasidim on campus seems to prove one could be anywhere, even in the university, and remain fully and visibly committed to Torah and mitzvahs.

Perhaps the single most important population, however, that the *shluchim* serve, and the ones who take up most of their energy and time, are those Jews who are marginally involved in Jewish life and observance and whose Jewish consciousness they try to arouse. These were *takhtn she'eyn takhtn mimenu*, "those in the spiritual abyss." ChaBaD's work with these Jews seems to be a kind of salvage operation, a chance to prevent complete assimilation and Jewish decline, and more concretely to get people to commit a Jewish act. While not everyone agrees with the goals or even the methods and details of Lubavitchers' outreach, it is undeniable that these *shluchim* are tireless and dedicated not only to holding back the tide of Jewish erosion but also, they believe, pushing the world forward toward a redemptive age. They use every tool at their disposal, learn new skills, and make friends with everyone simply to enhance Jewish practice and awareness, which makes them admired by many committed Jews and true to their mission. As Fishkoff put it, "The black-hatted, long-bearded men and their modestly dressed, bewigged wives move into your town without notice and before you know it, they're koshering your home, teaching you Bible, giving your kid a bar mitzvah, and running daily prayer services—most of it for free."[36] And when they encounter those who oppose them, they do not fold their tents and run but rather stay and resist the efforts to remove them. [37]

Some *shluchim* have become well-known personalities in their own right. They are exemplars of accomplishment, often with a large organization into which young novices are assimilated. For example, the already mentioned Berel Lazar has become chief rabbi in Moscow. He has a large network into which he can place all sorts of emissaries. Avremel Shemtov, starting in Philadelphia and moving on into Washington, D.C. (with the help of one of his sons), has sharpened his legendary ability to influence people at all levels of government. Shemtov's ChaBaD-style Hanukkah menorah is now a part of the Washington landscape, and some of his children have found work in his enterprise. Baruch Shlomo Cunin, the Lubavitcher in Los Angeles, has become the *shaliach* to Hollywood stars, famous for his national telethon begun in 1980 and its ability to raise huge amounts of money and attention. The program raises money "to provide food, clothing, shelter, and hope to thousands of people of all faiths," as he explains, and according to its Web site, it raised $6 million in 2006.[38] To be sure, the bulk of the money was presumably targeted for the Chabad National Drug Rehabilitation and Sober Living Center in Los Angeles and the more than twenty-five schools and thirty summer camps offering scholarship grants for underprivileged children and military families, as well as the Friendship Circle, which provides companionship for children with special needs and crisis intervention for individuals struggling with bereavement, medical emergencies, and major financial setbacks— institutions perhaps only tangentially attached to the specific Jewish and religious mission on which the Lubavitcher Hasidim have been sent by their rebbe.[39] Nevertheless, the spillover of funds and good will that these nonsectarian institutions garner for ChaBaD cannot help but benefit the sectarian goals of Lubavitch.[40]

At the local level, there are *shluchim* who have become well-established presences in communities or regions, often serving Jews who are not ready or willing to connect through established synagogues or other Jewish institutions. In part their apparent willingness to offer a Jewish connection without requiring either a payment for service or membership commitment attracts people who are more marginal to Jewish life in ways that the more conventional community structures cannot. While the *shluchim* might hope for more commitment from those they serve, they will live with less.

The college campus, where Jewish young people are often lost to Jewish involvement, offers new opportunities for outreach, and as the twentieth century drew to a close, the race to create a ChaBaD presence on every campus where even a few Jews were to be found was on. Here some *shluchim* found great success, as for example the already mentioned Hirschy and Elkie Zarchi at Harvard or Baruch and Sarah Goodman at Rutgers, who had overseen the construction of a 90,000 square foot building that they claimed as "the largest campus facility for Jewish students in the world."[41]

Even in the elite and sometimes aloof environs of Cambridge University in the United Kingdom, Reuven and Rochel Leigh have moved from the London-based Lubavitcher community and built a thriving "Chabad Jewish Society," including a Hebrew School for children, an Institute for Jewish Studies, and a Wisdom Centre, where the hard theological issues of Lubavitcher thinking are supposedly explored.[42]

Other *shluchim* are perhaps less publicly successful, toiling in smaller fields and counting their achievements far more modestly. They might succeed in offering a lunch-and-learn program in the college gym or bringing a few students to share in discussion and a homemade Sabbath meal, as do Mendel and Henya Matusof at the University of Wisconsin at Madison. After working thirty-five years on a campus with more than five thousand Jewish students, they are up to hosting thirty on a Friday night. They might offer Jewish astrology workshops, weekly kabbalah classes, and kitchen koshering, as Mayshe and Shifra Schwartz at the Chabad Chai Center of Brookline, Massachusetts, do. They might run a Gan Menachem pre-school, as for example Yisrael and Chana Greenberg do in El Paso, Texas. *Shluchim* might reach out to Jewish travelers or businessmen who come through town on a Sabbath, as do Eli Dovid and Mindy Borenstein, the ChaBaD emissaries in Bologna and Florence, Italy. On many days, Mindy makes kosher sandwiches and her husband goes to the convention center in Bologna looking for Jews to whom he can offer this food so they will not have to eat food that is prohibited by Jewish law. And during the tourist season, the entire family decamps to nearby Florence and prepares (with the help of young Lubavitcher volunteers and novices who come to Tuscany for a summer of work in the vineyards of outreach) Sabbath meals in a small storefront room, sometimes even renting a nearby pub in the neighborhood of the synagogue for tourists who want to observe something of the day. This is hard labor, and they do it all for a chance to get a few minutes in which to try to raise Jewish consciousness and enhance the religious observance of those passing, however briefly, through their orbit.

Yet as we have noted, Lubavitch has become a Hasidic movement that increasingly attracts and often serves mainly non-Orthodox Jews.[43] Moreover, when they do so, they hold on to them only tenuously. These people more often than not become Jews who do *some* of the acts that the *shluchim* encourage them to do but commonly do little more on their own. In the marketplace of ideas that the modern world has become, where religion is a lifestyle choice and no longer a matter of fate, Orthodox Judaism, let alone ChaBaD Hasidism, is not an easy sell. Lubavitchers need to make the Judaism they peddle comprehensible and attractive to people who would not at first blush be interested in being anything like the Hasid who is reaching out to them. Even within the domains of religion, the mission is no longer to turn Jews from complete secularity to some sort of Judaism or even from less restrictive forms to an Orthodox or Hasidic version, as it once might have been. ChaBaD now also has to compete successfully with all sorts of other spiritual attractions, from Yoga to New Age, from feel-good-pop psychology practices to the sports fanaticism or base popular culture, to say nothing about the increasing competition from other Orthodox Jewish outreach organizations (such as Aish HaTorah) that attract contemporary Jews.

Lubavitchers increasingly make a practice of creating Jewish events that have high symbolic value. Besides the popular Hanukkah lighting and getting Jewish men and boys to try on tefillin, they might blow a shofar, as Motti Seligson and Saadya Notik did in Novi Sad, Serbia, in front of the synagogue for the first time in fifty-five years, or bring freshly baked challah for earthquake victims in Peru. Or they might, as did Bentzion Shemtov, seek out one of the last two living Jews living in Bella Unión, Uruguay, and help him affix a mezuzah to the doorpost of his home. In an even more highly symbolic accomplishment, the *shaliach* in Dnepropetrovsk, the childhood home of the Rebbe, launched a massive effort at ChaBaD outreach. With an initiative to place mezuzahs on the doorways of any Jewish household that wanted one, Elisha Baram of the city's Nachlas Levi synagogue sent students from the Levi Schneerson yeshiva out into the city, where they managed to place more than four hundred mezuzahs on the homes of the elderly and impoverished families with children and promised hundreds more would be given to anyone who could not afford the holy scrolls.[44] While in the elite environs of University College in London's Bloomsbury, Yisroel and Devora Lew offer a free "mezuzah bank" for those who need these signs of Jewish identification on the doorpost of their dorm room or flat.

These acts, however, do not necessarily lead to people turning toward greater Jewish attachments or abandoning their non-Jewish ones. Thus, when Mendel Rivkin, the *shaliach* in New Orleans, persuaded Tamar George, who built a porch on the upper storey of her house, to put a railing around it in line with the biblical injunction to do so, she did so happily, but not before also checking with her feng shui consultant.[45]

Symbolic acts are an ideal strategy when the mission proves too complex, as it had become by the late twentieth and early twenty-first centuries, for they are dramatic but also relatively simple. These symbolic acts could either be cynically described as public relations stunts or else as acts that have for the Lubavitchers some cosmic or mystical meaning that will change the balance of good and evil in the world. The *shaliach* in Uruguay, father of the young man who went to put up the mezuzah, put it thus: "One single Mitzvah can tip the scales and bring the redemption for the entire world," and hence end *goles hanefesh*, the exile of the Jewish soul. "One mezuzah in Bella Unión transforms the entire Bella Unión."[46]

Yet in adapting the message this way, Lubavitchers also run the risk of simplifying it to the point of demeaning its ontological meaning and making it staggeringly undemanding. This was precisely the accusation that Jewish Orthodoxy had long ago made of those who sought to reform or reframe the demands of Judaism. They had accused these new movements of just this sort of watering down of Judaism in the quest for accommodation and to try to hold on to those who were abandoning Judaism willy-nilly.[47] Lubavitchers find themselves often doing the same, having to attract followers in ways that at best downplay the deep religious transformations that their last two rebbes sought to impose on Jewry and at worst exchange them for something far less comprehensive.

In a sense, as Fishkoff has noted, they put themselves in contradiction with their own life choices. "They avoid college because Schneerson . . . decided that America's college campuses would have a detrimental effect on his followers," yet they have and continue to establish a presence on campuses. They jet all over the world on a moment's notice and live in the most exotic, un-Jewish locales, but they seek to maintain a style of life that ignores their being in these places. "They are zealous about their own kashrut, but they open their arms to Jews who eat pork and drive on Shabbat."[48]

Thus, for example, at the Rutgers University ChaBaD House, students are courted with the following message: "This is the place to be for all incoming freshmen. Scared you won't fit in? Scared you won't find friends? Scared you'll be sitting at home while all the parties are happening? Well look no further this is THE best place to meet fellow students, whether it's at our massive 500 student Friday night dinners, our wandering Jew Wednesdays or, our Thursday night challah/dessert baking or any of our other amazing programs. You can celebrate being Jewish with us, no experience necessary!"[49] Hirschy Zarchi at Harvard echoes this sentiment when he asserts that "to participate in Shabbat, you don't have to be, quote unquote, religious."[50]

At Rutgers, much as at other campuses, those who come to such events "talk about feeling 'closer' to Judaism, more comfortable with the rituals, more willing to identify with the American Jewish community," but not about becoming either Lubavitcher Hasidim, believers in the messianic message, or even becoming significantly more observant.[51]

Even when Lubavitchers do succeed in getting Jews to enhance their ritual behavior, there is the possibility that the acts themselves may become carried out in a very different "key," to use Erving Goffman's terms, than what the *shaliach* might have hoped for, with a transformed meaning not all like its original one.[52] Thus, in the donning of tefillin, one of the signature rituals with which ChaBaD has become identified, an act that in traditional Judaism requires repeated commitment and accompanying prayer, one finds Lubavitchers often turning it into a ritual unhinged from its normal context as part of a daily routine of prayer. For the most part, in the Lubavitcher key this ritual has become a one-time act by someone stopped on the street by a *shaliach*. In at least one recent case, it even became a kind of burlesque and regrounded display of the mystical and spiritual act it was meant to be, as reported in a local Jewish newspaper on Long Island:[53]

Jay Greenfield, a forty-six-year-old fan of the New York Giants, had been disappointed with the failure of the football team to win its first two games. But Yisrael Shemtov, a Lubavitcher, assured him "that if he wanted to see the Giants turn things around, he should agree to put on tefillin with greater frequency." As the weeks progressed, Jay kept his commitment and the Giants kept winning. At the same time, Shemtov "kept on visiting and leaving notes at the *kever* [gravesite] of his Rebbe . . . apparently asking that in the Rebbe's merit the football Giants keep on winning." Other Lubavitchers would meet the fans and their friends when they went to out-of-town games "in order to supply and put on tefillin with them prior to each game, sort of the way others might make a barbecue in the stadium parking lots. Before some games, sometimes as many as 20 men participated in the tefillin tailgate party." On the day of the Super Bowl when the Giants were the underdogs to the favored New England Patriots, Jay traveled to the big game, representing the group of tefillin-wearing fans.

One of the latter asked, "Rabbi, what if the Giants lose? You'll fall on your face; the whole thing will fall apart." But the rabbi had been to the Rebbe's grave earlier on that day, and he replied that "he was not concerned about that." Back home on Long Island, about 70 men—most in their forties and fifties and who had never put on tefillin in their lives—gathered in two homes for a bash that was preceded earlier in the day by all the men donning the leather boxes. When the Giants miraculously won the big game, the fans agreed to keep putting on tefillin and some said they might even "consider putting up mezuzos on the doorposts of their homes."[54]

These fans' agreement to put on tefillin in the future or checking their mezuzahs, or even singing songs of *Moshiach*, on the predicated hope that this will help their home team "utterly changes," as Goffman might explain, what a religiously observant Jew would say is supposed to be the motivation for and meaning in these rituals.[55] The *shaliach* might reply that while of course he wanted Jewishly grounded long-time commitments, if he could get someone to observe one mitzvah, that was a start. An act done in the wrong key could be corrected in time. If they could get a group of men to commit to put on tefillin or check their mezuzah for any reason, that was enough. If one could get a Jew to come to a Passover seder or host someone for a Sabbath meal who would otherwise not even know it was Passover or Sabbath, that was good. Motivations could evolve and develop; actions mattered more. These unhinged acts are not meant to be the final goal, which still remains bringing about the day of redemption and making sure that the Jews are deserving of it. Some, however, look at these sorts of actions as over the top.

Is there a risk in this approach? Living in an environment of openness, where the possibilities of the messenger's becoming corrupted by the surrounding society and culture, is a sometimes unclear but always present danger. What happens when the *shluchim* who descend to the spiritual abyss are pulled down by those they seek to retrieve? How does one avoid "going native" in societies that are so seductively open? *Shluchim* know that is always a risk.

In the eyes of the ChaBaD establishment, some were not sufficiently protected by being emissaries of the Rebbe, contrary to his assurances. They were pulled out of the orbit of ChaBaD in their efforts to carry out the mission; others were pushed out.

Consider three examples. The first was Zalman Schachter (today Schachter-Shalomi), who was ordained as a rabbi by ChaBaD in 1947. As we have seen, he served as an early Lubavitcher emissary of both the sixth and seventh rebbes in America, and was close to them. But by the late 1960s, Schachter was experimenting with stretching the limits of being a *shaliach*, and by 1968, after receiving a degree from Hebrew

Union College (the Reform Jewish institution), was "effectively 'divorced' from the Lubavitcher Hasidim over issues relating to his controversial engagement with modern culture and other religions."[56] Today he is hailed as an important force in the development of the Havurah movement and of the Jewish Renewal movement. But he is no longer a Lubavitcher Hasid.

Shmuley Boteach, the *shaliach* at the University of Oxford in the 1990s, had achieved enormous success on campus and become a guide for many seeking greater understanding of religion. But after he published his best-selling book, *Kosher Sex*, and became a media personality, he found himself increasingly estranged from his Lubavitcher connections. "As Shmuley's stature on campus grew, his relations with the Lubavitch leadership began to fray." His L'Chaim Society attracted as many non-Jews as Jews—its president one year was an African American Baptist—and his peers felt Shmuley was spending too much time courting Gentiles, "thereby diluting outreach efforts and possibly even encouraging intermarriage."[57] The British heads of Lubavitch in London saw this as inimical to the Rebbe's mission; he had reached too far out, and he was ultimately separated from them and from the ChaBaD operation.

Not too many years later in London, two Lubavitchers, Rabbis Yosef and Mendy Vogel, members of a distinguished family of *shluchim* whose father, Rabbi Faivush Vogel, was director of Lubavitch in Stamford Hill and the main fundraiser for the movement's schools in England, opened what some called a "glitzy" establishment, the Gaon Club, off Bond Street, as part of their outreach work, particularly to young professionals and business people. The club had been opened with great pomp by no less than Britain's chief rabbi, who characterized it as a place where Jews could come "to relax, unwind, refresh physically and spiritually." The place was to be in line with the Rebbe's goals. "Its motto is a phrase, often repeated by the late Lubavitch Rebbe," ChaBaD reported on its news page Web site, "which states that "where two Jews meet, a third should benefit." The club was described to be outfitted with "plasma TV screens and internet terminals," and undoubtedly looked like a place in which these Jewish princes of industry would feel at home. After what some in Lubavitch called "lavish expenditures," the club, which even its critics claimed had "laudable" activities and goals, amassed a huge debt, and this led to a rift that divided the Lubavitchers and to the London Jewish religious court (a non-Lubavitcher authority) ruling that the two should not run outreach activities for six months without permission, and the resignation of their father as well, followed by recriminations and accusations that created an ugly controversy within the emissary community.[58]

The lesson in all of these examples is that those who strain the limits of outreach might snap the bonds to Lubavitch. Those who take too many liberties with the mission and descend too low into the spiritual abyss can no longer be connected to the one who dispatched them.

Although the Rebbe had persuaded *shluchim* that they would be protected by him, these cases show it was not always an ironclad protection. The internal contradiction between being emissaries, who are instruments for the one who dispatched them, and missionaries, who have to take initiatives and be inventive, is always a trap. The former might be too passive; the latter might get carried away by their enthusiasm and cross the line. Perhaps that was why Rabbi Kotlarsky reminded the *shluchim* at the *kinus* in 2006 about the need for them "to inspire, encourage and bond with one another." Their coming together as a fraternity (and for the *shluchos* with their own separate *kinus*, as a sorority) served at some level to help them not only learn from but also emulate one another and thus discipline and coordinate their creativity, avoiding an inventiveness that could lead to their crossing some red lines. Those who went out too much on their own ended like Schachter, Boteach, and the founders of the Gaon Club in London.

Indeed, after the Rebbe's passing, *shluchim* were finding they were increasingly in need of one another and the experience that they could share in order to maintain a sense of security and group identity. To do that they created an apparatus that many large corporations might envy. They developed self-help seminars, workshops and even a resource fair in which a variety of products, skills, and strategies to be used in outreach work are shared. Indeed, except for their beards and in some cases snap brim hats, the gathering of the *shluchim* might easily be mistaken for some corporate seminar.

In practice, Lubavitcher emissaries have to confront precisely the problems that modern Orthodox Jews have been dealing with for years: how to stand with one foot in the world beyond their own religious commitments and the other firmly planted in their own traditions. The difference is that the modern Orthodox Jews see ontological value in the outside culture and society—or at least have for a generation or more before its perceived moral decline—while the Lubavitchers are entering it only in order to retrieve Jews from it.[59] Yet both live a kind of double life, one in which they look at the world outside as a threat as well as an opportunity, and perceive the world from inside their Jewish attachments differently than when they are outside.

In this double life Lubavitchers remain on the one hand open, compromising, and willing to be engaged by the people and the society they seek to transform. In that life, they accept the legitimacy of all sorts of rabbis with whom they have to cooperate, including the non-Orthodox and women. They allow that a supporter or congregant could be less than fully committed to Jewish practice and still be someone of value, and tolerance is the name of the game.

In their other life, however, they remain rooted in their own sectarian values and maintain powerful attachments to the highly parochial and esoteric world of ChaBaD Hasidism. But there are neither easy solutions nor ironclad guarantees that they will not end up adrift.

∭

At the heart of the Lubavitcher mission today is the question of defining success. If the goal is redemption, clearly that point has not been reached. If the objective is simply to hasten that day, there is no way to know if the *shluchim* are succeeding. For those who seek to define success by the ability to manipulate events in history or the real world, there are always "miracles" to point to, and every *shaliach* has a bunch of these to report. The tradition of the *zaddik* as miracle worker goes back to the earliest Hasidim, to the *ba'aley shem*. But these signs are meaningful largely to those who already believe; they seldom convert outsiders.

Looked at from another perspective, one could define Lubavitcher success in its institutional building. In this regard the record is impressive. For a group whose actual numbers remain relatively small—about ten thousand in Crown Heights, five thousand in Kfar Chabad, and perhaps another twenty-five thousand worldwide, including about three thousand *shaliach* families—their ability to establish a presence in so many places and to become well known way beyond the borders of their community is surely a measure of success. There are rabbis, teachers, counselors, and even hospital and prison chaplains in thousands of outposts of Jewry serving every manner of Jew. If, however, the measure of success is their ability to change the orientation of Jews so that they truly become observant Lubavitchers, success has to be redefined in far more modest terms.

The final question, and perhaps the most important for Lubavitch today, is whether this group of Hasidim can continue to sustain themselves and their mission in the absence of a living rebbe and ultimate authority. In the short run, the movement, as it developed in the Rebbe's lifetime, continues to provide sufficiently for most Hasidim's intellectual, spiritual, and even economic needs: they live *for* ChaBaD and *off* ChaBaD. Additionally, familial social and cultural ties to other Lubavitchers and ChaBaD institutions buttress continued affiliation. Likewise, the plethora of publications that are part of a seemingly endless supply of material from their rebbes provides writings for them to explore and bond to. The absence of a rebbe, moreover, has allowed all sorts of Lubavitchers to contribute even more to the cultural, spiritual and intellectual life of the movement, and has also enabled a greater flexibility for including in the camp a larger degree of variation and even some deviants who might in the past have been banished. This means there may be greater latitude in the long run in defining what makes one Lubavitcher. As long as ChaBaD continues to provide what they need and nothing else does the job better, they are unlikely to abandon it. Where else would they go?

Rabbi Shimon Lazaroff, the first *shaliach* to Texas, exemplified this, as he distinguished himself from "some of the young people who became carried away by the belief that the Rebbe was the Moshiach."

"One time right after Gimmel Tammuz," he recounted, "everyone was all broken up, and the young people were all crazy with this Moshiach business. I told one guy, 'Look you young guys have no past that's why you're looking for crazy fantasies in the future. I have a past. The present is bitter? I'm living in my past.' I told the young man this. I have a beautiful past. If the present is wretched, I'm going back to my beautiful past."[60] How did he do that? He would sing a tune that the Rebbe had taught him, and each time he sang it he would teach it to other Hasidim, and as they sang it together they would sense, and he would recall, the Rebbe. Of course, that was just what the *shluchim* continued to do.

The outlook for the longer term, when those like Lazaroff who can recall the charisma of the Rebbe as an actual living leader and the excitement he generated are outnumbered by those for whom he is a historical figure or a video image, is not as clear. Can emissaries continue to go out to the periphery, missionizing among the uncommitted or very marginally committed without becoming changed by those among whom they find themselves? Will the moral protection the Rebbe gave them to go far away continue to prevent the erosion of their Hasidic beliefs and practices? Without being able to return and be revitalized in their Lubavitcher identity by a living Rebbe, can they be thus revitalized by a dead one? Are isolated *farbrengens* in New York or Kfar Chabad or elsewhere with other *shluchim* enough to keep them Lubavitchers through and through for generations? Will the organization of Merkos have sufficient authority to prevent deviant forms from emerging or even defining the group and its mission? Certainly the pressures of appealing to all sorts of Jews on the periphery can in principle and practice change the missionaries no less than the target of their efforts. Indeed, even success in making converts could ultimately prove to be the movement's undoing, for they can bring along their own foreign elements into the group. Will feng shui or some other outside influence infect ChaBaD?

And even if all these external influences can somehow be controlled, the question of how long *shluchim* can expand their numbers remains open. As children and grandchildren of *shluchim*, members of families that grow exponentially, continue to want to go "into the family business," are there sufficient venues in which they can ply their trade? How much can a territory be carved up, how many new *shluchim* can the mission absorb, particularly if the Messiah continues to tarry? There have already been territorial disputes, and while the Lubavitchers have been creative in finding new ways and situations in which to do their work, how long can the effort sustain itself economically and spiritually without some sort of change?

Life and the changing world bring all sorts of challenges to religious groups that try to hold on to tradition as the Lubavitchers do. That is why their Rebbe always had to respond to these changes with new religious interpretations of events. But will it be sufficient for some Hasid or other to now plumb the already written messages to find the Rebbe's interpretations of developing and unprecedented events? And if so, which Hasid will that be? Would such a universally accepted interpreter not then become a Rebbe? These are questions that suggest that continuity in the longer term cannot be taken as a given.

〰〰

The concept of the routinization of charisma was first articulated by Max Weber, the twentieth-century German sociologist of religion.[61] It is based on the understanding that charisma, the possession of extraordinary personal characteristics, charm, and magnetism that inspires people to admire or even love, follow, obey, and become attached to another, is ephemeral and transitory. Either the charismatic, whose powers are often viewed as near divine or supernatural, passes from the scene or loses the charisma, or those who have been attracted by it for whatever reason fail to retain their attachments. In Weber's analysis, charismatic authority "cannot remain stable, but becomes either traditionalized or rationalized, or a combination of both."[62] Put differently, this means that one of three possibilities ensues for those who once constituted the charmed: dissolution; the transformation of charismatic authority into a traditional authority whose influence is based on the sanctity of tradition, a dependence on the "eternal yesterday," and a desire to leave life unchanged; or finally the evolution of the charismatic authority into an authority governed by rational rules and regulations, a predictable system. Hasidism, particularly Lubavitcher Hasidism, has proved to be a perfect example of these processes. If the first rebbe, Schneur Zalman of Lyady (1745–1813), was endowed with charismatic authority, each of his successors faced the problem of how to continue to charm and inspire followers. They were helped by the charisma of their office and the "sacred" writings he left behind, along with the unique calendar of ChaBaD holidays and special events that would systematize the meaning of being a Hasid so that continued attachment to the group, even after the change from one rebbe to another, would be assured. But each also needed in some way to add to his own charisma above and beyond that which he gained by tradition or office.[63] Not all succeeded in the same measure, and accordingly in some cases the ascendance of a new Rebbe led to a loss of some follow-ers—dissolution, while in other cases it led to gains, and sometimes it led to a combination of both. We have seen how Menachem Mendel made use of all these mechanisms in his ascent to and continued hold on power. We have also seen how his personal charisma, enhanced by both traditional authority and the power of his office, as well as the devotion of his followers, his writings, and his attachment to his prede-cessor, raised him to a position perhaps unprecedented in the history of his movement. And then he was gone, with no one in line to replace him—for the first time in Lubavitcher history.

This left only the system in place—the writings, video record, cus-toms, rules, holidays, and beliefs—and of course the mission, but it also left uncertainty and elements of chaos. We have seen that the in-stitution of the emissaries has continued to grow over time. Their sense of mission remains powerful and, because it is attached to a career pat-tern and way of life, has continued to draw new recruits and enthusi-asm among a new generation of Lubavitchers of both sexes. We have seen how the feeling that they are still connected to the Rebbe and can draw inspiration from him via a seemingly endless series of publica-tions and video images can blur the line between his absence and his presence, allowing many Lubavitchers to continue on in the short run as if little has changed. Of course, those who never encountered the Rebbe in life and know him only as an image or through the words of a book cannot be as connected as those for whom he was once a living presence in their lives.

Accordingly, the latter have slowly been endowed with some bor-rowed charisma by virtue of having had this contact. We have wit-nessed older Hasidim who can share their memories of the Rebbe attract younger ones like a magnet, and some of their pronouncements carry some of the charm of the Rebbe. But what happens after these people are no longer around? Who will have charisma or ultimate au-thority, be it an individual or a group? Furthermore, can those who have come of age after the passing of the last rebbe become endowed with such charisma or authority? We believe that in the absence of some sacred institutions and a way of controlling deviation that would endow such individuals or groups with this kind of authority or cha-risma of office, continuity will be endangered by competing territorial claims and interests as well as by outside influences, as in the case of the Gaon Club affair in London and similar conflicts.

On the other hand, as the need for the services provided by Lubavitcher *shluchim* continues to grow with the geographic dispersal of Jews seeking religion and its benefits, the people who are ready to fulfill that need will at the very least find a calling to continue their mission. But will that calling continue to be driven by the robust enthusiasms of messianic dreams, or will it instead come about by a redefinition—as we have seen it seems to have done—a reappraisal and routinization of what it means to toil in the vineyards of outreach in the twenty-first century? Will the Lubavitcher yeshivas continue to produce new recruits ready to leave home and the way of life they have known to dedicate themselves to these missions without a feeling that a living rebbe or a sacred institution has elected and dispatched them to these distant outposts, which are often in the Jewish wilderness? Will they be able, as *shaliach* Ari Solish put it, "to continue to do the Rebbe's work faithfully," even if they do not see the fruits of their labors "with the coming of the Messiah?" Will giving people a passing taste and connection to Judaism be enough to reward their sense of mission?

What about the alternative of the unrestrained *meshikhistn*, who as we have seen have chosen reaffirmation, a reaction that disputes the failure of the prophecy and declares its partial or complete fulfillment? More than fifteen years after the death of the Rebbe, can they continue to believe he never really died and remains the Messiah, albeit in occlusion? Can a group that announced that on July 6, 2008, Gimmel Tammuz, they would gather in an amphitheater in Bat Yam, Israel, for a program that included "greeting the Rebbe, may he live many long good years, the King Messiah," continue to draw adherents and enthusiasms as if nothing happened when he failed to appear?[64]

Clearly, these believers are in total denial of reality. They continue to look for what one of them has called "ammunition against what our eyes can see."[65] To be sure, an irrational belief and a denial of reality are by no means a death sentence for religious groups. Some will argue that precisely the need to maintain these hard-to-believe ideas sustains and drives believers to prove repeatedly to themselves and to others that keeping the faith in the messianic identity of the Rebbe against all odds is the true sign of a Lubavitcher. While they continue to wave their "Moshiach" flags, flaunt their slogans, sing their songs, and even claim sightings of their leader and wait for his physical reappearance, their numbers seem not to have grown significantly in the last fifteen years.* We must ask, finally, whether these believers can stand seeing year after year pass without the appearance of their redeemer without becoming embittered and coming to grief. Of course, one always receives the answer that the disappointments will soon be over.

From the long view of the history of religion, fifteen years, the time that as of this writing has elapsed since the Rebbe's passing, represents an insignificant period. One needs to wait at least two generations to begin to see how religious change develops and whether movements die, fractionalize, or are sustained. Knowingly or unknowingly, Menachem Mendel Schneerson succeeded in building a structure and movement that could survive him and sustain itself for the near term. His "children," his emissaries, could continue his mission, as he had continued his predecessor's. But would they not ultimately change it?

§§§

In May 2009, Yehuda Krinsky, today one of the two most senior Lubavitcher Hasidim in the ChaBaD organization and not known for being among the unrestrained *meshikhistn*, repeated a story to one of us about an encounter he had had with a reporter in the years when the "Rebbe was alive and in full vigor."[66] The discussion inevitably came around to the question of whether or not Rabbi Krinsky believed that the Rebbe was Moshiach, the Messiah.

He replied, as he repeated that day and often on other occasions: "We know that the *Moshiach* is a human being who lives among us. He's in the world someplace today. I don't know who *Moshiach* is. But if you're talking about the candidacy for it. . . ." And again, as he had learned to do many times, he concluded that his Rebbe, Menachem Mendel Schneerson, was the most suitable candidate.

But now that Rabbi Menachem Mendel was no longer among the living, did Rabbi Krinsky still believe he was that candidate? There

---

* To be sure, there are no authoritative numbers and no census of the divisions in the group.

were some rabbinic commentators, he answered, who raised the possibility of the Messiah coming from among the dead. Did he agree with them? Did that mean he still believed his Rebbe was the candidate? Rabbi Krinsky paused for a long time; he offered no further reply.

𝕸

Simon Dein has argued that "religious movements need not deliver on their promises in this world—their most valuable rewards are obtained in a reality beyond inspection."[69] Yet one may wonder whether a reality beyond inspection will continue to be sufficient for a movement that wanted Moshiach *now*. When he was alive, Menachem Mendel Schneerson brought his Hasidim to such a peak of expectations, hopes, and organization in spreading the wellsprings that in his absence, should the Messiah continue to tarry, the future can only promise disappointment or the emergence of a new sort of Judaism.

GLOSSARY

Hasidic, Hebrew, Yiddish, and Lubavitcher Terms

𝄢

bale-batim: lay leaders, literally householders

bayis neemen: a faithful Jewish household

chatzi kadur tachton: Lubavitcher hasidic conception of the other side of the globe, the spiritually lowest hemisphere, the exile of America

cheshbon ha nefesh: soul searching

chevra shas: the group assembled around the study of Talmud and its associated commentaries and glosses

didan notzach: our side won

dirah b'tachtonim: a dwelling place for the Almighty among those in the lower spiritual realm, i.e., the physical world

farbrengen: Lubavitcher Hasidic gathering

galut be'tokh galut: living in the lowest level of exile, said of those who are nearly completely assimilated and secularized; living among the barely observant

gartl: black sash Hasidim wrap about their waists during prayer and with which they separate the higher from the lower parts of the body and the mind from animal inclination

gematria: mystical numerology in which Hebrew letters are converted into corresponding numbers

gevalt (expletive): for heaven's sake

haftarah: selection from prophetic literature read weekly after the Torah portion on Sabbath in the synagogue

haredi: ultra-Orthodox, literally God-fearing

hiskashres (Hebrew: *hitkashrut*): declaring a spiritual bonding between Hasidim and their leader, sometimes put in documentary form

histalkes: leave-taking or death

Igros Kodesh: letters or correspondence, specifically of the "holy" Rebbe

Kaddish: memorial prayer, said only in the presence of a *minyan*

kapote or *sirtuk*: the knee-length frock coat common to Hasidim, often black

kheyder (Hebrew, *heder*): Jewish school, literally a room

khoyzer: the Lubavitcher Hasid who could and would repeat from memory all the Rebbe's talks

khutse she'eyn khutse mimenu: spiritually the lowest point on earth

kiddush: the holy day benediction over wine or alcohol

kinus: gathering

kitel: the white smock Jewish grooms traditionally wear at the marriage ceremony, often worn on the high holy days of Rosh Hashanah and Yom Kippur

l'altar l'geula: to a swift redemption

lekhayim or *l'chaim*: literally "to life"; to make a toast over alcohol

ma'amar or *DACh*: Lubavitcher Hasidic discourse given by a Rebbe and recited in a special singsong

maftir: section of scripture preceding *haftarah*

mazl-tov: congratulations, literally, "a good star"

melamed: tutor for children

meoras: fiancé

meshikhistn: those who believe the Rebbe Menachem Mendel is the Messiah

minyan: quorum of ten males over the age of thirteen to make a communal prayer

mitnaggedim: religious opponents to Hasidism

mitzvah: religious commandment

Moshiach or *Mashiach*: Messiah

neshamah yeterah: mystical concept of the extra soul each Jew has on the Sabbath

neshome (Hebrew, *neshamah*): soul

nesi: prince or leader, a term in Lubavitch for their Rebbe

ohel: room attached to a tomb or bier (literally, tent)

pidyones: personal notes on which the names of the petitioners and their requests are listed and handed to the Rebbe; a sign of loyalty to the Rebbe, often accompanied by a monetary donation

pnimi: insider, one of us, one in the know with the special wisdom of ChaBaD

rav mi-ta'am: officially government-appointed rabbi

rebbetzin: rebbe's wife

rosh hodesh: holy day of the start of the lunar month

seforim: holy books

shaliach: emissary

sheva berakhot: seven blessings, the gathering part of the seven days of festive meals that follow a traditional Jewish wedding

shiva: seven-day mourning period

S*hkhine* or *Shechinah*: Divine Presence

shlita: acronym for "may he live for many good years, amen," used only for the living rabbi

shluchim: emissaries

shokhtim: ritual slaughterers of kosher meat

shtibl: small synagogue

shtrayml: fur hat worn by married hasidic men but no longer used by Lubavitchers

shul: synagogue

sichos: Lubavitcher rabbinic talks

sirtuk: see kapote

takhtn she'eyn takhtn mimenu: lowest spiritual realm

talis: prayer shawl worn by men

Tanya: basic text of ChaBaD Hasidism, written by the founding rebbe

tefillin: phylacteries, black leather amulets containing scripture worn by Jewish males older than age thirteen as part of daily prayer

tefillin d'shimusha rabba: strapping on an additional pair of tefillin, in which the order of the scripture placement includes an alternate version, reversing the standard (Rashi) one

tehillim or *tilim*: Psalms

temimim: the perfect or unblemished, pure of heart; often a term for students of a ChaBaD yeshiva, Tomekhei Temimim

tena'im: the ceremony prior to marriage that symbolizes a couple's formal engagement

teshuva: repentance and return

Torah-im-derech-eretz: philosophy that emerged among neo-Orthodox German Jewry urging the study of Torah and Jewish sources alongside secular university study

toras hasidus: the wisdom and philosophy of Hasidism; in ChaBaD a mixture of mysticism and their own Hasidic philosophy

tsiyen: tomb or bier

Tzivos Hashem: Army of God, Lubavitcher youth organization

uforatzto: A Lubavitcher anthem having the words "you shall break out from your boundaries and limits:, also the name of the Lubavitcher outreach campaign

yarzheit: anniversary of the day of death

yatir mi behayekhon: above and beyond the limitations of life and working even harder, a reference to the Rebbe's greater power in the afterlife

yihudim: mystical procedures and contemplation by which the living can continue to be attached to the soul of the departed saint who exists in the afterlife

zaddik: holy man, saint, or rebbe

Zohar: primary text of Jewish mysticism or Kabbalah

NOTES

〰〰

PREFACE

1 In this book we refer to him as "Menachem Mendel" when he becomes Rebbe and as "Mendel" (as he signed himself) in the years before he was crowned.

2 Clifford Geertz, *The Interpretation of Cultures* (New York: Basic Books, 1973), 35.

CHAPTER 1
Farbrengen: The Gathering of the Emissaries

1 The precise Hebrew or Yiddish word for emmisaries would be "*shlichim*," but for whatever reason, Lubavitchers have chosen to use the term "*shluchim*," perhaps to distinguish themselves from all other types of emmisaries, religious or otherwise.

2 Moshe Bogomilsky, *Hei Teves Didan Notzach* (Brooklyn: privately published, 2007), 18–19. The three-story house, built in 1933, was purchased in 1940 by Agudas Chassidei ChaBaD after the doctor was arrested.

3 Generally, Menachem Mendel spelled his last name without an "h," whereas his predecessor and almost all the other rebbes spelled it "Schneersohn." In all events, they took the name from the first rebbe, Schneur Zalman, and thus became Shneur's "sons."

4 There are versions of this letter that the Ba'al Shem Tov, Israel Ben Eliezer, founder of Hasidism, wrote to his brother-in-law, Gershon Kitover. See Naftali Loewenthal, *Communicating the Infinite: The Emergence of the Habad School* (Chicago: University of Chicago Press, 1990), 221 n. 43. On the relatively recent adoption of this exchange between the Besht and the Messiah as one of ChaBaD's outreach slogans, see now Naftali Loewenthal, "The Baal Shem Tov's *Iggeret Ha-Kodesh* and Contemporary HaBaD Outreach," in *Hasidim and the Musar Movement*, vol. 1 of *Let the Old Make Way for the New: Studies in the Social and Cultural History of Eastern European Jewry Presented to Immanuel Etkes*, ed. David Assaf and Ada Rapoport-Albert, 2

vols. (Jerusalem: Shazar Institute, 2009), English section, 69–101, esp. n. 2. On unifications, see chapter two.

5 See Loewenthal, *Communicating the Infinite*, 6, 14. See also Mor Altshuler, *The Messianic Secret of Hasidism* (Boston: Brill, 2006), esp. 3–13.

6 Quoted in Sue Fishkoff, *The Rebbe's Army: Inside the World of Chabad-Lubavitch* (New York: Schocken, 2003), 22.

7 "HaShaliach V'haMeshaleach" [The One Who Dispatches and the Emissary], *Sichat HaShavua* 775 (November 9, 2001) (translation by Samuel C. Heilman). On the Noahide "7 for 70" campaign that sought to ensure the observance of the seven commandments given to Noah and his offspring (the seventy nations), all non-Jews, see http://www.7for70.com/site/index-4.asp?depart_id=51179 (accessed May 28, 2008).

8 Hecht went on to be a *shaliach* in a variety of places in the United States, establishing Lubavitcher yeshivas in Boston, Buffalo, Newark, and New Haven.

9 Abraham Hecht, speaking on the video "The Early Years III" (Jewish Educational Media, www.jemedia.org).

10 The programs and mission of Harvard's ChaBaD House are described on its Web site, http://www.hcs.harvard.edu/~chabad/wisdomcenter.html (quotations as of May 26, 2008).

11 Shalom Greenberg, in conversation with Samuel C. Heilman, November 22, 2008, Shanghai. For more details (in Hebrew), see http://www.col.org.il/show_news.rtx?artID=11149 (accessed January 10, 2008). For a discussion of ChBaD in Shanghai, see http://www.chinajewish.org/index.htm (accessed June 22, 2008).

12 Asher Federman, in conversation with Samuel C. Heilman, November 2006, New York.

13 Fishkoff, *The Rebbe's Army*, 41.

14 Address by Moshe Kotlarsky at the 2009 *Kinus HaShluchim* November 16, 2009.

15 See chapter three.

16 Of course, as early as the nineteenth century ChaBaD had communities of Hasidim in the Holy Land, in Jerusalem and Hebron, but these were small and not very active.

17 See *Encyclopedia Judaica* (Jerusalem: Keter, 1972), 10:883, and *Sichat Ha-Shavua* (Israel), 1097, January 11, 2008, 2, quoting Menachem Mendel Schneerson.

18 Emile Durkheim, *The Elementary Forms of the Religious Life*, trans. J. W. Swain (Glencoe, IL: Free Press, 1965), 475; Friedrich Nietzsche, *Thus Spake Zarathustra* (New York: Cosimo Books, 2006 [1911]), 59.

19 See, e.g., Robert Wuthnow, *The Restructuring of American Religion: Society and Faith since World War II* (Princeton, NJ: Princeton University Press, 1988), and Graham Murdock, "The Re-enchantment of the World: Religion and the Transformations of Modernity," in *Rethinking Media, Religion and*

Culture, ed. Stewart Hoover and Knut Lundby (Thousand Oaks, CA: Sage, 1997), 91.

20 Menachem Mendel Schneerson, letter of 10 Elul 5720 (September 2, 1960), in *Igros Kodesh*, 19:428.

21 Erik H. Erikson, "Identity and Uprootedness in Our Time," in idem, *Insight and Responsibility* (New York: Norton, 1964), 91.

22 Rabbi Shalom Greenberg, in conversation with Samuel C. Heilman, November 16, 2008.

23 See Yitzchak Kraus, *The Seventh: Messianism in the Last Generation of Habad* [in Hebrew] (Tel Aviv: Yediot Ahronoth and Chemed Books, 2007), 26–28.

24 C. Bader, "When Prophecy Passes Unnoticed: New Perspectives on Failed Prophecy," *Journal for the Scientific Study of Religion* 38 (1999): 119-31.

25 Elie Kaunfer, "Rebbe's Death Throws Some into Confusion," *Boston Globe*, June 13, 1994, 4.

26 In the course of the Lubavitch dynasty, all of these had occurred. See Avrum M. Ehrlich, *Leadership in the HaBaD Movement: A Critical Evaluation of HaBaD Leadership, History and Succession* (Northvale, NJ: Jason Aronson, 2000).

27 See Rachel Elior, *Torah HaElohut b'Dor HaSheni shel Chasidut Chabad* (Jerusalem: Magnes, 1982), 5–14, and Loewenthal, *Communicating the Infinite*, 5. See also Samuel C. Heilman, "What's in a Name? The Dilemma of Title and Geography for Contemporary Hasidism," paper presented at University College London, November 2009.

28 A few Bobriusk and Nezhin Hasidim were to be found in New York, but their leaders, especially Rabbi Yisrael Jacobson, ultimately accepted the leadership of the sixth rebbe and unified under the Lubavitch banner, although even then there were a very few who did not accept his leadership. See Ehrlich, *Leadership in the HaBaD Movement*, 278.

29 RaMaSh is often used as an acronym for the Rebbe Menachem Mendel Schneerson (1902-94). This is in line with common nomenclature in Lubavitch, where his predecessor is called RaYaTZ, an acronym for the Rebbe Yosef Yitzchak Schneersohn (1880-1950), and the fifth rebbe is called RaSHaB, an acronym for the Rebbe Shalom DovBer (1860-1920), and so on.

30 Kaunfer, "Rebbe's Death Throws Some into Confusion," 4.

31 The exact term for "Previous Rebbe" was the Yiddish *Frierdiker Rebbe*.

32 *Living Torah*, disk 6, words spoken at the conclusion of the *shiva* for Chaya Mushka.

33 A *pidyen* is often accompanied by a monetary donation.

34 See Jonathan Garb, "The Cult of the Saints in Lurianic Kabbalah," *The Jewish Quarterly Review* 98, no. 2 (Spring 2008): 203-29, esp. 211–19.

35 See Ada Rapoport-Albert, "God and the Zaddik as the Two Focal Points of Hasidic Worship," *History of Religions* 18 (1979): 296-325.

36 *Zohar* 3 *Acharei Mot*, 71b. See also Garb, "The Cult of the Saints," 211.

37 We thank Ada Rapoport-Albert for calling our attention to this source.

38 *Zohar* 3 *Acharei Mot*, 70b–71a; Garb, "The Cult of the Saints," 212–13. Not all rabbis endorsed the idea of communicating with the dead. Some saw this practice as a transgression of the prohibition against "*dorshim el ha-metim*" (inquiring of the dead) (cf. Deut. 18:11). As one medieval Karaite critic put it, "How can I remain silent when some Jews follow the customs of idolators. They 'sit among the graves and lodge in the vaults' (Isaiah 65:4) and 'inquire of of the dead.'" No less an authority than Maimonides discouraged visiting graves at all (*Mishneh Torah* [Laws of Mourning], 4:4). The opponents of Hasidism often focused on what they saw as "the Hasidic cult of the dead" as particularly transgressive. See also Elliot Horowitz, "Speaking to the Dead: Cemetery Prayer in Medieval and Early Modern Jewry," *Journal of Jewish Thought and Philosophy* 8 (1999): 303–17.

Even such a known rationalist as the famous Rabbi Ezekiel Landau (1713–93), known as the *Noda' bi-Yehudah,* argued that there were distinct benefits in petitioning the dead *zaddik* for intercession on high. See Landau, *Ahavas Zion, Drasha 6,* "Eulogy on 19 Shevat 5525 [February 10, 1765] for Rabbis Samuel Heilman and Anschel Ozers" (Prague, 5587 [1827]).

39 *Igeret Kodesh Tanya*, epistle 27, http://www.chabad.org/library/article_cdo/aid/7972/jewish/Epistle-27.htm (accessed May 26, 2008). See also *Sefer Hahishtatchus* (Brooklyn: Kehot, 1996), 3–9. On the *Tanya* as a mediator between Hasidim and the *zaddik*, see, e.g., Loewenthal, *Communicating the Infinite*, 47ff.

40 Yoram Bilu has recently published interesting work on various modes of "concretizing" the dead rebbe's presence even after his death. See, e.g., his "'Itanu yoter mi-tamid': Hankhahat ha-Rabbi mi-Lubavitch ba-Peleg ha-Meshihi shel HaBaD," in *Leadership and Authority in Israeli Haredi Society*, ed. Kimmy Caplan and Nurit Stadler (Tel Aviv: Van Leer Jerusalem Institute/Hakibbutz Hameuchad, 2009), 186–209 [in Hebrew].

41 See Samuel C. Heilman, "Still Seeing the Rebbe: Pilgrims at the Lubavitcher Grand Rabbi's Grave in Queens," in *Killing the Buddha*, http://www.killing thebuddha.com/dogma/still_seeing_rebbe.htm. The question of whether 770 or the cemetery was the right place to encounter the absent rebbe was one that some saw as symbolic of the division between those who denied he was actually dead—the extreme messianists—and those who admitted that he was. See Michal Kravel-Tovi, "To See the Invisible Messiah: Messianic Socialization in the Wake of a Failed Prophecy in Chabad," unpublished manuscript, Hebrew University, Sociology Department.

42 On the use of bibliomancy in folk religious belief, see Stith Thompson, *Motif Index of Folk-Literature* (Bloomington: Indiana University Press, 1975), and Michal Kravel-Tovi and Yoram Bilu, "The Work of the Present:

Constructing Messianic Temporality in the Wake of Failed Prophecy among Chabad Hasidim," *American Ethnologist* 35 (February 2008).

43 Abba Refson, interview by Samuel C. Heilman, July 7, 2006, New York.

44 On the visits of Sephardic Jews to holy places and graves of the saints, see Y. Bilu, "The Sanctification of Space in Israel: Civil Religion and Folk-Judaism," in *Jews in Israel*, ed. U. Rebhun and C. I. Waxman (Hanover, NH: Brandeis University Press, 2004), 371–79, and Y. Bilu and E. Ben-Ari, "The Making of Modern Saints: Manufactured Charisma and the Abu-Hatseiras of Israel," *American Ethnologist* 19, no. 4 (1992): 29–44.

45 Yisrael Shmotkin, interview by Samuel S. Heilman, June 19, 2007, New York.

46 See William Shaffir, "When Prophecy Is Not Validated: Explaining the Unexpected in a Messianic Campaign," *Jewish Journal of Sociology* 37, no. 2, 126.

47 These enumerations of visitors and *pidyones* are available at http://www.crownheights.info/index.php?itemid=7036 (accessed May 12, 2008).

48 Max Weber, *The Theory of Social and Economic Organizations,* trans. A. M. Henderson and Talcott Parsons (New York: Free Press, 1947), 358-92.

49 For further information, see the Crown Heights, Brooklyn, Web site, http://www.crownheights.info/index.php?itemid=9240&catid=27 (accessed July 6, 2008), in which a *farbrengen* with Kahan, a senior Lubavitcher, on President Street is documented.

50 See Levi Sudak, "A True Chossid," http://www.shmais.com/pages.cfm?page=chabaddetail&ID=524 (accessed April 1, 2008).

51 Berel Shemtov, interview by Samuel C. Heilman, June 19 (Gimmel Tammuz), 2007, New York.

52 See Yosef Y. Kaminetsky, comp., *Days in Chabad*, trans. Yosef Kohen (Brooklyn: Kehot, 2002), 26.

53 Rabbi Menachem Mendel, talk delivered December 18, 1990 (the eighth day of Hanukkah).

54 Ibid.

55 Leizer Shemtov, interview by Samuel C. Heilman, December 11, 2007.

56 Jeffrey Shandler, *Jews, God, and Videotape: New Media and Religion in Twentieth-Century America* (New York: New York University Press, 2009), chap. 6.

57 Trailer, *Living Torah*, http://www.thelivingarchive.org/home/home_video.html.

58 *Living Torah*, disk 16, program 61 (Jewish Educational Media, www.jeminc.org) (italics ours). Rabbi Menachem Mendel goes on to explain that as a Gentile, the captain's resolution to think about God was surely a fulfillment of one of the Seven Noahide Commandments to abandon idol worship and believe in the One God. This talk, made in the context of the seven (Noahide commandments) for seventy (nations, a Talmudic term to identify the non-Jewish world, which is traditionally considered to be made up

of this number of nations) campaign (a clear play on "770"), was an extension of his overall mission to prepare the ground for the messianic redemption, which he argued also required getting Gentiles to observe these commandments so they too could be redeemed, a line of reasoning he took from Maimonides.

59 Shandler, *Jews, God, and Videotape.*

CHAPTER 2
Death and Resurrection

1 See *Der Tog*, January 30, 1950, 1, 3.

2 The description that follows is based in large measure on Raphael Nachman Hacohen, "*Shmuos v'Sipurim* [News and Stories] (New York: Yitzchak Gansburg, 1990–), 3:135–45.See also Bryan Mark Rigg, *Rescued from the Reich* (New Haven, CT: Yale University Press, 2004), 37.

3 Seligson was both a Hasid and a physician. See the ChaBaD Lubavitch news page at http://www.crownheights.info/index.php?itemid=1636 (accessed August 14, 2008).

4 Hacohen, *Shmuos v'Sipurim*, 3:135–45.

5 Of Lieberman (1892-1991), see Yehoshua D. Levanon (Mondshine), *Toldot Adam—Rabbi Chaim Leiberman Ha-Ish U'Mechkarav*, in *Alei Sefer* 6, no. 7 (Nissan 5739 [1979]): 5-25, esp. 7–8. Until the 1980s he was part of the Lubavitcher court, but after the trial over the Lubavitcher library, he became estranged from the court. He spent his final years in the Eishal Avrohom Home in Williamsburg. A number of Satmar Hasidim (who viewed ChaBaD with hostility) took on his care during his final years. He is buried in Israel. His two-volume *Ohel Rachel* is a classic in Jewish bibliography and Yiddish linguistics.

6 It was Levitin who had been at Rabbi Yosef Yitzchak's side when the latter's mother had died in January 1942, who had even recited kaddish on his behalf at the gravesite, because Rabbi Yosef Yitzchak had been too ill at the time to stand outside at the grave. See Menachem Mendel Schneerson, *Torat Menachem: Reshimat HaYoman* [Diary Notes] (Brooklyn: Kehot, 2006), 411.

7 Kaminetsky, comp., *Days in Chabad*, 115–16.

8 See Moshe Dovber Rivkin, "Ashkavta D'Rebbe" (Brooklyn: Vaad L'hadpasat HaKuntres, 5713 [1953]), 94-95. See also Ehrlich, *Leadership in the HaBaD Movement*, 343, and *Kfar Chabad*, April 3, 1997.

9 *HaRabanit: Roshei P'rakim MiToldot HaRabanit HaZadkanit*, ed. M. M. Kaminker (Brooklyn: Va'ad Talmidei HaTemimim HaOlami, 5763/2003), p. 7.

10 See Weiner, *Nine-and-a-Half Mystics*, 183. After the death of Zemah Zedek, the third rebbe, his sons engaged in a dispute about who would take his crown. Then a will was discovered that handed it to Shmuel, the youngest. His brothers claimed the will was a forgery, and its discovery did not

immediately end the dispute (see Chaim Tchernovitz, *Pirkei Chaim* [New York: Bitzaron, 1954], 104–6). Hence, even if there had been a will (and in an interview with Menachem Friedman, Barry suggested there was one that gave him the crown but that that will had been made to disappear), there are no guarantees the question of who would next lead the ChaBaD Hasidim would have solved easily.

11 This was not the first time in the history of this dynasty that a rebbe had died without making clear who if anyone should lead the Hasidim after him. Already at the passing of the first rebbe, Schneur Zalman, there were those who wanted to follow his most prominent disciple, Aharon HaLevi Horowitz (later of Strashelye, Belarus), rather than the younger Dovber, Schneur Zalman's son. See Ehrlich, *Leadership in the HaBaD Movement*. See also See Emanuel Etkes, "Controversy over Inheritance in ChaBaD Hasidism," paper presented at the Institute for Advanced Studies of the Hebrew University, July 10, 2008.

12 See *A Prince in Prison* (an extract from *Likkutei Dibburim* by Rabbi Yosef Yitzchak Schneersohn of Lubavitch), trans. Uri Kaploun (1997), http://www.sichosinenglish.org/books/prince-in-prison/04.htm, and Zalman Alpert, review of *The Heroic Struggle*, *Jewish Action*, Summer 2000.

13 See *A Prince in Prison*, section 11, http://www.sichosinenglish.org/books/prince-in-prison/04.htm (accessed June 23, 2009), and Alpert, review of *The Heroic Struggle*. The relationship between Barry and his grandfather was discussed by Barry Gourary in an interview by Bryan Rigg, May 2003.

14 Comments made by Shaul Shimon Deutsch in an interview by Samuel C. Heilman, March 9, 2008.

15 Gourary, interview by Rigg, May 2003. We thank Dr. Rigg for sharing his interview tapes with us. Barry would add that it was ironic that his Uncle Mendel would end up choosing the life that he himself would spurn, almost as if the two had exchanged futures.

16 Gourary, interviews by Menachem Friedman and Bryan Rigg, and attendance records from Monica Rivera of Brooklyn College.

17 Yosef Yitzchak Schneersohn, letter to the Jews of America and Canada, April 1940, in *Collected Letters and Talks* (Brooklyn: Kehot, 1942), 7. See also Yosef Yitzchak Schneersohn, *Igrot Kodesh* (Brooklyn: Otzar Hasidim), 13:295–97, and Menachem Friedman, "Messiah and Messianism in Habad Hassidic Sect," in *Gog and Magog Wars*, ed. David A. Joel, Maya Lebovitz, Yehoram Mazor, and Moti Anbari (Tel Aviv: Yediot Aharanot-Hemed, 2001), 174–229, esp. 204–14 [in Hebrew].

18 Zalman Schachter, interview by Samuel C. Heilman, May 10, 2008. Schachter was one of those posting these stickers. See also Yosef Yitzchak Schneersohn, "Tevet, the Month of Collective Soul-Searching," *Machane Yisrael B'Eretz Yisrael* (Jerusalem), May 1943, 6. See also Yosef Yitzchak Schneersohn, *Kovetz Michtavim v'Sichos* (Brooklyn: Machane Yisrael, Sivan

5701 [1941]), 10–12. Repentance did not bring redemption—the Messiah would come anyway. Repentance simply put one among the saved.

19 Kaminetsky, *Days in Chabad*, 115.

20 *New York Times*, January 30, 1950, 2.

21 See Yosef Y. Jacobson, "Stalin vs. Schneersohn," http://www.algemeiner.com/ generic.asp?id=3606 (accessed January 15, 2008).

22 *HaKri'ah Vehakedusha*, August 1941, 2. See also Yosef Yitzchak Schneersohn, *Igros Kodesh*, 6:170–73; Friedman, "Messiah and Messianism," 208–15; and Rigg, *Rescued from the Reich*, 181.

23 Yosef Yitzchak Schneersohn, "The Truth about the Destruction of the Jewish People Today," *HaKri'ah VeHakedusha* (New York), Sivan 5701 (June 1941); idem, letter to Rabbi Solomon Joseph Zevin of Jerusalem, February 23, 1942, in *Igros Kodesh*, 6:209.

24 See *Der Morgen Zhornal* (in Yiddish), January 27, 1950, 2; January 29, 1950, 1; January 30, 1950, 4.

25 *Der Tag*, January 30, 1950, 3.

26 Zalman Schachter, interview by Samuel C. Heilman, May 18, 2008.

27 Barry Gourary, interview by Menachem Friedman, September 1, 1991. The practice of Jewish mourning lasts a year. See Samuel Heilman, *When a Jew Dies* (Berkeley and Los Angeles: University of California Press, 2001).

28 A letter written 5 Tammuz 5695 (July 6, 1935), quoted in Kaminetsky, *Days in Chabad*, 135.

29 According to one source, Menachem Mendel had been asked to join the Rebbe on this last trip, but he refused (Shimon Deutsch, interview by Menachem Friedman, July 29, 1997).

30 See chapter three.

31 Evidence of this is difficult to find. Chances are if he did this work it was more mathematical than in the area of design, and for a very brief time. See chapter five.

32 Actually, their first address was 346 New York Avenue in Crown Heights (as indicated on the arrival record of June 16, 1947, when Menachem Mendel accompanied his mother, Chana, whom he brought to America aboard the *Mauritania*). See List of U.S. Citizens in the U.S. Archives.

33 Shmuel Marcus, *Rebbetzin Chaya Mushka Schneerson* (Brooklyn: Kehot, 1999), 15. See also *HaRabanit*, 85–94, and Menachem Kirschenbaum, *The Rebbe Inspiring a Generation* (Brooklyn: Avner Institute, 2008), 12-15.

34 See chapter five.

35 Zalman Schachter, interview, May 18, 2008. On the matter of the Rebbe Yosef Yitzchak's sentence, see Beizer (*The Jews of Leningrad*, p. 222), who asserts that a search of Soviet files reveals no evidence of a death sentence.

36 Cf. Deuteronomy 3:23 and 34:9. To be sure, if there were *only* a will and no indications of the Rebbe's plans for succession during his lifetime, such a

will could still be contested. But here there was no undeniable indication during the Rebbe's lifetime, and no will.

37 Weiner, *Nine-and-a-Half Mystics*, 175.

38 From a letter sent by the distinguished ChaBaD Hasidim Avraham Chen, Nachum Sosonkin, and Solomon Joseph Zevin in Israel; see Laufer, *Yemei Melech*, 1157.

39 Laufer, *Yemei Melech*, 1151.

40 Zalman Schachter, the Hasid in question, interview by Samuel C. Heilman, May 27, 2008. See also Laufer, *Yemei Melech*, 1159.

41 For the Hasidim's concerns about his childlessness, see also Weiner, *Nine-and-a-Half Mystics*, 172.

42 See Ehrlich, *Leadership in the HaBaD Movement*.

43 See also Laufer, *Yemei Melech*, 1164.

44 Ibid., 1163.

45 Ibid., 1166.

46 *Kfar Chabad* 14, 7 Adar I, 5741 (February 11, 1981), 18.

47 See Laufer, *Yemei Melech*, 1136.

48 See, e.g., http://www.chabad.org/calendar/view/day.asp?tDate=1/17/2008 (accessed January 31, 2008).

49 Kaminetsky, *Days in Chabad*, 118.

50 *Likkutei Dibburim*, 4:244–45. See also Rigg, *Rescued from the Reich*, 25.

51 See Ehrlich, *Leadership in the HaBaD Movement*, 351 n. 10, who cites the unpublished diary of Lubavitcher Hasid Eli Gross (New York, 1950–53).

52 Kahan Diaries, 11 Tishrei 5711 (September 22, 1950). Much of what follows in this page comes from Kahan's diaries.

53 Allon Dahan, "Maavakei HaYerusha B'Chasidut ChaBaD," *Kivunim Chadashim* 17, January 2008, 212.

54 Kaminetsky, *Days in Chabad*, 119.

55 Ibid.

56 See *Beit Moshiach*, 19 Shevat 5759 (February 5, 1999), 34.

57 Yehuda Krinsky, interview by Samuel C. Heilman, May 10, 2009.

58 This is a corruption of Proverbs 3:4.

59 Yosef Y. Schneersohn and Menachem Mendel Schneerson, *Basi L'Gani*, ed. Uri Kaploun (Brooklyn: Kehot, 1990), 82, 84, 96.

60 Kraus, *The Seventh*.

61 That some saw Menachem Mendel as the new Moses is clear. See, e.g., Weiner, *Nine-and-a-Half Mystics*, 159.

62 See Allon Dahan, "*Dira BaTahtonim* [A Dwelling Place in the Lower Levels]: The Messianic Ideas of Menachem Mendel Schneerson," Ph.D. diss., Hebrew University of Jerusalem, 2006, and Faital Levin, *Heaven on Earth: Reflections on the Theology of the Lubavitcher Rebbe Rabbi Menachem M. Schneerson* (Brooklyn: Kehot, 2002).

63 Schneerson (Kaploun edition), *Basi L'Gani*, 99, 88.

64 Kaminetsky, *Days in Chabad*, 119.

65 See Yoel Kahan, "Excerpts from a Diary," *Kfar Chabad*, 5 Adar II, 5741 (March 11, 1981), 20

66 See *Der Morgen Zhornal*, January 21, 1951 (14 Shevat), 1, 4, and *New York Times*, January 21, 1951, "Events Today." In the *Times*, the speaker was listed as Lazarus Joseph.

67 There are several important sources for the events of those days from which we are drawing. They include the diaries of Yoel Kahan, at the time an eager student at the Lubavitch yeshiva Tomekhei Temimim, some of which were published in the Hebrew newsletter, *Kfar Chabad*, between January and September 1981. Kahan would go on to become the respected *khoyzer*, the one who memorized every talk of the Rebbe (particularly those given on Sabbaths and holy days, when nothing could be recorded or written) and then repeat it exactly. The unpublished diaries of Eli Gross, at the time also a student in the yeshiva, are another source. Large sections of these diaries are quoted in Ehrlich, *Leadership in the HaBaD Movement*, 359–61, 401–2, which also serves as a source.

68 *HaPardes* 25, no. 8 (Iyyar 5711): 24. ADMOR is an acronym for the Hebrew phrase "Our master, our teacher, and our Rabbi," and is generally the term used to refer to Hasidic rebbes or rabbinic leaders.

69 *HaPardes* 25, no. 8 (Iyyar 5711): 24, and 9 (Sivan 5711): 81.

70 Letter to Nechama Dina Schneersohn, 26 Adar I 5711 (March 14, 1951) (collection of Menachem Friedman). In the letter they also refer to the aggravation (*agmes nefesh*) Shmaryahu Gourary had once caused Rabbi Yosef Yitzchak, "when once he sought to grab all the affairs of Lubavitch into his hands," suggesting thereby that the Previous Rebbe had not wanted to cede control and leadership to this son-in-law.

71 Ehrlich, *Leadership in the HaBaD Movement*, 399.

72 See chapter seven.

73 Ehrlich, *Leadership in the HaBaD Movement*, 399, citing the Kahan diary, 61.

74 Shaul Shimon Deutsch, citing an interview with Jacobson's daughter, personal communication to Samuel C. Heilman, March 2008.

75 In a case brought in 2003 in New York State Supreme Court (and not in a rabbinical court), the fact that Shmaryahu Gourary's empire was gradually diminished financially and politically became clear when a struggle between Merkos L'Inyonei Chinuch (the Rebbe's empire, now overseen by Yehuda Krinsky) and ULY (overseen by Shmaryahu Gourary's executers; he had died in 1989) ensued over access to funds in an estate left by Juda Weinstock. See http://www.nycourts.gov/comdiv/Law%20Report%20Files/January%202004/Merkos.htm (accessed May 20, 2008). Weiner, *Nine-and-a-Half Mystics*, 83.

76 See Kaminetsky, *Days in Chabad*, and Zalman Alpert, "Counterpoint," *Jewish Action*, Winter 5761 (2000).

77 It means literally "we together with God, won." See *Vayikra Rabbah* 24 and http://www.shmais.com/pages.cfm?page=chabaddetail&ID=280 (accessed January 16, 2008). Shimon Deutsch and Shalom DovBer Levine, interviews by Menachem Friedman, July 18, 1995. See also Bogomilsky, *Hei Teves Didan Notzach*.

78 Kaminetsky, *Days in Chabad,* 90.

79 Bogomilsky, *Hei Teves Didan Notzach*, 56–57.

80 Ibid., 7 n. 4.

81 Ibid., 80-81, where the verdict is reproduced in full.

82 See http://www.sichosinenglish.org/books/sichos-in-english/34/08.htm (accessed June 17, 2009).

83 Rabbi Shmuel Lew, interview by Samuel C. Heilman, June 20, 2007.

84 Irving Spiegel, "Jews Exhorted on School Help," *New York Times*, November 17, 1962, 25. On school prayer, he asserted that the Torah demanded that Jews oppose the Supreme Court ban on prayer in public schools, since such prayer would offer the only opportunity for children to make some contact with God every day, a matter he considered essential. "With the exception of a small number of secularists and atheists, there is no parent who could in all conscience object to a nondenominational prayer per se," he was quoted as saying. "Rabbi Scores Ban on School Prayer," *New York Times*, November 27, 1962, 25.

85 Interview by Menachem Friedman. He was also seen working on mathematical problems with his Uncle Mendel in New York in the 1940s (Schachter, interview by Heilman, May 18, 2008).

86 Miriam Yuval (a cousin of Moussia Schneerson), interview by Menachem Friedman, July 9, 2001. Tamar Otenzaufer (a cousin of the fifth Lubavitcher rebbe), interview by Menachem Friedman, April 26, 1998.

87 Shaul Shimon Deutsch, interview by Samuel C. Heilman, April 2008.

88 See Loewenthal, *Communicating the Infinite*, 5, who explains this is the way knowledge was expected to affect a Hasidic master.

89 See, e.g., Menachem Mendel Schneerson, *Torat Menachem: Reshimat Ha-Yoman* [Diary Notes] (Brooklyn: Kehot Otzar Hasidim, 2006). These notes are filled with everything from the tale of a story he heard about the Rebbe Shalom DovBer while walking on a Saturday night with the Rebbe Yosef Yitzchak in the summer of 1930 (156) to the importance of being "sanctified" at the time of intercourse (174).

90 Loewenthal, *Communicating the Infinite*, 3.

91 Yosef Yitzchak Kaminetzy, *Dates in the History of ChaBaD: Persons and Events in the History of ChaBaD* (Kfar Chabad: Kehot, 5754 [1994]), 153 [in Hebrew].

92 Menachem Mendel Schneerson, *Sichos Kodesh*, 24 Shevat 5710 (February 11, 1950). *Hisvaadus* 5710 (1950), 1, 11-12. See also Kraus, *The Seventh*, 280 n.16.

93 Menachem Mendel Schneerson, *Sichos Kodesh*, 24 Shevat 5710 (February 11, 1950), 8.

94 "Sections from a Diary," *Kfar Chabad*, 25 Shevat 5741 (January 30, 1981).

95 Menachem Mendel Schneerson, *Sichos Kodesh*, April 9, 1950, 10 (translation by Samuel C. Heilman).

96 See the Babylonian Talmud *Sanhedrin* 98B, where these birth pangs are described as an inevitable precursor to redemption.

97 Yosef Yitzchak Schneersohn, "The Truth about the Destruction of the Jewish People Today," *HaKri'ah V'Hakedusha* (New York), Sivan 5701 (June 1941).

98 Menachem Mendel Schneerson, *Farbrengen* 5711 (1951), pt. 1, 2:325–26.

99 Ehrlich, *Leadership in the HaBaD Movement*, 388.

100 In a way, he acted in a manner that Moshe Idel describes in his study of Hasidism as being shamanistic, mediating between the sacred dead rebbe and the community. See Moshe Idel, *Ascensions on High in Jewish Mysticism* (Budapest: Central European University Press, 2005), 154.

101 Shalom DovBer Wolpe, "Two Stories and a Conclusion," *Kfar Chabad*, 4 Cheshvan 5750 (October 2, 1989) (italics added; translation by Samuel C. Heilman).

102 Garb, "The Cult of the Saints," 215. See also Moshe Idel, "The Secret of Impregnation as Metempsychosis in Kabbalah," in *Vervadlungen*, ed. A. and J. Assmann (Munich, 2006), 341–79; and Friedman, "Messiah and Messianism." Isaac Luria (1534–72) was the central figure in kabbalah in Safed in the circle that formed there after the expulsion of Jewry from the Iberian Peninsula.

103 Ganzburg, *B'Kodesh P'nima*, 82. See also Bogomilsky, *Hei Teves Didan Notzach*, 43.

CHAPTER 3
Coming of Age in a Time of Transition

1 See Deutsch, *Larger than Life*, 1:204 n. 5, for a full explanation. See also Mordecai Zalkin, "Between the 'Sons of God' and the 'Sons of Man': Rabbis, Yeshiva Boys and the Draft into the Russian Army in the 19th Century" [in Hebrew], in *Peace and War in Jewish Culture*, ed. Avriel Bar-Levav (Jerusalem: Shazar Center, 2006), 165–222. Given that we find a letter to Mendel from his father in 1937 greeting him on his thirty-fifth birthday, we tend to believe the 1902 date to be the true one. See Levi Yitzchak Schneerson, *Igros Kodesh*, 387.

2 See his application for a French passport, about which more in chapter four.

3 Date and address from Mendel Schneerson's affidavit in his application for French citizenship. See next chapter. There was a small synagogue next door at number 3 at which craftsmen were known to pray.

4 See James A. Duran, "Catherine II, Potemkin and Colonization Policy in Southern Rusia," *Russian Review* 28, no. 1 (January 1969): 23–36.

5 Yehuda Slutsky and Shmuel Spector, "Dnepropetrovsk," in *Encyclopaedia Judaica*, ed. Michael Berenbaum and Fred Skolnik, 2nd ed. (Detroit: Macmillan Reference USA, 2007), 5:724–25.

6 See Shmarya Levin, *Youth in Revolt: The Autobiography of Shmarya Levin*, trans. Maurice Samuel (London: Routledge & Kegan Paul, 1939). To be sure, such rabbis as the latter were often regarded with suspicion by the more Orthodox elements of the Jewish community.

7 See Yehuda Slutsky, "Kazyonny Ravvin," in Berenbaum and Skolnik, *Encyclopaedia Judaica*, 12:47–48.

8 See Deutsch, *Larger than Life*, 1:90, and Sefer Yekaterinoslav, 122-24, as well as Schneerson's French affidavit for naturalization.

9 See Deutsch, *Larger than Life*, 1:53, 69.

10 Ibid., 1:134, citing Laufer, *Yemei Melech*, 2:891.

11 A. B. Yaffa, "A Shlonsky, Hameshorer V'Zmano," 12-13, and *Kfar Chabad* 485.

12 Testimony of Yeshia Shor, *Bais Moshiach*, 21 (5 Shevat 5755 [January 5, 1995]). This is a newsletter of the Lubavitcher messianists that began publishing weekly in Israel on August 11, 1994 (4 Elul 5754). See Deutsch, *Larger than Life*, 1:81.

13 Testimony of Yeshia Shor, *Bais Moshiach*, 21. See Deutsch, *Larger than Life*, 1:81, and also Zvi Harkavy in *Sefer Yekaterinoslav*, 119, and Hadassah Rachel Berman in *Sefer Yekaterinoslav*, 54.

14 National Library catalogue Barukh Ben-Anat, Praot Ukraina 1919–21 (Herzliya: privately published, 1996), esp. 63–64. See also Rachel Feigenberg, *B'Yemei Za'am* (Tel Aviv: La'am, 1942). On Jewish defense in Yekaterinoslav, see *Sefer Yekaterinoslav*, 72–73.

15 *Sefer Yekaterinoslav*, 34.

16 This comes from the ChaBaD publication *Bais Moshiach*, 35, of D. Markish, who quotes the recollection of a conversation his wife had in 1975 with Mendel in which he claimed to have served with her father-in-law, Peretz Markish, in the Jewish Defense Forces in 1919. But another internal source claims that he spent the year 1919–20 in Kremenchug (where Trotsky was at the time), studying in a yeshiva *not* affiliated with Lubavitch (even though there was a Lubavitcher yeshiva in the city). We have found no evidence to support these claims.

17 Yehuda Slutsky, "Denikin, Anton Ivanovich," in Berenbaum and Skolnik, *Encyclopaedia Judaica*, 2nd ed., 5:580, and Yehuda Slutsky and Shmuel Spector, "Dnepropetrovsk," in Berenbaum and Skolnik, *Encyclopaedia Judaica*, 2nd ed., 6:141–42.

18 See Schneerson's affidavit statement for French citizenship in the appendix on the book's Web site. According to a timeline of Mendel's life posted by Lubavitchers on their official Chabad.org site, in 1921–22 he visited the

Lubavitcher Tomekhei Temimim yeshiva in Kharkov, and in 1923 he traveled to Rostov to meet for the first time with Rabbi Yosef Yitzchak (see *HaRabbanit*, 29, and also http://www.chabad.org/therebbe/timeline_cdo/ aid/62151/jewish/1923-Soviet-Jewry.htm [accessed September 8, 2008]). (We find no independent confirmation of this visit and no documentation of it.) This would be a visit when the possibility of a marriage to Rabbi Yosef Yitzchak's middle daughter, Moussia, was broached. Nothing was, however, agreed upon at the time.

19 See Schneerson, French citizenship application affidavit.

20 Without a high school diploma, he could not enroll as a full-time student. Although records of his studies at the university were destroyed, we have found letters from the university asking for his academic record from Yekaterinoslav. Deutsch Archive.

21 The address can be found in the Leningrad telephone directories for 1925, 1926, and 1927 under the entry Schneersohn, Jos. Shalom[ovitch]. See also http://www.encspb.ru/en/article.php?kod=2804008026 (accessed February 21, 2008). This was the address he later listed as his residence in Leningrad on his French passport application affidavit.

22 See, e.g., the "Timeline" description in which they write, "Travels to Leningrad, where he is present for the first time at a Farbrengen of the Rebbe, Rabbi Yosef Yitzchak, who shows him special affection" (http://www .chabad.org/library/article_cdo/aid/1262/jewish/Timeline-Sketch.htm [accessed February 20, 2008]).

23 On the matter of his succession, see Ehrlich, "*Leadership in the Habad Movement*, 252–57.

24 See Alpert, Review of *The Heroic Struggle*.

25 See chapter five.

26 See Friedman, "Messiah and Messianism," 199-201, and Yosef Yitzchak Schneersohn, *Sichos Kodesh*, 5680-5700 [1919-1939] (*Kfar Chabad* 5741 [1980]), 95.

27 Abba Ahimeir and Shmuel Spector, "Dimanstein, Simon," in Berenbaum and Skolnik, *Encyclopaedia Judaica*, 2nd ed., 5:662. Dimanstein was ultimately arrested during the Stalin purges and died in prison, probably in 1937. On the Yevsektsiya, see M. Altshuler, *Reshit ha-Yevsektsiya*, 1918–1921 (Jerusalem: Ha Aguda l'Cheker Tefutzot Yisrael, 1966). See also Abraham Greenberg, "The Rabbinic Conference at Korostin 1926," *Shvut* 4, no. 20 (1996): 53–58, and Michael Beizer, "The Leningrad Jewish Community: From the NEP through its Liquidation," *Jews in Eastern Europe* (Hebrew University of Jerusalem, Center for Research and Documentation), Winter 1995, 16–42. See also Zvi Gittelman, *Jewish Nationality and Soviet Politics* (Princeton, NJ: Princeton University Press, 1972).

28 There were also concerns about a planned conference of Orthodox rabbis (the so-called LERO or Jewish Community of Leningrad) supported

by Zionists and other so-called "enlightened" Jews, which Rabbi Yosef Yitzchak opposed because he believed it would be used by the Yevsektsiya to infiltrate itself into religious matters (something other rabbis did not believe) and also feared it would be dominated by unbelievers and Zionists. See Michael Beizer, *The Jews of Leningrad: 1917–1939* (Jerusalemi Shazar, 2005), 210–23, and Zalman Alpert, *Counterpoint*, Summer 2000. See also Hacohen, *Shmuot v'Sippurim* (Brooklyn: Ganzburg Press, 1957), 1:207–9, as well as Shalom DovBer Levin, *Toldot ChaBaD b'Russia Hasovietit 5678–5710* [1918-1950] (Brooklyn: Kehot, 1989), 78–96.

29 Barry Gourary, personal communication to Menachem Friedman. Gourary also claimed they had been at a Habimah performance, but Habimah had left Russia by January 24, 1926. See Shimon Lev-Ari, *HaMa'avar shel Teatron HaBimah MeEropa L'Eretz Yisrael* [The Move of the Habimah Theatre from Europe to the Land of Israel], in *Toldot Hayishuv Hayehudi Be'Eretz Yisrael Me'Az HaAliya HaRishona*, vol. 3, pt. 1 (Jerusalem: Israel Academy of Science, 2008), 57–68.

With regard to that night, a huge mythology grew. Moussia Schneerson herself pointed out, "They tell a lot of stories about the arrest on the 12th of Tammuz that never happened" (*HaRabanit*, 25).

30 This is the phrase used in Lubavitcher hagiography to describe Mendel Schneerson in those days.

31 See Deutsch, *Larger than Life*, 1:180–200. See also Yehoshua D. Levanon (Mondshine), *Toldot Adam—Rabbi Chaim Leiberman HaIsh U'Mechkarav*, in *Alei Sefer* 6, 7 (Nissan 5739 [1979]): 5–25.

32 Deutsch, *Larger than Life*, 1:201, citing *Yemei Melech*.

33 See *A Prince in Prison*, trans. Uri Kaploun (1997), a version of Yosef Yitzchak's diary, and Alpert, review of *The Heroic Struggle*.

34 See *A Prince in Prison* and "Di yesurim fun libavitshn rebn in Sovet-Rusland—zayn arest fun 'Tshika,' zayne leydn in 'Shpalyarke,' zayn farurteylung tsum toyt, zayn farshikung keyn Kostroma un zayn bafrayung" (Riga: D. Apt Press, 1930).

35 "Borah Sees War if We Don't Recognize Russia," *New York Times*, December 3, 1922, 2. See also Rigg, *Rescued from the Reich*, 27.

36 Stephen Wise Archives at the American Jewish Historical Society, folders 64/7, 65/2, 70/2, 71/3, 71/4. See also Shaul Shimon Deutsch, "*Gimmel b'Tammuz—Ma yadu, ma osu yehude artzot habrit b'ikvot ma'asaro shel ha rabbi* [5687], in *K'far Chabad* 576, 5 Tammuz 5753 [June 24, 1993]. See also Israel Jacobson, *Zikaron L'Beis Yisrael* (Brooklyn: Kehot, 1996), 150–52.

37 "Di yesurim fun libavitshn rebn in Sovet-Rusland."

38 *HaRabanit*, 26.

39 On Oscar Cohen, see also a letter reproduced in *Admorei ChaBaD v'Yahadut Germania*, 111-13.

40 Kaminetsky, *Days in Chabad*, 25–26.

41 See Shalom DovBer Levin, *Toldot Chabad B'Russia Ha Sovietit 5678* [1917]–*5710* [1949] (Brooklyn: Kehot Publishing, 5749 [1988]).

42 Yehoshua Mondshine, *Derech HaMelech*: A Souvenir for the World. *Kinus HaShluchim* 5761 (2001), 7.

43 *Degel Yisrael* (a rabbinic monthly edited by Rabbi Horowitz) (New York: Horowitz, March 1928), 10–12. This publication published in full the protocols of the meeting of "*Vaad L'Chizuk HaTorah V'Hadat B'Russia*" [Committee for Strengthening Torah and Religion in Russia].

44 See Levin, *Toldot Chabad B'Russia Ha Sovietit 5678* [1917]–*5710* [1949].

45 See M. Laserson, "Jewish Minorities in the Baltic Countries," *Jewish Social Studies* 14, no. 3 (1940), esp. 280, and Deutsch, *Larger than Life*, 2:8–19.

46 See Deutsch, *Larger than Life*, 2:26–39. Hodakov would later become a key aide to Rabbi Menachem Mendel, as we have already noted.

47 Yehoshua Mondshine. "*Derech HaMelech*: A Souvenir for the World," *Kinus HaShluchim*, 5761 (2001), documents each of the stamps on Mendel Schneerson's Soviet passport.

48 Laufer, *Yemei Melech*, 218-25.

49 According to Shaul Shimon Deutsch (personal communication to Samuel C. Heilman), as a son of a then respected rabbi who was traveling for studies to Berlin, Mendel Schneerson was able to get these travel documents. Moreover, the government authorities also knew they could control his behavior abroad by virtue of the fact that his parents were "hostages" who remained within their jurisdiction.

50 Mondshine, *Derech HaMelech*, 7–8.

51 Yosef Yitzchak Schneersohn, letter of 2 Shevat 5689 (January 13, 1929)· *Igros Kodesh*, 153, and idem, letter to Dr. Pinhas Cohen, Ha'Hed 11, Av 5688 (August 1928).

52 See Laufer, *Yemei Melech*, 295–97. See also *Kfar Chabad* 5741 (1981), 103.

53 It was a question that others asked as well. See, e.g., Reuven Kimmelman, "Rabbis Joseph B. Soloveitchik and Abraham Joshua Heschel on Jewish-Christian Relations," *Modern Judaism* 24 (2004): 251–71. An online source is *The Edah Journal* (Kislev 5765), reprinted in *The Edah Journal*, vols. 3:1–4:2, Elul 5763–Kislev 5765 (2005), 1–2, n. 9, in which Soloveitchik, then a student at the university asked the same question. No answer is given in this source. (http://www.edah.org/backend/JournalArticle/4_2_Kimelman.pdf [accessed August 26, 2008]).

54 Zusha Wolf, *Admorei ChaBaD v'Yahadut Germania* [ChaBaD Rebbes and German Jewry] (Jerusalem: Heichal Menachem, 5767 [2007]), 100. He would also pay for his expenses later in Paris (see chapter four).

55 See, e.g, Wolf, *Admorei ChaBaD v'Yahadut Germania*, 99-100.

56 Mordechai Eliav and David Derovan, "Hildesheimer, Azriel," in Berenbaum and Skolnik, *Encyclopaedia Judaica*, 2nd ed., 9:103–4. See also David

Ellenson, *Rabbi Esriel Hildesheimer* (Birmingham: University of Alabama Press, 2003).

57 Alexander Carlebach, "Hildesheimer, Meir," in Berenbaum and Skolnik, *Encyclopaedia Judaica*, 9:105. The distinguished Slobodka yeshiva student J. J. Weinberg, who became rector of the seminary, was perhaps the best example of such students. See Marc Shapiro, *Between the Yeshiva World and Modern Orthodoxy: The Life and Works of Rabbi Jehiel Jacob Weinberg, 1884–1966* (Oxford: Littman, 1999).

58 See Deutsch, *Larger than Life*, 2:74.

59 See the registration book at Friedrich Wilhelm University. See also Golan, "Messiah Flesh and Blood," and Wolf, *Admorei ChaBaD v'Yahadut Germania*, 129.

60 Perhaps this arrangement to be registered at the seminary had been made at the meeting in Riga. See Mondshine, *Derech HaMelech*, 14. See also Wolf, *Admorei ChaBaD v'Yahadut Germania*, 129.

61 Laufer, *Yemei Melech*, 332, 353.

62 Yosef Yitzchak Schneersohn, *Igros Kodesh* (1982), 2:6–7 and n. 11. See also Wolf, *Admorei ChaBaD v'Yahadut Germania*, 77.

63 Mondshine, *Derech HaMelelch*, 9.

64 Levin, *Toldot ChaBaD B'Russia HaSovietit*, 119–24. See also Wolf, *Admorei ChaBaD v'Yahadut Germania*, 80, which describes other aspects of Gourary's work on behalf of Soviet Jewry as the sixth rebbe's personal emissary.

65 Wolf, *Admorei ChaBaD v'Yahadut Germania*, 77, 79.

66 Yosef Burg, communication to Menachem Friedman. Burg during these years was a student at the Hildesheimer Seminary and often visited Hasidic congregations, but never encountered Mendel Schneerson or heard about his activities.

67 See next chapter.

CHAPTER 4
Entering the Court of Lubavitch

1 Yosef Yitzchak Schneersohn, *Igros Kodesh* (2001), 1:328. See also Wolf, *Admorei ChaBaD v'Yahadut Germania*, 257.

2 Shlomo Zalman Duchman, *Yalkut Lshema Ozen—Zichronot Pitgamin Kadishin* (Brooklyn: no publisher, 1963), 151–52.

3 In 1900 the average age at marriage for formerly Russian men was between 28 and 30 years old, and for women it was between 25 and 26. See June L. Sklar, "The Role of Marriage Behaviour in the Demographic Transition: The Case of Eastern Europe Around 1900," *Population Studies* 28, no. 2 (July 1974).

4 *HaRabanit*, 31, suggests it was Monday, but Mondshine, *Derech HaMelech*, 9, notes it was the evening; hence the Hebrew date of the following day. See also *Reshimot Chatunah*, 8.

5 *Michtavei HaChatunah* (Brooklyn: Otzar Hasidim, 5759 [1999]), 9, 11.

6 For the letter, see the introduction to Yosef Yitzchak Schneersohn, *Igros Kodesh*, 2:10, and Deutsch, *Larger than Life*, 2:209.

7 Shaul Shimon Deutsch, personal communication to Samuel C. Heilman, March 9, 2008. As we shall see later, even when her husband became a rebbe, she refused to be engaged by parochial Hasidic affairs.

8 Deutsch, personal communication to Heilman, March 9, 2008; Miriam Horensztajn Yuval (grandniece of the fifth Lubavitcher rebbe), interview by Menachem Friedman, July 9, 2001. Miriam Horensztajn Yuval suggested that the marriage between Shmaryahu Gourary and Chana was far from idyllic and that her sisters knew it.

9 *HaRabanit*, 18, 67–68. To be sure, he also wrote to her in Yiddish. See, e.g., a long published letter in Yosef Yitzchak Schneersohn, *Igros Kodesh*, pt. 3, 156–279.

10 See a document executed on December 4, 1924, and quoted in Marcus, *Rebbetzin Chaya Mushka Schneerson*, 8.

11 Mondshine, *Derech HaMelech*, 7.

12 Ibid., and Yoef Yitzchak Schneersohn, *Igros Kodesh*, 11:90.

13 Wolf, *Admorei ChaBaD v'Yahadut Germania*, 101–2.

14 See enrollment record in *Mitteilungen*, March 23, 1929, no. 3.

15 See Geeertz, *The Interpretation of Cultures*, 114, and Heilman, *The People of the Book*, 97–98.

16 *Haynt*, November 30, 1928, 1.

17 Ibid.

18 Mondshine, *Derech HaMelech*, 9.

19 *Moment*, November 29, 1928.

20 Deutsch, *Larger than Life*, 2:226–27. See also *HaRabanit*, 35.

21 This is the date noted on Mendel Schneerson's French citizenship petition. See also Deutsch, *Larger than Life*, 2:216. According to his passport, Mendel did not enter Poland until November 25. This throws this date of his civil marriage into some question. We therefore believe that the young Schneersons actually married civilly in Latvia and then Moussia and her mother left for Poland later that day. The reason Mendel had told the French that he was married in Poland was not to confuse matters; for him the true marriage was the Jewish one, which did take place in Poland on November 27, 1928.

22 Kaminetsky, *Days in Chabad*, 62. The ceremony was witnessed by Berel Moshe Shmotkin and Mendel Koparstock. *HaRabanit*, 35.

23 On the parallel celebration, detailed in letters from Mendel's father and uncle, see *Michtavei HaChatunah*, 13-14, 21-23.

24 These are slightly different from the more common version of phylacteries worn by Jewish males, commonly called "Rashi" tefillin.

25 Letter from Levi Yitzchak Schneerson to his son, in *Igros Kodesh Levi Yitzchak*, 207.

26 See Deutsch, *Larger than Life*, 2:217–18.

27 *Moment*, November 29, 1928, 1, and *Haynt*, November 30, 1928, 1.

28 See Deutsch, *Larger than Life*, 2:294–95.

29 See Deutsch, *Larger than Life*, 2:238, and *Reshimot Chatunah*, 6 n. 9.

30 See Menachem Mendel Schneerson, *Reshimos* (Brooklyn: Kehot, 2003), 1:4, and *Reshimot Chatunah*, 7.

31 Yosef Yitzchak Scheersohn, *Igros Kodesh*, 2 Shevat 5689 (1929), 2:153.

32 See later discussion in this chapter.

33 Notes from the journal of one of the yeshiva students and quoted in Kaminetsky, *Days in Chabad*, 61.

34 Mondshine, *Derech HaMelech*, 12.

35 Recollections of Barry Gourary in Deutsch, *Larger than Life*, 2:134.

36 Mondshine, *Derech HaMelech*, 12. No doubt Rabbi Yosef Yitzchak tried hard to keep them close, fearing they would otherwise be absorbed by a life different from the Hasidic one.

37 Letter from January 3, 1932, in *HaTamim*, Warsaw, Kislev 5696 (December 1935), 56–65. Ironically, the performance of "miracles" would become a greater aspect of Menachem Mendel's reign.

38 See, e.g., in late 1932, when he sent a book of Torah commentaries; Wolf, *Admorei ChaBaD v'Yahadut Germania*, 115.

39 Letter of 10 Elul (1932), in Wolf, *Admorei ChaBaD v'Yahadut Germania*, 114–17.

40 Levi Yitzchak Schneerson, *Likkutei Levi Yitzchak Igros Kodesh* (Brooklyn: Kehot, 2004 [1985]), 443–44.

41 For a list of these, see Levi Yitzchak Schneerson, *Likkutei Levi Yitzchak Igros Kodesh*, 453–58.

42 See affidavit 45677 submitted by Mendel Schneerson to the French authorities on behalf of his application for naturalization.

43 Barry Gourary, interview by Deutsch, *Larger than Life*.

44 This would be the closest they lived to the university and the Jewish Community Administration building. On her claim to study mathematics, see her testimony at the trial, p. 84 of the transcript (Deutsch, *Larger than Life*, 2:95).

45 For more on the trial, see chapter two. For the deposition in the court case, see vol. 2, exhibit VI 3, p. 115, and the transcript.

46 *HaRabanit*, 236.

47 Mondshine, *Derech HaMelech*, 7.

48 Ibid., 14.

49 See Deutsch, *Larger than Life*, 2:94, citing Rabbi Yosef Yitzchak's diary.

50 From his records at the engineering school he later attended in Paris (see below), we can see his time was well spent, because he did gain such a certificate.

51 Mondshine, *Derech HaMelech*, 7.

52 See Deutsch, *Larger than Life*, 2:295, and Mondshine, *Derech HaMelech*, 16.

53 See Deutsch, *Larger than Life*, 2:293–94, quoting Barry Gourary. To be sure, this disappointment must have been tempered later, as Mendel began handling more tasks for the court. See below.

54 See Menachem Mendel Schneerson, *Igros Kodesh*, 21:7, and Mondshine, *Derech HaMelech*, 16.

55 Deutsch, *Larger than Life*, 2:293, citing Laufer, *Yemei Melech*, 1:247.

56 Schneerson, *Reshimos* pamphlet 65, 205–9.

57 On his notation of the traditions and practices of his father-in-law, see, e.g., Menachem Mendel Schneerson, *Reshimos* [notes or impressions], 5 and 8. See also Mondshine, *Derech HaMelech*, 23–33.

58 The name and identification papers belonged to a friend of his father who had drowned. Although spelled differently, this was the same family from which Shmaryahu Gourary came.

59 Testimony from Barry Gourary in Deutsch, *Larger than Life*, 2:134.

60 Zionist archives, folder 506/45/433.

61 For the marriage date, see a letter from the Immigration and Nationality Department of Great Britain, ref. no. G49571, October 20, 1995, reproduced in Deutsch, *Larger than Life*, 2:135. Leibel would later move to England, where he died.

62 *Kovetz Chof Menachem-Av*, 54–56, 60–64.

63 See Deutsch, *Larger than Life*, 2:136. For Leibel's secular lifestyle, see Yona Cohen, interview by Menachem Friedman, April 25, 2008. Yona Cohen was a friend and co-worker of Leibel's in Bloomstein's Bookstore. Cohen worked with Leibel in his store. Rebecca Shternschuss, Leibel's landlady, with whom the Gurarys shared an apartment in Tel Aviv at 2 Yochanan HaSandlar Street and who kept kosher, noted that she had to insist that Leibel keep their joint kitchen kosher, even though he himself no longer strictly abided by the Jewish dietary laws. Rebecca Shternschuss, interview by Menachem Friedman, November 9, 2005.

64 "Yisroel Aryeh Leib's Final Voyage," March 21, 2006, http://mentalblog.com/2006/03/yisroel-aryeh-leibs-final-voyage.html (accessed August 12, 2008).

65 Letter from the Immigration and Nationality Department of Great Britain, ref. no. G49571.

66 See the City of Otwock archives of the Gymnasium, 1933–36.

67 Barry Gourary, interview by Menachem Friedman, September 1, 1991.

68 Menachem Mendel Schneerson, *Reshimot Chatunah*, B'nai B'rak 22 Adar 5759 (March 19, 1999), 12–13. This booklet was created in honor of the wedding of Yosef Yitzchak Schneersohn and Chana Ruth Halperin

69 Mondshine, *Derech HaMelech*, 29 n. 13.

70 Ibid. Rabbi Yosef Yitzchak had requested his contact and supporter in the Latvian parliament, Mordecai Dubin, who had arranged for his own acquisition of Latvian citizenship, to arrange the same for his daughter Moussia and

her husband Mendel. (See Schneersohn, *Igros Kodesh*, pt. 3, 18–19, n.) However, they never received it and continued to use the Latvian *laissez passer* until they applied for French citizenship. In fact, they remained stateless refugees until they received their American citizenship on November 14, 1946.

71 Yosef Yitzchak Schneersohn, *Igros Kodesh*, introduction, pt. 2, 27, and pt. 11, 209.

72 Ibid., pt. 11, 210, and Menachem Mendel Schneerson, *Sichos Kodesh*, 5726, 435.

73 For the dates, see Mendel Schneerson's application for French naturalization, in which he details his date of arrival and all his residences.

74 Weiner, *Nine-and-a-Half Mystics*, 167. We find no recorded evidence of Moussia's studying architecture.

75 City of Paris Archives, census materials.

76 Monique Y. Wells, "The Literary Women of Montparnasse," *Discover Paris* http://www.crossculturedtraveler.com/Archives/SEP2004/Montparnasse .htm (accessed March 19, 2008).

77 National Archives of Paris, AJ16/5016. Academie de Paris Université de Paris, Faculté des Lettres. Edmea's father, a brother of Rabbi Shalom DovBer, was viewed as the black sheep of the family. He lived many years in Corsica, with no Jewish life there, but when he died, his body was brought to and buried in Safed, the city of mystics in the Land of Israel.

78 Yosef Yitzchak Schneersohn, *Lebn und Kampf von Yidn in Tsarishn Russland 1905–1917: Zichronos* (Paris, Éditions du Centre, 1968). On a return trip to Paris in 1947 (see next chapter), Mendel would make a special trip to visit him (see Laufer, *Yemei Melech*, 975).

79 Boris Schneersohn (son of Yitzchak), interview by Menachem Friedman, March 7, 2000.

80 In general, according to Emanuel Somer, a student at the school twenty years later and who graciously helped us understand the transcripts and the organization of the school, few received grades above 16. For the entire academic record, see this book's website at www.therebbebook.com.

81 See the report in Yosef Yitzchak Schneersohn, *Igros Kodesh*, pt. 3, 18–19. We also thank Baruch Oberlander, whose painstaking recording of all of Rabbi Menachem Mendel's travels (unpublished) serves as an important source.

82 Laufer, *Yemei Melech*, 413.

83 Menachem Mendel Schneerson, *Torat Menachem: Reshimat HaYoman* [Diary Notes] (2006).

84 The listed editors of the publication were Yechezkel Feigen, Yehuda Eber, and Shmuel Zalmanov. For the role of Mendel Schneerson, see an unpublished letter from Rabbi Yosef Yitzchak to Moussia, 22 Sivan 5695 (June 23, 1935), cited in an unpublished document from Baruch Oberlander.

85 See the police questionnaire in his naturalization application file available on the book's website, www.therebbebook.com.

86 Emanuel Somer (a student at ESTP), personal communication to Menachem Friedman, May 19, 1998.

87 Yosef Yitzchak Schneerson, *Sichos Kodesh*, pt. 3, 762.

88 Oberlander, unpublished, 37, cites a letter for Passover that Rabbi Yosef Yitzchak wrote to his children in Paris. Obviously, had they com back for the holiday, this would have been unnecessary.

89 The Rebbe Rabbi Yosef Yitzchak writes a letter to the couple in honor of Passover, clearly indicating they are not in Otwock with him at the time. See Oberlander, manuscript, 37 n. 460.

90 See *Kovetz Chof Menachem-Av* (2004), 53, 56. "Eng." was underscored.

91 See Oberlander, manuscript, 38 n. 480. There is a reference to Mendel's coming the following week for the Simchat Torah, but the Lubavitcher source (Laufer, *Yemei Melech*, 484) is not always reliable and the dates are not always exact there. Moreover, it seems unlikely that Rabbi Yosef Yitzchak would have sent a letter for Yom Kippur if he expected to see his children the next week.

92 *Kovetz Chof Menachem-Av*, 60–64.

93 In the 1939 Paris telephone directory he was registered as "Schneerson, M. Eng. Electr. Mecan. LECOURBE 83.23. The French poet and screenwriter, Jacques Prévert, would move into the apartment in 1945. (See http://www.terresdecrivains.com/Jacques-PREVERT,348 [accessed June 9, 2008].)

94 *Kovetz Chof Menachem-Av*, 60–64.

95 *Kovetz Chof Menachem-Av*, 54–56.

96 Vicki Caron, *Uneasy Asylum: France and the Jewish Refugee Crisis 1933–42* (Stanford: Stanford University Press, 1999), 2.

97 Ibid., 43ff.

98 See ibid., 47. Gone were the easier times of 1927 when the French naturalization law had actually reduced the residency requirement for citizenship from ten to three years; see ibid., 57.

99 See ibid., 278, quoting a November 2, 1938, editorial entitled "Les Étrangers en France."

100 See Caron, *Uneasy Asylum*, 237, and Ellen Furlough, "Selling the American Way in Interwar France: Prix Uniques and the Salon Des Arts Menagers," *Journal of Social History* 26, no. 3 (Spring 1993): 515 n. 45.

101 On the value of French franc to dollars at the time, see http://www.trussel .com/maig/franc.htm (accessed March 23, 2008).

102 *Kovetz Chof Menachem-Av*, 65.

103 In fact, as noted earlier, he registered with the French army before leaving Paris. See *HaRabanit*, 62.

104 *Kovetz Chof Menachem-Av*, 54–56.

105 On anti-Nazi activity in France, see Renée Poznanski, "La résistance Juive en France," *Revue d'Histiore de la Deuxième Guerre Mondiale* 137 (1985): 18–20, who cites the leftists who were engaged in anti-fascism. See also Michael

Marrus, "Jewish Resistance to the Holocaust," *Journal of Contemporary History* 30, no. 1 (1995): 99; and Hillel Kieval, "Legality and Resistance in Vichy France: The Rescue of Jewish Children," *Proceedings of the American Philosophical Society* 124 (1980): 354. See also David Weinberg, *A Community on Trial: The Jews of Paris in the 1930s* (Chicago: University of Chicago Press, 1977).

106 Weinberg, *A Community on Trial*, 108, 138 n. 17, and Shmuel Jatzkan, *Pariser Haynt*, May 12, 1936.

107 Weinberg, *A Community on Trial*, 195, and Phyllis Cohen Albert, review of David Weinberg, *A Community on Trial: The Jews of Paris in the 1930s*, *American Historical Review* 83, no. 4 (1978): 1029.

108 Weinberg, *A Community on Trial*, 217.

109 See Yosef Yitzchak Schneersohn, *Igros Kodesh*, introduction, pt. 4, 14–15. See also the letter that Rabbi Yosef Yitzchak writes to Mendel and Mouusia for Passover, a clear indication they were not with him (Oberlander, manuscript, 40 n. 501). Interestingly, when referring to the Rabbi Yosef Yitzchak and his impending visit in a March 13 letter to his parents, he refers to his father-in-law simply as "Moussia's father" rather than in the usual way that a rebbe is called "His honor the Holy master, teacher and rabbi." This may have been to avoid arousing the attention of the Soviet censors. See *Kovetz Chof Menachem-Av*, 51–52.

110 Yosef Yitzchak Schneerson, *Igros Kodesh*, pt. 1, 15.

111 Ibid., pt. 1, 23.

112 Levi Yitzchak Schneerson, *Likutei Levi Yitzchak Igros Kodesh*, 422.

113 *Lifkod* (to remember) one with a child is the language of the Bible for fertility, particularly among those barren. See Genesis 21:1.

114 This is captured in the Talmudic notion (B.T. Moed Katan 28a) adopted in the Hasidic expression, "*b'nai, chayai, um'zonai*," that rebbes may assist one in gaining children (sons), life, and sustenance. See Menachem Mendel Schneerson, *Igros Kodesh*, 20:237 and n., and also *Zohar Genesis*, 24a.

115 Levi Yitzchak Schneerson, *Likutei Levi Yitzchak Igros Kodesh*, 422–23.

116 For details of this practice, which entails wearing four sets of phylacteries rather than the standard one, see Menachem Mendel Schneerson, *HaYom Yom*, 80, and Menashe Elyashiv, "Weekly Page" 560 (August 17, 2004), Bar Ilan University.

117 Shmaryahu Gourary had also adopted this practice, although he never became a rebbe.

CHAPTER 5
From Survival to *Uforatzto*

1 Rigg, *Rescued from the Reich*, 153, quoting Israel Jacobson, "Journey to America," *Di Yiddishe Heim*, 1956, 7.

2 Rigg refers to Rabinovitz as "Oscar," but the record in the U.S. Archives (811.111 Refugees/834) and other places make clear he was "Arthur," or "Asher,"

as Lubavitchers referred to him, who was both an insurance agent and lawyer as well as the son of David Meyer Rabinovitz, a Lubavitcher Hasid. See *HaRabanit*, 65. On Ernst Bloch, see also Bryan Rigg, *Hitler's Jewish Soldiers* (Lawrence: University of Kansas Press, 2002).

3 Rigg, *Rescued from the Reich*, 121. The comment is in a December 12, 1939, memo to a State Department official. See Deutsch Archives.

4 See Exhibit 268, Library trial, CV 85-2909.

5 He adds that "Certainly, the Roosevelt administration did not have to worry about its domestic Jewish support. But the administration may have presumed that the high-profile rescue would deflect Jewish pressure for the entry into America of many more Jewish refugees." Rigg, *Rescued from the Reich*, xv. The use of Orthodox or even Hasidic rabbis with long beards (the longer the better) as icons who symbolize support for Jews is a continuing ploy of political leaders to this day, who rush to have their pictures taken with them in their efforts to court Jewish support.

6 Menachem Mendel Schneerson, letter 16 in *Igros Kodesh*, 1:30–31. See also exhibit 260, Library trial, CV 85-2909.

7 Hacohen 3:116–35, quoting the diary of Joseph Wineberg, who was with Rabbi Yosef Yitzchak in Poland. See also Rigg, *Rescued from the Reich*, 44–50.

8 Rigg, *Rescued from the Reich*, 90.

9 Ibid., 58.

10 Yosef Yitzchak Schneerson, *Igros Kodesh*, 13:282.

11 Ryan, *The Holocaust and the Jews of Marseille*, 52. See also Joseph Billig, *Le Commissariat Général aux Questions Juives 1941–1944*, 3 vols. (Paris: Centre de Documentation Juive Contemporaine, 1955–60).

12 Doris Bensimon-Donath, "France," in Berenbaum and Skolnik, *Encyclopaedia Judaica*, 2nd ed., 7:146–70 (online edition). Hebrew University of Jerusalem, March 24, 2008.

13 Rigg, *Rescued from the Reich*, 128; see also 118. *Der Morgen Journal*, December 17, 1939.

14 Rigg, *Rescued from the Reich*, 34, 129.

15 Ibid., 120, 131, 89.

16 Ibid., 99.

17 *Igros Agudas Hasidei ChaBaD*, 12 (19 Tammuz 5700). See also exhibit 316, Library trial, CV 85-2909, in which Rhoade suggested Kramer tell the Lubavitchers to keep the list of those in its hierarchy "open" so that other names could be added to it as needed.

18 Rigg, *Rescued from the Reich*, 101.

19 Ibid., 162.

20 Yuval (niece of Mendel), interview by Friedman, July 9, 2001.

21 See Avraham Chenoch Glitzenstein, ed., *Sefer Toldos RaYaTZ* (Brooklyn: Kehot, 5747), 4:69–71; and National Archives, Washington, D.C., 20408/immigration and naturalization, roll 6451, beginning March 16, 1940.

22 Kaminetsky, *Days in Chabad*, 136.

23 Mindel, *Rabbi Joseph I. Schneersohn: A Short Biography*, 15.

24 See *HaRabanit*, 62.

25 Barry Gourary repeated this statement in interviews with both Menachem Friedman and Bryan Rigg (May, 2003).

26 On the first visa request of Mendel as an engineer, see exhibit 317, Library trial, CV 85-2909.

27 *Collection of 28 Sivan Jubilee* (Brooklyn: Kehot, 1991), 9–21.

28 Schachter, interview by Heilman, May 12, 2008. Zalman Schachter was present in Marseille on this occasion.

29 National Archives, file811.1 Refugees/855.

30 Ibid.

31 Ryan, *The Holocaust and the Jews of Marseille*, 130.

32 Ibid., 131.

33 *HaRabanit*, 70; microfilm roll 6555, National Archives, Washington, D.C.; Kaminetsky, *Days in Chabad*, 203–4.

34 Gottleib, *Toldos Levi Yitzchak*, 2:507, 523.

35 Letter on Passover eve, 13 Nisan 5708, "Introduction *Torato Shel Ha-Mashaich* 109, 28 Sivan–3 Tammuz 5755 (1995), 1.

36 See http://www.sichosinenglish.org/books/sichos-in-english/34/08.htm, 5 Teves 5747 (accessed June 17, 2009).

37 See Laufer, *Yemei Melech*, 937.

38 Ibid., 937 n. 2.

39 Ibid., 939.

40 The hotel (see http://www.jpmoser.com/hoteledouardvii.html [accessed May 14, 2008]), where the eponymous king had stayed, required guests to wear neckties, as a Lubavitcher who tried to visit and was turned away discovered. But Mendel obviously still knew his way around the more cosmopolitan side of Paris, and he wore modern clothes. See Laufer, *Yemei Melech*, 942, 978.

41 Laufer, *Yemei Melech*, 999.

42 See Laufer, *Yemei Melech*, 958-60, and Yosef Yitzchak Schneersohn, *Igros Kodesh*, 9:233, 243-44. Rabbi Shmaryahu Gourary was there too, although he also traveled in Austria, Germany, and Czechoslovakia.

43 Laufer, *Yemei Melech*, 949, 955–70.

44 See the reproduced invitation in Laufer, *Yemei Melech*, 981.

45 Laufer, *Yemei Melech*, 982, 1003. No doubt news of his charm and abilities would be spread by Hasidim and others in attendance, who soon would likewise make their way to America and would help pave the way for his conquest of Lubavitch.

46 Weiner, *Nine-and-a-Half Mystics*, 192.

47 Exhibit 513, Library trial, CV 85-2909.

48 See memo in Samuel Kramer files, Deutsch Archive. In this same memo, Mendel Horensztajn (who never got to America) was described as an

expert in education and a psychologist, and head of the ChaBaD religious classes and study circles.

49 See http://www.chabad.org/therebbe/timeline_cdo/aid/62165/jewish/1943 -Author-Teacher.htm (accessed April 1, 2008).

50 Marcus, *Rebbetzin Chaya Mushka Schneerson*, 10.

51 See Friedman, "Messiah and Messianism."

52 Hacohen 3:116.

53 "Aviezer" (anonymous nom de plume), "*Mafteach HaZahav: Kav L'Demuto Haruchaint shel Ha'Admor MiLubavitch*" [The Golden Key: A Line in the Spiritual Image of the Rebbe of Lubavitch], in *Kol Mevaser*, ed. Moshe Epstein (Tel Aviv, Herzliyya Publishing, Cheshvan 5702 [November 1941]), 10.

54 Rodric Braithwaite, *Moscow 1941: A City and Its People at War* (New York: Random House/Vintage, 2006), 27. See also John Garrard, "The Twelve: Blok's *Apocalypse*," *Religion and Literature* 35, no. 1 (Spring 2003): 45–66, and L. Viola, "The Peasant Nightmare: Visions of Apocalypse in the Soviet Countryside," *Journal of Modern History* 62, no. 4 (1990): 747–70.

55 Yosef Yitzhak Schneersohn, "Kol Kore fun'm Lubavitsher Rabin," *Hakriya v'Hakedusha* 1, no. 9 (May 26, 1941): 15–16.

56 See *Kuntres Bais Rabbeinu Sheb'bavel* (5752 [1992]): 416–32, and Kraus, *The Seventh*, 22.

57 Friedman, "Messiah and Messianism," 209.

58 Yosef Yitzchak Schneersohn, *Igros Kodesh*, 13:295–96.

59 Gershon Greenberg, "Redemption after Holocaust According to Mahane Israel—Lubavitch 1940–1945," *Modern Judaism* 12 (1992): 61.

60 Greenberg, "Redemption after Holocaust," 62.

61 Ibid. See also *Hakriya v'Hakedusha* 1, no. 7 (March 28, 1941): 1.

62 Greenberg, "Redemption after Holocaust," 63. See also *Hakriya v'Hakedusha* 1, no. 10 (June 24, 1941): 1–2.

63 Greenberg, "Redemption after Holocaust," 62.

64 *Hakriya v'Hakedusha* 3, no. 30. See also Greenberg, "Redemption after Holocaust," 67.

65 Ish Yehudi [A Jew], "Bakent zikh mit der Varnung, "L'altar l' teshuvah," *Hakriya v'Hakedusha* 3, no. 25. Cited in and translated from the Yiddish in Greenberg, "Redemption after Holocaust, 69.

66 Gershon Greenberg, "The Rebbe's Response to the Holocaust," paper presented at New York University, November 6–8, 2005.

67 *Hakriya v'Hakedusha* 3, no. 37 (September 11, 1942), 1–2. See also Greenberg, "Redemption after Holocaust," 72.

68 See Friedman, "Messiah and Messianism," 208–14.

69 See, e.g., Menachem Mendel Schneerson, *Sichos Kodesh* 5720 (1960), 175, for a description and summary of the events on 10 Shevat 5720 (February 2, 1960).

70 Greenberg, "The Rebbe's Response to the Holocaust." See also Menachem M. Schneerson, "4:226" (March 23, 1956), in *Igros Kodesh* (1989), 12:412–14.

71 See Dahan, "*Dira BaTahtonim*," 2006.

72 See, e.g., Weiner, *Nine-and-a-Half Mystics*, 188–91.

73 Samuel Heilman, *Portrait of American Jews: The Last Half of the Twentieth Century* (Seattle: University of Washington Press, 199), 8.

74 The five-day workweek began formally in the late 1920s but became the norm after the Second World War. See Robert Whaples, "Hours of Work in U.S. History," http://eh.net/encyclopedia/article/whaples.work.hours.us (accessed April 1, 2008).

75 This is the term used after the names of venerated rabbis.

76 See, e.g., a letter of 25 Iyyar 5711 (May 31, 1951), in which he writes to a petitioner who has asked for a blessing for his family that "when I visited the *tsiyen* of my father-in-law . . . I mentioned all of them and I know that he has aroused God's mercy to help every one of you." Menachem Mendel Schneerson, *Igros Kodesh*, 4:297. See also Bogomilsky, *Hei Teves Didan Notzach*, 43, 64, where the practice of the Rebbe announcing *azkir al HaTziyon* (I'll raise it at the gravesite) is described.

77 Kirschenbaum, *The Rebbe Inspiring a Generation*, 43.

78 See Kraus, *The Seventh*, 26–28.

79 Yosef Yitzchak Schneersohn, *Igros Kodesh*, 8:118. See also Kraus, *The Seventh*, 27–28.

80 Yosef Yitzchak Schneersohn, *Igros Kodesh*, 8 (2):492. See also Menachem Mendel Schneerson, *Dvar Malchus, Parshat Ki Tissah* 5751 (1991), and *Likutei Sichos* (Brooklyn: Kehot, 1994), 23:274, for a talk given in the summer of 1986.

81 Israel Jacobson, *Zikaron L'Beis Yisrael* (Brooklyn: Kehot, 1996), 94.

82 See Rachel Elior, *The Paradoxical Ascent to God: The Kabbalistic Theosophy of Habad Hasidim* (Albany: SUNY Press, 1993).

83 See chapter one.

84 Menachem Mendel Schneerson, *Dvar Malchus*, 29 Kislev 5746 (December 31, 1986).

85 Midrash Rabbah Leviticus 29, quoted in *Basi L'Gani*. See also Midrash Tanchuma (Buber edition) Naso 24, (Warsaw edition) Naso 16.

86 Schneerson (Kaploun edition), *Basi L'Gani*, 87.

87 Ibid., 88.

88 To be sure, in 1926, on 2 Nisan (March 17), the anniversary of the passing of his father, Yosef Yitzchak had given a talk entitled "All Sevens Are Dear to God," noting that his father had been the seventh generation after the Ba'al Shem Tov, the man whom the Messiah had told about the spreading of the wellsprings in order to bring him. Menachem Mendel undoubtedly knew that talk, as he knew so much about the Lubavitcher past. Menachem Mendel, however, had a different set of seven in mind.

89 Kirschenbaum, *The Rebbe Inspiring a Generation*, 48.

90 Rabbi Shubert Spero, in discussion with Samuel C. Heilman, March 28, 2008. Rabbi Spero was at the time a student in Torah VeDaas and heard the

remark. From 1922 to 1948 the yeshiva was headed by Rabbi Shraga Feivel Mendlowitz. Other prominent Orthodox leaders reacted similarly.

91 Erik Erikson, *Childhood and Society* (New York: Norton, 1950 [1963]), 262. See also idem, *The Identity, Youth and Crisis* (New York: Norton, 1968).

92 See Robert Bellah, "Civil Religion in America," *Journal of the American Academy of Arts and Sciences*, special issue, "Religion in America," 96, no. 1 (Winter 1967): 1–21.

93 Pledge of Allegiance to the Flag of the United States of America," *Encyclopædia Britannica*, Encyclopædia Britannica Online, http://www.britannica.com/eb/article-9060389 (accessed March 31, 2008), and *Congressional Record*, 1956, 13917.

94 For example, Yehuda Nir, a psychiatrist whose clientele is heavily populated by members of the Satmar Hasidic community in Brooklyn, asserts that there is no one who does not have some immediate contact with the Holocaust (Yom Ha Shoah address, April 29, 1992, Young Israel of Scarsdale, New York). In general, most American Orthodox Jews (and their institutions) trace their origins to the years just before or after the Second World War.

95 See Rabbi Norman Lamm, cited in Chaim Dov Keller, "Modern Orthodoxy: An Analysis and a Response," *Jewish Observer* 6, no.8 (June 1970): 3–14.

96 He had over the first years of his leadership been increasingly active in organizing his Hasidim both in America, Europe, and Israel. In 1951, for example, he created the youth organization of ChaBaD and in 1953 the Lubavitch Women's Organization (see http://www.chabad.org/therebbe/timeline_cdo/aid/62170/jewish/1953-Chassidic-Feminism.htm [accessed April 3, 2008]). That same year he sent out special hand-baked matzos to important political leaders as a kind of political outreach. But 1958 was bigger; it sought something that would impact the world beyond Lubavitch. For the proclamation of the year of *U'fortazto*, see *Kfar Chabad* 13, 25 Shevat 5741 (1981), 10–11, and *Kfar Chabad* 763, 22 Iyar 5757 (1997), 56–60. See also http://www.chabad.org/therebbe/article_cdo/aid/550721/jewish/12-Tammuz-5718-Sicha-3.htm (accessed April 3, 2008).

97 See Rashi and Targum Onkelos. This is a reference also to the promise of God to Abraham in Genesis 13:16 that "if a man can number the dust of the earth, [then] shall thy seed also be numbered."

98 Menachem Mendel Schneerson, letter from 1 Kislev 5745, in *Likutei Sichos* 35, pt. 9, vol. 1 (Brooklyn: Kehot 5764 [2003]), 274.

99 Menachem Mendel Schnnerson, from a talk on 9 Kislev 5725 (1964), in *Likutei Sichos* 5, pt. 3, vol. 1(1999), 382

100 See also Menachem Mendel Schneerson, *Sichos Kodesh*, 5720 (1960), 188.

101 Letter of 15 Teveth 5751, in *Kuntres Torato shel Ha Mashiach*, 109, 28 Nisan 5755 (1995), 1.

102 See http://www.chabad.org/therebbe/article_cdo/aid/550718/jewish/12-Tammuz-5718-Sicha-1.htm (accessed April 3, 2008). He would repeat it

again on July 4, 1963 (12 Tammuz 5723), the same year he would begin taking public stands on American issues such as the Supreme Court decision on prayer in the public schools (see chapter two, note 28); http://www .chabad.org/therebbe/article_cdo/aid/551117/jewish/12-Tammuz-5723 -Sicha-6-Rebbe-Uforatzto.htm (accessed April 3, 2008).

103 "Shlichus": http://www.chabadlibrary.org/exhibit/ex5/exeng5.htm (accessed January 7, 2008).

104 See Dahan, "*Dira Ba Tahtonim*," and Levin, *Heaven on Earth*. To be sure, in desires to dwell.

105 John F. Kennedy, "Statement upon Order Establishing the Peace Corps," March 1, 1961, http://www.jfklibrary.org/Historical+Resources/Archives/Ref erence+Desk/Speeches/JFK/003POF03PeaceCorp03011961.htm (accessed December 30, 2008). See also "Kennedy Sets Up U.S. Peace Corps to Work Abroad," *New York Times*, March 2, 1961, p. 1.

106 We thank Elkanah Shmotkin for pointing us to this speech. See http://www .chabad.org/multimedia/media_cdo/aid/779312/jewish/Mission-of-Love .htm (accessed December 30, 2008). According to his aide, Yehuda Krinsky, the Rebbe and his wife regularly read the *New York Times* (interview by Samuel C. Heilman, May 10, 2009).

107 See http://www.chabad.org/multimedia/media_cdo/aid/140798/jewish/ Ufoatzto.htm (accessed April 3, 2008). See also, e.g., Menachem Mendel Schneerson, *Igros Kodesh* (Winter 5717): 14: 11–12. He would in the years of *Uforatzto* often request that everyone sing this song. See, e.g., *Sichos Kodesh*, 5720 (1960) (1986), 175, a description and summary of the events on 10 Shevat 5720 (February 2, 1960), which began with the singing of "*Uforatzto*."

108 Menachem Mendel Schneerson, *Igros Kodesh*, Winter 5717, 14:11–12.

109 Weiner, *Nine-and-a-Half Mystics*, 191.

110 Fishkoff, *The Rebbe's Army*, 11.

111 Weiner, *Nine-and-a-Half Mystics*, 159.

112 Loewenthal, *Communicating the Infinite*, 95. The reference here is to what the emissaries of the first rebbe, Shneur Zalman, were wont to do.

113 Friedman, "Messiah and Messianism," 195.

CHAPTER 6
On a Mission from the Rebbe in Life

1 See, e.g., *New York Times*, November 26, 1961, 84.

2 *New York Times*, September 20, 1962. The call, originally published in the May–June issue of the *The Jewish Forum*, was reprinted in the Catholic weekly *The Commonweal*, along with pieces by three other Jewish American leaders and thinkers. See also *New York Times*, November 27, 1962, and chapter two, this book.

3 Letter written in 1964, http://yiddisheheim.org/2.html (accessed April 2, 2008).

4 See Menachem Friedman, "Haredim Confront the Modern City," in *Studies in Contemporary Jewry*, ed. P. Medding (Bloomington: Indiana University Press, 1986), 2:74–96.

5 See Friedman, "Messiah and Messianism," 197.

6 We thank Professor Eliezer Witztum for this insight.

7 On the peace corps, see http://www.peacecorps.gov/index.cfm?shell=Learn (accessed April 14, 2008). See also Fishkoff, *The Rebbe's Army*, 28.

8 See Rivka Schatz-Uffenheimer, "Anti-Spiritualism be-Hasidut: Iyyunim be-Torat Schneur Zalman Mi-Lyadi," *Molad* 20, nos. 171–172, 5723 (November 1962), esp. 527–28 [in Hebrew]. For an alternative view of Schneur Zalman's view, see Isaiah Tishbi.

9 Loewenthal, *Communicating the Infinite*, 186, and Josef Dan, "Hasidut," *Encyclopedia Hebraica*, v. 17, 789–93 (Tel Aviv, 1949). See also DovBer Schneuri, *Sha'ar ha-Emunah* (Kopys, 1820), 114a, and Levin, *Heaven on Earth*, http://www.chabad.org/library/article_cdo/aid/294285/jewish/A-Synopsis-of-the-Dirah-Betachtonim-System.htm (accessed April 10, 2008).

10 Levin, *Heaven on Earth*. See also Simon Dein, "From Chaos to Cosmogeny," *Anthropology and Medicine* 11, no. 2 (August 2004): 136. On "conquering" the world, see Menachem Mendel Schneerson, letter to the Tzeirei ChaBaD (Lubavitcher Youth Organization) in the summer of 1956, *Igros Kodesh* (1987), 11:50.

11 Rachel Elior, "Between 'Casting off Corporeality' and 'Extension of Love even Within Corporeality': Tensions between the Spiritualist Approach and Social Reality in the Hasidic Milieu" [in Hebrew], in *Tzaddik ve-'Edah: Hebetim histori'im ve-hevrati'im be-heker ha-Hasidut*, ed. David Assaf (Jerusalem: Merkaz Zalman Shazar, 2001), 465, and Levin, *Heaven on Earth*. To be sure, Ada Rapoport-Albert has noted that the "Rebbe advocated that the performance of mitsvot was the ordinary person's best route to spiritual ascent (with the help of the charismatic leaders, the elite, who alone could achieve it even by performing any mundane, non-ritual act, such as eating)." However, she adds, the capacity of mitzvah "to change, purify, repair and 'conquer' the world" was something that the kabbalists had always believed, ascribing immense theurgic power "to the performance of mitsvot by man, which they believed to be capable of bringing about cosmic change." The Rebbe was thus using "traditional ideas as his building blocks" but changing emphases, and "repackaging" those notions. He "was not overturning classical Hasidic doctrines." Rapoport-Albert, personal communication.

12 Menachem Friedman, "Habad as Messianic Fundamentalism," in *Accounting for Fundamentalisms: The Dynamic Character of Movements*, ed. Martin E. Marty and R. Scott Appleby (Chicago: University of Chicago Press), 345.

13 Ibid., 349.

14 Menachem Mendel Schneerson, *Igros Kodesh* (1990), 17:52.

15 Mindel, *Joseph I. Schneersohn*, 15, 16.

16 Ibid., 18.

17 Schachter, interview by Heilman, May 2008. The description below is adapted from Arye Coopersmith, *Holy Beggars*, http://www.holybeggars .com/book.html (accessed May 13, 2008). See also Yaakov Ariel, "Hasidism in the Age of Aquarius: The House of Love and Prayer in San Francisco, 1967–1977," *Religion and American Culture: A Journal of Interpretation*, 13, no. 2 (2003): 139–65.

18 Berel Chaskind was the father-in-law of Barry Gourary.

19 Dahan, "*Dira BaTahtonim*," iv.

20 See http://www.sichosinenglish.org/general/thrust.html and http://www .chabad.org/therebbe/article_cdo/aid/62228/jewish/10-Point-Mitzvah -Campaign.htm (accessed April 8, 2008).

21 One of us (S.C.H.) was a student and present there at the time.

22 Fishkoff, *The Rebbe's Army*, 27.

23 Menachem Mendel Schneerson, *Sichos in English*, vol. 34, 28 Kislev, http:// www.sichosinenglish.org/books/sichos-in-english/34/06.htm (accessed April 13, 2008).

24 Charles S. Maier, "The Two Postwar Eras and the Conditions for Stability in Twentieth Century Western Europe," *American Historical Review* 86, no. 2 (1981): 327. See also Henri Theil, and S. D. Deepak, "The GDP's of Three Regions in Western Europe, 1950–1990," *Journal of Agricultural and Applied Economics* (2003).

25 Truffaut, quoted in Richard Brody, "Auteur Wars," *The New Yorker*, April 7, 2008, 62. On the year 1968 in Europe, see, e.g., Arthur Marwick, *The Sixties: Cultural Revolution in Britain, France, Italy and the United States ca. 1958–1974* (Oxford: Oxford University Press, 1998); Michael Seidman, *The Imaginary Revolution: Parisian Students and Workers 1968* (New York: Berghan Books, 2004); Wolff Dietrich Webler, "The Sixties and the Seventies: Aspects of Student Activism in West Germany," *Higher Education* 9 (1980): 155–68; and Stuart J. Hilwig, "'Are You Calling me a Fascist?' A Contribution to the Oral History of the 1968 Italian Student Rebellion," *Journal of Contemporary History* 36, no. 4 (2001): 581–97.

26 Maya Katz, "Chabad Iconography of the Diaspora," Institute for Advanced Study, Hebrew University of Jerusalem, January 10, 2008.

27 See David Berger, *The Rebbe, the Messiah, and the Scandal of Orthodox Indifference* (New York: Littman Library, 2001). While Berger takes the Orthodox to task for allowing Lubavitchers to provide for their religious needs, he shows how much they do so.

28 See *Farbrengen* 5752 (1992), 2:184, reporting on a gathering on 13 Shevat (January 18).

29 See Laufer, *Yemei Melech*, 1001, and Schneerson, *Igros Kodesh*, 14:156.

30 See Naftali Loewenthal, "Women and the Dialectic of Spirituality in Hasidism," in *Within Hasidic Circles: Studies in Hasidism in Memory of*

Mordecai Wilensky, ed. Immanuel Etkes et al. (Jerusalem: Bialik Institute, 1999), English section, 7-65; Ada Rapoport-Albert, "The Emergence of a Female Constituency in Twentieth-Century HaBaD Hasidism," in *Let the Old Make Way for the New,* ed. David Assaf and Ada Rapoport-Albert, vol. 1, English section. See also Bonnie J. Morris, *Lubavitcher Women in America* (Albany: SUNY Press, 1998).

31 Betty Friedan, *The Feminine Mystique* (New York: Norton, 1963), and Executive Order 11375.

32 See http://www.chabad.org/global/about/article_cdo/aid/244377/jewish/The -Woman.htm (accessed May 26, 2008).

33 See his letter in *Kfar Chabad* 1111.

34 See http://www.kinus.com (accessed May 26, 2008). See also, e.g., *New York Times,* May 13, 1974, 35, and http://www.portraitofaleader.org (accessed July 2, 2009).

35 Interview with Shlomo Riskin, *Kfar Chabad* 1119. All the quotations on this episode come from Riskin's interview. We also interviewed Riskin ourselves (Samuel C. Heilman) on July 16, 2008, and he confirmed the version in *Kfar Chabad.* We thank Ada Rapoport-Albert for calling this episode to our attention. See also her article, "'Making a Home for the Divine on Earth': Women in the Teaching of the Last Lubavitcher Rebbe," forthcoming.

36 According to Daniel Greer, a disgruntled member of Lincoln Square who had moved to the Young Israel of the West Side, when *he* asked Rabbi Soloveitchik if he approved Riskin's decision, Solevitchik had replied, "a Torah scroll is not a toy," presumably an expression of disapproval. See Zev Eleff, ed., *Mentor of Generations: Reflections on Rabbi Joseph B. Soloveitchik* (Jersey City: Ktav, 2008).

37 David Dunlap, "Women Sponsoring Torah," *New York Times,* October 5, 1981.

38 Riskin, personal communication to Heilman, July 16, 2008.

39 See Irving Spiegel, "Where Women Go to Find Judaism—and Themselves: A Sense of Worth," *New York Times,* April 17, 1974, 48, and Lynn Davidman, *Tradition in a Rootless World: Women Turn to Orthodox Judaism* (Berkeley and Los Angeles: University of California Press, 1991).

40 See Herbert J. Gans, "Symbolic Ethnicity and Symbolic Religiosity: Towards a Comparison of Ethnic and Religious Acculturation," *Ethnic and Racial Studies* 17 (1994): 577–92.

41 Katz, "Chabad Iconography of the Diaspora."

42 Avremel Shemtov, interview by Samuel C. Heilman, August 13, 2008.

43 Katz, "Chabad Iconography."

44 Menachem Mendel Schneerson. *Hilchot Beit HaBechira L'HaRambam,* in *Chidushim u' Biurim* (Brooklyn: Kehot, 1986), 46–52.

45 Katz, "Chabad Iconography," and Menachem Mendel Schneerson, *Hilchot Beit HaBechira,* 48.

46 Ironically, the Rebbe himself did not use this sort of menorah when he lit his own candles but instead used a more traditional one, with a back against which candles were arranged in a straight line. See Shalom DovBer Ganzburg, *B'Kodesh P'nima* (Kfar Chabad: Yossi Ashkenazi, n.d.), 23.

47 Fishkoff, *The Rebbe's Army*, 285–86.

48 See Menachem Daum and Oren Rudavsky, *A Life Apart*, http://www.pbs.org/alifeapart (accessed May 26, 2006), and Katz, "Chabad Iconography."

49 Louis Reinstein, "The Growth of Chabad in the United States and the Rise of Chabad Related Litigation," *Nova Law Review* 30, no. 2 (2005–6): 303–31.

50 Menachem Mendel Schneerson, *Likutei Sichos*, 5:223–24.

51 Gans, "Symbolic Ethnicity and Symbolic Religiosity."

52 Menachem Mendel Schneerson, *Igros Kodesh*, 4: 297.

53 Ibid., 1:298–301.

54 See Friedman, "Habad as Messianic Fundamentalism," 173–96. The question of who was a Jew, so much a matter of debate over the years, was crucial for Lubavitchers. They wanted a yes answer to their inquiry to be simple and reliable. They did not want varying definitions of who was a Jew, for it would undermine their campaign. See below.

55 Bernard Collier, Hasidic Jews Confront Hippies to Press a Joyous Mysticism, *New York Times*, May 27, 1968, 49.

56 See "The Power of Jewish Pride," talk given on 19 Kislev 5743 (December 5, 1982), *Living Torah*, Program 61 (Jewish Education Media, www.jeminc.org).

57 Ibid.

58 Yehuda Lukacs, *Documents on the Israeli-Palestinian Conflict 1967–1983* (New York: Cambridge University Press, 1984), 17–18; Abba Eban, *Abba Eban* (New York: Random House, 1977), 358.

59 See http://www.chabad.org/therebbe/timeline_cdo/aid/62173/jewish/1967-The-Six-Day-War.htm (accessed May 20, 2008) and Schneerson, *Sichos Kodesh*, 111–27, http://sichoskodesh.com/pdf/5727v2.pdf (accessed May 20, 2008).

60 See http://sichoskodesh.com/pdf/5727v2.pdf, 113.

61 http://sichoskodesh.com/pdf/5727v2.pdf, 133.

62 http://www.chabad.org/therebbe/timeline_cdo/aid/62173/jewish/1967-The-Six-Day-War.htm (accessed April 13, 2008).

63 *Sod Siach*, pt. 1, 20 Av (Brooklyn, 1991), 32–33.

64 Moshe Brilliant, "Hasidic Jews, in Flowing Beards and Black Hats, Bring Religion to Golan Trenches," *New York Times*, December 10, 1972, 25.

65 See *Der Algemeiner Journal*, December 7, 1973. Aryeh Morgenstern, personal communication. See also *Azure*, winter, 5770/2010, p. 7.

66 See Fishkoff, *The Rebbe's Army*.

67 See Menachem Mendel Schneerson, *Sichos Kodesh* 5714 (1954), 131–34.

68 Menachem Mendel Schneerson, *Likutei Sichos*, 28 Sivan 5746 (1986, 1994), 276.

69 See Seth Farber, *An American Orthodox Dreamer: Rabbi Joseph B. Soloveitchik and Boston's Maimonides School* (Waltham, MA: Brandeis University Press, 2003). On women's Torah education before the war, see Deborah Weissman, "Bais Ya'akov as an Innovation in Jewish Women's Education: A Contribution to the Study of Education and Social Change," *Studies in Jewish Education* 7 (1995): 278–99.

70 See Heilman, *The People of the Book*, 1–28. See also Gershom Scholem, "Jewish Awakening," in *From Berlin to Jerusalem* (New York: Schocken, 1980).

71 Maya Katz, "Trademarks of Faith: Chabad and Chanukah in America," *Modern Judaism*, 2 (May 2009):239–67.

72 Menachem Mendel Schneerson, letter of Friday, 24 Tishrei 5723 (October 21, 1962), *Igros Kodesh*, 22:340.

73 Yaakov Yehuda Hecht, http://www.shmais.com/pages.cfm?page=archivenews detail&ID=31288 (accessed April 23, 2008).

74 Chaim Zohar, interview by Menachem Friedman, December 21, 2007.

75 See Ganzburg, *B'Kodesh P'nima*, 71.

76 Yehuda Krinsky, interview by Samuel C. Heilman, May 7, 2009. See also Kirschenbaum, *The Rebbe Inspiring a Generation*, 16.

77 See Ganzburg, *B'Kodesh P'nima*, 34, 43, 60, 76.

78 Kirschenbaum, *The Rebbe Inspiring a Generation*, 14.

79 Dr. Ira Weiss, interview by Menachem Friedman, May 9, 1999. Dr. Weiss was the Rebbe's cardiologist and regularly visited the Schneerson home. Moussia treasured the few objects and mementos she had from her sister Sheina (see Laufer, *Yemei Melech*, 1254), perhaps because they reminded her of an earlier life and all its exciting promise.

80 Ada Rapoport-Albert, "The Emergence of a Female Constituency in Twentieth-Century Habad Hasidism," appendix 3, "Women and Food at the Court."

To be sure, there is evidence that they dined together on Sabbaths and holidays. See Ganzburg, *B'Kodesh P'nima*, 35.

81 See Laufer, *Yemei Melech*, 1256, quoting her testimony at the book trial. On her loneliness and solitude, see idem, 1262.

82 On his interactions with children, see Laufer, *Yemei Melech*, 973–75, 1002, and especially 988, note 121, who describes the "sparkle on his face" when he addressed children.

83 Adam D. Galinsky, Joe C. Magee, M. E. Inesi, and Deborah Gruenfeld, "Power and Perspectives Not Taken," *Psychological Science* 17, no. 12 (2006): 1068–74, argue that the more power a person has, the less capacity he has to see another's perspective or understand the world through another's eyes. On the culture of delusion, see H.B.M. Murphy, "Cultural Aspects of Delusion," *Stadium Generale* 20 (1967): 684–92.

CHAPTER 7
From Resurrection to Death: We Want Moshiach Now

1 Laufer, *Yemei Melech*, 1268.
2 Yisrael Eldad (Sheib), "My Encounter with the Rebbe," *Yedioth Acharanoth*, June 17, 1994. These words, Eldad reports, were spoken more than thirty years earlier.
3 Miscellaneous Collection, the National Library Jerusalem, Menachem Mendel Schneerson, Correspondence, vol. 1816.
4 This was in contrast to those who, like the disciples of Rabbi Abraham Isaac Kook and his son, Zvi Yehudah, did see it as the start of the era of redemption. See Marty and Appleby, *Accounting for Fundamentalisms*. When asked about Rabbi Kook and his ideas, Menachem Mendel expressed disapproval (see Weiner, *Nine-and-a-Half Mystics*, 174).
5 See, e.g., S. Sidon, *Efo Yosele* [in Hebrew] (Tel Aviv, Ha'Olam Ha'Zeh, 1962); Isser Harel, *Mivtsa Yosele* [in Hebrew] (Tel Aviv: Idanim, 1982); and Ian Black and Benny Morris, *Israel's Secret Wars* (New York: Grove, 1991), 191–94.
6 Michael Lando, "Israeli Unites with New York Woman Who Helped in His Abduction," *Jerusalem Post*, June 7, 2007, http://www.jpost.com/servlet/Satellite?cid=1181228570097&pagename=JPost%2FJPArticle%2FShowFull (accessed May 25, 2008)
7 Schneur Zalman Berger, *The Partisan* (Kfar Chabad, Vilimovsky, 2005), 213–17. See also http://www.chabad.info/index_new2.php?&id=10456&print=true&url=article_he (accessed May 25, 2008), in which the statement, missing in the book, is made that "the degree of his [the Rebbe's] involvement in the Yossele affair, is still foggy."
8 Shazar's attachment to the Lubavitcher Rebbe was noted at least by the *New York Times* (May 23, 1963, 16) from the moment he became president of Israel.
9 Israel Shenker, "Lubavitch Rabbi Marks His 70th Year With Call for 'Kindness,'" *New York Times*, March 27, 1972, 39. The point of this comment was to suggest that not only was the Lubavitcher Rebbe above the president of the state of Israel, but perhaps as well even above the president of the United States.
10 *Diglenu*, Iyyar 5718 (May 1958). There was one more possible reason for his not going to Israel, which we discuss later.
11 Weiner, *Nine-and-a-Half Mystics*, 166.
12 Joseph Berger, "Hasidim Confront the Secular While Living a Life Apart," *New York Times*, July 4, 1987.
13 See Miscellaneous Collection, the National Library Jerusalem, Menachem Mendel Schneerson Correspondence, vol. 1816. See also Marty and Appleby, *Accounting for Fundamentalisms*.

14 Menachem Mendel Schneerson, *Igros Kodesh* (1994), 22:338–39.

15 See, e.g., *New York Times*, December 8, 1968, 86, and March 27, 1972, 39, which had begun adding to its regular news items about Lubavitch the fact that President Shazar was a supporter and adherent.

16 Menachem Mendel Schneerson, *Hisvadus Parshat Shlach* 5710 (1950), 106.

17 *New York Times*, January 18, 1970, 24. David Berger in his book *The Rebbe, the Messiah, and the Scandal of Orthodox Indifference* (New York: Littman Library, 2001) would thirty years later take the Orthodox to task for not rejecting Lubavitcher leadership and teachings when the messianism of the movement became more adamant and, as he saw it, idolatrous.

18 See Riskin interview, *Kfar Chabad* 1119.

19 Frances X. Clines, "A Pilgrimage to Eastern Parkway," *New York Times*, September 24, 1977, 13.

20 See, e.g., *New York Times*, June 22, 1970, 40. Of course, other Hasidic rebbes—some of whom opposed ChaBaD—like the Satmar leader also became targeted for such political visits, but only the Lubavitcher got Israeli, American, and other international leaders, for he had the *shluchim*.

21 Shenker, "Lubavitch Rabbi Marks His 70th Year."

22 Irving Spiegel, "Hasidim from Abroad Gather Here," *New York Times*, October 2, 1972, 41.

23 Yirmiyahu Branover, "Kol Tuv, Sela," *HaGeula* 418, 24 Sivan 5768 (June 27, 2008).

24 See http://www.chabad.org/therebbe/timeline_cdo/aid/62151/jewish/1923-Soviet-Jewry.htm (accessed May 25, 2008).

25 Mordecai Staiman, *Secrets of the Rebbe that Led to the Fall of the Soviet Union* (Brooklyn, Mendelson Press, 2001), 58.

26 Ibid., 23.

27 Among these were Russian Lubavitchers. See ibid., 28.

28 Ibid., 56. The first Jew holding a doctor of science degree and the title of full professor to receive an exit visa to leave the USSR, Branover was among the initiators of the Jewish revival movement in Soviet Russia during his fifteen-year struggle to leave the Soviet Union.

29 This event became part of a popular documentary shown repeatedly on American Public Television and throughout the world. *A Life Apart* http://www.pbs.org/alifeapart (accessed May 30, 2008). In fact, the Rebbe's appearance on a huge screen in front of the Kremlin was prerecorded. By the time this took place, in 1993, he could no longer speak.

30 Shenker, "Lubavitch Rabbi Marks His 70th Year."

31 See, e.g., Irving Spiegel, "Jewish Homes Aid Aimless Youths," *New York Times*, August 24, 1975, 27.

32 See, e.g., *Dvar Malchus*, 6 Elul 5751 (August 16, 1991).

33 See *New York Times*, August 8, 1976, 38.

34 Ibid.

35 Laufer, *Yemei Melech*, 1264.

36 Ibid., 1268, quoting Chesed Halberstam, Moussia's assistant. See also *Kfar Chabad*, 322, 38.

37 The account was most likely Leibel Groner's (see http://portraitofaleader .blogspot.com/2007/09/doctor-rebbe-do-you-feel-pain-around.html [accessed May 26, 2008]).

38 As Talcott Parsons (*The Social System* [Routledge, 1951], 193) noted, the sick role emphasizes vulnerability and passivity. This is not something a messianic leader can afford.

39 *Beit Chayenu*, no. 3 (102) vol. 4, 1 Cheshvan 5738 (October 13, 1977), JNUL PA11337, 8.

40 Yehuda Krinsky, interview by Samuel C. Heilman, May 10, 2009.

41 *Tishrei with the Rebbe*, vol. II, video. See http://home.jemedia.org/update .asp?aid=565341 (accessed July 6, 2008).

42 Yori Yanover and Nadav Ish-Shalom, *Rokdim V'Bochim* [English title, *Dancing and Crying*] (New York: Meshi, 1994), 15–16.

43 "Jacob J. Hecht: Radio Broadcaster, 66," *New York Times*, August 7, 1990.

44 See Shandler, *Jews, God and Videotape*.

45 See "Rabbi Using Modern Medium in Call for Traditional Values," *New York Times*, January 23, 1983. This article was describing his annual Yud (10th) Shevat talk, the anniversary of his ascension.

46 Susan Heller and David Dunlap, "Lubavitcher Leader Marks 35th Anniversary," *New York Times*, February 2, 1985.

47 Ganzburg, *B'Kodesh P'nima*, 10–11. On weekdays, of course, the Rebbe could be driven from his home on President Street, but on Sabbaths he would have had to walk, in line with the prohibition against driving on this day.

48 Laufer, *Yemei Melech*, 253.

49 National Jewish Library in Jerusalem, Manuscript Archive, Miscellaneous Papers, vol. 1816, reference to a talk on 24 Tevet 5738 (January 3, 1978).

50 *B'Sod Siach* (Brooklyn: Uforatzto Press, 1991), 94-95; E. D. Halperin, "The Belief in the Messiah." *Kfar Chabad*, 25 Shevat 5741 (January 30, 1981).

51 *Kfar Chabad*, 10 Shevat 5741 (January 1, 1981), back page.

52 "The War of *Tzivos Hashem* for the Redemption of Israel Is on the Rise," *Kfar Chabad*, 9 Adar I, 5741 (February 13, 1981). Of course, children had been associated in Jewish tradition with the days after the arrival of the Messiah. As the prophet Isaiah (11:6) had promised, at the end of days "a little child shall lead them." In parallel fashion, Christians had seen the role of the child in leading to the redemption. Jesus was said to have said, "Let the little children come to me, and do not hinder them, for the kingdom of heaven belongs to such as these" (Matthew 19:14). To Christians, children were the key to the messianic future.

53 Ari Goldman, "Hasidic Group Expands Amid Debate About Future," *New York Times*, September 5, 1988.

54 Israel Shenker, "Hasidic Feat: Simple as Aleph, Beth Gimel," *New York Times*, November 3, 1977, 5. See also Alastair Gee, "Lubavitchers Fight Russia for Schneersohn Documents," July 10, 2009, http://jta.org/news/article/2009/07/10/1006451/lubavitchers-fight-russia-for-schneersohn-documents (accessed July 13, 2009). The Lubavitchers continued to try to retrieve these papers, and in 2009 they turned to the American courts in their quest.

55 *New York Times*, March 26, 1982.

56 See Menachem Mendel Schneerson, *Hisvadus*, 5743, 2:1097 (see chapter one, this book). On the claims of the capacity of the Rebbe to control world events, see, e.g., Staiman, *Secrets of the Rebbe*.

57 See Kaminetsky, *Days in Chabad*, 163; Moses Maimonides, *Mishneh Torah Hilchot Melachim u'Milchamot*, 11. See also E. D. Halperin, "The Belief in the Messiah."

58 Shenker, "Lubavitch Rabbi Marks His 70th Year." See also Halperin, "The Belief in the Messiah."

59 Goldman, "Hasidic Group Expands."

60 Shalom DovBer Kovalesky recalling his father Nachman Kovalesky's outburst, *Kfar Chabad* 592, November 4, 1993.

61 Francis X. Clines, "In Honoring the Rebbe, a Caterer Did Well Too," *New York Times*, March 25, 1983.

62 *Sicha*, 22 Nissan 5742 (April 15, 1982). See Moshe Slonim, *Beit Moshiach*, 23 Tammuz 5755 (July 21, 1995),

63 See *Beit Moshiach*, 23 Tammuz 5755, 20.

64 *Sefer HaSichos* 5752, 362–76. See also the pamphlet *Dvar Malchut*, *Mishpatim*, 27 Shevat 5755 (January 28, 1995).

65 Lis Harris, *Holy Days* (New York: Summit Books, 1985); Ari Goldman, "For Torah, Community, and Rebbe," *New York Times*, November 10, 1985.

66 Alistair Gee, "Lubavitchers Fight Russia for Schneersohn Documents," *JTA*, July 10, 2009.

67 Verdict of Judge Sifton, in Bogomilsky, *Hei Teves Didan Notzach*, 81.

68 Bogomilsky, *Hei Teves Didan Notzach*, 106, from the Court of Appeals decision.

69 Ibid., 22–23, 29.

70 Ibid., 33–34.

71 David Margolick, "Suit on Books Gives Look at Hasidim," *New York Times*, December 18, 1985.

72 Ibid. See also http://failedmessiah.typepad.com/failed_messiahcom/2006/01/the_beating_of_.html (accessed May 26, 2008).

73 See photo, http://failedmessiah.typepad.com/failed_messiahcom/2006/01/the_beating_of_.html (accessed May 26, 2008). See letter from Chana Gourary to *Der Yid* (July 8, 1988), in which she describes the attack.

74 Ari Goldman, "Judge Awards Rabbi's Library to Hasidic Unit," *New York Times*, January 7, 1987.

75 Verdict reproduced in Bogomilsky, *Hei Teves Didan Notzach*, 81.

76 Eli and Malka Touger, *To Know and To Care* (Brooklyn: Kehot), chap. 9, http://www.chabad.org/library/article_cdo/aid/78667/jewish/Chapter-9 -A-Dollar-For-Tzedakah-Fountain-of-Blessing.htm (accessed June 1, 2008).

77 *New York Times*, May 29, 1973, 31, and May 30, 1973, 42. See also Deutsch, *Larger than Life*, vol. 2.

78 Adam Kirsch, "Jesus and the Jews," *New York Sun*, May 1, 2007.

79 Ernest Becker, *The Denial of Death* (New York: Free Press, 1973), 84. On the posters welcoming King Messiah, see Herb Keinon, "Habad: Schneerson is Messiah," December 27, 1992, and "No Doubt for Habad: The Rebbe is the Messiah," *Jerusalem Post*, January 1, 1993.

80 See also Glen Hughes, "The Denial of Death and the Practice of Dying," http://staff.washington.edu/nelgee/lectures/speeches/hughes_1.htm (accessed June 22, 2008).

81 Bogomilsky, *Hei Teves Didan Notzach*, 74.

82 See, e.g., *HaRabanit*, 107. Many of the details that follow come from this same source, 107–29.

83 Ganzburg, *B'Kodesh Pnima*, 38.

84 Ibid., 38.

85 The Rebbe had told Ganzburg that the others would try to send him back to be by his side, but he should not do so: "Tell them," the Rebbe added, "that I am over bar mitzvah" (Ganzburg, *B'Kodesh P'nima*, 37).

86 *HaRabanit*, 111.

87 Ganzburg, *B'Kodesh P'nima*, 55.

88 *HaRabanit*, 115.

89 Ganzburg, *B'Kodesh P'nima*, 40–42.

90 Anson Rabinbach, "Between Enlightenment and Apocalypse: Benjamin, Bloch, and Modern German Messianism," *New German Critique* 34 (Winter 1985): 81.

91 See Ari L. Goldman, "U.S. Orthodox Rabbis Break with Israeli Religious Parties," *New York Times*, November 23, 1988.

92 See M. E. Schach, *Michtavim u'M'amarim* [Letters and Articles], vol. 5 (Benei-Brak: unknown publisher, 5755 [1995]), 172–74; letter 568 is dated 28 Shevat 5752 (February 1992). See also Gershom Scholem, *The Messianic Idea in Judaism* (New York: Schocken, 1972), and idem, *Sabbatai Sevi* (Princeton, NJ: Princeton University Press, 1976).

93 Ari L. Goldman, "'Who Is a Jew' Debate in Israel Attracts Leading Figures of U.S. Judaism," *New York Times*, December 3, 1988. Lubavitch, which raised much of its money from non-Orthodox Jewry, acknowledged subsequently that it had lost some financial backing because of its support for the legislation (see Ari L. Goldman, "Religion Notes," *New York Times*, March 24, 1990).

94 Ari L. Goldman, "'Who Is a Jew' Remains a Volatile Issue in U.S." *New York Times*, January 9, 1989.

95 All of the events described here and following are part of a diary of pseud-
onymous M. Moshe published in a special edition of *Kfar Chabad*, 20 Adar
5751 (March 6, 1991), 18–21.

96. Testimony of a Lubavitcher Hasid, interview, June 23, 2008.

97 Testimony of a Lubavitcher Hasid, interview, June 23, 2008.

98 Menachem Mendel Schneerson, *Der Aibeshter vet noch Visen Gresere Nisism*
[The Almighty will yet show us Greater Miracles], leaflet, in *Igros Kodesh*, 21
Adar 5751 (March 7, 1991). See also "Words of the Lubavitcher Rebbe," *Der
Algemeiner Journal*, 28 Nisan 5751 (April 12, 1991), 1.

99 See also *Sichat HaShavua*, 27 Elul 5751 (September 6, 1991).

100 Ernest Becker, *Escape from Evil* (New York: Free Press, 1975), 37.

101 Interview, June 23, 2008.

102 Zvi Aranoff (Lubavitcher Hasid), interview, June 23, 2008.

103 See Rashi in B. T. Arachin, 11b.

104 Rodney Stark and Roger Finke, *Acts of Faith: Explaining the Human Side of
Religion* (Berkeley and Los Angeles: University of California Press, 2000),
145.

105 What follows is from *Moshiach I'fi Tumo*, 3 Iyar 5751 (April 17, 1991), 10.

106 Kaminetsky, *Days in Chabad*, 119.

107 "Messiah Plain and Simple," *Yom HaShishi*, 3 Iyar 5751 (April 17, 1991), 10.

108 Leaflet, 27 Nisan 5751 (April 11, 1991), Friedman Archives.

109 Yanover and Ish-Shalom, *Rokdim V'Bochim*, 74–75. See also http://www
.chabad.org/therebbe/timeline_cdo/aid/62185/jewish/3-Tammuz-1994
-Transmission.htm (accessed July 4, 2008).

110 Schneerson, *Basi L'Gani*, 87.

111 "Messiah Plain and Simple."

112 Testimony of a Hasid who was there that evening. All of the subsequent
descriptions come from this testimony.

113 Further details were to be learned by contacting "your regional Chabad
House." The idea of appreciating the significance of miracles was stressed
by the Rebbe. See *Der Algemeiner Journal*, April 12, 1991, 1.

114 See, e.g., James L. Franklin, "Hopes for the Messiah: Rabbi's Followers Say
Redemption Near," *Boston Globe*, September 9, 1991, 28, and Martha Allen,
"Lubavitcher Rabbi Says Messiah Is Here," *Star Tribune* (Minneapolis), No-
vember 11, 1991, 10C.

115 See, e.g., Tom Hundley, "Billboards Herald Messiah's Arrival," *Toronto Star*,
March 10, 1992, A2.

116 Menachem Mendel Schneerson, *Sichos in English*, 7 Elul 5751 (August 17, 1991),
vol. 49, http://www.sichosinenglish.org/books/sichos-in-english/49/20.htm
(accessed August 12, 2008).

117 "Kol Koreh," pamphlet from the Rabbis of ChaBaD, December 31, 1991.

118 *D'var Malchus* (Brooklyn: Kehot, 5768 [2008]).

119 *Sichat HaShavua*, 3 Cheshvan 5752 (October 11, 1991).

120 Francis X. Clines, "Russian Court Backs Lubavitchers on Documents," *New York Times*, October 6, 1991.

121 The Lubavitchers claim this statement comes from Talmudic or midrashic sources (see http://www.mnow.co.il/html/mashiach_achshaiv.html and http://www.pnimi.org.il/00etzchaim/04nefesh/torathanefesh/aniemloj.asp [accessed June 10, 2008]), but we find the reference in the medieval book by Rabbeinu Bahya, *Kad Ha'Kemach*.

122 See http://www.mnow.co.il/psak_din.pdf (accessed June 10, 2008).

123 Reprinted in *Dvar Malchus*, 27 Shevat 5755 (January 28, 1995), 362–76.

124 Shachar Ilan, "Chabadniks Demand That Schneerson Announce That He Is the King Messiah," *Haaretz*, January 20, 1992; Harvey Shepherd, "Preparing the Way: Lubavitchers Believe Messiah is Already Here," *Montreal Gazette*, April 7, 1992, A3.

125 Schach, *Michtavim u'M'amarim* [Letters and Articles], vol .5 (Benei-Brak: unknown publisher, 5755 [1995]), 172–74; no. 569 written 5752 (February 1992), see also no. 570. In Deuteronomy 13, scripture berates the false prophet who entices and misleads (*mesit u'madiach*) believers to departing from the true path of God. Such false prophets are to be punished by death. Cf. B.T. Sanhedrin 67A, "a *mesit* is a [enticing] layman [as opposed to true prophet], and he who seduces an individual . . . to idolatry" and a *maddiach* is one who says, 'let us serve idols." See also Maimonides, *Mishneh Torah* [Laws of Repentence], chap. 4, Law 1.

126 Simon Dein, "What Really Happens When Prophecy Fails: The Case of Lubavich," *Sociology of Religion* 62, no. 3 (2001): 392.

127 Shlomo Shamir, "The Condition of the Lubavitcher Rebbe," *Haaretz*, March 4, 1992.

128 Ganzburg, *B'Kodesh P'nima*, 19.

129 On Yosef Yitzchak as a prophet, see Menachem Mendel Schneerson, *Sichos in English*, 7 Elul 5751 (August 17, 1991), vol. 49, http://www.sichosinenglish .org/books/sichos-in-english/49/20.htm (accessed August 13, 2008).

130 Yanover and Ish-Shalom, *Rokdim V'Bochim*, 9–18.

131 Nadine Brozan, "Chronicle," *New York Times*, March 5, 1992.

132 "A Year Since 27 Adar 1 5752," *Kfar Chabad* 565, 25 Adar 5753 (March 18, 1993).

133 Ari Goldman, "As Leader Lies Ill, Hasidim in Brooklyn Wait and Pray," *New York Times*, March 9, 1992.

134 Clyde Haberman, "Special Prayers in Israel for Brooklyn Rabbi," *New York Times*, March 7, 1992.

135 See Bader, "When Prophecy Passes Unnoticed."

136 R. Stark, "Why Religious Movements Succeed or Fail: A Revised General Model," *Journal of Contemporary Religion* 11, no. 2 (1996): 137. See also Leon Festinger, H. W. Riecken, and S. Schacter, *When Prophecy Fails* (New York: Harper & Row, 1956).

137 Festinger, Riecken, and Schacter, *When Prophecy Fails*, 3.

138 See J. F. Zygmunt, "When Prophecies Fail," *American Behavioral Scientist* 16, 2 (1972):245–68.

139 Dein, "What Really Happens When Prophecy Fails," 383.

140 Nadine Brozan, "Chronicle," *New York Times*, April 7, 1992.

141 Alison Mitchell, "Convoy of Mitzvah Tanks Celebrates Birthday of Rebbe," *New York Times*, April 13, 1992.

142 Goldman, "As Leader Lies Ill."

143 Dein, "What Really Happens When Prophecy Fails," 394. See also Shmuel Haber, "Messiah and Redemption," *Kfar Chabad* 566 (March 25, 1993), 16–17.

144 See 1 Peter 2:21–25.

145 Kenneth Woodward, "Doth My Redeemer Live?," *Newsweek*, April 27, 1992, 53. See also Shachar Ilan, "Lubavitcher Rabbis Decree: The Rebbe Is Truly the Messiah and He Will Live Forever," *Haaretz*, April 27, 1992.

146 "HaGeula Ha'Amitit VeHashelemah" (The True and Complete Redemption), leaflet, March 3, 1992, Friedman Archive. See also "There Will Be Healing Soon, with Song and Singing," *Sichat HaShavua*, March 13, 1992; "Some Conclusions in Light of Recent Events," *Sichat HaShavua*, March 27, 1992; and "The Situation before the Redemption," *Sichat HaShavua*, April 10, 1992.

147 Dein, "What Really Happens When Prophecy Fails," 395. For a variation on this argument, see Menachem Ohav, "As the First Redeemer so the Last Redeemer," leaflet, March 16, 1992, Friedman Archive.

148 See, e.g., *Sichat HaShavua*, August 14, 1992.

149 *Chadshot Beit Chayenu*, 21 Adar II, 5752 (March 26, 1992).

150 Yosef Halevi Weinberg, "Completely Beyond Nature," *Kfar Chabad* 519, 27 Adar II, 5752 (April 1, 1992), 34–35.

151 See Yanover and Ish-Shalom, *Rokdim V'Bochim*. See also "Report on the Medical Condition of the Rebbe," *Kfar Chabad* 592 (November 4, 1993), 56–58. See also a leaflet distributed at the time, Friedman Archive. Interviews with some of the physicians were conducted June 23, 2008, and June 25, 2008.

152 Goldman, Religion Notes, *New York Times*, October 3, 1992.

153 On pseudo-events, see Daniel Boorstin, *The Image* (New York: Vintage, 1961), esp. chap. 1.

154 Ari L. Goldman, "Debate Splits Lubavitcher Hasidim; Showdown Nears on Whether Grand Rabbi is the Messiah," *New York Times*, January 29, 1993.

155 Michael Winerip, "On Sunday: The Watch for the Messiah in Crown Heights," January 3, 1993.

156 See Vanessa L. Ochs, "Waiting for the Messiah, a Tambourine in Her Hand," *Nashim* 2005, 144–69, and Laurie Goodstein, "Followers Cope with Void of Failed Expectations: Internal Debate Pits Pragmatists Against Those Seeking the Messiah," *Washington Post*, June 19, 1994, A3.

157 Ari L. Goldman, "Rebbe, But Not the Messiah, as Lubavitchers Compromise," *New York Times*, February 1, 1993.

158 Goldman, "Debate Splits Lubavitcher Hasidim."

159 Editor's note, *Kfar Chabad*, April 29, 1993. See also *New York Times*, April 26, 1993.

160 Elsa Brenner, "Two Groups Contest Role in Promoting Lubavitch Judaism's Cause in the County," *New York Times*, April 3, 1994.

161 Goldman, "Rebbe, But Not the Messiah."

162 David Gonzalez, "For Rebbe's Followers, Hospital Becomes a Yeshiva," *New York Times*, May 13, 1994.

163 "Leader of Lubavitch Is Worse, an Aide Says," *New York Times*, March 17, 1994.

164 David Gonzalez, "For Lubavitch Hasidim Caravan of Mitzvah Tanks Honors Rebbe," *New York Times*, March 24, 1994.

165 See letter from the rabbinic court of Lubavitch, 3 Tammuz 5754, Friedman Archive.

166 Elie Kaunfer, "Rabbi's Death Throws Some into Confusion," *Boston Globe*, June 13, 1994, 4.

167 Dein, "What Really Happens When Prophecy Fails," 397.

168 David Gonzalez, "Holding onto Faith in the Face of Unexpected Loss," *New York Times*, June 14, 1994.

169 Dein, "What Really Happens When Prophecy Fails," 398.

170 Gonzalez, "Holding onto Faith."

171 Dein, "What Really Happens When Prophecy Fails," 399.

172 David Gonzalez, "Lubavitchers Learn to Sustain Themselves Without the Rebbe," *New York Times*, November 8, 1994.

CHAPTER 8

On a Mission from the Rebbe in His Afterlife

1 Nathaniel Popper, "Lawsuit over Chabad Building Puts Rebbe's Living Legacy on Trial," *Jewish Forward*, March 16, 2007 (italics added).

2 Leon Festinger, Henry Riecken, and Stanley Schachter, *When Prophecy Fails: A Social and Psychological Study of a Modern Group That Predicted the Destruction of the World* (New York: Harper & Row, 1956).

3 See chapter two.

4 See Don Handelman and Leah Shamgar-Handelman, "The Presence of Absence: The Memorialism of National Death in Israel," in *Grasping Land*, ed. Eyal Ben-Ari and Yoram Bilu (Albany: SUNY Press, 1997), 85–128.

5 See http://decisions.courts.state.ny.us/fcas/fcas_docs/2006mar/230040288 2004100sciv.pdf (accessed June 22, 2008).

6 See Popper, "Lawsuit over ChaBaD Building."

7 See http://decisions.courts.state.ny.us/fcas/fcas_docs/2006mar/230040288 2004100sciv.pdf, pp. 5–6.

8 Popper, "Lawsuit over ChaBaD Building."

9 See http://decisions.courts.state.ny.us/fcas/fcas_docs/2006dec/2300402882 004101sciv.pdf (accessed June 22, 2008).

10 Decision 40288/004 2007 NY Slip Op 52495U; 18 Misc. 3d 1111A; 856 N.Y.S.2d 499; 2007 N.Y. Misc. LEXIS 8584; 239 N.Y.L.J. 16

11 See http://decisions.courts.state.ny.us/fcas/fcas_docs/2008apr/2300402882 004102sciv.pdf (accessed June 22, 2008).

12 See http://www.moshiach.net/blind/hebrew/sg-index.htm and http://www .chabad.org.il/Magazines/Articles.asp?CategoryID=30 (both accessed June 24, 2008).

13 The quotation is from Menachem Mendel Schneerson, *Sichos Kodesh*, April 9, 1950, 10; see chapter two.

14 See, e.g., "The Repair for the Sin of the Spies," *Sichat HaShavua*, 1120 (June 20, 2008), in which the decline is attributed to an Israeli government "suddenly engaged in talks with Syria and Hamas" as well as "educational and moral erosion that has reached a new low" and " unconcern with the turmoil of the vulnerable classes."

15 Interview by Samuel C. Heilman, January 2008. The identity of the *shaliach* remains anonymous.

16 Yosef Chaim Kantor, *shaliach* in Bangkok, Thailand, keynote address at the 2006 *kinus shluchim.*

17 See *Likkutei Sichot*, 35:113–19, and sources cited there.

18 See, e.g., the weekly *Sichat HaShavua* 775 (November 9, 2001), http:// chabad-il.org/sh/701-800/sh775.htm, and the missives to Tzeirei ChaBaD youth organization nos. 487 (November 11, 2003) (http://www.chabad.org .il/Magazines/Article.asp?ArticleID=485&CategoryID=404) and 642 (November 10, 2006) (http://www.chabad.org.il/Magazines/Article.asp?Article ID=3426&CategoryID=907) (all accessed February 6, 2008).

19 Remarks offered at the 2006 *kinus shluchim.*

20 See http://www.shturem.net/index.php?section=news&id=26799&lang= hebrew, accessed June 23, 2008.

21 Schneerson (Kaploun edition), *Basi L'Gani*, 97.

22 *Sichat HaShavua* 775 (November 9, 2001) (translation by Samuel C. Heilman).

23 Keynote address, *kinus shluchim.* 2006.

24 "An Emissary Like Him—Like Him Literally," missives to Tzierei ChaBaD youth organization no. 487 (Nov. 11, 2003) (translation by Samuel C. Heilman).

25 For a sense of how well organized the system has become, see the "Online Shlichus Center," http://www.shluchim.org/main/default.asp (accessed June 19, 2008).

26 The Talmud suggests a more complicated formula. See, e.g., BT Sanhedrin 97a and b, where a whole variety of conditions are presented for determining when the Messiah will come.

27 In 1971 he inserted himself vigorously into the process of converting refugees in Vienna who were coming out mostly from the Soviet Union. See
Harold Branin, "Conversions Stir a Jewish Dispute," *New York Times*, February 21, 1971, 10.

28 Interview by Samuel C. Heilman, May 10, 2009.

29 See http://lubavitch.com/subsection.html?task=618 (accessed June 20, 2008).

30 Marvin Schick, "A Census of Jewish Day Schools in the United States,
2003–2004," Avi Chai Foundation, 2005.

31 Mission statement, http://www.myjli.com/dc.php?ID=10 (accessed June 17,
2009).

32 Sjaak Van Der Geest, "Anthropologists and Missionaries: Brothers under
the Skin," *Man* 25, no. 4 (December 1990): 588.

33 Van Der Geest, "Anthropologists and Missionaries,"589, 593.

34 Some observers, most prominently David Berger in his *The Rebbe, the
Messiah, and the Scandal of Orthodox Indifference*, argue that those who
remained committed to a resurrection of their rebbe as a messiah cannot legitimately continue to be called Jews, let alone Orthodox. And, Berger adds,
allowing such Lubavitchers to be appointed or considered "Orthodox rabbis
betrays Judaism" (see David Berger, "Response to David Singer," in *Orthodoxy Today*, http://orthodoxytoday.org/articles2/BergerSingerResponse.php
[accessed June 23, 2008]).

35 Samuel C. Heilman, *Sliding to the Right: The Contest for the Future of American Jewish Orthodoxy* (Berkeley and Los Angeles: University of California
Press, 2006), esp. 278–90.

36 Fishkoff, *The Rebbe's Army*,11.

37 For a review of a number of lawsuits against them, see Louis Reinstein, "The
Growth of Chabad in the United States and the Rise of Chabad Related
Litigation," *Nova Law Review* 30, no. 2 (2005–2006): 303–31.

38 See http://www.chabad.com/site/apps/nlnet/content3.aspx?c=eeJNIWOz
ErH&b=1986735&content_id=%7BE46E6CB0-AC78-482A-873D-B1DCF
6AE1F74%7D&notoc=1 (accessed February 9, 2008).

39 Indeed, ChaBaD of California, which is listed as a public nonsectarian
charity, claims to have an income of less than $25,000. See Guidestar for its
official information: http://www.guidestar.org/pqShowGsReport.do?npoId
=1512&partner=justgive (accessed February 9, 2008).

40 Exactly how was not always clear, since ChaBaD of California, according to
Guidestar, "is not required to file an annual return with the IRS because its
income is less than $25,000."

41 The Goodmans worked under Yosef Carlebach, who was the overall head of
Central New Jersey ChaBaD.

42 See http://www.cuchabad.org/templates/articlecco_cdo/aid/157067/jewish/
Wisdom-Centre.htm (accessed June 23, 2008).

43 Fishkoff, *The Rebbe's Army*, 11.

44 Joshua Runyon, "Free Mezuzahs for Residents of Ukraine Port City," February 26, 2008, http://www.chabad.org/news/article_cdo/aid/643173/jewish/Free-Mezuzahs-in-Ukraine.htm (accessed May 20, 2008).

45 See http://www.chabadneworleans.com/templates/articlecco_cdo/aid/239674/jewish/Rare-Mitzvah-on-the-Avenue.htm (accessed February 10, 2008).

46 Leizer Shemtov, email to Samuel C. Heilman. February 10, 2008

47 See Stephen Sharot, "Jews and the Secularization Debate," *Sociological Analysis* 52, no. 3 (1991), 257.

48 Fishkoff, *The Rebbe's Army*, 27.

49 See http://www.chabadnj.org/page.asp?pageID=%7B5BA9F3EB-F2DA-4B64-B6BC-96A5AD1DD0EE%7D (accessed February 10, 2008).

50 Quoted in Leon Neyfakh, "Gefilte Fish Slithers into Harvard Yard," *Jewish Forward*, February 17, 2006.

51 Fishkoff, *The Rebbe's Army*, 91.

52 Erving Goffman, *Frame Analysis* (Cambridge, MA: Harvard University Press, 1974), 40–82.

53 Larry Gordon, "Tefillin Tailgate Party," *5 Towns Jewish Times*, February 7, 2007, http://www.5tjt.com/news/read.asp?Id=2066 (accessed February 10, 2008).

54 In Israel in the upper Galilee, at a basketball tournament, a similar thing happened: a song calling for the Moshiach, led by Lubavitchers from Safed, was turned into an anthem, which fans believed accounted for their team's victory. See http://tam.co.il/12_8_2005/magazin2.htm (accessed June 24, 2008).

55 Goffman, *Frame Analysis*, 45.

56 See http://www.rzlp.org/index.cfm?objectid=3609552C-D612-00A6-A9085C6A13DBEF56 (accessed May 26, 2008).

57 Benjamin Soskis, "Who Is Shmuley Boteach?" *Slate*, http://www.slate.com/id/103323/ (accessed June 24, 2008).

58 See the online Crown Heights information page, http://www.crownheights.info/index.php?itemid=4848; Simon Rocker, "Cash Crisis Tears Apart Lubavitch," *Jewish Chronicle*, December 28, 2007, http://www.thejc.com/home.aspx?ParentId=m11s18&SecId=18&AId=57123&ATypeId=1; and idem, "Chabad Rabbis Remain Defiant," *Jewish Chronicle*, January 4, 2008, http://www.thejc.com/Home.aspx?ParentId=m11&AId=57190&ATypeId=1&secid=11&prev=true (all accessed February 6, 2008).

59 On the Modern Orthodox relationship with contemporary general culture and society, see Samuel C. Heilman, *Sliding to the Right: The Contest for the Future of American Jewish Orthodoxy* (Berkeley and Los Angeles: University of California Press, 2006).

60 Shimon Lazaroff, interview by Samuel C. Heilman, June 29, 2006, Crown Heights.

61 Max Weber, *The Theory of Social and Economic Organization* (New York: Free Press, 1947), 358–92. See also Talcott Parsons, *The Structure of Social Action* (New York: Free Press, 1937), 658–72; Edward A. Shils, "Charisma, Order and Status," *American Sociological Review* 30, no. 2 (1955): 199–213; Robert C. Tucker, "The Theory of Charismatic Leadership," *Daedalus* 97, no. 3 (1968):731–56; Ann Ruth Willner, *Charismatic Political Leadership: A Theory* (Princeton, NJ: Center of International Studies, 1968).

62 Weber, *Theory of Social and Economic Organization*, 364.

63 See Ehrlich, *Leadership in the HaBaD Movement*.

64 See *Sichas HaGeula* 703 (June 20, 2008), http://www.torah4blind.org/hebrew/sg703h.pdf (accessed June 25, 2008). Note the name of the Web address, "torah4blind," those blind to the truth of these beliefs.

65 Kravel-Tovi, "To see the Invisible Messiah."

66 Krinsky, interview by Heilman, May 10, 2009.

67 Dein, "What Really Happens When Prophecy Fails," 384.

INDEX